OPEN FOR BUSINESS
THE ROOTS OF FOREIGN OWNERSHIP IN CANADA

Gordon Laxer

Toronto   OXFORD UNIVERSITY PRESS   1989

For Edna May and Robert Laxer

In memory of George Grant, Walter Gordon, and T.C. Douglas

Oxford University Press, 70 Wynford Drive, Don Mills, Ontario, M3C 1J9

Toronto   Oxford   New York   Delhi   Bombay   Calcutta   Madras   Karachi
Petaling Jaya   Singapore   Hong Kong   Tokyo   Nairobi   Dar es Salaam
Cape Town   Melbourne   Auckland

and associated companies in
Berlin   Ibadan

CANADIAN CATALOGUING IN PUBLICATION DATA

Laxer, Gordon, 1944-
Open for business : the roots of foreign
ownership in Canada

Includes bibliographical references.
ISBN 0-19-540734-2

1. Canada – Economic policy. 2. Investments,
Foreign – Canada. 3. Populism – Canada.
I. Title.

HC113.L38 1989   338.971   C89-093587-4

Cover photograph: William Toye

Contents

Preface

This book endeavours to explain the unique level of foreign ownership of the Canadian economy from a new comparative perspective. I begin with the assumption that Canadians have largely determined their own history—surely not a very startling point of departure, but one that is at odds with the standard explanations of Canadian economic development. Rejecting the conventional perspectives (external, geographic, technological, and élite influences) as unduly deterministic, I examine instead the *internal* social and political factors that have shaped Canadian development policies. This change in focus leads to fresh perceptions of familiar facts never before associated with the emergence of a branch-plant economy. It casts new light on an old debate.

Students of Canadian economic history usually place Canadian development within the context of the North Atlantic triangle (Britain, the United States, and Canada). Such an approach makes Canada's failure at independent economic development appear inevitable, since the focus is on the influence of powerful external forces. When, however, one looks at how other equally undeveloped countries, which I call 'late followers', overcame similar economic and external pressures, the assumptions of inevitability become questionable. Canada had a far broader range of development alternatives during its period of initial industrialization and early statehood than has generally been acknowledged. Comparison allows us to explore these alternatives and examine why Canada did not consider, let alone follow, the development routes of other countries in similar circumstances.

It is the central thesis of this book that Canada's uniqueness lay not in its resource-exporting orientation, in its proximity to a powerful and expanding industrial economy, or in the influence of merchants and bankers in the economic élite, but rather on the weak impact that agrarians had on the state during initial industrialization. In this respect Canada has differed socially and politically from other late-follower countries, indeed from almost all countries that developed independently.

The book studies the effects of agrarian weakness in Canada during the National Policy years in the areas of banking and domestic credit for industry, on the extent of state-created demand for foreign capital, on defence and technological policies, and on restrictions on foreign direct investment.

The idea that agrarians were important midwives in the birth of modern economic and political systems is not new. This was the central point in Barrington Moore's pathbreaking *Social Origins of Dictatorship and Democracy: Lord and Peasant in the Making of the Modern World* (Boston: Beacon Press, 1967). As a graduate student in the late 1960s I absorbed this work and that of others using comparative historical approaches. This background made me sceptical of the standard explanations of Canadian historiography. They relied too heavily on supposedly unique factors in Canadian development, which upon examination turned out not to be unique. When I resumed graduate work in the mid-1970s, debate raged over R.T. Naylor's thesis that the dominance of merchants and bankers in nineteenth-century Canada retarded independent industrial development and left a void that US branch plants filled. At first I was an adherent of this perspective, but I quickly rejected it as overly deterministic and moved on to comparative studies. I was drawn to European intellectual traditions of social, economic, and political thought. Alexander Gerschenkron, Karl Marx, Eric Hobsbawm, Max Weber, and Herbert Norman stand out among the many thinkers who influenced my ideas on the relation between social life and economic development. In considering Canadian development in the light of European and Japanese experiences, I was drawn to earlier writers who emphasized the role of popular-democratic movements in Canadian history, in particular J.M.S. Careless, A.R.M. Lower, Stanley Ryerson, and Frank Underhill. My study of popular movements in nineteenth-century Canada led to an examination of the impact of French/English and religious conflicts and tensions. Later I undertook an in-depth examination of Sweden's successful emergence out of a 'staple trap', as an example of a small country's development possibilities. I was impressed with the many thoughtful works by Swedish political and economic historians. To all of these writers I owe an intellectual debt.

Many writers approach historical studies from a theoretical perspective and search for factors that confirm their theory. This is the deductive method. My approach was different. I first immersed myself in the history of early industrial development in seven countries, including Canada, and then looked for common and divergent elements. The empirical evidence led me to abandon some early presuppositions. I then developed a framework inductively from what I had learned. Theoretical purists will decry the resulting eclecticism, but I view it as a strength that has allowed me to discard preconceived ideas.

This book is bound to disappoint the discipline specialist who assumes that only primary research can make an original contribution to knowledge. For him or her, this book is far too ambitious in its scope. The historian will look in vain for archival research, the economic historian for econometrics, and the political scientist for detailed political-party analysis, while the specialist sociologist may be put off by the economic focus of the book.

With all of them I beg to differ. Narrow disciplinary concerns and methodologies restrict the range of comparisons and questions that can be addressed. The real world is not divided along the lines of the academic disciplines. Originality comes from combining elements never before brought together. Long ago Max Weber argued that creativity lay in the middle ground between narrow empiricists and grand theorists:

> There are, to use the words of F. Th. Vischer, 'subject matter specialists' and 'interpretive specialists'. The fact-greedy gullet of the former can be filled only with legal documents, statistical worksheets and questionnaires, but he is insensitive to the refinement of a new idea. The gourmandise of the latter dulls his taste for facts by ever new intellectual subtleties. That genuine artistry which, among the historians, Ranke possessed in such grand measure, manifests itself through its *ability to produce new knowledge by interpreting already known facts according to known viewpoints.* (Max Weber, "Objectivity in Social Science and Social Policy" in Weber, *The Methodology of the Social Sciences* [New York: Free Press 1949], p. 112. [Emphasis added])

Comparative research allows us to analyze why certain things happened in one society and not in another. Without comparison we are left to unearth and interpret only those events pertaining to the society under study; we cannot address the question of why certain alternatives were debated and implemented in one society and not even conceived of in another. The value of this book lies, I hope, not only in the specific issues it addresses, but in the type of analysis it presents.

Many people helped in the progress of this study, and to all of them I am grateful. Ulf Olsson of the University of Umea went over the chapter on Sweden with a fine-toothed comb. Gregory Kealey and Wallace Clement made substantial critical comments on Chapter 4. Michael Percy, Kenneth Norrie, and two anonymous reviewers were helpful with Chapter 1. An anonymous reviewer made incisive and detailed criticisms of an early draft of the book. Sven Nordlund allowed me access to portions of his doctoral dissertation on Sweden. David Moss reviewed a section on nineteenth-century British banking changes.

Others provided more general help. David Wolfe, Ed Shaffer, John Hutcheson, David Mills, Garth Stevenson, and John Gartrell were helpful at various points. I owe a special gratitude to Melville Watkins for several years of debate, suggestion, encouragement, and criticism as an instructor, member of my thesis committee, and friend. Other members of my thesis committee, Dennis Magill (chairman) and Lorna Marsden, deserve special acknowledgement. I would like to thank Graham Lowe, friend and colleague, for editorial, intellectual, and moral support throughout this lengthy project. I am grateful to Larry Pratt for encouragement when it was most needed. Any shortcomings that remain in this book are my responsibility.

Many other people helped in the preparation of the manuscript. Peter Milroy gave several years of support. Thanks are extended to Pat Leginsky, Barry Lang Hodge, Karen Hughes, Dennis Prior, Cam Stout, and Sophia Papaioannou for research help. Val Irwin and Shirley Stawnychy spent many frustrating hours typing the manuscript into the computer. The University of Alberta supported the project by granting release time from teaching that enabled me to write two chapters. I would also like to thank several people at Oxford: Richard Teleky had faith in me through a difficult period; Sally Livingston, working from several versions of the manuscript, brought it order and clarity; and Phyllis Wilson did an outstanding job sorting out the editing for the computer.

To Judith Beirs, my wife and companion, I owe a special gratitude. Her support and loyalty through trying times, her tolerance of my preoccupations, and her impatience helped to propel me forward.

Kitchener-Waterloo
December 1988

Introduction

It is in the power of the Imperial Government, by sanctioning a confederation of these Provinces, to constitute a Dependency of the Empire.

Alexander Galt, Inspector-General of Canada, first politician to propose confederation, 1858.

Protection means much more than this. It will secure the influx of a large amount of foreign capital for manufacturing purposes that would never reach us as long as our present Free-trade tariff exists.

John Rykert, Conservative member (Ontario) during the National Policy debates, March 1879.

Are we the servile and supple tool of foreign capitalists, or are we going to preserve this country for our own people?

Representative James Burns Belford of Colorado, 1884.

A great proportion of our manufacturing is done with English money, and its profits go to England. A great bulk of the stock of our mines and ironworks is held in England, and the profits go into foreign pockets . . . Interest, earnings, rents, and profits are the shackles Americans have to fear; they are the modern development of the gives, the manacles, and the clanking chain.

The National Economist, *organ of the Southern Farmers Alliance (USA), July 1889.*

United States capital in Canada is not invested or used for the exclusive benefit of the Canadian people. As American production increases and there is a growing surplus to dispose of, not only will markets be found for it, but accumulating capital will be invested more and more abroad and will make a rich return for its use.

Eugene Foss, Governor of Massachusetts, 1913.

It is natural that Canada should depend largely on outside help for the financing of its development. Its population is small, its investment power weak, and its resources and possibilities most striking . . . Notwithstanding that Canadian banks have several million dollars on deposit in New York,

Canadian industrial development seems to attach more naturally to
Philadelphia and Boston.

Fred Field, editor of the Monetary Times *(Canada), 1914.*

There are businessmen, labor representatives and media commenta-
tors—even, I suppose, an occasional banker—all of whom have encouraged
this myth of the superiority of Canadian capital. That kind of nationalism is
economic nonsense. Canada cannot meet its capital needs from within its
borders. Unless we want a steady decline in our living standards, there is no
choice about importing capital. Provided that the bulk of those funds are
productively invested, there is little reason for concern.

Rowland Frazee, Chairman, Royal Bank of Canada, 1981.

We believe that US foreign direct investment has also made a contribution to
employment in the United States through the link between exports and
investment. Much of our trade with foreign countries originates with orders
placed by the subsidiaries of US companies located overseas. For example, 75
percent of our exports to the 300 largest companies in Canada originates from
the subsidiaries of US firms.

Harvey Bale, Assistant US Trade Representative for
Investment Policy, July 1981.

You've been talking of economic nationalism. I'm speaking of 1.5 million
unemployed who are not concerned with where investment comes from. They
are concerned with attracting investment to Canada so that they can have
jobs.

Prime Minister Brian Mulroney, September 1984.

At a black-tie affair at the Economic Club of New York on 10 December
1984, newly elected Prime Minister Brian Mulroney heralded a new era in
Canadian-American relations when he proclaimed that 'Canada is open for
business again'. Foreign investment was welcome and freer trade with the
United States desired. On the same evening that the prime minister made
his declaration of dependence to the financiers of New York, Bob White,
the Canadian director of the United Auto Workers, issued his call for
independence in Detroit: Canadian auto workers would separate from the
international and form an independent Canadian union.

These statements made on American soil were the opening salvoes in the
debate about Canada's future course that culminated in the passionate and
divisive free-trade election of 1988. It was a revival of an old and recurrent
debate about the nature and independence of Canadian society. Should
Canada defy the market forces of North America and try to make its way as
an independent society, or should it hitch its star to the economic colossus
to the south? Ever since the Annexation Manifesto of 1849 Canadians have
pondered this question.

Especially in their opening stages, these debates have been conducted
largely in the cold and technical language of economists, but the issues

involved have always signified more than trade, investment, and resources: as Rudyard Kipling said in 1911, they touch Canada's 'own soul'.[1] Choosing closer economic integration with the United States has always meant choosing the American power and value systems as well. Those values have represented pure classical liberalism—what in the 1980s came to be called 'neo-conservative' economics, in which the marketplace is virtually the only arbiter of social values, the power of big business is unrestricted, and the values of extreme individualism are paramount. Choosing a more independent economic course for Canada has always meant not only emphasizing trade links outside North America and government strategies to diversify the economy beyond resource exports, but also embracing communitarian values to partially offset those of the predominant economic liberalism. The Canadian soul has wanted a more peaceful and ordered society and has shown a greater willingness to use government and public institutions to compensate for the economic or social shortcomings of pure capitalism.

Brian Mulroney and Bob White also symbolized the class divisions and conflicts of economic interests that underlie the current Canadian debate on continental economic integration. Mulroney, the former President of the American-owned Iron Ore Company of Canada, represents well the position of continental corporate power that so resented the way the border restricted its ability to make controlling investments in whole sectors of the economies in both countries, constrained the movement of goods and personnel between head office and subsidiary, and hindered access to Canadian energy resources. White, the son of an immigrant farm labourer, quit school at fifteen and worked his way up the union ladder to become an eloquent spokesman for popular organizations and Canadian nationalists working to preserve Canada's mildly social democratic traditions in the areas of social services, regional development, and industrial policy.

In an unprecedented demonstration of near political unanimity, continental corporate business put its money and prestige into the campaign for free trade and the Conservative Party. On the other side, in an equally unprecedented fashion, popular organizations of feminists, church groups, unions, farmers, environmentalists, and many members of the arts community joined together in nationalist appeals to support the opposing side, represented by the Liberal and New Democratic parties. The result was an impassioned debate about the roles of business, government, and ordinary people in shaping the life of Canada that divided people along class lines. An Environics poll conducted a couple of weeks before the 1988 election showed how deep the class division was: 52 per cent of free-trade supporters earned more than $60,000 per year, while 57 per cent of opponents earned under $20,000 per year.[2]

The opponents narrowly won the free-trade debate, gaining a popular vote—52 per cent—equal to that of the Conservative Party's anti-reciprocity victories of 1891 and 1911,[3] but they lost the election because their votes were split between the Liberals and New Democrats. Mulroney's victory and the ensuing Free Trade Agreement completed his government's dismantling of most of the mild economic-nationalist policies, begun in the 1960s, that had started to reverse, to a small degree, the overwhelming extent of foreign ownership and control of Canada's manufacturing and resource sectors. In terms of foreign-ownership legislation, the 1984 and 1988 elections meant a return to Canada's historical open-door policy.[4]

Canadian business leaders have never been strongly nationalist, and since the Second World War they have been overwhelmingly continentalist. 'Continentalism'—meaning 'a closer and more cooperative relationship with the United States'—is a 'respectable word', according to journalist Anthony Westell, that 'needs to be brought back into the language of debate' on Canada-US relations.[5] George Grant, a twentieth-century professor of philosophy with the sensibilities of a nineteenth-century Tory, observed that

> after 1940 it was not in the interests of the economically powerful to be nationalists. Most of them made more money by being the representatives of American capitalism and setting up the branch plants. No class in Canada more welcomed the American managers than the established wealthy of Montreal and Toronto . . . Capitalism is, after all, a way of life based on the principle that the most important activity is profit-making. That activity led the wealthy in the direction of continentalism. They lost nothing essential to the principle of their lives in losing their country.[6]

Rowland Frazee, former chairman of the Royal Bank of Canada, typifies the economic élite in his overwhelming support for continental integration. Despite Canadian bankers' recent and massive exports of Canadian savings to foreign countries, especially in the Third World, Frazee advised that 'Canada cannot meet its capital needs from within its own borders. Unless we want a steady decline in our living standards, there is no choice about importing capital.'[7] This was not a new stance for Canadian bankers: when Walter Gordon introduced tax proposals in his 1963 budget to increase private Canadian ownership of the economy, it was the bankers who lobbied hardest in the successful effort to force the government to back down.

The historian Michael Bliss succinctly expressed the conventional wisdom about foreign investment: 'On the whole Canadians continue to believe—wisely, I think—that a limited but prosperous national existence is preferable to a pure, poor nationality.'[8] Ordinary Canadians, however, do not necessarily accept the conventional wisdom. Canadian nationalism is a subterranean movement. The idea that foreign investment makes Canadians richer but less Canadian has been incorporated into a standard Gallup poll question on the subject.[9] In response to the poll's unpalatable choice between prosperity and country, 36 per cent of Canadians agreed in 1986 that Canada should buy back the economy even if it meant a big reduction in living standards; 50 per cent were opposed.

For a brief nine-month period in 1980-81 the Canadian government, through the National Energy Program (NEP), departed from tradition by engaging in a serious, though high-priced, attempt to Canadianize the petroleum industry. Until then the industry had been only one-fifth Canadian-controlled.[10] Much to its chagrin, the Canadian Petroleum Association, dominated by multinationals, found that 84 per cent of Canadians approved the government's target of 50 per cent Canadianization by 1990.[11] Despite this approval, the effort did not move much beyond a one-third Canadian-control level before enormous pressure from the multinationals, combined with howls of protest from western premiers and the opposition parties, forced the government to retreat from one of the most popular policies in Canadian history.

Continually fed continentalist opinion by the media, Canadians swing back and forth between the assumptions of the élite and their own gnawing concerns over Canadian sovereignty. In good times, when confidence in the country is high, Canadians support independence in defiance of their opinion leaders.[12] In recessions, and sometimes in their aftermaths, a sense of desperation descends and the élite view prevails.

THE FAILURE OF CONSERVATIVE NATIONALISM

If the overwhelming majority of Canadian business leaders and much of the political élite are now continentalists, surely this was not always true. Donald Creighton, Canada's great conservative historian, spent much of his life canonizing the élite's nationalism during the National Policy era that John A. Macdonald initiated in 1879. 'Macdonald's whole plan for Canada', wrote Creighton, 'was essentially nationalist; every policy, political or economic, was conceived as a means to the same great nationalist goal.'[13] Macdonald 'had the temerity to suggest that the British connection, far from being a constitutional fetter, was a valuable alliance by which Canada could correct the imbalance of power on the North American continent and help ensure her own survival as a distinct and separate nation.'[14]

When E.P. Taylor, the Conrad Black of the 1960s, quipped 'Canadian nationalism? How old-fashioned can you get?' this was the sort of British-Canadian nationalism he had in mind.[15] Ironically, George Grant agreed with Taylor when he wrote his eloquent lament for the defeat of Canadian nationalism. In the 1920s 'the character of the country was self-evident', wrote Grant:

> To say it was British was not to deny it was North American ... We were grounded in the wisdom of Sir John A. Macdonald, who saw plainly more than a hundred years ago that the only threat to nationalism was from the

South, not from across the sea. To be a Canadian was to build, along with the French, a more ordered and stable society than the liberal experiment in the United States.[16]

Later in his book Grant stated: 'Those who loved the older traditions of Canada may be allowed to lament what has been lost.'[17]

What exactly was lost? The nationalism of the Canadian élite. In that nationalism there was certainly a powerful attachment for things British-Canadian: respect for rank, principle, law and order, stability, and non-materialist values, all symbolized by the British Crown. There was as well an element of what Canadians in later generations would call 'anti-Americanism', although it was more a fear of Americanization than a genuine hostility to the American people. 'Our freedom to develop our own resources, in our own way, by our own people, is to be curtailed by [reciprocity] with a foreign nation,' thundered George Tate Blackstock in 1911 to an overflow anti-reciprocity meeting at Massey Hall in Toronto. 'Our influence as a unit of the great British Empire would be diminished. And this in favor of the Stars and Stripes!' he proclaimed, amid hisses and cries of 'Never'![18] But conservative economic nationalism was curiously contradictory. While its adherents vociferously opposed free trade and economic union with the United States as 'veiled treason', they positively welcomed foreign ownership and control of the economy.[19]

As early as 1879, the year the National Policy was introduced, some politicians understood that the tariffs would lure American branch plants into Canada. 'Protection', said John Rykert, an Ontario Conservative, 'would secure the influx of a large amount of foreign capital for manufacturing purposes that would never reach us as long as our present Free-Trade tariff exists.'[20] This argument was commonly heard by the time of the debate over reciprocity (free trade) in the historic 1911 election campaign. Influential politicians and businessmen, who led the conservative nationalist and protectionist side to an upset victory over the Laurier Liberals with the cry 'No truck or trade with Yankees', were the same ones who proudly pointed to the tariffs as encouraging the establishment of American branch plants in Canada.

Observed the *Financial Post* in 1910:

> Our ministers at Ottawa have not the slightest desire to do anything . . . that will have any tendency whatever to check the movement of United States manufacturers to establish large plants in this country . . . It seems that the existence of our moderate tariff against United States manufactured goods has been instrumental in many cases in bringing us these industries. Hence a strong argument exists for not meddling overmuch with the duties.[21]

As Michael Bliss noted of the tariffs, it 'was a peculiarly self-defeating kind of economic nationalism. The funny thing was that we always wanted the enemy to jump over them. Some walls!'[22]

In fact, once American companies had located in Canada they joined the 'nationalist' brigade, hoping to exclude their rivals confined to the United States.[23] In 1920 an American government study pointed out that 'American manufacturers with branch establishments in Canada were opposed to reciprocity because it promised to open the Canadian market to other American products in competing lines.'[24] Harold Innis, Canada's brilliant political economist, carried the observation further:

> As part of her east-west programme, Canada had built up a series of imperial preferential arrangements in which Great Britain had felt compelled to acquiesce and which proved enormously advantageous to American branch plants. Paradoxically, the stoutest defenders of the Canadian tariff against the United States were the representatives of American capital investors. Canadian nationalism was systematically encouraged and exploited by American capital. Canada moved from colony to nation to colony.[25]

One may object that these are unfair judgements made with the benefit of hindsight. How could conservative nationalists have anticipated that foreign domination of Canadian industry would result from these meagre beginnings? After all, multinational corporations did not become major players in the world until after the Second World War. Can Canada's early conservative nationalism be faulted?

Yes. It did not take great prescience to understand the long-run implications of foreign ownership; indeed, Canada's apparent blindness to the consequences of a foreign-controlled economy was notable even at the time. The pre-First World War era, during which American branch plants first established a commanding presence in Canada, was the age of autarky and fierce nationalist rivalries among western countries.[26] In this climate it was common for countries to take actions designed to protect their economic sovereignty. Consider Sweden, a country that, like Canada, was a resource-exporter and industrially immature. In the early 1870s Britain and Germany, already industrial giants, began buying Swedish land, iron mines, ironworks, and forest resources. Alarmed by the long-run implications, the Riksdag, Sweden's parliament, launched an investigation and concluded that

> if this movement [foreign acquisitions] was allowed to continue, a large part of Sweden would gradually be bought up by rich foreign firms and companies, because [Sweden] . . . was in the first phase of economic development, with practically untouched natural resources and a scarcity of capital . . . Welcome as the capital these foreign firms and companies brought with them was, it could be obtained at too high a price, namely if all the profit of Swedish industry was to go abroad.[27]

Laws were passed over the next fifty years to restrict or reverse foreign ownership of Swedish land, resources, railways, and manufacturing industries.[28]

Late-developing Japan was even more wary of the political and economic implications of foreign investment. Not only did Japan forbid foreign control of its industries, but from the mid-1870s to the mid-1890s, a period of extreme shortage of Japanese capital, it even refused to borrow foreign funds. 'Neither the government nor the people', said Marquis Masayoshi Matsugata, 'favoured foreign debts because, as the world's history shows, such obligations were liable to cause trouble politically between the two countries concerned as creditor and debtor when no stable financial system was as yet established by the latter.'[29] In other words, foreign debts could lead to the loss of sovereignty.

Nationalist policies in Europe and Asia had little salience for Canadians at the turn of the century, but similar actions were taken closer to home. Many Americans became alarmed when foreign ownership of their economy reached levels long considered insignificant in Canada.[30]

As part of the American farmers' populist uprising against metropolitan control over prices, railways, and land monopoly (in a word, the 'trusts'), there was a campaign against 'alien land holders' and foreign ownership generally. Britain, America's old enemy, was the target. Echoing sentiments expressed in Sweden about foreign landownership, the *National Economist*, the official paper of the Southern Farmers' Alliance, charged that

> The hold of this deadly monster [English landlordism] is at last being loosened on the green sod [Ireland], but it has seized upon the fresh energy of America, and is steadily fixing its fangs into our social life, until even now thousands of so-called free Americans are as much the vassals of English masters as the most oppressed of Ireland.'[31]

But American farmers did not limit their complaints to foreign landownership. The same paper used strong invective about English control of American manufacturing and resource companies:

> . . . a great proportion of our manufacturing is done with English money, and its profits go to England. A great bulk of the stock of our mines and ironworks is held in England, and the profits go into foreign pockets . . . Interest, earnings, rents, and profits are the shackles Americans have to fear; they are the modern development of the gives, the manacles, and the clanking chain.[32]

Although farmers' organizations and trade unionists in the Knights of Labor were the driving force behind these sentiments, such ideas were not limited to a populist minority. Alien landownership was a central issue in the 1884 presidential election. James Blaine, the Republican candidate, ran his campaign on the theme of 'America for Americans' and asserted that land 'should be disposed of only to actual settlers and those who are citizens of the Republic, or willing to become so'.[33] The Democrats, not to be outdone, made similar promises. But the first concrete steps came at the state level, mainly in the west. In the end, congressional action against alien landownership was mild, but the heated campaign was said to have driven home the 'swarm of American sharpers' who had been selling American real estate in London and 'scared the hitherto credulous English' away from American investments.[34]

Such sentiments found little support in Canada at the time.[35] Canadian economic nationalism was a strange brew in the National Policy era: free trade was bad but foreign ownership was good. Canada's curiously incomplete nationalism during its early industrialization goes a long way to explaining Canada's unique level of foreign ownership in the late twentieth century.

FOREIGN OWNERSHIP IN COMPARATIVE PERSPECTIVE

In 1978 the United Nations studied foreign-ownership levels in thirty countries and found great disparities among them.[36] Canada, a member of the annual economic summit of the seven major industrial powers, found itself in unaccustomed company. According to the UN study, Nigeria had the most foreign ownership of its industry, followed by Canada, Malaysia, Ghana, and Brazil. The advanced country closest to Canada was Australia, hardly a strong manufacturing economy; it occupied seventh place. Old-industrial Belgium ranked number ten. Canada's colleagues at the economic summit were in the bottom half of the list, with Japan and the United States dead last.

Since the 1978 survey the 'foreign direct investment' levels (the technical term for foreign ownership) in Canada and the US have converged a little. The 57 per cent foreign-ownership level of Canadian manufacturing in 1974 had shrunk by 1986 to 49 per cent of manufacturing profits and sales and 44 per cent of assets. Part of the decline can be attributed to the establishment of the Foreign Investment Review Agency in 1974 and other Canadianization measures.[37] American corporations made up the bulk of the foreign-controlled sector in Canada, accounting for 72 per cent of the assets and an astounding 88 per cent of the profits of this sector in 1983.[38] On the other hand, foreign direct investment in American industry increased dramatically from the 3 to 4 per cent level of the UN study (1974) to about 10 per cent in manufacturing and 5 to 6 per cent of total US assets by 1987.[39]

In recent years the two great foreign-investing nations of the past century or more, Britain and the United States, have experienced a little of what it's like to be on the receiving end of foreign ownership. Since 1973 the nineteenth-century absentee-ownership issue, long forgotten except in the Midwest and Rocky Mountain states, has been resurrected in the US. The country's leaders are ambivalent about foreign direct investment. On the international stage American governments champion the unrestricted investment of capital, and roundly criticize resistance to foreign economic control as nationalistic and discriminatory. On the other hand, there is growing concern about the effects of foreign direct investment in the United States itself.

In December 1985 *The New York Times* prominently displayed a three-part series, 'Buying into America'. Although considerable support for foreign direct investment was expressed, a growing number of critics voiced concerns familiar to Canadians. Governor Richard Lamm of Colorado was one of several politicians to raise the spectre of what he called 'economic colonialism'. Uneasiness was evident on a wide range of issues. Many worried about the loss of American independence as a result of political campaign contributions by foreign companies and foreigners buying into key strategic sectors. Concern was raised as well about branch plants restricting exports and at the same time importing from parent companies rather than buying from local suppliers. Others feared that America would lose its technological lead because research and development is usually conducted in the parent company rather than in branch plants.[40]

American legislators have not come to grips with all these problems, but they have acted quickly on many of them. The 1974 Federal Election Campaign Act prohibits foreign nationals from making campaign contributions, and since 1975 a standing interagency watchdog committee has monitored foreign control of strategic industrial sectors. Foreign ownership is restricted in many sectors. In important areas such as defence, radio and television operators, and domestic air carriers, foreign control is prohibited outright. In many other sectors foreign ownership is restricted by legislation, or foreign companies are deemed ineligible for state aid. Domestically owned industries with important defence contracts (for example, electronics or auto production) are heavily subsidized, especially in research and development, while foreign-owned firms cannot obtain defence work.[41] State governments often have even stricter legislation than the federal government and in some cases ban foreign control of industry altogether.[42]

In the mid-1980s Britain experienced some of the same debates about foreign direct investment. 'I'm not', said Edward Heath, former Conservative prime minister, 'anti-American'.[43] He had to make the ritual disclaimer when opposing General Motors' attempted buy-out of British-Leyland and Ford's bid to take over Austin-Rover (a group within British-Leyland). These were Britain's two remaining domestically-owned auto companies. It was a humiliating experience for Britain, the oldest foreign investor in the industrial era. Many Britons worried about the threat of foreign, especially American, ownership to British independence. As the *Guardian* put it: 'America is stripping Europe of its independent manufacturing capacity. And even more crudely in cultural, political and economic terms: we're willy nilly becoming the 51st state'.[44] In the end, neither company fell into American hands.

Yet despite the growth of foreign-ownership levels in the United States and Britain, the extent of foreign ownership in Canada remains unparalleled among developed nations. If Canada is unique in this respect, the obvious questions are, why is this so? and when did it happen? The latter question will be dealt with in the following pages. Why Canada developed in this peculiar way is the subject of this book.

FOREIGN OWNERSHIP ESTABLISHED EARLY

Canadians know less about their own collective history than do most other peoples. An outsider could easily conclude that Canadians had recently experienced a traumatic accident and that its people were suffering from historical amnesia. In this state of mind, misconceptions abound. Peering dimly at the forgotten past, many Canadians believe that industry only recently came to Canada with the American branch plants. This is not the case. Industry is not new to Canada. A century before Confederation Canadian iron was said to be of better quality than English and American iron, and perhaps as good as Swedish. When England was the only country undergoing the industrial revolution Canadian foundries were producing cast-iron stoves that matched English imports in quality as well as in price.[45] The engines that powered the *Royal William*, the first steamboat to cross the Atlantic, were built in Canada.

In the late 1800s, before the age of the automobile, the manufacturing of farm machinery was a dominant industry. Implement companies staged popular field competitions to demonstrate the superiority of their horse-drawn machines. The Paris Exposition of 1889 featured the Eiffel Tower and the greatest farm-machinery contest ever, in which all the major international firms were represented. Massey's Toronto light binder, designed and made in Canada, took first prize and a special trophy of honour. Within a few years Canada was exporting its harvesters, mowers, and ploughs to over forty countries, with Britain, Germany, and France buying almost two-thirds of the total.[46]

These examples are not exceptions. According to one set of estimates, Canada was the eighth largest manufacturing country in the world in 1870 and seventh largest by 1900.[47] Thus, despite its small population, Canada was in the big leagues both as a producer and as a consumer of industrial goods. At the time of Confederation Canada manufactured more than Japan and Sweden and had the world's third largest merchant marine, if Prince Edward Island's and Newfoundland's fleets are counted.[48]

On the ceiling of the Sistine Chapel in Rome Michelangelo painted a striking picture of God the Creator stretching out his arm to impart life to man, the inert mortal. In a similar way, it is commonly thought, American capitalists bestowed on Canada the gift of modern industry through their expert management, advanced technology, and infusion of risk capital. Without American help Canadians would still be eking out a primitive existence as 'hewers of wood and drawers of water'.

Not so. Canadian industry had a promising start, and then the branch plants came—not the other way round. In fact, it was Canada's industrial development that attracted American capital to invest in Canadian manufacturing. It is only recently that American industrial investment has been shifting to low-wage countries, particularly in the Pacific Rim. In the early twentieth century US companies invested heavily in manufacturing only in the already advanced countries[49] (Western Europe and Canada).

Contemporary scholars usually refer to the beginning of the Second World War as the time when Canada passed into the American economic orbit. The American-born rugged individualist C.D. Howe has been portrayed as the ring-leader in Canada's headlong rush towards continental integration in the 1940s and 1950s.[50] As Minister of Munitions and Supply he used the War Measures Act to commandeer factories and develop a formidable Canadian war-goods industry, only to sell most of it back to private, often American, interests after the war.[51] And in the mid-1950s Howe was at it again. His approval of American ownership and control of the trans-Canada natural-gas pipeline from Alberta to Ontario led to John Diefenbaker's charge that the government's 'touching solicitude' for American big business would make Canada 'a virtual economic forty-ninth state'.[52] The 1952-60 period witnessed the largest inflow of American capital in Canadian history, confirming the idea that it was during the war and immediately thereafter that American branch plants came to dominate the economy.

In *Silent Surrender* (1970) Kari Levitt emphasized the shift from British portfolio (loan) capital to American direct (ownership) capital that started in the 1920s and 1930s and become decisive by 1946. It was this shift, argued Levitt, that signalled Canada's transition from the British to the American economic sphere of influence.[53] This view made intuitive sense because the shift coincided with Canada's switch in political and military allegiance from the declining British to the rising American empire, first under the Permanent Joint Board on Defence (of North America) in 1940 and later under the American-led alliances of NATO (North Atlantic Treaty Organization) and NORAD (North American Aerospace Defence Command). But despite its logical appeal the theory ignores evidence of substantial American domination of Canadian manufacturing and resource industries at a much earlier time.

At the turn of the century Europeans used the terms 'American invasion' and 'Americanization' to describe both the penetration of their markets by American exports and the spectacular purchases of some of their venerable industries by American capitalists.[54] Alarmed at American attempts to capture the British retail tobacco trade, Phillips, a British tobacco company, carried advertisements depicting Uncle Sam kidnapping England and crushing workmen. The House of Morgan's purchase of part-ownership of the Leyland shipping line in Britain caused the greatest clamour. Sir James Woodhouse suggested in Parliament that 'Americans are gradually capturing our industries', while Admiral Sir E.R. Fremantle naturally saw the threat in strategic terms: 'What is the use', he asked of the Morgan takeover, 'of soldiers and sailors sacrificing their lives for a country so disposed?'[55] But despite the hue and cry in Europe, the real American 'industrial invasion' occurred in Canada. By 1929, the date of the first survey of American investments abroad, the value of US direct investments in Canada was 50 per cent greater than in all of Europe.

As early as 1914 there were already 450 American branch plants and subsidiaries in Canada.[56] Most were obscure, and some soon went out of business; others became household names to generations of Canadians. Several have since reverted to Canadian ownership. In chemical and related fields there was Kodak, Parke Davis, United Drug, Sherwin Williams, Glidden, Dominion Paint, Benj. Moore, Goodyear Tire, Uniroyal, and United States Rubber. Westinghouse, RCA, Hot Point, and Northern Electric (now Northern Telecom) were among US-owned electrical companies. In the iron-products group were such notables as IBM (called Computing-Tabulating Recording Company until 1924), Ford Motor Company, National Cash Register, Remington Firearms, Singer Sewing Machines, Pratt and Whitney, Frost Wire Fences, Algoma Steel, Gillette Safety Razor, American Can, Dominion Bridge, and Yale Lock. In food processing there were Heinz, Quaker Oats, Coca-Cola, Swift Canada, Chase and Sanborn, Borden's Milk, and Wrigley's (chewing gum); in agricultural implements, John Deere, International Harvester, and J.I. Case. Several American companies established themselves early in the financial field, especially in insurance: Traveler's Life, New York Life, Prudential Life, Aetna Life, and Dun and Bradstreet, a credit-rating company. In miscellaneous fields were Columbia records, the Thermos Bottle Company, and Waterman's Pens.

By the First World War American capital was already important in the resource sector as well, with such companies as Imperial Oil, International Nickel (INCO), British American (later renamed Gulf), Dome Mines, Asbestos Corporation, Crown Zellerbach, and Johns-Manville. There were also numerous American-owned companies that, through mergers, would prove to be building-blocks in the formation of later US giants in Canada: General Motors (McLaughlin-Buick), du Pont, General Foods, Union Carbide (Canadian National Carbon), Aluminum Company of Canada (ALCAN), Canadian General Electric, Canadian International Paper, and the F.W. Woolworth Company.[57]

After the war American ownership and control increased dramatically. By 1926, the date of the first comprehensive survey on the question, it accounted for 30 per cent of Canadian manufacturing and 32 per cent of Canadian mining and smelting. By 1962, after the C.D. Howe era had ended, US control had climbed further, to 45 per cent in manufacturing and 51 per cent in mining and smelting.[58] Only part of that increase resulted from new infusions of American capital into Canada: after 1926 much of it was due to the reinvestment of earnings of US subsidiaries, concentrated as they were in the growth industries of the twentieth century. Clearly American business had established a powerful position in this country before the Second World War. So much for another misconception.

The early influx of American branch plants was part of a broader American trade 'invasion' of Canada. Before the First World War imports of American manufactured goods soared to unprecedented levels. In 1899, when the American invasion was first noticed in Europe, nine of the most advanced countries on that continent, with a combined population thirty-five times larger than Canada's, imported four times the value of American manufactured goods that Canada did.[59] Fourteen years later a large number of American branch plants had entered the country and the value of Canada's US imports was more than half that of the US goods imported by the European countries.[60] By 1929, at the end of the second great influx of US branch plants into Canada, these same European countries, now twenty-two times as populous as Canada, imported only 12 per cent more American goods than did this country.

The National Policy was intended to encourage the replacement of foreign imports with Canadian-made goods and so provide jobs for Canadians. 'We have no manufactures here,' exclaimed John A. Macdonald, exaggerating a little for effect. 'We have no work people . . . If Canada had a judicious system of taxation [tariffs] they would be toiling and doing well in their own country.'[61] Unfortunately, the outcome fell short of the promise. The American branch plants, which were supposed to contribute to the goal of replacing the imports, had the opposite effect, acting instead as conduits for American parts, machinery, and brand names. Even if Canadians were reluctant to acknowledge it, foreign observers were well aware of this effect at the time. A US Senate report in 1931 noted that the 'branch factory, by and large, is merely a more intensive method of selling an American product in foreign markets; the branch factory, theoretically at least, takes up the work where ordinary sales methods stop.'[62]

British Empire countries had a similar perception in the 1920s. Canadian trade officials claimed that the products of US branch plants were Canadian-made and therefore eligible for a preferential trade arrangement then being set up within the British Empire. But the Australians, who were considering adopting preferential Empire tariffs, were not fooled by a 'made in Canada' label stamped on a product largely made in the United States and assembled in Canada. 'I find', complained one Australian politician in 1924, that business people in the United States of America are investing capital in Canada and opening up factories there, where parts of machinery manufactured in the United States of America are assembled in order to get the benefit of the preferential tariff granted by Britain to Canada. As soon as the Americans know that preference is to be granted to Canadian goods by Australia, this country will be flooded with articles of Yankee origin.[63]

Fifty-four years later a Canadian government study belatedly acknowledged the connection between American branch plants and the massive imports of finished goods into Canada. Foreign-controlled importers, the 1978 study found, accounted for fully 72 per cent of Canada's imports by companies.[64] Clearly, the 'American invasion' occurred in Canada more intensively than in Europe; the result was that this country imported articles with a high job content and exported low-job-content resources in exchange. This became an enduring pattern. The National Policy, an import-substitution strategy, was not compatible in the long run with full industrialization.

The late twentieth century is a time of rapid technological change that promises to remake the nature of our society. Our sights are set on the future, often with more than a little trepidation. Robotics, fibre-optics, lasers, the new ceramics, software systems, the 'chip', small-batch custom-tailored production, biological engineering, and a Star Wars generation of weapons are among the changes leading us into a very different society in the twenty-first century. Many of these changes hold the promise of jobless growth, especially in the high-wage economies of the industrialized world, as new technique after new technique streamlines production and services; fewer workers are able to produce more. The term 'future shock'[65] has entered the language to describe the rapidity of these and other changes. In such times it is easy to forget that the technological and social revolution our great grandparents experienced at the turn of the twentieth century was, if anything, more profound than the one we are experiencing now. The way Canada responded to economic change when our industrial structure was still in its fluid formative stage has a bearing on our prospects for adapting to the demands of the late twentieth century.

The first thirty years of this century saw the rise of three important new industries: automobile, chemical, and electrical. The latter had such profound implications that even Vladimir Lenin, the leader of the Russian Revolution, claimed effusively that 'Soviets *plus* electrification equals communism'.[66] It was in these three new industries, as well as in the machinery sector that underlay them, that American branch plants gained an early and decisive grip on Canadian manufacturing. By the early 1930s over 40 per cent of machinery and chemical products were made in American-owned factories, while in electrical goods the figure was 68 per cent and in automotive products 83 per cent.[67] Henry Ford, the Michigan farm boy turned inventor, then racing-car driver, and finally captain of industry, produced the world's first cheap car to replace the family horse. 'I will build a motorcar for the great multitude,' he insisted. 'As the volume goes up, it is certain to get cheaper per unit produced.' He fixed his design on the Model T and set out to lower the price by pioneering assembly-line, mass-production techniques. Soon a Model T was being turned out every twenty-four seconds, and by 1913 the price was down to $490. The next year he doubled his workers' wages and shortened the working day all in one stroke to solve the problem of worker turnover. A riot broke out among thousands of would-be employees desperate to join the new industrial order. The Employers Association of Detroit accused Ford of undermining the capitalist system. Meanwhile profits and sales soared.[68]

The Ford Motor Company of Detroit had been capitalized at a mere $100,000 in 1903, with Henry Ford and a partner holding 51 per cent of the shares. The next year Gordon MacGregor, a Canadian carriage-maker, struck a deal with Ford to establish an affiliate in Canada. MacGregor would supply the capital for the Canadian subsidiary (capitalized, incidentally, at a higher value than the parent firm the year before) in return for all Ford rights and processes in perpetuity in Canada, New Zealand, Australia, India, South Africa, and British Malaya. The Ford Motor Company of Detroit received 51 per cent of the shares of the Canadian subsidiary in return for its patent rights.[69] Over the next twenty-two years Ford's profit from its Canadian affiliate was enough to make a pirate blush:

> On an initial capitalization of $125,000, only part of which was paid in cash, the company paid cash dividends of $14,551,238 between 1905 and 1927. Since the increase of $6,875,000 in issued capital during those years was entirely by way of stock dividends, the profits can only be matched by the much more unbelievable earnings—on an equally tiny initial investment—of the parent company.[70]

Thus on the basis of providing technology rights but no investment, Ford of Detroit had acquired a Canadian subsidiary (worth over $55,000,000 by 1933) that sent handsome profits back across the border. By 1927 American investors had acquired 85 per cent of the Canadian subsidiary.[71]

Imperial Oil earned similar profit levels in Canada for Standard Oil and the Rockefellers. On an initial investment of $315,884.16 in 1898 and later infusions of about $23 million before 1921, Standard Oil of New Jersey (later Exxon) received generous cash dividends of $13 million from 1907 to 1921, $52 million in the 1920s, and $177 million in the 1930s. Meanwhile the value of its assets in Canada mushroomed and Exxon invested no new money in Imperial between 1921 and 1951.[72] These are illustrations, more extreme than most, of a more general phenomenon. Reinvestment of profits made in Canadian subsidiaries grew from small amounts to gigantic sums through the parent companies' control of the new growth industries.[73]

Many Canadian subsidiaries began as partnerships struck between US and Canadian businesses. Some carriage-makers made the jump from the horse and buggy to the automobile, bringing proven production techniques and business-organization methods with them. William C. Durant's company turned out 200 carriages a day by assembling already-finished parts in specialized plants making bodies, wheels, upholstery, paint, varnish, axles, and springs before moving into automobiles and creating General Motors Corporation.[74] It was only natural that the McLaughlins of Oshawa, Ontario, largest carriage-makers in the British Empire, would team up with Durant and establish an auto company in Canada.

R.S. McLaughlin, later affectionately known as 'Colonel Sam', initially had a more independent relationship with General Motors than MacGregor had had with Ford. The McLaughlin Motor Car Company, 51 per cent owned by the McLaughlin Carriage Company, started producing its own car in 1907—the McLaughlin-Buick—using engines from GM. Yet a decade later, at the close of the First World War, GM bought out the McLaughlin interest and made Colonel Sam head of the Canadian subsidiary, a position he held until his death in 1972 at the age of 100.

When assessing American economic influence in 1914 or 1926, it is not enough to look at percentage ownership of Canadian industry. US subsidiaries became powerful in the early years of this century and gradually extended their grip from this base long before C.D. Howe strode across the Canadian political horizon.

CONCLUSION

Canada was unique among the industrialized countries in permitting and encouraging so much foreign ownership. Moreover, the foundations for a branch-plant economy were laid much earlier than is commonly believed. In the nineteenth century Canada showed promise as an industrial power and thereby attracted American companies to locate in Canada. Clearly, then, American-based technology, management, and investment did not create Canada's industry in the first place.

This fact raises some intriguing questions. Was it inevitable that Canada would become a northern extension of American industrialism? Was geography, a comparative advantage in resources, or external American pressure the cause? Alternatively, were factors internal to Canadian society largely responsible? Most important, did Canada ever have a chance to develop an independent economy? These issues are taken up in Chapter 1.

Chapter 2 examines the problems and opportunities in countries beginning to industrialize in the late nineteenth century. Did other countries, at a level of development similar to Canada's, face the same dilemmas regarding foreign control and technological dependence? If so, how were they able to develop more independently than Canada?

The intriguing case of Sweden is explored in depth in Chapter 3. Like Canada, Sweden began to industrialize well after its dominant neighbours, Britain and Germany, had become well-established industrial and military powers. Both had designs on Sweden's bountiful resources, but the Swedes resisted their numerous attempts to make the country an economic dependency. Why did geographic proximity and external economic pressure not mould Sweden into a branch-plant economy like Canada? What characteristics of Swedish society made Sweden react so differently from Canada to similar conditions?

Chapter 4 examines the social and cultural milieu that made Canadians receptive to the idea that foreign ownership, management, and technology were crucial for development. The influence of an economic élite, French/English antagonisms, and Canada's relations with Britain are all considered, and some basic questions are addressed. Were Canadian business leaders less protective than those in other developing countries regarding proprietary control over their own country? Why were popular-democratic movements so feeble during the formative period when the nation-state and the branch-plant structure were established? Why has the latent nationalism of ordinary Canadians had so little impact on government policies regarding foreign investment?

'Canada is a nation created in defiance of geography,' wrote W.A. Mackintosh.[75] Not so, rejoined Harold Innis, his colleague: 'Canada emerged as a political entity with boundaries largely determined by the fur trade . . . The present Dominion emerged not in spite of geography but because of it.'[76] Whether Canada was created in defiance of geography is open to dispute, but it is difficult to challenge the idea that Canada was created in defiance of the market forces of North America.[77] Throughout Canadian history, the state has been instrumental in developing and maintaining a distinct economic unit in the northern half of North America.[78] The Canadian Pacific Railway, the St Lawrence Seaway, Trans-Canada Pipelines, Petro-Canada, and other economic institutions were possible only because of the active intervention of the Canadian state. The nature of this intervention is explored in Chapter 5. Why did the actions of governments, predicated as they were during the National Policy era on the creation of an independent society, lead to a branch-plant economy? And what were the long-term consequences of this type of economic development?

Scholars who have focussed on government restrictions on foreign ownership in recent decades have given little attention to such restrictions in the nineteenth and early twentieth centuries. Chapter 6 explores early attempts at restrictions on foreign control over land and resources, banks, oil, hydroelectricity, and transportation, and accounts for successes and failures in those attempts.

The concluding chapter discusses the lessons to be learned from Canada's early 'open for business' policy. Are the political and social conditions that gave rise to Canada's uniquely anti-nationalist responses still present? Once vested interests have become entrenched, is it as easy to reverse foreign economic domination as it was to bring it about in the first place? Finally, how do these questions bear on Canada's transition to the third industrial revolution as we near the twenty-first century?

NOTES

[1]Castell Hopkins, *The Canadian Annual Review of Public Affairs 1911* (Toronto: Annual Review Publishing Co., 1912), p. 221.

[2]*Globe and Mail*, 19 Nov. 1988, p. A1.

[3]Winning a bare majority of votes was more difficult for free-trade opponents in the 1988 election because whereas in 1891 and 1911 the economic élite threw its weight behind the opposition, in 1988 it had abandoned the cause. The Conservative Party's reversal of its previous opposition to free trade is understandable, however: the party remained loyal to the economic élite. It was the latter that changed its position first. In 1891 and 1911 the Conservatives won 51 per cent of the vote. See Hopkins, *Canadian Annual Review of Public Affairs 1911*, p. 265.

[4]The opening of Canadian banking to American investment and control in the Free Trade Agreement was a new departure, reversing 170 years of legislation protecting Canadian control. See Chapter 6.

[5]Anthony Westell, 'Economic Integration with the USA', *International Perspectives*, Nov. and Dec. 1984: 4.

[6]George Grant, *Lament for a Nation* (Toronto: McClelland and Stewart, 1965), p. 47.

[7]Rowland Frazee, 'Working Smarter: Improving Productivity in Canada' in G. Lowe and H. Krahn, *Working Canadians* (Toronto: Methuen, 1984), p. 176.

[8]Michael Bliss, 'Canadianizing American Business: The Roots of the Branch Plant' in I. Lumsden, ed., *Close the 49th Parallel Etc.* (Toronto: University of Toronto Press, 1970), p. 40.

[9]'Some experts are suggesting that Canada should buy back a majority control—say 51 per cent—of US companies in Canada. Even though it might mean a big reduction in our standard of living, would you approve of this or not?' (*Toronto Star*, 7 Aug. 1986, p. A3).

There was no polling in the late 19th and early 20th centuries. Canadians usually supported closer integration with the United States more strongly during or immediately after recessions than during periods of prolonged prosperity.

[10]Canada, Petroleum Monitoring Agency, *Canadian Petroleum Industry. 1983. Monitoring Survey* (Ottawa: Minister of Supply and Services Canada, 1984), p. 6-1. Canadian control moved up from 23.1% to 36.5% between 1980 and 1981 as measured by upstream revenues or from 18.7% to 25.9% as measured by petroleum-related revenues. Petro Canada's buy-out of Petrofina and Dome's purchase of Hudson's Bay Oil and Gas were the largest in a series of Canadian takeovers. See G. Bruce Doern and Glen Toner, *The Politics of Energy: The Development and Implementation of the N.E.P.* (Toronto: Methuen, 1985), pp. 109-10, 228-30, 355-8.

[11]*Nickle's Daily Oil Bulletin*, 15 Sept. 1981.

[12]Canadian Gallup Polls, *Canadians Speak Out* (Toronto: McNamara Press, 1980), pp. 135-7.

[13]Donald Creighton, 'Macdonald and the Anglo-Canadian Alliance' in *Towards the Discovery of Canada* (Toronto: Macmillan, 1972), p. 224.

[14]Ibid., p. 214.

[15]Cited in Kari Levitt, *Silent Surrender: The Multinational Corporation in Canada* (Toronto: Macmillan, 1970), p. 144.

[16]Grant, *Lament for a Nation*, pp. 3-4.

[17]Ibid., p. 96.

[18]*Toronto Telegram*, 10 March 1911, p. 16.

[19]Some Liberals took the opposite tack by favouring free trade and criticizing foreign ownership. For example, H.H. Miller (Liberal, South Grey) commented: 'If I am to make a choice as between a large factory built in Canada with United States capital, and a large factory built in Canada with Canadian capital, I will every time choose the latter . . . the net profit from that American institution will be taken to the United States to further develop that country' (Canada, *House of Commons Debates*, 9 March 1911), p. 4954.

[20]Rykert was quoting approvingly from A.T. Wood, a Liberal Protectionist (Canada, *House of Commons Debates*, 28 March 1879), p. 789.

[21]Cited in Bliss, 'Canadianizing American Business,' p. 29.

[22]Ibid., p. 32.

[23]See *The Independent* (a New York newspaper), 28 Sept. 1911, pp. 709-10.

[24]United States Tariff Commission, *Reciprocity with Canada: A Study of the Arrangements of 1911* (Washington: Government Printing Office, 1920), p. 76.

[25]Harold Innis, 'Great Britain, The United States and Canada', *Essays in Canadian Economic History* (Toronto: University of Toronto Press, 1973), p. 405.

[26]This argument is elaborated in Chapter 2.

[27]E.E. Fleetwood, *Sweden and Capital Imports and Exports* (Geneva: Journal de Genève, 1947), pp. 30-1.

[28]These policies are summarized in Gordon Laxer, 'The Social Origins of Canada's Branch Plant Economy, 1837-1914' (Ph.D. dissertation, University of Toronto, 1981), pp. 287-92.

[29]Marquis Masayoshi Matsugata, 'Japan's Finance', in Count Shigenobu Okuma, ed., *Fifty Years of New Japan* (London: Smith, Elder & Co., 1909), p. 375.

[30]To my knowledge there has not been a full-length study of American responses to foreign ownership of the US economy in the 19th century. W.A. Williams had the same impression in *The Roots of the Modern American Empire* (New York: Random House, 1969). There are some excellent journal articles on the subject. See, for example, Richard Clements' 'British Investment and American Legislative Restrictions in the Trans-Mississippi West, 1880-1900', *Mississippi Valley Historical Review* 42 (1955): 207-28, and his 'Farmers' Attitudes Toward British Investment in American Industry,' *Journal of Economic History* 15 (1955): 151-9.

[31]From the *National Economist* (Washington) 1 (June 1889): 229, cited in Clements, 'British Investment and American Legislative Restrictions', p. 215.

[32]Clements, 'Farmers' Attitudes', p. 155. In 1890 the Southern Farmer's Alliance (whites only) had between one and three million members. See John Hicks, *The Populist Revolt* (Minneapolis: University of Minnesota Press, 1931), pp. 76-127.

[33]Williams, *The Roots of the Modern American Empire*, p. 282.

[34]Harold Dunham, *Government Handout* (New York: Da Capo Press, 1970), p. 300. The House and the Senate passed separate bills and had difficulty harmonizing their policies. Bills restricting alien landownership were finally signed by the president in 1887 and 1891. The laws did not apply to existing holdings.

[35]The first major criticisms of foreign direct investment were voiced in the 1920s. See Chapter 5.

[36]United Nations Commission on Transnational Corporations, *Transnational Corporations in World Development: A Re-Examination* (New York, 1978), p. 263. Criteria for determining foreign ownership and date of surveys differed among the countries.

[37]Statistics Canada, Industrial Organization and Finance Division, *Annual Report (CALURA)*,

Part 1—Corporations 1986 (Ottawa: Minister of Supply and Services, 1988); D.G. McFetridge, Canadian Industry in Transition, vol. 2, Royal Commission on the Economic and Development Prospects for Canada (Macdonald Commission) research report (Toronto: University of Toronto Press, 1986), p. 24.

[38]Canada, Minister of Supply and Services, Annual Report of the Corporations and Labour Unions Returns Act 1983 (CALURA) (Ottawa, 1986), p. 58.

[39]Toronto Star, 29 July 1988, p. C3, citing a study by the Congressional Economic Leadership Institute. See also R. David Belli, 'Foreign Direct Investment in the United States: Highlights From the 1980 Benchmark Survey,' Survey of Current Business (US Dept. of Commerce) 63, no. 10 (Oct. 1983): 27. The United States applies a much more stringent definition of foreign ownership than does Canada. Foreign direct investment in the US is deemed to exist when one foreign person directly or indirectly owns or controls 10% or more of the voting securities of a US business (ibid., p. 25.) In Canada foreign control is said to exist when non-residents own a majority of a corporation's voting rights (Canada, CALURA 1983, p. 105.)

[40]New York Times, 29, 30, 31 Dec. 1985.

[41]The US Department of Defense supports between one-third and one-quarter of all scientists and engineers in the United States. The Free Trade Agreement dismantles most Canadian restrictions against foreign ownership and control but does not touch existing US regulations, which are grandfathered under article 1607 (Canada, External Affairs, The Canada-US Free Trade Agreement, [Ottawa: External Affairs, 1988], pp. 237-8).

[42]Foreign Investment Review Agency, 'Barriers to Foreign Investment in the United States' (Policy, Research and Communications Branch, staff document, n.d.). Missouri prohibits foreign control of all companies located in the state (p. 49).

[43]The Guardian, 7 Feb. 1986, p. 14.

[44]Ibid., p. 14.

[45]Benjamin Sulte, 'Les Forges Saint Maurice', Mélanges Historiques, vol. 6 (Montreal: Malchelosse, 1920), pp. 179-80.

[46]Merrill Denison, Harvest Triumphant (Toronto: McClelland and Stewart, 1948), pp. 95-113; Canada Year Book (1901), p. 228.

[47]League of Nations, Industrialization and Foreign Trade (New York: League of Nations, 1945), p. 13. Levels of manufacturing development are discussed in Chapters 1 and 2.

[48]Globe, 1 July 1867, p. 1.

[49]Only Canada received substantial amounts of American industrial and resource capital. The usual pattern was for industrial capital to go to Europe and resource capital to flow to the underdeveloped world. See Mira Wilkins, The Emergence of Multinational Enterprise: American Business Abroad from the Colonial Era to 1914 (Cambridge: Harvard University Press, 1970), and United States, American Direct Investments in Foreign Countries (Washington: Trade Information Bulletin #731, 1930).

[50]Grant, Lament for a Nation, pp. 40-1; Clarkson, Canada and the Reagan Challenge, pp. 6-7.

[51]Robert Bothwell and William Kilbourn, C.D. Howe: A Biography (Toronto: McClelland and Stewart, 1979), pp. 128-96.

[52]Ibid., p. 305.

[53]Levitt, Silent Surrender, pp. 58-70.

[54]The term 'American invasion' was first used in 1897 by Austria's foreign minister. Three books were written about the phenomenon in 1901-2. See Wilkins, Emergence of Multinational Enterprise, pp. 70-1. The term was soon used regarding Canada; see for example Robert H. Montgomery, 'Our Industrial Invasion of Canada,' World's Work V, Jan. 1903, pp. 2978-98.

[55]Richard Heindel, The American Impact on Great Britain 1898-1914 (Philadelphia: University of Pennsylvania Press, 1940), pp. 148-51.

[56]F.W. Field, *Capital Investments in Canada*, 3rd ed. (Montreal: Monetary Times of Canada, 1914), pp. 39-42.

[57]The list of US-owned companies was compiled from several sources: Field, *Capital Investments in Canada*, pp. 39-52; H. Marshall et al., eds, *Canadian-American Industry* (Toronto: McClelland and Stewart, 1976), pp. 29-174; Wilkins, *Emergence of Multinational Enterprise*, pp. 135-48, 216; Wallace Clement, *The Canadian Corporate Elite* (Toronto: McClelland and Stewart, 1974), pp. 401-28. Canadian General Electric was organized in 1892 out of several US subsidiaries. It was Canadian-owned from 1895 to 1923, when its control reverted to General Electric (US). When Canadian-owned it was technologically dependent on G.E. See Marshall et al., *Canadian-American Industry*, pp. 72-3.

[58]A.E. Safarian, *Foreign Ownership of Canadian Industry*, 2nd ed. (Toronto: University of Toronto Press, 1973), p. 14.

[59]The nine countries consisted of Belgium/Luxembourg, France, Germany, Italy, The Netherlands, Norway, Sweden, Switzerland, and the United Kingdom. Alfred Maizels' detailed trade statistics cover only these countries for the years 1899, 1913, and 1929. See Maizels, *Industrial Growth and World Trade* (London: Cambridge University Press, 1963), pp. 444-53, 540. Percentages were calculated using the raw data in Maizels' tables.

[60]By then these countries were twenty-eight times as populous as Canada.

[61]Cited in R.T. Naylor, *History of Canadian Business*, vol. I (Toronto: Lorimer, 1975), p. 7.

[62]US Senate, 'American Branch Factories Abroad' (71st Congress, 3rd Session, Document No. 260), p. 5.

[63]Cited in Glen Williams, *Not for Export: Toward a Political Economy of Canada's Arrested Industrialization* (Toronto: McClelland and Stewart, 1983), pp. 89-90.

[64]Statistics Canada, *Canadian Imports by Domestic and Foreign Controlled Enterprises* (Ottawa: Minister of Supply and Services, 1981), p. vii.

[65]This was the name of a popular book by Alvin Toffler, *Future Shock* (New York: Random House, 1970).

[66]Maurice Dobb, *Soviet Economic Development Since 1917* (London: Routledge & Kegan Paul, 1948), p. 315.

[67]Marshall et al., *Canadian-American Industry*, pp. 60-80.

[68]Carol Gelderman, *Henry Ford The Wayward Capitalist* (New York: Dial Press, 1981), pp. 50-8.

[69]Cleona Lewis, *America's Stake in International Investments* (Washington: Brookings Institute, 1938), pp. 300-1

[70]Marshall et al., *Canadian-American Industry*, pp. 64-5.

[71]Floyd Chalmers, *Financial Post*, 20 May 1927, p. 2.

[72]David Crane, *Controlling Interest: The Canadian Gas and Oil Stakes* (Toronto: McClelland and Stewart, 1982), p. 109.

[73]I have not seen comprehensive calculations for the years 1900 to the present of the percentage contributions of (1) new foreign funds, (2) reinvestment of earnings, and (3) borrowing from the Canadian capital market. Kari Levitt calculated that 85% of the funds used to expand US-controlled industry in Canada between 1957 and 1965 came from Canadian domestic savings (*Silent Surrender*, p. 137). Kenneth Buckley's data points to the importance of the 1901-15 period in establishing US branch plants and their capital in Canada. Capital imports accounted for 57% of capital formation in Canada between 1901 and 1915; they made up only 9% of it from 1916 to 1930. In the latter period, when domestic savings were able to supply over 90% of Canada's capital demand, the value of foreign capital trebled. After 1915 reinvestment of profits made in Canada, rather than new infusions of foreign direct capital, accounted for much of the rise in value of US-owned branch plants and resource industries

(Buckley, *Capital Formation in Canada, 1896-1930* [Toronto: McClelland and Stewart, 1974], pp. 99-103).

[74] Alfred Chandler, *Strategy and Structure: Chapters in the History of the American Industrial Enterprise* (Cambridge: MIT Press, 1962), p. 116.

[75] W.A. Mackintosh, 'Economic Factors in Canadian History', *Canadian Historical Review* 4, no. 1 (1923): 25.

[76] Harold Innis, *The Fur Trade in Canada* (Toronto: University of Toronto Press, 1975 [1930]), p. 393.

[77] W.J. Eccles disputes Innis's connection between the fur trade and Canada's boundaries ('A Belated Review of Harold Adams Innis, The Fur Trade in Canada', *Canadian Historical Review* 60, no. 4 [1979]: 419-41).

[78] Hugh Aitken, 'Defensive Expansionism: The State and Economic Growth in Canada' in Aitken, ed., *The State and Economic Growth* (New York: Social Science Research Council, 1959), pp. 79-114.

1

Clearing Away the Myths

The fear that American capital is buying us out body and soul should recede before the figures of increasing Canadian ownership of resources and industries. And if, as the economists inform us, we are passing from the necessary stage of capital-import into that of capital-export, we are doing so because of a development largely conditioned upon American investment in this country. Safety from financial annexation ought to go some way to cure the 'inferiority' complex.

P.E. Corbett, The Dalhousie Review, *1930.*

Canada, from the beginning of its history, has been a vulnerable economy, exposed to pressures and stimuli from more advanced nations . . . Canada has never been master of its own destiny; as a satellitic staple-producing economy, it reflected, and still reflects, in its rate of development the imperatives of more advanced areas.

Hugh Aitken, 1959.

Where capitalism followed the more rigid channels of surviving commercialism, or where it arrived later in a highly centralized state, it was part of governmental machinery. In Germany, Italy, and Japan, and in the British Dominions, the state became capital equipment.

Harold Innis, 1938.

Our economy is closely, increasingly closely, geared to that of the United States. We need United States markets. We need United States capital. We need United States industrial 'know-how'. Clearly our economic policy will be shaped by our needs.

W.A. Mackintosh, 1959.

The lack in a backward country of many things that could be reasonably regarded as 'prerequisites' did not prevent the industrial development from taking place . . . it proved possible to find substitutions for the missing factors.

Alexander Gerschenkron, 1962.

People have a wonderful capacity to rationalize their past failures and present predicaments. Canadians have accepted several myths that make it easier to live with high levels of foreign investment, with compromised political independence, and with a continuing reliance on resource exports. On the reassuring side there are the familiar refrains: Canada is a young country, just beginning on the path to independent industrial development; without the help of American capital and technology over the years, Canada would still be an economic backwater. Those of a more fatalistic bent point to the legends of Canada's vast distances as barriers to development, or to US or British external control as having inhibited Canadian development. Unfortunately, far from exposing these myths to critical scrutiny, social scientists and historians have helped to create them. The late-bloomer theory, America's role as friend or enemy, and the land-is-bigger-than-the-people theory are all comforting because they place the blame for Canada's dependent existence elsewhere.

We have seen that, despite its small population, Canada was already the eighth largest manufacturing country in the world at the time of Confederation. We have also seen that Canada's economic achievements were impressive before the first major wave of American branch plants came after 1900. These facts do not fit the myths. If Canada had such a promising industrial start, why did it not generate an independent and fully developed manufacturing economy? Instead of being a late bloomer, with its future still ahead of it, why did Canada peak some time ago?

Students of Canadian development neither ask nor answer these questions. They either accept Canada's past as having been unique or do not venture beyond matters relating to the North Atlantic triangle of Britain, Canada, and the United States. The first view does not get us anywhere: whatever occurred in Canada, it is assumed, was inevitable because of Canada's unique position.[1] The second view emphasizes Canada's relations with superior external forces in Britain and the United States, again leading to notions of determinism.[2] Because geographic factors are givens, undue focus on them perpetuates a fatalistic view as well.[3] In each case our attention is misdirected. As an alternative to such thinking I will set out a historical/comparative approach to explain the path of Canadian development. By comparing Canada with countries in a similar economic position during the formative period of industrialization, this approach may remove the blinkers of inevitability and allow us to see that, in fact, there was a period when the external situation provided Canada with the opportunity to develop independently. The first step, however, is to clear away the myths. Doing so will take us part of the way towards understanding the real reasons for the pattern of Canadian economic development.

CRITIQUES

The staples approach

Pioneered by Harold Innis and W.A. Mackintosh in the 1920s, the staples approach has been Canada's greatest contribution to the study of economic history.[4] According to this school of thought, hinterland development was determined externally by the pattern of demand and the level of technology in the metropolitan countries and internally by God-given geographic and resource endowments. By and large, the initiatives came from the metropolitan countries in the form of changing cultural tastes, economic demands, and new techniques, especially in transportation and communications. The limits to development largely rested in the availability of resources within the staple economies.[5] The theory purportedly explained export-oriented growth in new settler societies.[6]

There are optimistic and pessimistic variants of the staples approach. The optimistic version saw Canada as a resource-exporter that, with the help of external sources of capital and know-how, would develop an independent industrial economy. This variant was associated with Mackintosh and easily merged with neo-classical economics. It also coincided with the Canada-is-young-and-full-of-promise theory. The pessimistic variant saw Canada as a resource-exporter that was blocked from development towards independent industrial maturation by external forces and their capitalist agents in Canada, and by internal geographic constraints. Innis, the founder of the pessimistic variant, put it this way:

> Energy has been directed toward the exploitation of staple products and the tendency has been cumulative . . . Agriculture, industry, transportation, trade, finance and governmental activities tend to become subordinate to the production of the staple for a more highly specialized manufacturing community.[7]

The staples approach was innovative in resisting the common assumption that each country is an island unto itself and can be analyzed in isolation. Yet its international perspective went too far in attributing most events in Canada to external causes. At the same time the approach was too narrow, in that it ignored the experiences of other undeveloped or staple economies.

The staples approach correctly stressed the role of the Canadian state in fostering economic growth. 'The creation of a national economy in Canada', wrote Hugh Aitken, an illustrious student of Innis's, 'and, even more clearly, of a transcontinental economy was as much a political as an economic achievement.'[8] But although followers of Innis focussed on government activities, politics, strangely enough, did not seem to exist for them.[9] Instead, they reverted to their familiar duo of factors for explanation: external domination and internal geographic features. The Act of Union (1841), joining Lower Canada (Quebec) with Upper Canada (Ontario), and

Confederation (1867) were attributed to the need to facilitate the financing of railways and canals, both of which were necessary for exporting staples to Britain. But the complex internal politics that preceded the Act of Union and Confederation, such as conflicting French and English views on the nature of Canadian nationality, or quarrels regarding the powers of the élites and the people, were ignored.

It was only a short step from neglecting domestic politics to developing a Canada-as-victim perspective. Hugh Aitken argued:

> Canada, from the beginning of its history, has been a vulnerable economy, exposed to pressures and stimuli from more advanced nations . . . Canada has never been master of its own destiny; as a satellitic staple-producing economy, it reflected, and still reflects, in its rate of development the imperatives of more advanced areas.[10]

Mel Watkins disagreed. 'Staple economies are often believed to be more at the mercy of destiny than they actually are,' he wrote in his first article outlining the staples approach.[11] Independent development could occur if several conditions were met: if there were (a) a favourable person/land ratio or, in other words, bountiful natural resources to be shared amongst a small population (conditions in much of the New World satisfied this requirement and implied a high standard of living from the outset); (b) strong external demand for resources that are readily available in the country; (c) the 'good fortune' to have developed staples that avoid labour systems such as slavery or other plantation-style social arrangements, producing great inequalities in income; (d) a sufficient domestic population and per capita income to permit economies of scale; and, finally, (e) institutions and values consistent with growth beyond the confines of a staple economy. If these conditions were satisfied, argued Watkins, staple economies could evolve into self-reliant industrial ones.

More recently, however, Watkins has moved to Aitken's position:

> What of the nature of the state that emerges out of staple production? And what is the likelihood of it showing the way out of the staple trap? Now, to transcend staple production, that is, to escape subservience to the rising American empire, would surely have required a state prepared to go well beyond the limitations of the actual National Policy. But the state itself is almost a by-product of the exigencies of staple production.'[12]

The Royal Commission on the Economic Union and Development Prospects for Canada (known as the Macdonald Commission) echoed this refrain in 1985 when it claimed that 'the intimate and extensive links' between Canada and the United States 'no longer allow Canadians room to manoeuvre; rather they make us more vulnerable'.[13]

The Canada-as-victim theme shows up in the work of Canadian writers as well as in that of economic historians. 'Let us suppose, for the sake of argument,' wrote Margaret Atwood in *Survival*, her celebrated book on Canadian literature, 'that Canada as a whole . . . is a colony. A partial definition of a colony is a place from which a profit is made, but *not by the people who live there*: the major profit from a colony is made in the centre of the empire. That's what colonies are for, to make money for the "mother country".'[14] There is a certain appeal to being a victim: like the drunken guest at a party, you are not responsible for what happens. Nevertheless, in the instance of Canadian economic development such a theme has defeatist implications that do not coincide with reality.

Underestimating the extent to which Canadian history was made in Canada is a consequence of failing to look beyond the examples of Canada, the US, and Britain. Sweden's transition from staple-exporter to manufacturing-exporter demonstrates the possibility of escape from dependency. In the middle of the nineteenth century Sweden had a resource-exporting economy strikingly similar to Canada's, with forest, farm, and mineral exports providing the basis for economic growth. It is true that Sweden still had a major primary iron industry, a holdover from the eighteenth century, but its technology was archaic and its importance dwindling. There was little secondary manufacturing. Railways were built on a grand scale to overcome harsh winters that immobilized the country for much of the year. They connected previously isolated communities in a large and sparsely populated land that bore a remarkable resemblance to the Canadian Shield. By 1914 Sweden's railway mileage was closer to the New World level than to the European.

Short of capital because it began industrialization late, Sweden borrowed an unprecedented amount of foreign capital (in relative terms) to finance its railways in the 1880s. Such a heavy reliance on foreign funds equalled Canada's record level three decades later. Nevertheless, with a smaller market than Canada's, Sweden avoided a staple trap and by the First World War was well on its way to becoming an independent industrial country. Engineering goods were exported on a large scale. State policies that blocked foreign ownership and emphasized economic independence contrasted sharply with Canada's 'industrialization by invitation', as R.T. Naylor put it. The key to Sweden's divergence from Canada lay in its different social formation, politics, and history (a theme to be discussed at length in Chapter 3). The point is that the internal social structure and politics of a staples-based economy had an effect on the course of its development. Staple traps do not inevitably follow from external and geographic factors.

Proponents of the staples approach would dismiss the Swedish case as irrelevant on the grounds that new settler societies were unique. 'Perhaps the most serious obstacle to effective work in Canadian economic history', argued Innis, 'is the lack of a philosophy of economic history applicable to new countries.'[15] Mackintosh, for one, cited the US economy as the logical model. Canada would, Mackintosh felt, develop with the help of foreign capital and technology: Canada was a backward United States, destined not to repeat all the steps by which the US progressed, but nevertheless to follow a similar trajectory.[16]

Innis and the pessimists did not share the view that Canada would follow in the glorious footsteps of the United States. Readers of their works are confronted with a curious historical gap: for the first three centuries of British North American contact with Europe, France and Britain are pictured as the metropolitan centres that determined events in what would become Canada. Then suddenly, in the middle of the nineteenth century, without examination of its transition away from staple-exporting dependence on Britain, the US enters these works as a dominant metropolitan country in relation to Canada.[17] The focus on Canada as victim does not, it would seem, lead to the study of countries that have escaped similar positions. Furthermore, these studies do not address the obvious question: if the United States, the oldest and most developed settler colony, was able to generate an independent and mature industrial economy, why was Canada, the second most developed colony, not able to do the same?

Innis's disciples have rarely compared Canada with other staple-exporting societies. This weakens their arguments. If comparisons were to be made, the logic of Innis's perspective, with its emphasis on the perpetuation of resource-exporting dependency, would suggest the 'white dominions' (Australia, New Zealand, and possibly South Africa, Argentina, and Uruguay) as the countries that ought to be compared with Canada. Their dominant cultures grew out of Europe, and they prospered as resource-exporting economies. Are these the right cases for comparison with Canada? Or is Mackintosh correct in regarding the US as the best model? These questions will be addressed below, after discussion of two other perspectives on Canadian development.

The élite approach

In the 1970s R.T. Naylor and Wallace Clement developed a new way of explaining Canada's continued dependence by combining several frameworks.[18] At first glance their work appears to be an amalgam of Innis's staples tradition with Marxism, but the latter element is more in the eyes of the authors than in the mode of their analyses. Both writers drew heavily on the élite approach that can be traced back to Gaetano Mosca, Vilfredo Pareto, Robert Michels, and later writers such as C.W. Mills and John Porter. This perspective largely ignores the role of classes in society that are not part of the ruling élite. For Naylor and Clement power relations were simple: in a capitalist Canada capitalists control the Canadian state. Dismissing political history, however, is hardly a Marxist approach. Naylor also drew on the American muckraking tradition of Gustavus Myers (1910) and others who viewed capitalists as thieves. In this approach the study of politics is reduced to unearthing spectacular cases of corruption and conspiracy.

Naylor and Clement attributed Canada's twentieth-century economic dependence to the peculiar longevity of rule by Canada's merchants and bankers.[19] According to their argument, the commercial capitalists promoted railways and financed the international movement of staples, but largely ignored industry. The resulting gap in the economy was filled by American branch plants after 1900.

Certainly this emphasis on the role of commercially oriented financial institutions has advanced our understanding of Canadian development. But Naylor's explanation of the causes of the continuing staples orientation of the banks and the state during the National Policy era is unsatisfactory.

Naylor's argument is based on an inappropriate extension into nineteenth-century Canada of Karl Marx's and Maurice Dobb's discussions of the conflict between merchants and manufacturers in the pre-industrial Europe of the sixteenth century:[20]

> There are two principal routes, with some minor variants, that an economy can follow on the road to industrialization. Manufacturing industry can grow up 'naturally' from a small scale, even artisanal mode of production when capital accumulation is a largely internal phenomenon based on the reinvestment of the firm's own profits. A second path implies direct development to large-scale oligopolistic enterprise where outside capital is invested to facilitate its expansion and where the state takes an active, direct role in its growth. The outside capital required could come from commercial capital accumulation, from the state, or from foreign investment. The first path, if successfully followed, would lead to the emergence of a flourishing and independent national entrepreneurial class. The second may or may not; it may simply reproduce the conservatism of commercial capitalism in a new guise, the development of inefficient, non-innovative, and backward industrial structures with a penchant for dependence on foreign technology, foreign capital, and state assistance.[21]

Naylor correctly outlined the difference between early and late industrialization, but his assumption that the latter was inferior cannot be sustained. It was the route followed by successful late-industrializing countries such as Germany, Sweden, and Japan. Canada's failure to make a success of this path demands an explanation.

Since the second path involved major state involvement in economic development, it is relevant to look at the social groups that influenced government policy. According to Naylor, Canadian commercial capitalists dominated politically as well as economically.[22] But he failed to ask why this was so. Surely the political power of a small commercial élite was a curious thing in a new settler society with a broad electoral franchise. After all, in the United States and Australia the rule of the commercial pretenders was ended quickly.

Clement's historical analysis of élite linkages in *The Canadian Corporate Elite* and *Continental Corporate Power* does not rescue Naylor's thesis. It cannot be determined why an élite is in power unless the élite is discussed in relation to the other classes in society. Clement did not do this in these books, although he has since moved to a class analysis. The problem with Naylor's exclusive interest in the economy, dominated as it was by Britain and the US, is that it gets us back to the staples Canada-as-victim explanation.[23]

While Innis and others working within the staples tradition were shy about making comparisons with resource-based economies other than that of United States, Naylor was not.[24] The difference, however, lies only in the explicit nature of the comparison. The logic of each approach points to the same conclusion: that of comparison with the white dominions.

In sum, the dominant perspectives on Canadian economic development perpetuate myths. Like Canada's boom-and-bust economy, they vacillate between undue pessimism and excessive optimism. The Innis and Naylor/Clement approaches tend to ignore evidence of considerable industrial output in Canada by the late nineteenth century. At the other extreme, the Mackintosh variant makes the naïve assumption that the American model of development can be copied at a later period. Is there another approach that can strike a more realistic balance about Canadian development?

In the midst of his transition from a neo-classical-staples to a Marxist-staples approach, Mel Watkins suggested that Canada, as a more backward nation than the US, would have done better to copy the German rather than the American model.[25] As evidence, he pointed to Alexander Gerschenkron's work on the successful industrialization of the economically backward nations of nineteenth-century Europe.[26]

The economic-backwardness approach

When Karl Marx wrote that the 'industrially more developed country presents to the less developed country a picture of the latter's future' he was not expressing a view peculiar to revolutionary socialists.[27] In the nineteenth century both Marxist and capitalist economists assumed that all countries must develop along English lines—a not-unnatural assumption, given that England developed first and thus for a time was the only case that could be studied. The problem was that the models built on the English case lived on long after the period in which England was the only industrial society.

Alexander Gerschenkron took strong exception to the notion that all countries must develop along English lines. The backward countries of nineteenth-century Europe, he said, evolved differently from England. There were gradations of backwardness, and the greater the backwardness of a country, the greater was the disparity of its path to industrialization from England's. It was this gap between the actuality of backwardness and the potentiality that industrialization could release that provided the tension and motivation to develop. Nevertheless, Gerschenkron did not break completely with a unilinear evolutionist view of progress. In his search for the 'substitutions' employed by backward countries in place of the methods used in England's classical liberal route to development, he assumed that England's route was the normal way.[28]

For Gerschenkron the backward countries of Europe faced two enormous problems: (a) capital shortage for industry and infrastructure, and (b) the need to create a free and disciplined labour force. Competition from the advanced countries forced the backward countries of Europe to industrialize quickly, adding to capital-shortage problems. Although there was often a mass of underemployed workers, only small numbers of skilled and disciplined labourers could be found. Hence backward countries, ironically, tended to adopt labour-saving technologies that consumed a great deal of capital.[29]

The abruptness of the industrialization process meant that industry had little opportunity to accumulate domestic capital. The situation had been different in the early-industrializing countries, where factories and infrastructure had been financed mainly by the reinvestment of profits within manufacturing and by short-term loans from commerce. These means were adequate for the more leisurely pace of the industrial pioneers, but were not enough to begin industrialization in the backward countries. These countries needed to find substitutes for the traditional sources of capital.

One such substitution emerged in the 1860s in the German states, where industrial development did not begin until almost a century after it had begun in England. It was here that universal investment banks were born. These were a new type of financial institution in that they tapped non-traditional sources of funds and placed increased amounts of long-term capital in heavy industry.

The universal investment banks proved a valuable alternative to the commercial banks that remained dominant in early-developing England and France. By the middle of the nineteenth century capital costs had escalated dramatically; the commercial banks, which had been designed to supply short-term capital for moving goods, were inadequate for starting advanced secondary industries. In still-more-backward Russia the state had to assume the substitution role because the banks were too feeble to support industry and infrastructure.

But capital alone was not enough. There had to be a large number of workers whose ties to the land had been broken (in other words, who would starve if they did not find employment) to run the factories, mills, and foundries. But the simple existence of these pools of labourers was not sufficient either. Workers had to be socialized to accept the idea of spending a lifetime of endless hard work in dreary surroundings for the benefit of someone else. Given our current image of hard-working Germans, it is ironic to read of the envious glances that nineteenth-century German writers such as Schulze-Gaevernitz kept casting across the Channel at the English worker, 'the man of the future . . . born and educated for the machine . . . [who] does not find his equal in the past'.[30]

The backward countries of Europe could not wait hundreds of years for aristocrats or agricultural capitalists to push peasants off the land and thus create a work force dependent only on wage labour. Here, in contrast to the situation in the first industrialized countries, the development of a free wage-labour force had to develop simultaneously with, rather than before, industrialization. Theories of uniform prerequisites for industrialization, usually drawn from the peculiar English case, are therefore impossible to sustain.[31]

Gerschenkron stressed the vast social and cultural changes that were necessary to grapple with the twin problems of capital shortage and semi-feudal social structures. New ideologies were needed to excite the imagination of the people:

> To break through the barriers of stagnation in a backward country, to ignite the imaginations of men, and to place their energies in the service of economic development, a stronger medicine is needed than the promise of better allocation of resources or even of the lower price of bread. Under such conditions even the businessman, even the classical daring and innovating entrepreneur, needs a more powerful stimulus than the prospects of high profits. What is needed to remove the mountains of routine and prejudice is faith—faith, in the words of Saint-Simon, that the golden age lies not behind but ahead of mankind.'[32]

Saint-Simonian socialism in capitalist France and Marxism in czarist Russia were among the new religions that helped to bring about the needed institutional changes.

But Gerschenkron's approach falters, and to be useful it must be modified in several respects. First, he fails to examine the economic and class forces behind the sudden shifts in ideas in these societies. His philosophically idealist approach ignores the social factors leading to the generation of the dominant ideas that formed the context for institutional substitutions.[33]

In addition, Gerschenkron underestimates the importance of foreign investment as a source of substitute funds. Large amounts of foreign capital were crucial for the development of Russia, Sweden, and Canada.[34] In some nations foreign capital was as important as domestic banking funds and state capital for industrialization.

A further problem with Gerschenkron's model for understanding Canada is that it is rooted in the old-world conditions of Europe. Canada did not resemble the backward societies of pre-modern Europe in its class structure: it had a seigneurial system designed for colonization but not a manorial structure with an aristocracy that had to be removed. In fact, Canada was a more quintessentially new society than the United States, where plantation slavery produced a social structure with similarities to old Europe. Moreover, Canada never faced the Gerschenkronian problem of having to create a free and disciplined labour force:

> The truth is that Canadian employers commanded throughout the nineteenth century a virtually inexhaustible labour reserve. The great reserve . . . was the

immigrant stream. Frequently it exceeded Canadian requirements, and flowed on to the United States. Whenever jobs were plentiful in Canada . . . whenever, that is, capital was found for large construction projects—immigration swelled in an appropriate volume . . . Kinds and quantities of skilled labour not at once available could be got from the United States for a little money, or from the United Kingdom for a little trouble.[35]

What of capital shortages? Did Canada share this feature with the backward countries of Europe? By the 1850s foreign capital flowed into Canadian railways and canals on a scale unknown in the first industrialized countries.[36] Long-term domestic investment, however, especially in manufacturing, was a different matter. Here there is evidence of the shortages typical of the backward countries of Europe during Canada's first four decades of industrialization.[37]

As noted, industrialization took firm root in Canada in the 1870s and 1880s, the period of the National Policy. Signs of the industrial revolution were everywhere: the factory system spread; steam power was used extensively; finished iron and steel products surpassed the leading resource-processing industry; and provincial and national markets for manufactured goods emerged. Similar events occurred at the same time among a handful of late-follower countries: Sweden, Russia, Italy, the Czech region of the Austro-Hungarian Empire, and Japan. Since Canada industrialized at the same time as the backward countries of Europe, can a modification of Gerschenkron's model—to suit Canadian conditions—explain the path of Canadian development? This question is addressed below.

MODELS OF DEVELOPMENT

The preceding section examined the conceptual adequacy of three approaches to understanding Canadian development; however, an empirical test is in order. Each approach suggests comparison with a different set of countries. The Mackintosh version and neo-classical perspective point to the US of thirty, fifty, or eighty years ago as the appropriate parallel.[38] On the other hand, the Innis staples and Naylor/Clement élite approaches suggest comparison with the other white dominions. Finally, Gerschenkron's economic-backwardness perspective invites comparison with Sweden, Russia, Italy, or Japan. Which approach explains the facts best?[39]

Before reviewing the models of development it is worth explaining what is meant here by 'independent industrial development', 'mature industrial economies', and 'successful industrialization'. I use these terms interchangeably to indicate countries that have wide freedom to manoeuvre in a crisis such as a war, an oil embargo, or a drastic fall in the price of one or more export commodities. Such countries are not necessarily self-sufficient, but they have the ability to produce nearly all the finished goods they require without incurring a major reduction in overall productivity.[40] This definition would exclude countries specializing in the export of a few lines of finished goods but importing most of their machinery. Those countries that make a wider range of manufactures but have to buy most of the high-technology items from abroad would also be excluded. A nation's ability to respond to a crisis that threatens its independence is determined both by the willingness of all sections of society to pull in the same direction and by the degree of domestic control over technology and management. The latter provides the basis for the creation of alternatives for imported goods. In the everyday world of normal trade relations as well, technological and managerial sovereignty are vital factors in international capitalist competition: product innovation has been crucial to the profitability of most corporations since the 1920s.[41] Domestic ownership and managerial control over most of the nation's productive enterprises and a high degree of technological sovereignty are the *sine qua non* of substantial product innovation.[42]

In the early 1960s, when Alfred Maizels conducted a comprehensive study of industrial development and its relation to international trade, he found Canada a difficult country to classify. Was it one of the dozen industrial countries in the world, or one of the equal number of semi-industrial countries, among them the white dominions? The fact that the value of Canada's staple exports greatly exceeded that of finished manufactured goods was not characteristic of the industrial countries. On the other hand, Canada's level of manufacturing productivity was very high. It was a puzzling case.[43] (Others have had similar difficulty working Canada into their models.)[44]

Canada has other anomalous features. It has balance-of-payments problems caused by the extensive outflow of dividend, interest, and royalty earnings to foreign investors and by its strong reliance on foreign-controlled technologies and management. These features characterize the white dominions as well as much of the Third World.[45] But, in contrast to these countries, Canada is still among the top ten industrial nations of the world.[46]

Is Canada a borderline case because it is transforming itself from a semi-industrial to an industrial country? This is the usual assumption of progressive development. But is not the reverse equally plausible? Perhaps Canada was developing along the lines of the late-follower countries and was thwarted for some reason. Is Canada regressing into the ranks of the semi-industrial countries? To answer these questions let us consider each of the three approaches in turn.

Canada as a latter-day America

Mackintosh and other neo-classical economists portray Canada as a backward United States with some differences. By invoking their favourite phrase, *ceteris paribus* (all other things being equal), neo-classical economists often throw away most of the useful variables for understanding development in one society and retardation in another. For example, it would be difficult, using economic variables alone, to explain how Japan was able to advance to a point where its industrial output is now three times that of Britain, when a hundred years ago it produced one-fiftieth as much.

If Canada is a backward United States (with a penchant for more state intervention), it should be following a similar trajectory towards industrial independence. A favourable balance of trade in finished goods, domestic ownership of the bulk of the productive industries, and internal control over technological progress are all signs of independent economic development. Has Canada's development been moving in this direction?

First, an industrially developed country is one that can supply most of its internal market with finished goods and break into another's territory. The extent of maturity can be measured by comparing exports to imports of finished manufactures. If a country has an export/import ratio of more than 1.0 (unity) it is a net exporter; if less than unity, it is a net importer. Let us compare Canada with the United States in this regard, giving the former a thirty-year time lag. By 1899, with a score of 1.3, the US was already a net exporter of finished goods. In 1929 and 1955, it had moved up to ratios of 5.2 and 4.0.[47] In contrast, Canada stagnated: in 1929 its score was 0.28 and by 1955 0.20. The situation has improved somewhat since the mid-1950s and by 1985-87 Canada's export/import ratio was 0.72. This ratio was inflated, however, by the 1965 Auto Pact, which gave a large boost to Canada's export statistics of finished goods without substantially changing the level of manufacturing in Canada. If such trade is removed from the calculation, the export/import ratio of finished goods equals 0.49 for the years 1985-87.[48] Whether the Auto Pact is included or excluded, however, an even balance in trade of finished manufactured goods is still a long way off. Canada's deficit in trade in all finished goods ranged from $17 billion to $24 billion in the years 1985 to 1987.[49] In short, Canada still pays its way in the world by massive exports of resources.

Second, the role of foreign investment is crucial in assessing dependence. Canada, along with Sweden, holds the record among advanced economies for the extent to which foreign funds contributed to its early industrialization. Most of this investment was in the form of portfolio or loan capital. Of a more permanent and cumulative nature has been the very high level of foreign direct (ownership) investment in Canada's manufacturing and resource industries. In contrast, Swedish governments have had a history of blocking foreign direct ownership since the 1870s, and current levels are low.[50] The 1972 Gray Report (*Foreign Direct Investment in Canada*) demonstrated that high levels of foreign ownership reduced the amount of research and development undertaken in Canada and led to the massive importation of machinery.[51] At the same time extensive foreign ownership restricted exports and hindered growth in the size of firms.

Perhaps Canada's experience with foreign ownership is a passing phase, and the country is on the road to greater development. To evaluate this possibility, one should question whether the United States went through a similar period of reliance on foreign funds and foreign control.

Foreign capital was important in the development of the American economy in the middle of the nineteenth century. Foreign contributions to net capital formation were almost 11 per cent in the decade following the Civil War.[52] In the manufacturing and transportation industries, European loans may have contributed as much as a fifth of total investment in the 1850s.[53]

But the American example cannot offer hope that foreign investment is a transitory phenomenon for Canada. American foreign indebtedness was never close to the Canadian rate, and it diminished rapidly. Most of the funds were of the portfolio variety, placed in government securities and railway bonds. These loans were either paid off or wiped out by a massive defaulting on debts in the late 1830s. (American business leaders conveniently forget this chapter in their history in their war against the current threat of loan defaults among Third World countries.) In contrast to portfolio investments, foreign direct investments, once made, tend to increase in value over time. This type of investment was never a large factor in the US: British direct investment was estimated at only $700 million in 1913,[54] and by 1987 foreign ownership of manufacturing was about 10 per cent. Douglass North estimated that American direct investments abroad were greater by the 1850s than were foreign direct investments at home.[55]

Finally, there is the role of technology in creating an independent economy. It is clear that no country can develop all the new technologies required for an advanced economy. But while imported technologies are indispensable, they need not imply dependence. Two elements are crucial for relative sovereignty: a substantial level of domestic innovation and the borrowing of technology through arm's-length arrangements. The Japanese have been masters of the latter, while the Swedes have shown an innovative vigour that is surprising for a small country. The ratio of patents issued to citizens to patents issued to foreigners is a crude measurement of the strength of domestic innovations. Canada's performance in this regard compared to that of the US is telling. In the US six of every seven patents issued went to native citizens in 1900; the ratio was the same in 1930 and 1955.[56] Canada has been moving in the opposite direction. In the early 1900s Canadians held 15 per cent of domestically issued patents,[57] and the road has been downhill since: 11 per cent in 1930, 6 per cent in 1955, and 7 per cent in 1986 and 1987.[58]

When domestic innovations are not forthcoming on a major scale, imitation is a way to import technologies while retaining managerial and corporate independence. Yet Canada did not pursue the successful Japanese and Italian strategies of copying their competitors. In the fifteen years preceding the First World War Canada imported almost 60 per cent of the new plant machinery installed, while much domestic production took place in US branch plants.[59] In recent years Canadian industry has actually become more technologically dependent: by the mid-1970s over 70 per cent of the

Canadian market for machinery was served by imports, and a similar percentage of the domestic machinery industry was foreign-owned.[60]

In sum, Mackintosh's late-bloomer thesis is not applicable. Canada has not progressed along the American path. The export/import ratio of Canadian exports of finished goods failed to rise to unity, and mammoth imports continue. As foreign investment has not been a temporary phase in Canadian development, it cannot be attributed to the youthfulness of the country. Finally, Canadian control over the processes of innovation has decreased over time.

Canada and the white-dominion model

It is ironic that the best defence of the Canada-as-a-white-dominion model comes not from the Innis staples perspective, nor from the Naylor/Clement élite approach, but from Marxists. Philip Ehrensaft and Warwick Armstrong make an exceptionally able and comprehensive case for the white-dominion model.[61] For them the nature and responses of the rural classes and the industrial working class in the white dominions played a crucial role in the establishment of the high-wage, low-industry pattern typical of these societies.

According to Ehrensaft and Armstrong, the white dominions include not only the legitimate British offspring—Canada, Australia, and New Zealand—but two unofficially adopted children as well: Argentina and Uruguay. The white dominions distinguished themselves from their poor cousins in the rest of the New World by inhabiting lands where the native population was too small for large-scale exploitation and where the climate did not favour extensive farming of the sort that required the importation of African slaves or indentured workers from the East Indies to work in the fields. Few slaves, of course, meant no plantation owners. New settlers from Europe provided the bulk of the labour force, and the large land reserves meant labour shortages and hence high wages. This situation had a number of implications: the adoption of labour-saving and therefore highly productive technology, urbanization, and a substantial level of manufacturing based on rich domestic markets.

The white dominions shared these features with the advanced capitalist countries, but fell short of full capitalist development. Primary products remained their major exports, while manufacturing was largely confined to supplying many, though not all, of their domestic needs with protected, inefficient industry and to processing, rather than finishing, resources. Subsidiaries of multinational corporations were prominent in the goods-producing sectors, and the white dominions all passed from the sway of the British Empire to that of the American in this century. Furthermore, the politics of the various classes perpetuated the orientation of these economies towards resource exports and stunted, domestically confined manufacturing. The working classes tended to support government strategies of shortcuts to industrialization through importing foreign factors of production: capital, technology, and management. But workers wanted to keep out a fourth factor, cheap Oriental labour, and in this regard they were largely successful.

From the vantage point of the late twentieth century Canada seems to fit the white-dominion category quite well—although if it does, it is clearly the most advanced in the group. But Canada's contemporary similarity to the other white dominions, especially Australia, may in fact point to a reversal in its fortunes rather than parallel development prospects in the past. Ehrensaft and Armstrong admit this possibility: 'Another hypothesis would be that Canada, as the senior dominion, possessed an industrial structure which was sufficiently profound to provide a far more autonomous development than we have experienced.'

Ehrensaft and Armstrong demonstrate current similarities between Canada and the other white dominions. Canada shares with Australia and the others both a low degree of finished manufactures as a percentage of total exports and a somewhat lower level of manufacturing production as a proportion of gross national product (GNP) than the advanced economies.[62] Canada is not ahead of the other dominions in relative terms (though its absolute level of manufacturing is of course much higher, as is its total GNP).

It is when we look to development prospects in the past that the sharp divergence between Canada and the rest is apparent. In their discussion of the early twentieth century, Ehrensaft and Armstrong shift their focus from exports and sectoral shares of the GNP to other measures of development: capital/labour ratios, agricultural productivity, the percentage of the labour force engaged in industry, and per capita incomes. In all these respects Argentina and Australia bore up well (though it is worth noting that, rather than signifying diversification into secondary manufacturing, high capital intensity [high capital/labour ratios] may indicate specialization in resource industries and the further processing of primary products before export: both sectors are notorious for the paucity of workers they employ). Canada was behind in capital/labour ratios and agricultural productivity; in the middle regarding the number of manufacturing workers; and only somewhat ahead in incomes in the period from 1910 to the 1930s. These are not, however, the best measures of prospects for independent industrial development. To determine the level of development it makes more sense to look at productivity in manufacturing than in agriculture. In this respect Canada was 50 per cent to 100 per cent ahead of Australia in the 1920s and 1930s and 140 per cent ahead of Argentina in the 1930s (the first time such figures are available for that country).[63]

Development prospects depended not only on productivity in industry but also on the absolute size of the manufacturing sector and its ability to penetrate foreign markets. It may be arbitrary to establish minimum levels of manufacturing necessary to permit sufficient specialization of factors of production and economies of scale. But it is difficult to argue with the cases of success and failure. The crucial question is whether Canada resembled the white dominions, which did not break free from a staples orientation, or whether Canada was as developed as the other late-follower countries.

Consider the scale of industrial production (Table 1.1). From 1905 to 1909 Canada's overall manufacturing output was behind that of populous Russia and Italy, but at the same level as that of Japan and Sweden and more than double Australia's. In the 1920s and 1930s Canadian production was in the middle range of the late-follower countries and at least two and one-half times that of either Australia or Argentina.

Ehrensaft and Armstrong's model specifies the inability of the white dominions to produce manufacturing products for anything but the protected home market (with minor exceptions). Was this true of Canada in the 1920s? No. Canada exported more manufactured goods per head than any of the late-follower countries, and its absolute level of such exports was in the middle of the late-follower range (see Table 1.2). On the other hand, Australia's manufacturing exports were six times lower than Sweden's—the lowest of the late-follower countries'—and eleven times lower than Canada's. Whereas Canada was ahead of any of the late-follower countries in per capita exports of finished goods, Australia's record was dismal: it exported less than

TABLE 1.1

WORLD NET INCOME FROM MANUFACTURING PRODUCTION IN MILLIONS OF INTERNATIONAL UNITS

	1870-74	1905-09	1925-29	1935-38
Late-follower countries				
Czechoslovakia	–	–	673	634
Italy	146	735	1395	1503
Japan	–	343	1533	2835
Netherlands	–	–	508	755
Russia	–	622	862	2740
Sweden	45	356	570	948
Median	1	489	768	1226
Canada	70	334	1090	1218
White dominions				
Argentina	–	–	363	479
Australia	–	150	433	475
New Zealand	–	63	127	172
Uruguay	–	–	–	43

SOURCE: Colin Clark, *The Conditions of Economic Progress*, 3rd ed., rev. (New York: Macmillan, 1960), Table VII.

[1] Not enough cases to warrant calculation.

one-fifth as much per capita as the average for the late-follower countries. New Zealand's per capita exports of finished products were worse. Comparable data for Argentina and Uruguay could not be found,[64] but there is no reason to suppose that either country performed better than Australia in the 1920s.

The historical timing of events had a profound effect on the nature of industrial development. A great chasm was created between the few countries that began serious industrialization before 1900 and those that did not get well into the process until the Second World War or its aftermath. For this reason it is important to determine whether Canada was among the pre-1900 developers, along with the late-follower countries, or whether it shared the much more difficult prospects of even later, white-dominion development.

To understand the profound changes in the 1890-1940 period that led to the chasm between the developed and the underdeveloped countries, it is first useful to note the significance of continuity. Despite momentous technological, military, and social upheavals in the twentieth century, the relative

TABLE 1.2

TRADE IN MANUFACTURED[1] ARTICLES PER HEAD 1926-29
(ANNUAL AVERAGES)

	Exports		Imports	
	Exports of manufacturing per head ($)	Gross value of manufacturing exports ($000,000)	Imports of manufacturing per head ($)	Gross value of manufacturing imports ($000,000)
Late-follower countries				
Czechoslovakia	27	395	11	156
Italy	10	401	6.4	259
Japan	7.3	451	3.9	241
Netherlands	33	254	52	397
Sweden	29	178	31	187
Median	27	395	11	241
Canada	35	336	64	627
White dominions				
Argentina	–	–	–	–
Australia	4.8	30	81	510
New Zealand	1.5	2	119	166
Uruguay	–	–	–	–

SOURCE: Adapted from League of Nations, *Industrialisation and World Trade* (New York: United Nations, 1945), p. 84.

[1] 'Manufacturing' refers to class IV of International (Brussels) Classification of 1913. Excludes manufactured foodstuffs and some semi-manufactured articles.

economic strength of nations has changed little. The Russian Revolution, the introduction of space-age electronics, the eclipse of Britain, and the rise of Japan have not greatly altered the international pecking order. Russia was the fifth largest manufacturing country before the 1917 revolution and is now in second place. Japan has moved up in spectacular fashion to third place.[65] But it should not be forgotten that Japan was already sixth in the 1930s and had an industrial base sufficiently advanced to conquer half of East Asia and challenge the Americans in the Second World War; by 1913 it was already about the tenth largest industrial country.[66] Britain has declined substantially, but only from first place a hundred years ago to sixth place in the 1980s.[67] Notwithstanding these fluctuations, the fact remains that all of the dozen or so advanced industrial countries of the late twentieth century had begun widespread industrialization before 1890. The obverse holds as well: no seriously industrializing country of the late nineteenth century has slipped into de-industrialized oblivion. Those ahead seventy or a hundred years ago are still ahead today.

Surprisingly, this striking fact about international development has been neglected. Much work has been done on economic problems in the Third World in the past thirty years and on specific countries over a longer period. But the increasing strength of the barriers to industrial success between 1890 and 1940 has received little systematic attention. A comprehensive treatment of the gap between the leading nations and the would-be followers during that time, along the lines of David Landes's *The Unbound Prometheus*, is clearly needed. Here I can list only a few of the main factors that worked against the attainment of industrial independence and maturity during that time.

Around 1900 there was a transformation in the nature of international capitalism. Observant contemporaries understood this. J.A. Hobson, a liberal, and Vladimir Lenin both labelled the phenomenon 'imperialism'.[68] Major corporations and cartels emerged in the advanced economies as a response to overproduction, increased international competition, and the high cost of new technologies. The scientific discoveries of the previous half century began to bear fruit: the turn of the century ushered in the automobile, electricity, and advances in communications, motors, and new chemical products for wear and for war. In contrast to earlier manufacturing, these industries required large capital outlays, scientifically educated workers and managers, complex techniques, and a modern communications system on a national scale. Shipping costs fell drastically as steam, metal hulls, and new propulsion techniques revolutionized ocean travel. Between 1874 and 1884, for example, ocean freight rates dropped by 60 per cent between New York and Europe. Strategically placed canals such as Suez (opened in 1869) and Panama (opened in 1914) cut thousands of kilometres from major shipping routes.[69] After the major networks were completed in northwestern Europe and North America, railways were pushed into Asia, Africa, and South America.

The developed countries could easily thrust their goods, their business organizations, their techniques, and their armies into every part of the globe. Most of Africa and Asia was conquered. Though nominally independent for the most part, the Latin American countries were reduced to economic satellites of the industrial countries. World trade in finished goods rose by 75 per cent in the 1899-1913 period alone, and imports doubled in the semi-industrial and small industrial countries.[70] For the first time large corporations began to set up foreign subsidiaries to overcome tariff barriers that were erected everywhere except in England and a few smaller countries. The US was the main centre for the emergence of the transnational corporation. While Canada and Mexico were the largest recipients of American direct investment, Europe was not neglected. All of these new developments in trade, transportation, technology, and the monopoly control of big business made it much more difficult for the pre-industrial countries to emulate the example of the advanced countries. A watershed had been crossed. The disadvantages of following the leader seemed to outweigh the advantages.

The timing of Canada's development is therefore significant. If Canadian manufacturing was weak prior to the First World War, the white-dominion model would seem to hold; a capitalist Canada probably never had the chance to break out of its staple trap. If, however, industry in Canada is as old as in the successful late-follower countries, then Canada's failure becomes more interesting. To help assess Canada's relation to the development gap, comparisons with Australia (the most advanced of the other white dominions) and Sweden (the smallest of the successful late followers) seem useful.

Soon after Confederation manufacturing in Canada accounted for just under one-quarter of the gross domestic product (GDP), compared to one-eighth for Sweden—whose manufacturing figures are somewhat inflated by the inclusion of mining statistics—and only one-twelfth for Australia (see Table 1.3). If absolute levels of production are considered, the difference between Canada and the other two was even greater. International comparisons of total output are always arbitrary, and the further back in time you go, the more tenuous the assessments become. But there is no doubt that in the 1870s Canada had the highest gross domestic production of the three countries, probably somewhere in the order of double the product of the other two. Thus Canadian manufacturing had a higher share of a greater output. Furthermore, Canada's industry in 1870 was of a different character than Australia's. Whereas half of Australian industry in 1900 still involved primary manufacturing, or the processing of staples before export, thirty years earlier between two-thirds and three-quarters of Canadian manufacturing was in secondary (i.e., finished) production.[71] Finished iron and steel was already the leading sector in Canada, slightly ahead of primary wood products.[72]

Industry developed so slowly in Australia that by the 1930s it accounted for only one-sixth of the gross domestic product. It was not until the Second World War that manufacturing outstripped agriculture in Australia—something that had happened in Canada during the First World War despite the wheat boom on the prairies. (Manufacturing took the lead slightly earlier in Sweden.) Canada had experienced considerable industrialization by the late nineteenth century, whereas Australia developed after the period that separates the mature economies from the rest of the world.

In sum, the Canadian case is clearly different from that of Australia and the

TABLE 1.3

AGRICULTURE AND MANUFACTURING AS A PERCENTAGE OF GDP
AVERAGES FOR SELECTED 5-YEAR PERIODS

	1871-75	1881-85	1891-95	1901-05	1911-15	1921-25	1931-35
Australia							
Manufacturing[1] (not incl. mining)	8.6	11.2	11.2	11.4	14.0	13.8	15.7
Agriculture (incl. pastoral but excl. dairying)	23.2	19.2	18.3	18.5	18.6	19.7	17.6
Canada							
Manufacturing[2] (not incl. mining)	23.2	24.0	23.9	22.6	20.1	21.8	21.7[4]
Agriculture	33.1	32.9	27.8	24.5	22.0	18.9	9.6[4]
Sweden							
Manufacturing[3] (incl. mining)	13.1	14.0	17.5	24.4	27.9	30.1	30.8
Agriculture	38.5	35.7	33.0	25.8	23.8	18.2	11.2

SOURCES: For Australia, N.G. Butlin, *Australian Domestic Product, Investment and Foreign Borrowing 1861-1938/9* (Cambridge: Cambridge University Press, 1962), pp. 12-13; for Canada, M.C. Urquhart, 'New Estimates of Gross National Product, Canada 1870 to 1926: Some Implications for Canadian Development', (Kingston, Ont: Institute for Economic Research, Queen's University, Discussion Paper #586, 1986); for Sweden, O. Krantz and C. Nilsson, *Swedish National Product 1891-1970* (Lund: C.W.K. Gleerup, 1975).

[1] Mining comprised the following percentage of Australia's GDP: 8.9 per cent (1871-75), 4.5 per cent (1881-85), 6.9 per cent (1891-95), 9.8 per cent (1901-05), 5.6 per cent (1911-15), 2.4 per cent (1921-25), 2.3 per cent (1931-35).

[2] Mining comprised the following percentage of Canada's GDP: 1.2 per cent (1871-75); 1.0 per cent (1881-85); 2.2 per cent (1891-95); 3.9 per cent (1901-05); 3.1 per cent (1911-15); 3.1 per cent (1921-25); 4.3 per cent (1931-35).

[3] Swedish statistics combine mining with metal industries and it is not possible to disaggregate the two. The inclusion of mining inflates the Swedish manufacturing percentages. According to a study by E. Lindahl, E. Dahlgren, and K. Kock (*National Income of Sweden 1861-1930*, part 2 [London: n.p., 1937]), mining made up roughly 15 per cent of the total of manufacturing production in the 1861 to 1895 period (pp. 185, 302).

[4] These figures are taken from M.C. Urquhart and K.A.H. Buckley, eds, *Historical Statistics of Canada*, 2nd ed. (Ottawa: Statistics Canada, 1983), F 59. They are compatible with Urquhart's recent data.

other white dominions.[73] We may conclude, therefore, that a pure staple-exporting model along the lines of the Innis or Naylor/Clement approaches is inapplicable to Canada.

Canada and late-follower development

We are left with the modified version of Alexander Gerschenkron's model. Did Canada resemble the late-follower economies with respect to their level of manufacturing activity in the late nineteenth and early twentieth centuries?[74]

By the 1870s and 1880s the United States, Britain, Germany, France, and, on a smaller scale, Belgium and Switzerland had already emerged as industrial powers in fierce competition with one another; the first four large industrial countries controlled over 75 per cent of world industrial production.[75] At roughly the same time a handful of countries began their initial phase of industrialization. These late-follower countries (not including Canada) were Russia, Italy, Sweden, the Czech provinces, Japan, and possibly the Netherlands.[76] In 1913, by which time industry had surpassed agriculture in most late-follower countries, their shares of world production had climbed. Individual totals were 5.5 per cent (Russia), 2.7 per cent (Italy), 1.4 per cent (Czechoslovakia), 1.2 per cent (Japan), and 1.0 per cent (Sweden and the Netherlands). Canada, with less than 0.5 per cent of the world's population, compared favourably with these countries. In 1880-85 it had 1.3 per cent of world manufacturing production, and 2.3 per cent by 1913. Only two of the six late followers produced more.

But gross production statistics tell only part of the story. Canada has a long history of exporting large quantities of semi-processed goods (primary manufactures), such as pulp and paper, but confining finished goods to the home market.[77] Nevertheless, in 1899 Canadian exports had the greatest proportion of finished to primary manufactures of any industrial nation. All late-follower countries for which statistics are available recorded ratios of exports of finished manufactures to primary manufactures of 1.0 (unity) or less. In contrast, the Canadian ratio was 5 to 1 (see Appendix, Table A). While it is true that Canada achieved this high ratio by exporting few manufactured goods, its exports of finished goods compared favourably in absolute terms with those of other late followers. In 1899 Canadian exports of fully finished goods totalled $15 million (US) compared to Sweden's $13 million, Japan's $24 million, and Italy's $53 million (see Appendix, Table B). The latter two achieved higher levels of finished exports by concentrating on textiles and clothing, items then accounting for half the world's trade but now making up only a small portion of it. When textiles and clothing are excluded on the grounds that they are not indicative of twentieth-century development prospects, Canadian finished exports were more comparable: Japan, $10 million; Canada, $12 million; Sweden, $13 million; and Italy, $23 million (see Appendix, Table C).

Lest the reader suppose that the aggregate figures hide more than they reveal, and that Canada's performance looks good only because of a quirk in the definition of finished goods, the breakdown of Canadian exports in 1899 is presented in Table 1.4. It was not canned fish that placed Canadian exports at a level comparable to those of other late-follower countries: processed foods are excluded from finished exports.

With 22 per cent of the total, agricultural implements led the list of Canada's finished exports in 1899. Consisting of such items as harvesters, mowers, and ploughs, 64 per cent of Canada's implement exports went to the competitive markets of Britain, Germany, and France. Manufactures of

TABLE 1.4

CANADIAN EXPORTS OF FINISHED GOODS[1] 1899 – RANK ORDER

	1899 prices ($Can.)	1913 prices[2] ($Can.)	Total exports (%)
Agricultural implements	1,863,468	2,627,490	22
Manufactures of leather including soles, uppers, boots and shoes	1,681,283	2,370,609	20
Manufactures of wood including doors, furniture, misc. and spools	1,545,432	2,179,059	18
Manufactures of iron and steel	706,411	966,040	8
Musical instruments including organs and pianos	561,836	792,189	7
Textiles and clothing	480,876	678,035	6
Chemicals including drugs, explosives and fertilizers	464,432	654,849	5
Vehicles including bicycles	303,757	428,297	4
Cordage, twines	134,522	189,817	2
Publishing	92,426	130,321	1
Other	739,971	1,043,359	9
Total	8,574,414	12,089,924	102

SOURCE: Canada, *Department of Agriculture Statistical Yearbook* (Ottawa, 1901), pp. 288-91.

[1] Using Maizels' definition of finished goods. See Maizels, *Industrial Growth and World Trade* (London: Cambridge University Press, 1963), Appendix D. Does not include food products or household effects (emigrants' effects).

[2] Prices adjusted using seventy-commodity index from K.W. Taylor and H. Michell, *Statistical Contributions to Canadian Economic History*, vol. 1 (Toronto: Macmillan, 1931) p. 56; 1899 prices were 71.1 per cent of 1913 prices.

leather, chiefly soles and uppers, and manufactures of wood, including doors, matches, and mouldings, made up an additional 38 per cent of all finished exports. More technologically advanced articles such as manufactures of iron and steel, musical instruments, chemicals, and vehicles accounted for another 24 per cent. Clearly, Canadian finished exports in 1899 were a balanced mix of the sophisticated and the simple.

Canada: failed follower

Thus Canada held its own with the other late-follower countries at the end of the nineteenth century. It began the initial phase of industrialization before 1890, and its absolute level of making finished products was high. Furthermore, industry surpassed agriculture's share in the economy during the First World War, a sure sign that Canada had passed beyond the precarious initial phase of industrialization. A modified Gerschenkron model appears to best explain Canadian economic development at that point. Canada was the only late-follower country that clearly failed to generate a mature and independent industrial economy. Two questions therefore need to be addressed. First, when did Canada diverge from the path of the other late followers? Second, why did it do so?

In the post-Second World War era the Canadian economy differed substantially from the economies of other late-follower countries. The familiar pattern of dependence on the export of raw materials and the massive disparity between importing and exporting finished goods was solidly established in Canada. In 1955, with only 3.2 per cent of the total population of the ten major capitalist economies, Canada accounted for over 25 per cent of all the finished manufactures imported by those ten countries. At the same time it exported only 2 per cent of the total. Some 80 per cent of Canada's manufactured exports were unfinished, while imports of finished goods were five times the level of exports. Canada paid its way in international trade through staple exports. None of the other late-follower countries exhibited a similar pattern.

There is evidence that Canada began to regress from late-follower development as early as 1899, when it showed a high propensity to import industrial goods. In that year, with only 1.8 per cent of the population of the ten major capitalist countries, Canada received 5.9 per cent of the imports of finished goods. But two points need to be made. First, an import surplus at that phase of development was not unusual: Japan's imports of finished goods were twice as much in value as those exported (three times as much if clothing and textiles are excluded). For Canada, however, the ratio was 4 to 1,[78] and Italy and Sweden had much better balances. Second, Canada had a higher standard of living than the other late-follower countries, and Canadians could therefore afford to import more. The pattern of large imports of finished goods, although present, was not overwhelming in 1899 and could have been reversed.

Between 1899 and 1913, however, a sharp divergence between Canada and the other countries developed. Although this was the period of Canada's most rapid growth ever in manufacturing output—the time when Canadian industry is supposed to have come of age—all the indicators point to a regression in development.[79] In 1913, 52 per cent of Canada's manufactured exports were finished, down from 83 per cent fourteen years earlier. The trend in those of the other late-follower countries for which there are complete statistics was in the opposite direction: Italy, 70 per cent (up from 41 per cent); Japan, 63 per cent (up from 39 per cent); and Sweden, 57 per cent (up from 50 per cent). While Canadian industrial output had more than doubled, the value of finished exports climbed by only one-half, confirming the argument that industrial production was aimed almost exclusively at the home market.[80] At the same time imports of manufactured goods more than trebled. The ratio of exports/imports of finished manufactured goods in 1913 tells the story (the 1899 ratio is given in parentheses): Canada, 0.10 (0.23); Japan, 1.3 (0.53); Sweden, 1.5 (1.1); and Italy, 1.4 (1.5). Even if textiles and clothing are excluded, the figures do not improve much: Canada exported only 14 per cent of the value of finished manufactures that it imported. For Sweden the comparable figure was 230 per cent, and even for the clothing- and textile-exporting countries the percentages indicate more-developed manufacturing economies: Italy, 79 per cent, and Japan, 66 per cent.

In the crucial capital-goods sector the same economic regression occurred. Imports of producer durables increased from 13 per cent of the Canadian market in 1880 and 1890 to more than 30 per cent between 1900 and 1915.[81] At the same time little Sweden made a spectacular breakthrough in this sector by exporting a wide range of Swedish-invented engineering goods (weapons, electronics, gas lighting, precision instruments, ball bearings). Canada's modern economic structure appears to have emerged by the First World War. Never again did Canada resemble the other late-follower countries.

In the 1920s Canada's exports of finished goods rallied to some extent as American corporations used their Canadian branch plants as assembly points for exports to British Empire markets. But the rally was more apparent than real. US transnational companies strove to disguise products of high American content with Canadian warehouse-assembly operations and made-in-Canada labels.[82] This strategy, which was supported by the Canadian Manufacturers' Association and the federal government, raised finished exports to the not-very-impressive level of slightly over one-quarter of imports by 1929. But the strategy was ephemeral and blew away with the British Empire after the Second World War.

What happened in the pre-First World War period to push Canada off the path to late-follower development? Two interrelated factors were of major importance. First, many Canadian manufacturers imported technology by entering into licensing agreements with American firms (the McLaughlin-General Motors arrangement is a good example). Usually the agreements specified that the rights to the technology applied to the Canadian market, and sometimes to other markets within the British Empire, but not to other areas. It would not do to have Canadian firms competing with their technological parent by exporting from Canada. Second, American branch plants came to dominate the most dynamic sectors of Canadian manufacturing, often by taking over the Canadian firms that had started out by licensing American technology. Subsidiaries were even more stringently restricted from competing with the parent company, while at the same time they tended to import parts and machinery on a major scale. Whether the cause was technological dependence or branch-plant ownership, Canada ended up importing a lot and exporting but little.

CONCLUSION

In this chapter I have examined the dominant paradigms in Canadian historiography and found them wanting. For the past century it has been incorrect to characterize Canada as a dependent resource economy presided over by a commercial élite, as the staples and Naylor/Clement approaches have been wont to do. It was not inevitable either that Canada would follow the American model of development at a later date or that it would fail to break fully free from a staple trap. The easy assumptions must be modified or discarded.

As we have seen, two contradictory tendencies must be explained: Canada's promising manufacturing development in the late nineteenth century and its failure to make good on that promise. None of the traditional approaches account for these tendencies satisfactorily. Instead, we saw that a modified Gerschenkron approach that focusses on the problems and possibilities of late development seems to explain the facts best. Because this approach is comparative, it breaks down the assumptions of uniqueness and inevitability. It poses the right questions. How did Canada deal with a shortage of domestic capital? Why did Canada develop a British commercial banking system rather than a German industrial one? How was state debt related to capital imports? How independent was Canadian technology and management? Answering these questions means examining the social and political forces underlying state policies and social-economic change. To move forward in our understanding of Canadian development, we must go beyond the givens of geography and external influence and look at the role of Canada's internal social formation. We may discover that Canadian history was made in Canada, not by geological forces millions of years ago, but by the people who later inhabited it.

NOTES

This chapter is a revised version of 'Foreign Ownership and Myths About Canadian Development', *Canadian Review of Sociology and Anthropology* 22, no. 3 (August 1985).

[1]This idea is akin to the prevalent notion of American exceptionalism. It is more an unstated assumption than something that is discussed. The power of this assumption can be seen in the paucity of comparative studies involving Canada. In correcting an earlier bias regarding importing economic theories unmodified to Canadian conditions, Harold Innis may have contributed to this assumption. See 'The Teaching of Economic History in Canada', in H.A. Innis, *Essays in Canadian Economic History* (Toronto: University of Toronto Press, 1973 [1929]), pp. 3-16.

[2]The idea that external forces determined Canadian development is related to the uniqueness-of-Canada assumption, of which, again, Innis was a major exponent. See H.A. Innis, *The Fur Trade in Canada* (Toronto: University of Toronto Press, 1975), pp. 385-86. John Hutcheson had a similar perspective in *Dominance and Dependency: Liberalism and National Policies in the North Atlantic Triangle* (Toronto: McClelland and Stewart, 1978).

[3]Although not a determinist, W.A. Mackintosh, in his 'Economic Factors in Canadian History' (*Canadian Historical Review* 4, no. 1 [1923]), emphasized geographic factors in thwarting Canadian development. The theme of overpowering geography is present in many Canadian works: for example, Donald Creighton, *The Commercial Empire of the St. Lawrence 1760-1850* (Toronto: Macmillan, 1970).

[4]Innis, *The Fur Trade*; Mackintosh, 'Economic Factors in Canadian History', p. 25.

[5]Staples economies have limited room for initiative. They can develop new wheat strains or encourage settlement, but they cannot create external demand, the crucial factor in the prosperity of staples economies.

[6]M.H. Watkins, 'A Staple Theory of Economic Growth,' *Canadian Journal of Economics and Political Science* 29, no. 2 (1963): 143.

[7]Innis, *The Fur Trade*, p. 385.

[8]Hugh Aitken, 'The State and Economic Growth in Canada', in W.T. Easterbrook and M.H. Watkins, eds, *Approaches to Canadian Economic History* (Toronto: McClelland and Stewart, 1967), p. 184.

[9]This is not true of Creighton and others who have written within the Laurentian or metropolitan approaches. See J.M.S. Careless, 'Frontierism, Metropolitanism, and Canadian History', in C. Berger, ed., *Approaches to Canadian History* (Toronto: University of Toronto Press, 1967), pp. 1-14.

[10]Hugh Aitken, 'The Changing Structure of the Canadian Economy', in Aitken et al., *The American Economic Impact on Canada* (Durham, N.C.: Duke University Press, 1959), p. 3.

[11]Watkins, 'Staple Theory', pp. 149-51.

[12]M.H. Watkins, 'The Staple Theory Revisited', *Journal of Canadian Studies* 12, no. 5 (1977): 89.

[13]Canada, *Report of the Royal Commission on the Economic Union and Development Prospects for Canada* (Macdonald Commission), vol. 1 (Ottawa: Minister of Supply and Services, 1985), p. 247.

[14]Margaret Atwood, *Survival: A Thematic Guide To Canadian Literature* (Toronto: Anansi, 1972), pp. 35-6.

[15]Innis, 'Teaching of Economic History', p. 10.

[16]W.A. Mackintosh, 'Canadian Economic Policy from 1945 to 1957—Origins and Influences', in Aitken et al., eds, *The American Economic Impact on Canada*, pp. 67-8.

[17]Innis, 'Teaching of Economic History', p. 208.

[18]R.T. Naylor, *The History of Canadian Business 1867-1914* (Toronto: Lorimer, 1975), 2 vols.; R.T. Naylor, 'Foreign and Direct Investment in Canada: Institutions and Policy, 1867-1914' (Cambridge, Ph.D. dissertation, 1978); W. Clement, *The Canadian Corporate Elite* (Toronto:

McClelland and Stewart, 1975); and Clement, *Continental Corporate Power* (Toronto: McClelland and Stewart, 1977).

[19]Naylor, *History of Canadian Business*, vol. 2, p. 282; Clement, *Continental Corporate Power*, p. 290.

[20]Karl Marx, *Capital: A Critique of Political Economy*, vol. 3 (Moscow: Progress Publishers, 1959) p. 323; M. Dobb, *Studies in the Development of Capitalism* (London: Routledge and Kegan Paul, 1954), p. 123.

[21]R.T. Naylor, 'Dominion of Capital: Canada and International Development' in A. Kontos, ed., *Domination* (Toronto: University of Toronto Press, 1975), p. 52.

[22]Naylor, *History of Canadian Business*, vols 1 and 2.

[23]Clement differs from Naylor in this respect. He attributes more strength, independence, and political influence to the Canadian corporate élite.

[24]Naylor, *History of Canadian Business*, vol. 1.

[25]Mel Watkins, 'The "American System" and Canada's National Policy', *Bulletin of the Canadian Association for American Studies*, 1966.

[26]Alexander Gerschenkron, *Economic Backwardness in Historical Perspective* (Cambridge: Harvard University Press, 1962).

[27]Marx, *Capital*, vol. 1, p. 19.

[28]Gerschenkron, *Economic Backwardness*, pp. 5-30.

[29]David Landes disagrees. See 'Technological Change and Development in Western Europe 1750-1914' in H.J. Habakkuk and M. Postan, eds, *The Cambridge Economic History of Europe*, vol. 6, part 1 (Cambridge: Cambridge University Press, 1965), p. 116: 'In Europe, the follower countries made the most of their cheap manpower by building more rudimentary but less expensive equipment, buying second-hand machines whenever possible, and concentrating on the more labour-intensive branches or stages of manufacture. Not until the last third of the century did the Continental economies conform to the usual theoretical model and avail themselves of the opportunity to adopt the latest techniques.' The late 1800s, however, was precisely the time when late-follower countries began to industrialize.

[30]Gerschenkron, *Economic Backwardness*, p. 9.

[31]Ibid., p. 31.

[32]Ibid., p. 24.

[33]Gershenkron did a fine class analysis in an early work, *Bread and Democracy in Germany* (New York: Howard Fertig, 1966 [1943]), but discussed ideas largely without reference to class in his later works.

[34]Gerschenkron *(Economic Backwardness*, p. 47) recognized foreign investment as a form of 'substitute' capital but did not think it a major source even in Russia in the 1890s. See O. Crisp, 'French Investment in Russian Joint Stock Companies 1894-1914', *British History* 2 (1960); E.E. Fleetwood, *Sweden and Capital Imports and Exports* (Geneva: Journal de Genève, 1947); Kenneth Buckley, *Capital Formation in Canada, 1896-1930* (Toronto: McClelland and Stewart, 1974).

[35]H.C. Pentland, 'The Role of Capital in Canadian Economic Development Before 1875', *Canadian Journal of Economics and Political Science* 26 (1950): 458.

[36]P. Hartland, 'Factors in Economic Growth in Canada', *Journal of Economic History* 15, no. 1 (1955).

[37]Not enough work has been done on secondary industries to show that this was true in every case. Something can be learned from the demand side, but the greater evidence lies with the supply side. The essence of investment banking was its ability to initiate change and consolidation in industry. If supply had been available in Canada through an investment-banking system, would demand have been far behind? The capitalization of Canadian industry was low in comparison with American industry in the 1870s and 1880s. See G.W. Bertram, 'Historical Statistics on Growth and Structure in Manufacturing in Canada 1870-1957' in J. Henripin and A. Asimkopoulos, eds, *Canadian Political Science Association Conference on Statistics* (Toronto, 1962), p. 115.

The consolidation movement did not begin until 1909-12, twenty years after mergers occurred in Germany, Russia, the US, and, to a lesser extent, Britain. See Clement, *Continental Corporate Power*, p. 45; Gerschenkron, *Economic Backwardness*; David Landes, *The Unbound Prometheus* (Cambridge: Cambridge University Press, 1969), p. 245; A.K. Cairncross, *Home and Foreign Investment 1870-1913* (Cambridge: Cambridge University Press, 1953), p. 38; W.G. Phillips, *The Agricultural Implements Industry in Canada: The Study of Competition* (Toronto: University of Toronto Press, 1956), p. 37.

38Most neo-classical economists do not concentrate on questions of long-term development. Among those that do, not all would agree with W.A. Mackintosh's scenario. Harry Johnson in *The Canadian Quandary* (Toronto: McClelland and Stewart, 1977 [1963]) and John Dales in *The Protective Tariff in Canada's Development* (Toronto: University of Toronto Press, 1966) accept the resource orientation of Canada's economy as its comparative advantage.

39International comparisons of industrial statistics present enormous problems. Different methods are applied in calculating national indices, and there are overlapping national series and a lack of uniform assumptions as to what constitutes manufacturing (prior to the Second World War). Currency valuations can be arbitrary. The further back in time we go, the more uncertain the conclusions. Despite the crudeness of the exercise, comparative estimates are crucial to assess comparative development levels.

We must rely on the handful of comparative studies on industrialization levels. For estimates of manufacturing output in the advanced industrial countries, there are basically two sets of data. One is the recent monumental work by Paul Bairoch, 'International Industrialization Levels from 1750 to 1980', *Journal of European Economic History* 11, no. 2 (1982), which for the first time includes estimates of handicraft production from the Third World. This provides a new view of relations between the developed and the underdeveloped world since the beginning of the Industrial Revolution. This is the main purpose of Bairoch's new methods of calculation (see his Appendix A).

The other set of data is older and includes the works of Hilgerdt for the League of Nations, *Industrialisation and World Trade* (New York: United Nations, 1945); Colin Clark, *The Conditions of Economic Progress* 3rd ed., rev. (New York: Macmillan, 1960); and Alfred Maizels, *Industrial Growth* and *World Trade* (London: Cambridge University Press, 1963.) These studies do not wholly agree among themselves, nor do they involve exactly the same methods of calculation. Nevertheless, there is considerable agreement regarding orders of magnitude and levels of industrial production among the countries we are interested in: late follower-countries, the white dominions, and the US in the period from 1870 to the 1930s. Furthermore, Simon Kuznets is in general agreement with their estimates as well, and he has a high regard for Hilgerdt's study. See Kuznets, *Modern Economic Growth: Rate, Structure and Spread* (New Haven: Yale University Press, 1969), p. 305.

I use the earlier sources rather than Bairoch's (for the period before the Second World War) for several reasons. First, Bairoch's estimates for Canada's aggregate level of Canadian manufacturing production in the 1881 to 1913 period is between one-third and two-fifths the level estimated by Hilgerdt. Estimates for the US in 1860 and 1880 are also much below Hilgerdt's (and others'), suggesting a systematic underestimation of North American manufacturing production at an early point in their industrial development. Bairoch's figures for the later period (starting about the First World War in the case of the US and about the Second World War in the case of Canada) are very similar to the earlier studies. Second, Bairoch's estimates for Canada do not coincide with what we know about the character as well as the quantity of Canadian manufacturing between 1870 and 1914. The following works are in general agreement with the earlier sets of comparative international statistics: Gordon Bertram, 'Historical Statistics' and 'Economic Growth in Canadian Industry, 1870-1915: The Staple Model and the Take-Off Hypothesis', *Canadian Journal of Economics and Political Science* 29, 1963; John Dales, 'Estimates of Canadian Manufacturing Output by Markets, 1870-1915, in J. Henripin and A. Asimkopoulos, eds, *Canadian Political Science Association Conference on Statistics* (Toronto: 1962); Duncan McDougall, 'The Domestic Availability of Manufactured Commodity Output, Canada 1870-1915', *Canadian Journal of Economics* 6, no. 2 (1973); and M.C. Urquhart 'New Estimates of Gross National Product, Canada 1870-1926: Some

Implications for Canadian Development' (Kingston, Ont.: Institute for Economic Research, Queen's University Discussion Paper No. 586, 1986). Finally, Bairoch does not reveal enough detail for the reader to make an independent assessment of his sources and assumptions. On the other hand, Hilgerdt, Maizels, and Clark have laid out their methods in much greater detail.

[40]The ability to produce most needed items in case of a sudden cut-off of supply cannot be determined by looking solely at a nation's economic indicators. As Dudley Seers pointed out, the strength and unity of national feeling is an important ingredient in potential self-sufficiency. See Seers, 'Patterns of Dependence', in J. Villamil, ed., *Transnational Capitalism and National Development New Perspectives on Dependence* (Hassocks, Sussex: Harvester Press, 1979).

[41]Alfred Chandler, *Strategy and Structure: Chapters in the History of the American Industrial Enterprise* (Cambridge: M.I.T. Press, 1962).

[42]Pierre Bourgault, *Innovation and the Structure of Canadian Industry* (Ottawa: Science Council of Canada, 1972).

[43]Maizels, *Industrial Growth and World Trade*, p. 58.

[44]Canada did not fit W.W. Rostow's model of 'economic take-off' because of the unusually high rate of gross investment in the pre-take-off stage. See Rostow, *The Stages of Economic Growth: A Non-Communist Manifesto* (London: Cambridge University Press, 1965).

[45]*Government of Australia Yearbook* (Canberra, 1981), p. 644; United Nations Department of Economic and Social Affairs, *Multinational Corporations in World Development* (New York: 1974).

[46]Bairoch, 'International Industrialization Levels', p. 284.

[47]By the mid-1980s the US no longer had a favourable trade balance in finished goods. But if the time-lag hypothesis of Canada as a backward US holds, Canada should not experience this reversal for decades.

[48]The Auto Pact treats North America as one entity for the auto producers, and most of the 'trade' consists of movement between parent and subsidiary. Maizels is the source for 1899, 1929, and 1955. Canada, Statistics Canada, *Summary of Canadian International Trade* (Ottawa, 1988) is the source for the mid-1980s (my calculations).

[49]Canada, *Summary of Canadian International Trade*, pp. 17, 23.

[50]Fleetwood, *Sweden and Capital Imports and Exports*; Harry Johansson, 'Foreign Businesses Operating in Sweden', in M. Norgren, ed., *Industry in Sweden* (Halmstad, Sweden: Swedish Institute for Cultural Relations with Foreign Countries, 1968).

[51]Canada, Dept. of Trade and Commerce, *Foreign Direct Investment in Canada* (Gray Report) (Ottawa: Dept. of Trade and Commerce, 1972).

[52]Simon Kuznets, 'Economic Growth: The Last Hundred Years' *National Institute Economic Review* (1961), p. 133.

[53]Ross Robertson, *History of the American Economy* (New York: Harcourt, Brace and World Inc., 1964), p. 231.

[54]John Dunning, 'United States Foreign Investment and the Technological Gap', in C. Kindleberger and A. Schonfield, eds, *North American and Western European Economic Policies* (London: Macmillan, 1971), p. 370.

[55]Douglass North, 'United States Balance of Payments, 1790-1860', in National Bureau of Economic Research, *Studies in Income and Wealth* (Princeton: Princeton University Press, 1960), vol. 24, p. 576.

[56]Regarding the utility of using patents as a measure of domestic innovation, see Statistics Canada, Science and Technology Division, *Patents as Indicators of Invention* (Ottawa: Minister of Supply and Services, 1985). Regarding US patents, see United States, *Reports of the Commission of Patents* (Washington, 1970), p. 957.

[57]Government of Canada, *Department of Agriculture Statistical Yearbook* (Ottawa, 1901), p. 612.

[58]Government of Canada, *Canada Yearbook* (Ottawa, 1931, 1956); Consumer and Corporate Affairs Canada, *Annual Report 1987-8* (Ottawa: Supply and Services, 1988), p. 19.

[59]Glen Williams, 'We Ain't Growin' Nowhere', *This Magazine* 9, (1975): 8-9.

[60]John Britton and James Gilmour, *The Weakest Link: A Technological Perspective on Canadian Industrial Development* (Ottawa: Science Council of Canada, 1978), pp. 48, 91.

[61]Philip Ehrensaft and Warwick Armstrong, 'The Formation of Dominion Capitalism: Economic Truncation and Class Structure', in A. Moscovitch, ed., *Inequality: Essays on the Political Economy of Social Welfare* (Toronto: University of Toronto Press, 1981).

[62]Argentina was an exception. Manufacturing comprised as high a percentage of its GNP as in the 'dominant economies'. See ibid., p. 115. This may not mean any more than that other sectors of the economy were even weaker than manufacturing.

[63]Clark, *The Conditions of Economic Progress*, p. 336.

[64]Neither the League of Nations nor Bairoch gives data on Argentinian or Uruguayan manufacturing exports.

[65]United Nations Development Organization, *Industry and Development: Global Report 1988/9* (Vienna: 1988). In 1986 USSR manufacturing value added was $526,741 million (US), while Japan's was $446,028 million (US); see pp. A-49, A-84.

[66]League of Nations, *Industrialisation and World Trade*, p. 13.

[67]Bairoch, 'International Industrialization Levels', p. 284.

[68]J.A. Hobson, *Imperialism: A Study* (London: Archibald Constable, 1905).

[69]S.B. Clough, *Economic History of Europe* (Boston: D.C. Heath, 1952), pp. 594-602.

[70]Maizels, *Industrial Growth and World Trade*, p. 136.

[71]Dales, 'Estimates of Canadian Manufacturing Output', p. 75; Bertram, 'Historical Statistics', p. 103; Colin Forster, *Australian Economic Development in the Twentieth Century* (London: George Allen and Unwin, 1970), p. 129.

[72]Bertram, 'Historical Statistics', pp. 112-13.

[73]I am not arguing the irrelevance of comparisons between Canada and other white dominions. Ehrensaft and Armstrong take us in fruitful new directions. But the white-dominion model is misleading in assessing early development prospects for Canada.

[74]The data for this section are derived from the tables of my doctoral thesis, 'The Social Origins of Canada's Branch Plant Economy, 1837-1914' (University of Toronto, 1981). To probe these figures further, consult as well the sources from which they were drawn: League of Nations, *Industrialisation and World Trade*: Maizels, *Industrial Growth and World Trade;* and United Nations studies: *Multinational Corporations in World Development, Statistical Yearbook*, and *Transnational Corporations in World Development: A Re-examination.* But was Canada advanced enough in all respects in the late nineteenth century to be one of Gerschenkron's late-follower countries? The 1920s and 1930s comparisons with Argentina and Australia are obviously not early enough to gauge this, and internationally comparable data are not available for Argentina before this time, but the situation is a little better for Australia. The League of Nations' estimates go back to 1908, at which time Australia had about 1% of world manufacturing production (*Industrialisation and World Trade*, p. 141). Bairoch's estimates go back to 1860 for Australia ('International Industrialization Levels', p. 330.) He estimated that in 1860 Australia produced 0.2% of the UK's 1900 level of industrial production and 2.3% of that level by 1913. The latter was about one-quarter of Canada's output in 1913. For a discussion of the validity of Bairoch's estimates, see note 39, above.

[75]A century later, an altered set of the top four industrial countries accounted for between 61% and 73% of the world's total. See Bairoch, 'International Industrialization Levels'.

[76]According to Maizels, there are no adequate figures for the Netherlands (*Industrial Growth and World Trade*). Bairoch ranks that country's industrial production level as very low for the 1880-1913 period ('International Industrialization Levels', p. 330). Czechoslovakia was not an independent country then.

[77]Glen Williams, *Not for Export: Towards a Political Economy of Canada's Arrested Industrialization* (Toronto: McClelland and Stewart, 1983).

[78]The ratio does not change appreciably whether textiles and clothing are included or excluded.

[79]Bertram, 'Historical Statistics', p. 103; O.J. Firestone, *Industry and Education: A Century of Canadian Development* (Ottawa: University of Ottawa Press, 1969), p. 25.

[80]Williams, *Not For Export.*

[81]The ratio of exports to imports indicate the same trend. In 1880, 1890, and 1900 the ratio was about 0.2, and it dropped to about 0.15 in 1905 and 1910. The 1915 figure indicates a gain (0.32), but this was due to a boost for exports because of the war. These figures, as well as those quoted in the text, are derived from Table I in McDougall, 'Availability of Manufacturing Commodity Output', p. 193. His Table is misleading: the 'producer durables' column should be read as percentages, not ratios.

[82]Williams, *Not For Export*, p. 80.

2

Late-follower Development

[If the province of Canada] is willing to devote all her resources both in men and money to the maintenance of her connexion with the Mother Country . . . the Imperial Government fully acknowledge[s] the reciprocal obligation of defending every portion of the Empire [including Canada] with all the resources at its command.

Edward Cardwell, British Colonial Secretary, 1865.

The battles of Canada cannot be fought on the frontier but on the high seas and at the great cities of the Atlantic coast; and it will be nothing but folly for us to cripple ourselves by spending fifteen or twenty millions a year to raise an army of 50,000 for the purpose of resisting an invasion of the country. The best thing that Canada can do is to keep quiet and give no cause for war.

A.A. Dorion, Rouge leader, 1865.

Because there were vast accumulations of capital burning holes in their owners' pockets they had to find an outlet for their investments. Most of it was sunk into the railways and much of it was sunk without a trace . . . much of it was rashly, stupidly, some of it insanely invested. Britons with surpluses, encouraged by projectors, contractors and others whose profits were made not by running railways but by planning or building them, were undeterred by the ex- traordinarily swollen costs of railways, which made the capitalization per mile of line in England and Wales three times as high as in Prussia, five times as high as in the USA, seven times as high as in Sweden.

Eric Hobsbawm, historian, re railway investment in
Britain in the 1830s and 1840s.

What do we most need to save us from the fate of China? A modern army and navy. On what does the creation and maintenance of modern armed forces depend? Chiefly on heavy industries, engineering, mining and shipbuilding, in a word strategic industries.

Herbert Norman, historian, characterizing the the Meiji
government in Japan (1868-1911).

In Russia a foreign company can be opened only by a special decree of the Committee of Ministers . . . Russian joint-stock companies in which foreigners are shareholders are permitted to have only a minority of foreigners on their board of directors. In [many provinces of Imperial Russia] neither foreign companies nor Russian companies with foreign participation are permitted to acquire property or exploit natural resources . . . In permitting the activities of foreign companies in Russia, the government retains the right to revoke at any time that permission and to demand the liquidation of any company.

Count Witte, Russian finance minister, 1899.

Thus, in war as in most other matters, Canadian interests are necessarily deeply involved with either or both of the great powers–Great Britain and the United States–but, except through them, very slightly with any others . . . To put it in another way, Canadians can go out into the international rain if they care to, but when they get drenched they can always scramble back under the Imperial umbrella . . . With the double-barrelled protection of the British Navy and the Monroe Doctrine, and Canada's relative inaccessibility to the armed forces of any invader, except those of a neighbor with whom the possibility of war is apt to draw smiles of amused incredulity, Canadians go about their business with a feeling of complete unconcern.

H.F. Angus, economic historian, 1938.

Monroe's creed of America for the Americans has been altered to mean America for the Americans and as much else of the world's surface as can be obtained at a profitable figure.

Stephen Leacock, 1909.

During his first year in office US President Ronald Reagan offered some advice to the underdeveloped countries of the world: the best path to prosperity was to be found through free trade and private investment. No nation had ever been less developed than the fledgeling United States of America–and look how far economic freedom had taken it.[1] The implication was obvious. Citizens of poor countries should stop complaining about the ubiquitous power of the multinational corporations and the unfairness of international institutions such as the World Bank, and follow the example of the sturdy American pioneer: work hard, save, and the economy will develop through the 'magic of the marketplace'.

With his ability to recount homespun American truths, President Reagan was undoubtedly 'the great communicator', but he was no historian. The American laissez-faire prescription is more utopian today than it was a hundred years ago when the late-follower countries wanted to join the exclusive club of developed nations and begin their own industrial revolutions. Emulating the 'least government is the best government' models of early-industrialized Britain and the United States was not appropriate for the late followers because the very success of the pioneering countries meant that their route could not be copied.[2]

England was the first to undergo the great transformation to an industrial society; for a short time it was the world's 'only workshop, its only massive importer and exporter, its only carrier, its only imperialist, almost its only foreign investor'.[3] Soon a handful of other countries—France, the US, Belgium, Switzerland, and later Germany—joined the march towards a society promising the multitudes freedom from the dreary burden of poverty. (For most people, of course, reality fell short of the promise.) Within a century of the first great inventions of the late 1700s a world economy had been created, but it involved very unequal players. On one side were a half dozen rapidly developing countries monopolizing over 80 per cent of manufacturing production for the world's marketplace; on the other were all the other countries, which did not possess the means to compete against the astounding new technical and social methods of production.

For the half-dozen or so late-follower countries that were undergoing the beginnings of the industrial revolution in the late nineteenth century there were basically two routes to industrialization. The independent route involved transforming the financial system to channel new pools of scarce domestic resources into industrial development and adopting defence and economic nationalist policies that ensured sovereignty over technological and managerial processes. The banks and the state were the central institutions to these ends. The use of foreign loan capital was generally compatible with independent development, but only as long as political sovereignty was not compromised. Foreign direct (ownership) capital, with its tendency to create managerial and technological dependence, had to be restricted in order for an independent, export-oriented manufacturing structure to evolve. For most countries nationalism and defence considerations were the main bases for state curtailment of foreign direct investment, especially in the technologically important sectors of machinery and other strategic goods.

Although the independent route to development was taken by most late-follower countries, another one was possible: the dependent or passive route. Instead of struggling to create all the necessary building blocks at home, a country could simply import as many of the factors of production as possible from the already-advanced countries.[4] Investment capital, the latest technologies, and enterprising management could all be imported as a package via branches of successful foreign companies. It was easy to induce foreign businesses to invest in branch plants as long as they could be assured of economic stability, secure access to resources, and a good market. But this route could lead to permanent dependence. Foreign direct investment would mean a growing external debt as the foreign companies built up their assets inside the country without injecting new infusions of capital. Political sovereignty could also be jeopardized as foreign capital became an internal political force, and the threat of its sudden withdrawal was enough to dissuade all but the most sanguine governments from attempting to reassert domestic ownership and control. As well, rather than educate home-grown youngsters to fill the new positions in industry, the state could import skilled and disciplined workers as immigrants, to save itself and business the expense of training them.

Late-follower countries could take one route to development or the other. This chapter explores the circumstances in which most took the independent route. Chapters 4, 5, and 6 will examine Canada's divergence from the usual course of late-follower development.

THE ROUTE TO INDEPENDENCE

The context of late-follower development

The industrial revolution had an effect that is hard for contemporary observers to understand. It drastically slashed the prices of many goods; for example, around 1800 cotton yarn, the basic building-block for a modern clothing industry, fell to less than one-fifth of its pre-industrial price. The same effect has been repeated over and over again as new techniques have been developed and new products have begun to be mass-produced and copied. Calculators, video-cassette recorders, and personal computers are recent examples of this process. But the effect was much more profound in the nineteenth century. Hand-made production methods fell one by one as new machine techniques were developed and a large number of workers were dispossessed from their land or their tools. In the already-industrialized countries new jobs were usually available to replace those in the declining pre-industrial sectors. This transition was never easy, as the sorry plight of England's weavers in the early 1800s attests.[5] For the vast majority of countries, however, the old jobs were threatened and new industrial jobs were not created to compensate for them. Modern transportation and communications systems removed the age-old barriers of distance that protected local producers in local markets. Suddenly all societies were part of this new world, whether they wanted to be or not.[6] For example, Japan's policy of keeping out the *Komo no yabanjin* (red-haired barbarians) from the west came to an end in 1853, when American gunboats entered Tokyo harbour and forced Japan to trade on unequal terms with the advanced countries.[7]

In the rapidly changing context of the late 1800s the social and technical revolution began to take hold in the late-follower countries. Being a follower had its advantages and disadvantages. On the positive side, it was possible to import advanced technology, capital, and management and to obtain supplies of skilled and disciplined labourers whose ties to the land had already been broken. On the other hand, the followers were bedevilled by shortages of domestic capital, the withering effects of foreign competition, and a myriad of internal social and political problems. One thing was certain: the late followers could not take the slow, laissez-faire path to independent industrialization.

Follower countries had social and political structures that were different from those of the industrial pioneers; indeed, that is why they developed later. They either had archaic class structures that were ill-adapted to the creation of a free wage-labour force, or else they belonged to areas of the world in which large nation-states had not yet formed (some countries, notably Italy, faced both problems at the same time). In the already-developed countries of the late 1800s, the social and political revolutions had taken place *before* industrialization. But in the late-follower countries the pressures of international competition and imperial threats to sovereignty forced the pace. The social revolution had to occur simultaneously with the economic revolution.[8] In the older societies, those with 'feudal'-like structures, the process of removing people from the land and breaking up rigid social hierarchies had to be greatly accelerated. New settler societies, such as British North America, largely avoided the problems associated with outdated social structures, but the pace of their development was forced as well. They had to establish independence and national unity at the same time as economic development. For both the older states and new settler societies, therefore, political and social questions loomed large.

Finally, late followers faced two problems in developing independent economies: a shortage of domestic capital and threats to technological and managerial sovereignty. The issues were often interrelated.

Late-follower countries did not possess enough of their own capital to finance rapid industrialization easily. The situation had been different in England during the initial phase of industrialization: costs had been lower and supplies of domestic capital more plentiful. For example, in cotton, perhaps the leading industry of the late 1700s, it cost only six pounds to equip a forty-spindle shop.[9] A hundred years later, when finished steel products—guns, sewing machines, typewriters, locks, and farm machinery—were the dynamic sector, the costs of starting up such industries were much higher. But by then England was not short of domestic capital: when it 'ruled the waves' profits from international trade surged through the whole economy. Because Britain faced no rivals, returns to industry were abnormally high in the first seven or eight decades of its industrialization.[10]

Thus capital was amassed for British industrialization through short-term loans from commerce and through the reinvestment of manufacturers' profits. This was the 'laissez-faire' path to capitalist progress, considered by most economists then, and by neo-conservatives now, to be the 'normal' course of development. These means had been more than sufficient for England. In fact, sixty or seventy years after the industrial revolution began, British capitalists were so bloated that they became the great financiers of other countries' economies.

Late followers were in a different situation. They had not been the major trading nations of the world and had no history of slowly amassing capital within industry. Because the costs of starting up industry and transportation had risen and pressures to develop quickly had increased, the laissez-faire path was not possible. In late-follower countries private enterprises did not have sufficient means and opportunities to begin industrial development on their own. Capital, knowledge, markets, and good transportation and communications were all deficient. The state had to take a leading role, at least in the initial phase of industrialization. But what was the route to take? This is where politics—in the broad sense of ideas, national culture, and class and ethnic structures—had significant influence. Whether the politicians and the public conceived of the development options or not, state policies had long-term consequences that led down one path or the other. Often it was less a matter of conscious choice than of a myriad of short-run decisions made to satisfy the premises and demands of important political groupings in each country.

The route to independence

The route to independence was taken by all the late-follower countries save Canada. It involved not only domestic control of productive capital but also a fair degree of technological and managerial sovereignty. The latter enables a society to generate industries that are in tune with its resource endowments, specialized skills, and market size. The Swedish iron and steel industry is a good example. Because Sweden had vast forest reserves but no coal, it continued to make steel on a competitive basis from charcoal, which is wood-based, long after the advanced countries had moved on to coal-using techniques. Then, around 1900, Swedish ironmasters pioneered methods of making high-grade steel using electric forges driven by Sweden's abundance of hydro power. Some coal for steel-making purposes did have to be imported, but Sweden had retained and then developed techniques appropriate to its own resource endowments.[11] Such are the advantages of a high degree of technological and managerial sovereignty.

Technological independence does not require autonomous invention. One country cannot expect to develop every product or technique on its own. But copying and adapting others' technologies within domestically run companies can also lead to technological sovereignty. This practice is sometimes called industrial espionage, or just plain stealing, but it is time-honoured. Certainly Japan and Italy used it successfully.[12]

In contrast, when techniques are imported and not adapted to local conditions, the result is technological dependence. Subsidiaries of transnational corporations are the classic case, buying machinery and techniques from the head office, often at exorbitant prices. Licensing inventions from other countries is a compromise that can lead to either dependence or independence. In 1907, for instance, Kawasaki purchased the right to manufacture ship turbines from American Curtis, and soon Japan was developing its own ship engines.[13] But licensing technology can also be the first stage towards takeover: in the same year the McLaughlin carriage works branched out to automobile production, bought Buick engines, and was soon absorbed into General Motors. Thus technological sovereignty is often intimately related to capital sovereignty.

How did Sweden, Japan, Italy, and czarist Russia avoid the pitfalls associated with capital shortage and technological backwardness in late-follower development?[14] Shortages of domestic capital were overcome in three ways: by modifying the banking system to facilitate the flow of funds to industry and infrastructure; by providing direct state aid for economic development; and by reducing the level of capital needed for development through a primitive form of government 'planning'. The dangers of technological dependence were generally avoided by two means: through the development of investment banks—with their emphasis on domestic control over industry—and domestic technology; and through defence policies aimed at independent armaments capability. In such endeavours an interventionist state played a central role.

Banks were crucial to financing both new industry and the transportation and communications systems needed to connect markets, move workers to jobs, and reach resources. Most countries began with a variant of British banking. During the early stages of the industrial revolution merchants required more capital than manufacturers; they also had better prospects. Consequently banks were, for the most part, geared towards the short-term financing of trade. Some bankers' and merchants' credit reached the industrialists, but usually only for short periods to facilitate the movement of their wares;[15] capital for long-term investment was usually not forthcoming. In late-follower countries, however, the sharply increased costs of industrial start-up made this arrangement unsuitable. In all of them either the banking system was modified or else the state stepped in to play the role of industrial financier—in all, that is, except Canada.

Facing some of the same conditions as the late-follower countries, Germany was the first to succeed with a new type of investment banking that broke with the British tradition.[16] German banks were much more oriented to the long-term capital needs of manufacturing and railway construction. Not only did they lend money more readily to industrialists who were just starting out, but they also sold the stocks of struggling as well as established companies. When banks financed and sold stocks for small manufacturers, a whole new source of domestic capital became available to industry. Small investors, who otherwise would not have touched anything as speculative as industrial stocks, were reassured by the commitment of the large banks. Thus it was through an institutional change, and not by the gradual accumulation of capital, that a new pool of domestic funds was made available to German industry. (The politics that gave rise to this kind of banking system are discussed in Chapter 4.)

As well as facilitating the creation of the building blocks necessary for an industry's success, investment banks often planned and developed whole new sectors of the economy. The Swedish electrical-generating business is a prime example. The Stockholms Enskilda Bank (SEB), a *de facto* investment bank owned by the Wallenbergs, the 'Rockefellers of Sweden', took over the financing of the giant engineering firm ASEA by 1898. The company had developed electrical generators but could not sell them because there was little demand. The task, therefore, was to create a demand for electricity. To do so the SEB became heavily involved in 'the building of power stations, the purchase of waterfalls, the promotion of urban electrification, including tramways, and the establishment of suitable industries to use the electricity generated'.[17] This was planning not by the state, but by a privately-owned Swedish bank.[18]

Banks were not the only means to finance and promote industry. The state itself could overcome the shortage of domestic capital and thus avoid the prospect of branch-plant industrialization. Japan's Meiji government, for instance, financed industry in the 1870s because domestic banks were too small, whether reformed or not, to initiate rapid industrialization.

Japan was in a race against time; it could develop rapidly on its own or become another China, humiliated and colonized by the Western powers. Except for the silk industry, which evolved largely under private auspices, virtually all modern Japanese industries had their beginnings as government enterprises. The state provided the capital, trained the first managers and skilled workers by importing foreign engineers for short periods, and brought in the latest equipment from abroad.

Later the state relinquished much of its economic role when it sold most of its modern industries at fire-sale prices to rich Japanese families, thereby in essence creating a small group of monopoly capitalists. The peasants were the unwilling financiers of capitalist industrialization, paying over half the value of their produce in taxes to the state.[19]

In czarist Russia and in Italy the state took a lesser but still important part in financing and aiding industrialization. Governments in both societies paid for large portions of the railway systems and used their influence over the railways and the military to procure supplies from domestically based and domestically owned companies.[20] Again, the unfortunate peasant was the source of much of this state largesse. Late-follower Sweden was a less backward country with a reformed banking system that was better able to plan and finance industry during the initial phase of industrialization (1870-1914). Nevertheless, Sweden's trunk rail lines too were built and operated by the government.

Another kind of state planning was equally important in the independent route to industrialization. If the costs of the early part of the process could be lessened, when domestic funds for development were still meagre, industry's need for foreign capital would be reduced. For example, in the enormously expensive undertaking of building railways, it was imperative to work as cheaply and as quickly as possible and to avoid duplication. Above all, England's laissez-faire example was not to be copied.

By the 1830s, after Britain had been industrializing for half a century, its problem was not a shortage of capital but a glut. Eric Hobsbawm describes the consequences of this capital surplus on British railway construction:

Most of it was sunk into the railways and much of it was sunk without a trace . . .

much of it was rashly, stupidly, some of it insanely invested. Britons with surpluses, encouraged by projectors, contractors and others whose profits were made not by running railways but by planning or building them, were undeterred by the extraordinarily swollen costs of railways, which made the capitalization per mile of line in England and Wales three times as high as in Prussia, five times as high as in the USA, seven times as high as in Sweden.[21]

Comparative estimates of railway costs for Italy, Japan, and Russia during initial industrialization (the 1870s until the First World War) are not readily available, but they could not have been as high as Canada's. Many Canadian railways were built according to the British standard and price, some of them by the very same British contractors, and duplication of lines was rampant. What had been a benign folly in Britain took on quite a different character in Canada. The size of the country, the small population, and the lateness of development magnified the consequences of such extravagance. In contrast, Japan built relatively few lines, even considering its island character. For example, in 1907, the year Japan launched the *Satsuma*, the world's largest battleship, it had only a quarter as many miles of railway as Britain.[22] Admittedly, Japanese railways are said to have been 'badly planned, poorly constructed and inefficiently managed',[23] and when the private lines were nationalized in 1906 the government paid 'about twice as much as the amount of their capital' (thus continuing the tradition of state munificence to the newly created capitalists, via taxes obtained from the peasants).[24] For all the inflated costs, however, the low overall mileage more than compensated.

Italy and Russia were not noted for strenuous efforts to reduce capital needs through careful railway planning. In fact, costs were pushed up in both countries by government procurement programs that encouraged high-cost domestically made products.[25] As well, military and national-unity considerations increased the costs of railway construction.[26] Nevertheless, railway expenditures were not wildly extravagant. Although greater Russia had the largest railway mileage of any European country by the First World War, its immense size and population meant that it had the fewest miles on both an area and a per capita basis.[27] Italy was close to the European average in these respects, but the state avoided much duplication by dividing the country into four non-competing networks.[28]

Thus building railways to unite a national community was not a constant factor in every country in terms of cost or economic consequences: these depended on a variety of circumstances. Perennially short of cash at first, late-follower countries had a tendency to adopt less wasteful methods than England. This was especially true of Sweden, which apparently built railways to an exacting standard, but managed to do so at a drastically reduced cost per mile.[29] To some extent this frugality was counteracted by a stress on 'development' railways, which, as in the new world, were built ahead of settlement in order to facilitate growth. But the pattern of low-cost railways in Sweden held nevertheless. Duplication of lines was usually reduced in late-follower countries if the railways were built by the state according to a central plan.

On the other hand, most late-follower countries spent extravagantly on defence. At the high end, Russia spent almost half its budget on the army and navy between 1866 and 1885.[30] In roughly the same period Japan spent about one-sixth of its revenue on the armed forces, while Sweden may have spent something in the order of 10 per cent of its budget on defence.[31] With its minuscule armed forces, Canada spent much less: about 4 per cent, on average, of federal expenditures.[32] Defence costs increased reliance on foreign loans, but also provided the strongest motive for blocking foreign ownership of industry. (The latter effect is discussed below.)

To sum up, most late-follower countries dealt with shortages of domestic capital by (a) changing the banking system so that new sources of funds would flow into industry; (b) providing direct state aid for economic development; and (c) engaging in state 'planning'. But the use of foreign capital was not eliminated completely. Sweden borrowed a great deal of foreign capital to finance its railways, although it did not allow much external ownership.[33] Czarist Russia blocked foreign ownership in certain strategic sectors but encouraged its use elsewhere. The threat of branch-plant industrialization was removed only when the Bolsheviks wiped out foreign debts in 1918 by refusing to recognize the obligations of their bourgeois predecessors.[34]

Japan and Italy made very little use of external capital, partly because foreigners did not view them as attractive prospects. Absence of natural resources was one deterrent. Another was state indebtedness incurred during social and economic modernization, which resulted in high inflation and, for a time, the inconvertibility of both countries' bank notes. A third factor in Japan was the domestic barriers erected to keep out foreign investment.[35]

Why did all the late-followers—save Canada—in varying degrees discourage foreign ownership? Restrictions on foreign direct investment were related to the issues of technological sovereignty, nationalism, and defence.

Technology, defence, and economic independence

The late 1800s were the years of classical imperialism. Major Western powers entered into a mad scramble to plant their flags, carve up the globe, and administer new colonies for their own benefit. Even the United States joined this largely European game with its occupation of Cuba and the Philippines and the creation of Panama. Most of the action was in Africa and Asia, but the backward Western countries were not immune from the threat of foreign tutelage.

Industrialization changed the nature of warfare. What had been a grandiose duel, fought at a leisurely pace and confined to aristocrats and professional military men operating according to strict codes of honour (such as observing the 'Truce of God' on the Sabbath), became total war involving sneak attacks aimed at exterminating civilian populations, mobilization of mass conscript armies, and national efforts to co-ordinate industrial output and railway timetables.[36] Gone were the days when the main military problem was to build a war chest large enough to finance the hiring of mercenaries, such as Swiss Guards. Securing the latest technologies of destruction became the principal concern. Only modern industry could turn out longer-range and more accurate guns, stronger armour, and the means to transport men speedily to battle. No longer could economically backward nations be on an even military footing with the advanced countries.

This fact was brought home to Russia in 1877-78. In its historic drive for access to the Mediterranean, and caught up in pan-Slav nationalism, Russia defeated Turkey in the Balkans only to lose most of the spoils at the negotiating table with Britain in Berlin.[37] Russia had to give up its military gains because its antiquated army was no match for an enemy with a well-developed industrial economy.

The Japanese 'economic miracle' of our time was built to a great extent on a base of military industries. The Japanese learned the hard way that they could not remain in splendid isolation unless they developed modern armed forces equipped by Western-style industry. They expressed this lesson in the slogan *fukoku-kyōhei*: rich country, strong army.[38] The reaction to Commodore Perry's intrusion in the 1850s was a modernizing revolution 'from above', carried through by an élite group whose cry was 'Revere the Emperor, expel the foreigner'. This élite's way of expelling the foreigner was to embrace Western technology and industry so closely that Japan's output could be turned against the predatory Western powers themselves. Herbert Norman, the son of a Canadian missionary in Japan and a great scholar of Japanese history, characterized the thinking of the Meiji government (1868-1911) in these terms:

> What do we most need to save us from the fate of China? A modern army and navy. On what does the creation and maintenance of modern armed forces depend? Chiefly on heavy industries, engineering, mining and shipbuilding, in a word strategic industries.[39]

The extraordinary determination that went into this effort is exemplified by the Mito clan, which in 1855 succeeded in constructing a reverberatory furnace for making iron. They had never seen a working model, had great difficulty in securing suitable materials, and built it by following the instructions of Dutch textbooks.[40] Thus it went with the early Japanese armaments industries from the 1840s to the 1860s.

The Western powers seemed able to recognize only two kinds of countries in Asia: subject nations or victorious empires. There was no halfway house of simple independence for Japan. To end unequal Western-imposed treaties and extra-territorial rights, Japan had to demonstrate that she was a great power. As Foreign Minister Inoue put it: 'We have to establish a new, European-style empire on the edge of Asia.'[41] Japan did this by defeating China and then Russia at war in 1894 and 1905. Once Japan was victorious, the West ceased to interfere in its internal affairs.[42]

In Sweden and Italy the military question was not as strongly related to economic development and national independence. But it was a factor. Sweden has a well-deserved reputation as a peaceful country. It has not gone to war since 1809, refuses to join military alliances, and was the birthplace of Alfred Nobel, dynamite king turned peace philanthropist. Yet Sweden has not purchased its neutrality and independence by renouncing all arms. The Swedish consensus during this century has been 'No adventure, no conquest, but plenty of arms for self-defence'.[43]

In the seventeenth century Sweden was one of Europe's great powers, controlling the Baltic Sea and able to push its armies deep into Europe. The cry 'The Swedes are coming' was enough to terrorize people from the Alps to the Ukraine.[44] Sweden was then a large munitions manufacturer and exporter, making 20,000 muskets in 1629-30 alone.[45] Even after it fell from great-power status in the next century, defence continued to be a major preoccupation. The state lavished funds on the strategic industries: iron and shipbuilding.[46] Although Sweden was at peace from 1815 to 1914, it came close to war in the Crimea, against Prussia over the Danish issue, and against Norway in 1905. It was also constantly apprehensive of Russian intentions. Thus the defence question continued to influence state policy and the direction of economic development: for example, Saab, the automobile company, developed as an offshoot of the firm that built airplanes for the Swedish air force.[47]

In the late 1800s, before unification, the Italian states fought hard against France and the Austro-Hungarian empire. After national unification was achieved, Italy had to develop modern armed forces to safeguard its newly won independence. As a country almost surrounded by water, it concentrated on sea power and by 1885 had the third largest navy in the world. But an effective navy needed more than an intelligent command and mere numbers of ships. It needed technical superiority—hence the state's interest in developing modern strategic industries located in Italy and thus under its control. To this end the state fostered the steel and munitions works at Terni and imported up-to-date technology through licensing arrangements and joint ventures with British munitions companies.[48]

Late-follower countries, then, emphasized the creation of independent armaments industries to support modern armed forces. This involved the establishment of a domestic engineering sector that coincidentally went a long way towards the general development of the technologies of the second industrial revolution: the internal combusion engine, chemicals, and electrical goods. Once generated, these industries produced for civilian as well as military purposes. These developments were not foreseen by state officials: they came about simply as by-products of the strategic requirements of the late-follower countries.

Restrictions on foreign investments flowed naturally from the late followers' concern with creating and sustaining independent armaments industries. Following Bismarck's advice, Japan not only forbade direct foreign investment in its industries but, during a period of extreme capital shortage in the 1870s to 1890s, even refused to borrow foreign capital, as it had seen Turkey and Egypt lose autonomy after defaulting on foreign debt repayments. As well, several foreign investments in mining and shipping were repatriated, mainly for strategic reasons.[49] Strategic industries remained in state hands after most of the publicly owned companies had been sold to private business. It was only after Japan was well along the road to becoming a great power in the late 1890s that restrictions on foreign investment were eased, but they were never lifted entirely. As a result foreign ownership did not play a large part in the Japanese economy.

Military strategy did not push the Russians as far as the Japanese in restricting foreign investment. But then, unlike Japan, Russia had not been marked out for colonial status by the Western powers. The temptation to overcome the extreme shortage of domestic capital was great, and about half the capital employed in early Russian industries, including mining, from the 1870s to 1916, came from abroad. This did not mean, however, that the military question had no consequences for foreign investment in Russia:[50] its character and nationality were affected.

Germany was to be a crucial factor in Russian development. Along with the US, it rose to industrial prominence in spectacular fashion in the late 1800s. As a consequence, like the Americans, German industrialists began to look abroad for scarce resources and new markets, and established subsidiaries in neighbouring countries at the same time as US firms did in Canada. Russian-occupied Poland was the target of German foreign investment, partly because the 1868 Russian tariffs had blocked German exports to the area.

It appeared that czarist Russia was simultaneously giving up its strategic independence and starting down the road to branch-plant industrialization. Foreign technology and engineers played an overwhelming role in early Russian industrialization. The foreign entrepreneurs assumed, as they tend to do everywhere, that what is good at home is good abroad. Thus conditions in Russia—plentiful supplies of cheap but unskilled and undisciplined labour, typical of most underdeveloped countries—did not affect factory design. Massive imports of fully developed, capital intensive technologies were the result.

But the push factors emanating from Germany were not the only ones that counted. The czarist state was ambivalent about foreign ownership, as were the politically important classes in Russia. On the one hand, there was unabashed praise for the benefits of foreign capital by Count Witte, finance minister from 1891 to 1903: 'The inflow of foreign capital is, in the considered opinion of the Minister of Finance, the only way by which our industry will be able to supply our country quickly with abundant and cheap products.'[51] But the actions of the state belied this open-door policy in important respects. In 1899 Witte disapprovingly enumerated Russian restrictions on foreign investment:

> In Russia a foreign company can be opened only by a special decree of the Committee of Ministers. . . . Russian joint-stock companies in which foreigners are shareholders are permitted to have only a minority of foreigners on their board of directors. In ten provinces of Poland, in eleven provinces of the western regions of Russia, in Turkestan, the steppe regions, and the Amur district, neither foreign companies nor Russian companies with foreign participation are permitted to acquire property or exploit natural resources . . . In permitting the activities of foreign companies in Russia, the government retains the right to revoke at any time that permission and to demand the liquidation of any company.[52]

He could have added that foreign-owned companies did not receive the same treatment as domestic ones regarding government contracts, including those for the state's railways, loans from the state bank, or receivership legislation.[53]

Preservation of Russian independence was a major objective in these restrictions. Russia permitted the establishment of German branch plants in strategic industries when it was allied with Germany in the League of the Three Emperors. Then, as relations with Germany deteriorated in the 1880s and a Franco-Russian alliance blossomed, the pattern of foreign investment altered. In 1887 Russia moved against German branch plants in Russian Poland by decreeing that shareholders of joint-stock companies there must be Russian.[54] In response, many Germans entrepreneurs accepted Russian nationality.[55] It is difficult to assess how much this affected German investment in all of Russia, since German capital continued to expand on an absolute basis in Russian corporations until the First World War. In the 1890s, however, Germany fell from first to third largest foreign investor in Russian industry.[56]

From the late 1880s on, France was at pains to make Russia an effective ally by hastening its development through infusions of French capital, technology, and know-how.[57] As Franco-Russian ties grew closer, French investment, often taking the guise of Belgian capital, gradually became more substantial than German investment in Russia.[58]

French and Belgian investment implied more industrial independence for Russia than did German investment. For one thing, 85 per cent of French capital in Russia was invested in bonds of a public nature.[59] Furthermore, even though French ownership capital was preponderant in mining, metallurgy, and engineering in south Russia, and French capitalists controlled several powerful industrial investment banks, in most cases the relationship was not the usual one between parent and subsidiary. Most French-owned companies were founded specifically for activity in Russia, and this was true of British- and Belgian-owned firms as well.[60] Thus there was less foreign technological and managerial control than is commonly the case with branch plants.

Russia did lose sovereignty, however, because it depended on foreign loan capital. For example, when its attempts to borrow funds in Paris failed, Russia reluctantly agreed to build a railway that its French allies deemed strategically advisable. Suddenly the loans became available.[61]

Russia's dependence on foreign direct investment in industry also undoubtedly compromised its economic and technological independence, and the country might well have followed the Canadian route towards branch-plant industrialization if the Bolshevik revolution had not intervened. It is significant, however, that czarist Russia was moving away from economic dependence on the eve of the First World War. Whereas in Canada foreign investment was at first largely portfolio (loan) capital and later largely direct (ownership) capital, in Russia during initial industrialization under the czars the reverse order was evident: before 1900 most foreign investment was direct; after 1900, and especially after 1908, most of it was passive portfolio investment, with Russian capitalists increasingly providing the entrepreneurship and control.[62] At the same time Russian investment banks took the lead in managing and lending to domestic industries, muscling out the foreign banks in several instances.[63]

With opposition to foreign investment, often mixed with anti-Semitism, strong amongst industrialists, the nobility, the intelligentsia, and the petite bourgeoisie, restrictions were placed on foreign ownership in pre-revolutionary Russia. Nevertheless, these restrictions pale in significance compared to the institutional changes that were to come in 1917, when the Bolsheviks led the country in an autarkic direction after the expected international socialist revolution failed to materialize.

In Sweden, finally, foreign ownership restrictions were put in place mainly for nationalist and economic reasons, but defence was a contributing factor. Growing concern over British and German ownership of Swedish resources in the late nineteenth century led to increasingly restrictive actions by Swedish governments. Tough concession laws on foreign ownership were passed in 1916, in the midst of the First World War. Sweden restricted foreign direct investment, but welcomed foreign portfolio investment on a vast scale. In fact, generous amounts of the latter allowed Sweden to use its scarce domestic capital to develop its own industries and resources. The politics and national circumstances that underlay Sweden's choice of the independent route to development are the subject of the next chapter.

CONCLUSION

Late-follower development provided both opportunities and constraints. Capital, technology, resources, labour, and even management could and did pass from the early industrial nations to the late followers. Partly for these reasons, economic and social transformation, often called 'the spurt', usually progressed more rapidly in the followers than it had in the industrial pioneers.

At the same time, however, the very ease with which factors of production could move across international borders created the possibility that the follower country would remain permanently dependent on at least some aspects of the foreign connection, impeding progress towards the greater self-reliance that was the desire of all late-follower states during the age of autarky in the late nineteenth century. Dependence on foreign capital, technology, and managerial expertise was difficult to reverse, especially when transnational corporations offered all three.

Most late-follower countries had certain characteristics in common that allowed them to avoid these pitfalls and follow the independent route to development. First, unlike Canada, they needed to defend themselves against foreign military threats. Second, the class basis and political ideology of the ruling circles were strong enough to move policies in the direction of economic independence. Hence when shortages of domestic capital arose, the measures taken to ease them followed a particular pattern: modified banking systems, state provision of capital for industrialization, and early forms of planning to reduce the amount of capital needed for development. Modern technology from the advanced countries was acquired through imitation and licensing arrangements, supplemented by autonomous invention.

All in all, the late followers—except Canada—marked out a path that was dramatically different from the branch-plant route to industrialization. In taking the independent path, as we shall now see, no country was more successful than Sweden.

NOTES

Much of this chapter appeared in 'The Political Economy of Aborted Development', in Robert Brym, ed., *The Structure of the Canadian Capitalist Class* (Toronto: Garamond Press, 1985).

[1] *The Atlantic*, January 1982, p. 7.

[2] The US was less laissez-faire than present ideologues would like to admit. The Erie Canal and many railways were built by state governments, and Pennsylvania was involved in over 150 mixed corporations in 1844. See Louis Hartz, *Economic Policy and Democratic Thought: Pennsylvania 1776-1860* (Cambridge: Harvard University Press, 1948).

[3] Eric Hobsbawm, *Industry and Empire* (Suffolk: Penguin, 1968), p. 13.

[4] Erik Dahmen, *Entrepreneurial Activity and the Development of Swedish Industry, 1919-1939* (Homewood, Ill.: Richard D. Irwin, 1970).

[5] William Cobbett, an early English radical, wrote of the rapid deterioration of the living standards of weavers after the power loom was adopted widely: 'It is truly lamentable to behold so many thousands of men who formerly earned twenty to thirty shillings per week, now compelled to live upon five shillings, four shillings, or even less . . . It is the more sorrowful to behold these men in their state, as they still retain the frank and bold character formed in the days of their independence' (cited in E.P. Thompson, *The Making of the English Working Class* [London: Victor Gollancz, 1965], p. 314).

[6] Marx and Engels made this point in 1848 in the *Communist Manifesto*: 'The bourgeoisie has

through its exploitation of the world market . . . drawn from under the feet of industry the national ground on which it stood. All old-established national industries have been destroyed or are daily being destroyed . . . the bourgeoisie, by the rapid improvement of all instruments of production, by the immensely facilitated means of communication, draws all . . . nations into civilization. The cheap prices of its commodities are the heavy artillery with which it batters down all Chinese walls . . . it compels all nations, on pain of extinction, to adopt the bourgeois mode of production' (K. Marx and F. Engels, 'Manifesto of the Communist Party', in L. Feuer, ed., *Marx and Engels* [Garden City, N.Y.: Doubleday, 1959], pp. 10-11).

[7]All foreigners and foreign trade were excluded from Japan from 1640 until Commodore Perry's forced entry in 1853. Japanese were not allowed to travel abroad and the size of ships was reduced by decree in order to prohibit international trade. A small window on the western world was kept open, however, in remote Nagasaki, where the Dutch (and Chinese) were allowed to trade on a small scale. In the 19th century scholars learned about western science through 'Dutch studies' See E.H. Norman, *Japan's Emergence as a Modern State* (New York: US Institute of Pacific Relations, 1940), pp. 13, 28-9, 37.

[8]Alexander Gerschenkron, *Economic Backwardness in Historical Perspective* (Cambridge: Harvard University Press, 1962).

[9]Was cotton or iron the leading industry of the early Industrial Revolution? In *The First Industrial Revolution* (Cambridge: Cambridge University Press, 1965), Phyllis Deane argues both were. Hobsbawm disagrees in *Industry and Empire* (p. 71). He points out that, like coal, iron 'did not undergo its real industrial revolution until the middle decades of the nineteenth century or about fifty years later than cotton'. David Landes concurs in 'Technological Change and Development in Western Europe 1750-1914', in H.J. Habakkuk and M. Postan, eds, *The Cambridge Economic History of Europe*, vol. 6, part I (Cambridge: Cambridge University Press, 1965), pp. 88-9: 'Not in men, nor capital invested, nor value of output, nor rate of growth could iron be compared with cotton in this period.' Although it cost much more to start up an iron company than a cotton firm in the 1700s, the sums involved were not that great. Some large enterprises were established with funds accumulated in 'artisan activities'. See François Crouzet, *Capital Formation in the Industrial Revolution* (London: Methuen, 1972), p. 166.

[10]France was an early industrial rival, but was set back by its revolution and Napoleonic Wars. See A.S. Milward and S.B. Saul, *The Economic Development of Continental Europe 1780-1870* (London: George Allen and Unwin Ltd., 1973), p. 262.

[11]Ibid., p. 495.

[12]Landes, 'Technological Change and Development in Western Europe,' p. 172; J. Quinn, 'Technology Transfer by Multinational Companies', *Harvard Business Review* 47 (1969).

[13]Yoshio Ando, 'The Formation of Heavy Industry', in S. Tobata, ed., *The Modernization of Japan*, 1 (Tokyo: Institute of Asian Economic Affairs, 1966), p. 125.

[14]Czarist Russia only partially avoided the pitfalls of dependent capitalist industrialization. See below.

[15]Crouzet, *Capital Formation in the Industrial Revolution*.

[16]Richard Tilly, *Financial Institutions and Industrialisation in the Rhineland 1815-1870* (Madison: University of Wisconsin Press, 1966). Under the leadership of the Pereire brothers and their Crédit Mobilier (founded 1852), France was actually the first country to experience investment banking. The idea spread rapidly from France to other countries in Europe. But the Crédit Mobilier experiment failed in France, and the great French banks continued in their security-conscious ways, only slightly altered by the experience. See Rondo Cameron, *France and the Economic Development of Europe 1800-1914* (Princeton: Princeton University Press, 1961). The US also broke away from a British type of commercial banking system in the 1830s. See Chapter 4.

[17]J. Potter, 'The Role of a Swedish Bank in the Process of Industrialization', *Scandinavian Economic History Review* 11 (1963): 67

[18]O. Gasslander, *History of Stockholms Enskilda Bank to 1914* (Stockholm: Stockholms Enskilda Banken, 1962), p. 212.

[19]Thomas Smith, *Political Change and Industrial Development in Japan: Government Enterprises 1868-1880* (Stanford, Cal.: Stanford University Press, 1965).

[20]Luciano Cafagna, 'The Industrial Revolution in Italy 1830-1914' in C.M. Cipolla, ed., *The Fontana Economic History of Europe*, vol. 4, part 1 (Glasgow: Fontana, 1973) p. 318; Olga Crisp, *Studies in the Russian Economy Before 1914* (London: Macmillan, 1976), pp. 31-2, 162.

[21]Hobsbawm, *Industry and Empire*, p. 113. Lars-Erik Hedin estimates that the actual cost of private Swedish railways (1876-1926) was about 30% higher than the amount given in official statistics. These revised estimates do not apply to state railways. See 'Some Notes on the Financing of the Swedish Railroads 1860-1914', *Economy and History* 10 (1967): 8.

British railway philosophy, born during a glut of capital, was to build solidly with high original cost and low upkeep in contrast to the American philosophy, born of capital shortage, to build cheaply and make improvements as revenue allowed. See G.P. de T. Glazebrook, *A History of Transportation in Canada*, vol. 1 (Toronto: McClelland and Stewart, 1964), p. 66. The following railways were built according to the expensive British methods: the Grand Trunk and the Great Western, in the 1850s (see ibid., p. 166); the Intercolonial in the 1870s (see W.T. Easterbrook and Hugh Aitken, *Canadian Economic History* [Toronto: Macmillan, 1956], p. 412); and the National Transcontinental (see Glazebrook, *History of Transportation*, vol. 2, p. 137). On the other hand, the CPR and Mackenzie and Mann's Canadian Northern were built according to the American standard. See Glazebrook, *History of Transportation*, vol. 2, p. 145; Harold Innis, *A History of the Canadian Pacific Railway* (Toronto: McClelland and Stewart, 1923), p. 102.

[22]Nobutaka Ike, 'The Pattern of Railway Development in Japan' *Far Eastern Quarterly* 14, no. 2 (1955): 226.

[23]Johannes Hirschmeier, 'Shibusawa Eiichi: Industrial Power' in W.W. Lockwood, ed., *The State and Economic Enterprise in Japan* (New Jersey: Princeton University Press, 1965), p. 230.

[24]Jon Halliday, *A Political History of Japanese Capitalism* (New York: Pantheon Books, 1975), p. 60.

[25]Peter Lyaschenko, *The History of the National Economy of Russia to the 1917 Revolution* (New York: Macmillan, 1949), p. 534.

[26]About 37% of the railways were built for political and military reasons. See Herbert Feis, *Europe the World's Banker 1870-1914* (New York: Yale University Press, 1930), p. 211.

[27]A.S. Milward and S.B. Saul, *The Development of the Economies of Continental Europe 1850-1914* (Cambridge: Harvard University Press, 1977), p. 541.

[28]S.B. Clough, *The Economic History of Modern Italy* (New York: Columbia University Press, 1964).

[29]Hedin, 'Some Notes on the Financing of the Swedish Railroads 1860-1914'.

[30]This proportion was arrived at after debt-servicing costs were removed. See Theodore von Laue, *Sergei Witte and the Industrialization of Russia* (New York: Columbia University Press, 1963), p. 22.

[31]Smith, *Political Change and Industrial Development in Japan* p. 71. Regarding Sweden, see Chapter 3.

[32]Desmond Morton, *Ministers and Generals: Politics and the Canadian Militia* (Toronto: University of Toronto Press, 1970), p. 202.

[33]See Chapter 3.

[34]L.J. Lewery, *Foreign Capital Investment in Russian Industries and Commerce* (Washington: US Government, 1923)

[35]Halliday, *A Political History of Japanese Capitalism*, p. 55.

[36]Maurice Pearton, *The Knowledgeable State: Diplomacy, War and Technology Since 1830* (London: Burnett Books, 1982), pp. 19-35.

[37]A.J.P. Taylor, *The Struggle for Mastery in Europe 1848-1918* (Oxford: Clarendon Press, 1954), p. 228.

[38]Marius Jansen, 'Modernization and Foreign Policy in Meiji Japan', in R. Ward, ed., *Political Development in Modern Japan* (New Jersey: Princeton University Press, 1968), p. 155.

[39]Norman, *Japan's Emergence as a Modern State*, p. 118.

[40]Ibid., p. 119.

[41]Jansen, 'Modernization and Foreign Policy in Meiji Japan', p. 175.

[42]Norman, *Japan's Emergence as a Modern State*, pp. 198-201.

[43]Franklin Scott, *Sweden: The Nation's History* (Minneapolis: University of Minnesota Press, 1977), p. 236.

[44]Hertha Pauli, *Alfred Nobel, Dynamite King, Architect of Peace* (New York: L.B. Fischer, 1942), p. 19.

[45]Scott, *Sweden: The Nation's History*, p. 189.

[46]Kurt Samuelsson, *From Great Power to Welfare State* (London: George Allen and Unwin Ltd., 1968), p. 102.

[47]Scott, *Sweden: The Nation's History*, p. 446.

[48]Clough, *The Economic History of Modern Italy*, p. 87; Pearton, *The Knowledgeable State*, p. 115.

[49]Halliday, *A Political History of Japanese Capitalism*, p. 55.

[50]J.P. McKay, *Pioneers for Profit: Foreign Entrepreneurship and Russian Industrialization 1885-1913* (Chicago: University of Chicago Press, 1970).

[51]Ibid., p. 11.

[52]von Laue, *Sergei Witte and the Industrialization of Russia*, p. 181.

[53]Foreign companies received more favourable treatment for a time after 1899-1901. See McKay, *Pioneeers for Profit*, p. 284.

[54]This decree applied outside towns, where most German branch plants were located.

[55]Germany passed a law allowing dual nationality. Thus the German naturalization movement in Russian Poland may not have been genuine. See Crisp, 'Foreign Entrepreneurship and Russian Industry'.

[56]McKay, *Pioneers for Profit*, p. 32.

[57]Pearton, *The Knowledgeable State*, pp. 102-4.

[58]O. Crisp, 'French Investment in Russian Joint Stock Companies 1894-1914', *Business History* 2 (1960); McKay, *Pioneers for Profit*.

[59]Crisp, 'French Investment in Russian Joint Stock Companies', p. 90.

[60]Lewery, *Foreign Capital Investment in Russian Industries*, pp. 3-5.

[61]Feis, *Europe the World's Banker*, p. 219.

[62]Crisp, 'Foreign Entrepreneurship', p. 189.

[63]McKay, *Pioneers for Profit*, pp. 286-9, 368-85.

3

Sweden: Out of the Staple Trap

The Swedes are coming.

> *A cry of terror in Central Europe as far away as the*
> *Alps and the Ukraine in the Middle Ages.*

No adventure, no conquest, but plenty of arms for self-defence.

> *Franklin Scott, historian, characterizing the Swedish*
> *consensus on defence, 1977.*

In viewing the relative painlessness of Sweden's way of overcoming her disabilities—one cannot fail to attribute a great deal of importance to the strong cultural tradition in Sweden.

> *Alexander Gerschenkron, economic historian, 1954.*

A variety of engineering products created new manufacturing and energy technologies, and these contributed massively to the transformation of industry in Sweden . . . industrialisation in Sweden depended to an unusual extent upon the genesis and growth of the engineering sector.

> *Jan Kuuse, economic historian, 1978.*

The historical connection between commerce and the new manufacturing firms is a conspicuous feature in almost all industries. The first engineering firms that were independent of the old iron works were usually founded by merchants. The same applies to the big new lumber mills, the pulp mills, and to the construction joineries and furniture factories . . . In the early decades of industrialisation . . . twenty or so names appear in connection with at least a hundred of the new firms during this period.

> *Erik Dahmen on the role of merchants in early Swedish*
> *industrialization, 1970.*

As long as [the conservative élite] were masters of the state apparatus, they took a positive view of the State. But when faced with the prospect that the Reform policy would be taken further by a democratized state authority, the Conservatives . . . repudiate[d] an extension of State influence.

> *Bo Jonsson, historian, referring to the struggle for*
> *the democratic franchise 1900-14.*

With God and Sweden's common people for King and fatherland.
Slogan of huge farmers' march to support rearmament,
February 1914.

It is necessary to change such rules, as allow Swedish land to be sold in rising proportions to foreigners, whose economic calculations will decide how our people and our land is treated ... What future will Norrland have if they are allowed to buy all the land? Those principles ... must be changed, if not, Norrland and our whole native country shall end up under a foreign yoke [and] the population turned into enslaved and indolent company workers. The free and wealthy farmer disappears ... The sawmill owners act like traitors, planning to sell the country to foreigners and exterminate the free farming population.

Norrland Farmers Manifesto, 1902.

THE RELEVANCE OF COMPARISON

A remarkable consensus emerged in the 1980s regarding Canada's economic prospects. It culminated in the Macdonald Commission's *Reports on the Economic Union and Development Prospects for Canada*. The consensus view goes like this: small economies such as Canada's cannot appreciably influence their terms of trade in the world and so must specialize in sectors where they have a comparative advantage. For Canada, trade advantages lie in resources and a limited number of manufacturing sectors.[1] The domestic market is simply too small to sustain a wide range of industries on a competitive basis, and the global move to regional trading blocs makes that prospect even less likely. The dream of developing a strong industrial economy, in which Canada would export finished goods on a scale to match its imports, is unrealistic and a delusion.[2] Some argue that Canadians should be happy with what they've got: a comparative advantage in resources.

Earlier generations of Canadians did not accept this bleak view of Canada's prospects. In the 1870s and again in the 1891 and 1911 reciprocity elections, the Liberal Party offered Canadians the continental vision of Canada as a resource supplier for industrial America. The vision did have its supporters: fishing and lumber interests in the Maritimes, export-oriented farmers, those who disliked British domination, some anti-French elements in Ontario, and many small-scale Ontario manufacturers.[3] Yet despite such support Canadians rejected this alternative. They did not want to become 'hewers of wood and drawers of water'.

The Conservative victory over Laurier's reciprocity scheme in 1911 severely limited public expression of the continentalist vision, and the dream was kept alive only in isolated pockets. After the staples tradition was eclipsed by professionalized neo-classical economics in the 1950s,[4] however, the idea was revived among the growing army of academic economists. Later, in the 1970s, it attracted new converts in resource-producing regions, and in the 1980s market liberalism came roaring back to assume, increasingly, the position of conventional wisdom.[5]

It is ironic that the strongest proponents of the market liberalism of the nineteenth-century Liberal Party of Canada are now in the Conservative Party. The new terms for this philosophy are 'neo-conservatism' and the 'magic of the marketplace'. In the English-speaking countries in the 1980s the dogma of two centuries of classical and neo-classical economics became the ideology of the powerful. Economists Richard Harris and David Cox, both free-traders, admit that the economists' views are to a great extent based on faith:

> The embarrassing fact is that the importance attached to free trade by economists is often a belief hammered into them by years of training ... This 'belief' translates into the assertion that it is 'self-evident' or 'well-established' that free trade is a major source of economic growth ... [but] by the conventional standards of evidence in economics, the claim is not well-founded.[6]

In Canada pure market liberalism is rejected by many in the Liberal Party and is not accepted by social democrats. Nevertheless, some tenets of market liberalism have seeped even into these groups.[7]

The view that resource exporting is what Canada does best is widely held.[8] Those who look forward to Canada's future in the post-industrial era often share the same pessimistic assumption: that Canada cannot make it in manufacturing. We must either stick with our resources or else catapult ourselves into the future with services and the new information industries— but by all means we should skip over the present stage of manufacturing, in many lines at least.[9] Environmentalists often concur because they associate manufacturing with smoke-stack pollution.

Whatever the source of its inspiration, the consensus view points to the same obstacles to secondary manufacturing and, especially, finished exports: a small domestic market, high transportation costs, high wages, and the comparative advantage of abundant resources.[10] In their narrow North American view of the world, Canadian academics and the general public often believe that these obstacles are axioms of development. They have taken on the aura of laws that need no proof.

The case of Sweden brings a breath of fresh air to these musty, pessimistic assumptions. Sweden was the late-follower country that most resembled Canada during the period of early industrialization. If proximity to powerful neighbours, a comparative advantage in resource exports, a small population, and distance from major markets are supposed to hinder or prevent a full transition to an industrial economy, how did Sweden manage to overcome them?

SIMILARITIES AND DIFFERENCES

Geography

The parallels between nineteenth-century Canada and Sweden are striking. Sweden is a northern country where winter is the dominant season; Gilles Vigneault's 'Mon pays, ce n'est pas un pays, c'est l'hiver' could just as well have been written about Sweden as about Quebec.[11] Similarities with Canada's historic St Lawrence/Great Lakes system are obvious: harsh winters freeze Sweden's abundant lakes and rivers for half the year, closing extensive water routes. In the nineteenth century, in both Sweden and Canada, ice and snow facilitated movement by creating winter roads ideal for hauling heavy goods even where no man-made roads existed.

Sweden's rugged terrain was deeply scarred by the last ice age, which bared pre-Cambrian rock and left numerous lakes, producing a landscape—the Baltic Shield—that is uncannily like the Canadian Shield. Less than 10 per cent of Sweden is farmland. Four populous areas are separated by wildernesses dominated by extensive northern woods of pine, spruce, and birch. Forests were the key to Sweden's nineteenth-century economy, and fast, unnavigable rivers proved ideal for floating logs and harnessing hydro power.

Sweden's topography and small population contributed to its early role as resource-exporter to more-advanced areas. The mix of staple exports was remarkably similar to Canada's in the last century: timber to Britain, grain for British cities, iron ore for Germany and Britain, pulp and paper to supply mass-circulation newspapers.[12] The ebb and flow of resources was heavily dependent on external demand.[13] 'The stream of influences to Sweden', wrote Eli Heckscher, 'considerably outweighed those from Sweden' in the late nineteenth century.[14] In other words, Sweden's was a hinterland economy.

To move resources to market, late nineteenth-century Sweden needed railways, but their enormous costs were compounded by great distances and sparse settlement. Swedish railways were like those of the New World. Instead of connecting established centres, they extended ahead of settlement in frontier fashion. By 1914 Sweden had more than twice the per capita railway mileage of any other European country.[15] Only by importing enormous amounts of capital and by exporting natural resources could a pre-industrial country finance railway building on such a scale in quick order. Sweden, like Canada, did both in spades.

Market size

Canadians assume that the domestic market sets limits to the scale of industrial output, though at times we have attempted to supplement this market by gaining privileged access to British or American markets. A domestic-market orientation is a Canadian mind-set[16] that strikes Swedes as peculiar, for they do not measure market size primarily in domestic terms. In view of that Canadian attitude, however, the size of the Swedish domestic market must be explored.

Sweden's home market was almost certainly smaller than Canada's between 1870 and 1914, the period when both countries industrialized. In 1871 Canada had 3.7 million people, half a million fewer than Sweden;[17] however, its population soared past Sweden's between the late 1890s and the First World War.

Alfred Maizels estimated that in 1899 Canadians consumed 150 per cent as much per capita in manufactured goods as did Swedes,[18] and by 1913 they had increased the gap to just under 5 to 2 per head. Thus the Canadian market was several times larger than the Swedish from 1899 to 1913. Canada must have had a larger market from the 1870s through the 1890s as well, but comparison is difficult because of the dearth of reliable statistics and the complicating factor of the Swedish customs union with Norway from 1873 to 1897.

Sweden was a poor country in the 1870s, with industrial wages below those of France and Germany, which in turn were several times lower than those in England.[19] American workers were paid almost twice as much as their English counterparts, while Canadian incomes were in between the English and the American; thus industrial wages in Canada were several times greater than those in Sweden. Swedish wages rose rapidly, but not more quickly than Canadian.[20] As well, since more Swedes were engaged in farming[21] and were often paid in kind rather than in currency, their purchasing power was low. Canadians were not as heavily involved in farming, and so were more apt to buy manufactured articles.[22]

Sweden's customs union with Norway counterbalances the comparison somewhat, but it could not have added more than 50 per cent or so to its market. (Norway had less than half Sweden's population.)[23] If Canadians consumed industrial goods at double the Swedish-Norwegian level, a conservative assumption, the market size advantage lay with Canada. Thus Sweden became an independent manufacturing country with a smaller home market than Canada.[24]

This leaves us with the question of access to foreign markets. American protectionism throughout early Canadian industrialization hindered Canadian industrial exports into the closest market. Sweden faced similar protectionist obstacles in nearby Germany, France, and Russia. But it had closer contact with countries associated with Britain's free-trade policy: Denmark, Norway, Finland, and the Netherlands. These neighbours provided Sweden with important markets in the early twentieth century when its engineering sector was getting started. Their relative affluence and less-advanced industry proved favourable for Sweden's exports.

Canada had access to comparable foreign markets at the same time: those of the white dominions. Industrially backward but more affluent than Scandinavia, the white dominions had the highest propensity to import manufactured goods of any region in the world (see Table 1.2). From 1903 to

1907 Canada gained access on preferential terms to New Zealand, South Africa, and other British colonies (with the important exception of Australia).[25] But it failed to use export opportunities in the British Empire as Sweden had done in Scandinavia (see below).[26] Canada had an advantage, though: the rapidly expanding Canadian west, which acted like an export market.

When size and potential of domestic and export markets are considered, then, the balance was, if anything, in Canada's favour. If Sweden was nevertheless able to overcome the disadvantages of a small domestic market, the idea that Canada was too small to develop fully needs to be re-examined.

New World/ Old World

There were other differences between Sweden and Canada. Sweden had a big-power past, symbolized by the original national anthem, 'du gamla du friska' (you ancient, you strong).[27] Despite proud claims of a 175-year history of neutrality, Sweden has had a militaristic bent. One of the principal powers of seventeenth-century Europe, it made the Baltic a Swedish sea, holding all of Finland, much of the Baltic states, and important coastal areas in Germany and Russia.[28] It lost most of its empire in 1719-21 but retained an enormous army: in 1760 there were 154,208 soldiers in a total population of fewer than 2 million.[29]

Sweden lost its remaining empire during the Napoleonic Wars, but was given Norway in a personal—not political—union: the two countries had a common monarch but separate governments and representative assemblies, though Sweden directed Norway's foreign affairs. The union was dissolved in acrimony in 1905.

As an old society, Sweden had a social structure quite different from Canada's. During its emergence from a staple economy, in the years 1870 to 1914, a state and landed nobility formed the ruling class, into whose ranks the leading capitalists were incorporated. As in Germany, the bourgeoisie never supplanted the old order, and so liberal democracy was weak. On the left in Sweden a politically conscious proletariat arose. This German pattern emerged from the prolonged influence of a landed aristocracy coupled with the precocious development of a class-conscious working class.[30]

In France, Britain, and the United States emerging capitalists were the early promoters of an enlarged democratic franchise, a pattern not followed by later-developing countries.[31] In the latter the fledgeling working classes often quickly adopted radical ideas that had evolved slowly elsewhere. As a result, in the German pattern the capitalists faced class enemies from above and below at the same time. Afraid to wrest control from the aristocracy for fear of touching off a revolution of the masses, the bourgeoisie usually allied with the old order. The end result was that liberal democracy was weak, ground between the upper stone of reaction and the lower one of socialism. Marx portrayed the dilemma of the German bourgeoisie in the failed revolution of 1848:

> It was, in fact, evident . . . that the Liberal bourgeoisie could not hold its ground against the vanquished, but not destroyed, feudal and bureaucratic parties except by relying upon the assistance of the popular and more advanced parties; and that it equally required, against the torrent of these more advanced masses, the assistance of the feudal nobility and of the bureaucracy.[32]

Sweden conformed generally to this pattern, but because its landlord class supported industrialization, conflict between noble and capitalist was minimized. Sweden retained an oligarchic structure throughout the period of initial industrialization. After the constitutional reforms of 1866, the right to vote was based on property-holding rather than social standing. This reform allowed only 22 per cent of adult males to vote for the lower chamber of the Riksdag (parliament). In the upper chamber, or Senate, 2 per cent controlled the election. The franchise was broadened in 1907-09 but was still based on rights according to wealth.[33] Only after the end of Sweden's initial industrialization was universal suffrage accepted.

The contrast with Canada could hardly have been greater, or so it would seem. But the real differences were less than they appear. Plutocratic politics had a surprisingly long life in Canada (a theme taken up in Chapter 4). On the other hand, Sweden was less repressive than most societies following the German pattern. Sweden has been described as a 'new' land resembling a rich, tradition-free, pragmatic America.[34] By the late nineteenth century Sweden had a long history as an open society evolving towards British-style parliamentarism. As one scholar has noted:

> of crucial importance were the deepseated devotion to legal rules, the liberal content of the rules long in effect, and the practice of division of powers within the government. Next to England, Sweden has the longest tradition of constitutional and representative government. A Freedom of the Press Act has been among the fundamental laws since the eighteenth century.[35]

In addition, Sweden never had a true feudal past. Freehold peasants did have to perform labour services for the state; peasants had to haul goods and passengers for a fixed charge and government officials for free; tithes had to be paid to the state church; and these feudal vestiges were removed rather late, between the 1850s and 1870s. Nevertheless, feudalism in Sweden was never entrenched. From time immemorial, Swedish peasants had not been enserfed (serfdom and slavery were forbidden in 1335).[36] They were tenants paying fees to noble landowners, not serfs whose work was overseen by feudal lords, and land was widely distributed. More unusual, peasants who held land and paid taxes had their own assembly (Estate) in the Riksdag. (Landless peasants had no recognized political rights.) The Peasant Estate played an important role in the struggles between nobles and the monarch in the seventeenth and eighteenth centuries, a period when no other European country granted peasants a legal voice.

By the 1800s Swedish farmers resembled the independent farmer-proprietors of the New World. The king, needing popular support to counteract noble opposition during a war in 1789, gave peasants landownership rights without their having to resort to a French-style revolution. By 1850, 60 per cent of the land was cultivated by owner/operators and another quarter by relatively independent tenant farmers.[37] (At the same time, many landless farm workers escaped poverty only by emigrating to North America in the late 1800s.)

In the 1870s and 1880s this movement towards the family farm provided the social basis for a farmers' reform party opposed to the oligarchy. Fifty years later another farmers' party emerged to form coalitions with the Social Democrats, a development reminiscent of farmer-labour alliances in Canada in the same period.

Summary

While politics and class structure produced less divergence between Sweden and Canada than might be expected, the two countries were far from being mirror images of one another. For one thing, whereas Canada has been an extremely heterogeneous society ever since the British Conquest of 1759 forced 'national' unity, Sweden has been very homogeneous, at least until recent decades. The long coastline and winter roads promoted migration and prevented the development of strong regional identities, except perhaps in the southern region where Danish influence was strong.

As well, Sweden has a long tradition of nationalism that is in stark contrast to Canada's divided nationalisms of English and French, its regional identities, and the anaemic pan-Canadian nationalism that in 1867 proclaimed the country a dependency of the British Empire.

Sweden's spirit of independence originated in the 1400s, when the country was ruled by Danish kings. It grew during Sweden's heyday as a great power in the 1600s, blossomed in the 1700s, and was further invigorated by the wave of romantic nationalism that arose throughout Europe in the next century. Whatever their differences over class privileges, Swedish conservatives and liberals were alike in their strong nationalist outlook.

In brief, Sweden and Canada shared similarities in terrain and in international economic roles, but diverged in their social structures, political traditions, and sense of national identity. If their economies parted company towards the end of initial industrialization, 1870 to 1914 (see Chapter 1), the explanation is likely to lie more in social and political factors than economic or geographic ones. For Canadian economic historians, these are largely un-explored waters.

THE BEGINNINGS OF ECONOMIC TRANSFORMATION

Delays in Swedish development

From a twentieth-century perspective Sweden's escape from a staple economy is something to marvel at, given the country's late development and its small population. But if we adopt an eighteenth-century perspective the issue is reversed. The advanced nature of Sweden's political economy in that period raises the question of why industrialization was so delayed. The explanations suggested below go only part of the way to providing a satisfactory answer.

After its fall from great-power status, Sweden entered the 'Age of Freedom' spanning the years 1718 to 1772. There was a turning inward, away from war and empire, towards peace and prosperity. Mortality rates declined, life expectancy rose, and utilitarian ideas swept the land. Educated Swedes showed a deep interest in the progress of science, technology, and manufacturing, and in social problems of every kind.[38] Sweden was at the forefront of the modern ways of thinking about humankind and the world that constituted the eighteenth-century enlightenment, the revolution in ideas underlying the great economic transformation that began in England in the 1760s and 1770s.

This era witnessed the emergence of a galaxy of scientific talent that included Anders Celsius, who developed the 100-degree thermometer, and the biologist Carl Von Linne (Linnaeus), who systematized the nomenclature of living species. Swedish scientists contributed to astronomy, medical research, chemistry, biology, and engineering;[39] scientific journals were started; universities emphasized science. Sweden was recognized as the leading European centre of metallurgy. Its scientists had a practical as well as a theoretical orientation that foretold Sweden's spectacular series of inventions more than a century later.

The industrial revolution did not go unnoticed in Sweden. Like other nearby countries, it sent industrial 'spies' to observe the latest English inventions and imported English technicians for its textile and engineering industries.[40] The Swedish Institute of Mechanics was founded in 1798—only four years after the world's first technical school opened in Paris—and other technical schools were established in the next few decades. Gymnasia—high schools along German lines—made their appearance in the 1600s, and by the next century were emphasizing modern subjects. In the mercantilist, interventionist tradition, Swedish governments encouraged and subsidized research.[41]

The new scientific and utilitarian spirit in Sweden took root in a setting conducive to rapid development. Sweden had no feudal structure to resist capitalism and technological progress, and the bourgeoisie's emergence was easily accepted by nobles. The centralized state, run by a reasonably honest, modern bureaucracy, probably gave a boost to capitalist progress. And, finally, Sweden had experience in international industrial trade: in the mid-1700s, for example, on the eve of England's industrial revolution, Sweden made half of Europe's iron, and most of it was exported, half to England itself.[42]

Yet despite state support for manufacturing, an atmosphere conducive to science and practicality, and the absence of feudal social barriers, Sweden stagnated. While nearby countries underwent the profound changes of the industrial revolution, Sweden, like the rest of Scandinavia, was largely immune. The question is, why?

This issue has been largely avoided. Franklin Scott was content to observe that 'to discover the reasons for Sweden's late start and rapid development is difficult'.[43] The reasons why one country experienced economic transformation before another have confounded some of the best minds. A country's economic transformation was not a matter of an accumulation of changes that, when added up, led to gradual development. Many specific factors needed to come together to provide momentum: credit, adequate transportation, entrepreneurial talent, a free, disciplined, and skilled labour force, and available markets. Contrary to the concept of 'prerequisites' to industrialization, however, all these elements did not have to be in place prior to development. Social and economic changes often evolved simultaneously. Once under way, the industrial revolution was often rapid, even violent, especially in late-follower countries; a sudden spurt would come, usually after decades of fruitless attempts at development.[44] This was the sort of growth that Sweden experienced.

Sweden's delayed development had a number of causes. The country had no coal that could be used in its iron industry. (This was not an obstacle for that other child of the industrial revolution, cotton textiles).[45] Most Swedes lived on subsistence farming, supplemented by forest activity and 'sloyd' production (a graded system of manual training in woodworking, etc.) Fewer than one person in ten lived in urban areas until as late as the 1840s,[46] which made the market for industrial goods very small indeed. The market was further hindered by the rough terrain that separated populated areas—it was no accident that industrialization waited until the 1870s, when Sweden's railway boom integrated its market and at the same time provided enormous work gangs with the means to purchase industrially made articles. Finally, the state misdirected its economic policies, choosing to shower its energies on the wrong industries—textiles, sugar refining, and tobacco—rather than build upon Swedish resources. The latter were key to Swedish development when it came.[47]

The agricultural revolution

Successful industrialization was not an inevitable outcome of living near developing countries. Eastern Europe witnessed rapid changes in Germany and Czechoslovakia, but remained on the sidelines. In the same way, Sweden passively observed the first century of England's industrial revolution. Its rapid progress in the late 1800s was not a sure thing, for while many countries advanced economically at that time, others regressed.[48] The two processes were related. Instead of holding up a mirror for the less-developed countries to see the image of their own future, as Marx had put it, the handful of advanced countries flooded the more backward ones with their low-priced wares,[49] often backing up these export salvoes with force or diplomatic pressure. For their part, backward countries usually adopted some elements of modernization but lagged behind in others. Success at development depended upon which elements of modernization progressed first.

In many of the societies that adopted modern nutrition and public health practices before economic transformation, the resulting demographic revolution produced rapid declines in the death rate and unprecedented population growth, since family planning emerged slowly everywhere. Instead of joining the small number of rapid industrializers, many more countries experienced stagnation and regression.

If growth in the number of mouths to feed was accompanied by agricultural stagnation and the decimation of handicraft production, the result would be lower consumption. If democracy also preceded development, the poor would demand immediate improvements, thus lessening the amount of capital that could be created out of savings—then, as now, the poor saved little unless coerced by a class of overseers or by the state. Thus it was usually important for agricultural development to precede or accompany the demographic and industrial revolutions. We can reject W.W. Rostow's rigid model of a critical threshhold of capital formation and still accept that industrialization needed increased savings and capital formation.[50] (Fundamentally, capital is simply a portion of today's production that is set aside for tomorrow's needs. The fact that in capitalism this process is accompanied by social inequality does not mean that such inequality is an inevitable part of investment in future production.)

Like other late-developing countries, Sweden progressed unevenly. The demographic transition occurred before industrialization, the product of 'peace, vaccine and potatoes', in the words of nineteenth-century poet Esaias Tegner, as well as the early spread of literacy, which facilitated knowledge of hygiene and nutrition.[51] The result was a rapidly growing army of impoverished rural dwellers consisting of crofters with too little land to support themselves, paupers with no land, and personal servants. By 1870 these groups made up half of Sweden's population in about three equal parts.[52] Between 1718 and the onset of industrialization around 1860, Sweden's population trebled but remained overwhelmingly rural, and famines still struck hard, especially during harsh winters or epidemics. Economic advance could have been washed away in a demographic tidal wave. (Indeed, Malthus used Sweden as proof of his theory.)

Fortunately, the plight of the rural poor was eased by major advances in agriculture and rapid industrialization. But before saw-mills and factories provided many jobs, there was a remarkable development of home-craft production, especially in rural areas where it supplemented farming. In addition, massive emigration to the United States helped to ease the problem of surplus population.

The transformation of Swedish agriculture began slowly in the 1700s, but by 1830, at the beginning of the agricultural revolution, rising food production had finally overtaken population growth. The turnaround came none too soon: Sweden had been unable to meet its own food requirements since the 1680s.[53]

Eighteenth-century rural progress was influenced by the new scientific agriculture in Holland and England. But whereas in England farm labourers worked the large estates, in Sweden consolidated lots were usually parcelled into smaller units to be farmed by independent owners.[54] Agricultural productivity improved, as in England, but Sweden's pattern led to a different social structure, in which farmer-proprietors were politically active during initial industrialization.[55]

Large-scale land reclamation and new crops, such as potatoes, were additional aspects of agricultural progress. The move away from animal husbandry reduced the quantities of grain needed to produce each calorie for human consumption, and was a response to growing population pressure.[56] Food still had to be imported, but the process was made easier by loss of empire: before 1718 Sweden used exports to finance military glory; afterwards foreign currency helped to feed the growing population.

Nineteenth-century rural life in Sweden encompassed more than farming. In the many areas where arable land was scarce, Swedish conditions resembled those of the North American frontier, with forest and sloyd production supplementing or surpassing farming output. In fact, the forests and uncultivated land were central to Sweden's economy. Agriculture depended on them for pasture for animals, fuel and timber for houses, much of the meat and fish of peasant diets, and hides and fur for clothing. The peasants' victory in gaining freehold ownership also meant that half of Sweden's forests were owned by small proprietors. (Today 60 per cent of this forest sector is worked in conjunction with farming.)[57]

A peculiarity of Swedish rural life was the relationship between the iron industry, forestry, and marginal farming. 'Actually,' wrote Eli Heckscher, 'the iron industry might well be described as a forest industry, since charcoal was by far the most important product of the forest.'[58] Owning much of the forest reserves, many nobles became iron manufacturers, while the ironmasters hired, at low wages, tenant farmers and the rural landless and bought charcoal from independent farmers who engaged in forest production to boost their incomes.[59] In fact, the iron industry knitted together Sweden's rural class structure.

By the 1830s Sweden's slow and uneven reforms had transformed the countryside from self-sufficient peasant communities to a collection of individualistic farmers with a penchant for technical progress and commercial sales, often to export markets. The rapid agricultural advance for which they were responsible was crucial for Sweden's later industrialization.

It is easy for the student of development to overlook agricultural progress. After all, the industrial revolution was more spectacular. The introduction of new ways of working, the wrenching of people away from rural communities, and the invention of new products and methods were changes of revolutionary significance. But for a long time these changes had less impact on Sweden than did progress in farming, and until about 1905 the value of farm production was greater than that of manufacturing. Thus changes in the agricultural sector had an enormous impact. (See Table 1.3).

Imports of grain ended in the 1830s, and thereafter exports of it grew so rapidly that in 1870 grain ranked with iron as Sweden's second greatest export;[60] by then 40 per cent of Swedish grain was sold abroad.[61] The turnaround gave Sweden a foreign-currency surplus, allowing it to import large amounts of loan capital, most of which financed capital-intensive farming and improved agricultural productivity. Luckily, Swedish financial institutions were sufficiently flexible to provide for these new needs.

Mortgage societies and rural savings banks emerged to cater to the farming community. Because of their local monopoly over the issuing of bank notes, rural savings banks could provide low-interest loans.[62] On the other hand, Swedish mortgage societies obtained over 70 per cent of their capital from abroad, freeing domestic savings for infant industries and improvements in transportation.

In the long run, the transformation of agriculture was beneficial to Swedish industrialization. The domestic market grew, and increased farm exports enabled Sweden to borrow large amounts of foreign capital to finance the railways of the 1870s.[63]

The role of forestry and railways in industrialization

Twentieth-century Sweden has excelled in well-engineered specialty-steel products—ball bearings, telephones, farm equipment, high-quality cars and trucks, stainless-steel ware, machinery, and combat aircraft; its strategy is to find specialist niches in international markets and make the best products in well-defined, narrowly based sectors. Recalling Sweden's domination of the world market in high-quality iron in the eighteenth century, we may assume that Sweden's industrial revolution began in the iron industry. Such was not the case, however.

Unlike Russia's iron exports, which were virtually eliminated by the revolutionary iron-making techniques pioneered in England in the 1780s, Sweden's were never shut out of the international market, even though instead of importing coal,[64] the fuel of early industrialization, Sweden relied exclusively on charcoal, an out-dated forest-based fuel, until the 1870s. Although it lost its dominance in iron in the European export market, Sweden managed to define a specialist position by turning out high-quality charcoal-iron, indispensable in making crucible steel.

The iron industry grew more slowly in the nineteenth century than the economy as a whole and had only a limited impact on finished manufacturing.[65] (Its survival did provide a foundation for one branch of engineering—fabricated metal products such as wires, sheet and plates—but it had little to do with the twentieth-century breakthrough in the machinery branch of engineering.)[66] Instead, the first stirrings of industrial development came from forestry, the sector of Canadian-Swedish rivalry for almost two centuries. Scandinavia had been Britain's main supplier of timber until Napoleon blockaded Scandinavian exports in 1808. Britain then turned to its North American colonies as a high-cost but secure source of supply, offering a preferential tariff that more than counterbalanced the higher freight rates from North America. This preference remained in place after Napoleon's defeat, and for some time British North America supplied half of Britain's needs.[67] When preferences were reduced, however, in the 1840s and 1850s, the Scandinavian industry revived, and Sweden's vast timber stands, the largest in Europe next to Russia's, were soon under assault.

At first Sweden enjoyed a lumber boom, but when its forest reserves became depleted in the 1860s, the industry expanded into finished products, demonstrating Sweden's knack for innovation. The first new product was the safety match, invented by Gustaf Pasch in 1846.[68] Initially the matches were made by hand, but soon another Swede discovered a mechanized process, and by 1913 Sweden supplied a quarter of Britain's matches.[69]

More important than the match trade, though, was pulp and paper. With the spread of literacy the daily press and the general demand for paper grew prodigiously, so much that the traditional—and expensive—linen rags could no longer meet the need. Sweden seized the opportunity and led in the development of chemical pulp, a substitute for linen paper. The world's first chemical pulp factory opened in Sweden in 1872, and within twenty years the industry was growing rapidly. By 1914 Sweden had become the world's leading pulp exporter.[70]

Forest products had diversified beyond simple resource processing, yet timber and lumber continued to have the largest impact, accounting for 51 per cent of total exports in 1900.[71] Swedish growth was thus typical of staple economies, where resource exports provided the main dynamic.

Lumber and timber had important backward linkages with machinery used in forest production. By the 1860s demand was high for Swedish-made steam engines and fine-bladed saws, products first developed by experts brought in from Norway, whose modern forest industry predated Sweden's. Sweden's machinery engineering started with the mechanization of forestry, which was later to transform the economy.[72] As well, export earnings from forestry enabled Sweden to borrow large amounts of foreign capital to build railways.

The few countries that had developed before the mid-1800s began in cotton textiles, not in the heavy industries associated with railways.[73] It could hardly have been otherwise: railways were the outcome, not the cause, of fifty or sixty years of industrial development in England. In Sweden, however, and most other late followers, it was the introduction of railways that sparked development. Industrialization did not get seriously under way until the railway boom of the 1870s.

In the 1850s a farsighted national railway plan had been devised. Instead of responding to immediate needs, the plan was to go through areas of sparse settlement in order to spur economic growth. Not counting the terminals, the four oldest trunk lines, built in the late nineteenth century, touched only eight of the ninety-four cities in existence.

Controversy surrounds the contribution of railways to Sweden's industrial development. Using econometric techniques, Hans Modig argued that 'the railroads did not bring about any "great leap forward" . . . of [the] Swedish mechanical engineering industry'. He based his argument on the fact that the 'railroads were something of a foreign affair . . . financed to a considerable degree by imported capital; the railroads themselves consisted of rails, 86 per cent of which were imports; locomotives burned fuel, of which roughly 95 per cent was imported.'[74] This is a narrow view. As development lines across hinterland regions, Swedish railways stimulated the construction of the modern infrastructure that the previously isolated communities required, and employed over 10 per cent of all adult males in the 1870s. Such massive projects increased the demand for a variety of domestically made goods and provided many of Sweden's rural poor with their first experience of wage employment. In addition, railways united Sweden into a truly national market and they reduced costs.

Although railway construction meant increased imports of the supplies required, it also benefitted domestic industry, which in time was able to compete with foreign suppliers. The specialized Swedish iron industry could not produce rails as cheap as those built in Germany and Britain, but in all Sweden produced almost half of the equipment, including about 30 per cent of the locomotives, bought by its railways in the early boom years. After 1877 all coaches and wagons were made domestically.[75]

To build railways at the same time as industries, Sweden borrowed record amounts of foreign capital. In fact, in the 1860s and 1870s foreign capital comprised half of net domestic capital formation, and by the 1880s it had reached an astounding 80 per cent.[76] Only Canada and Australia imported comparable levels of capital during early industrialization.[77]

FROM STAPLE- TO MANUFACTURING-EXPORTER

Engineering

Adam Smith, the father of modern economics, the 'dismal science', could reconcile himself to the loss of the American colonies because he was confident that England would retain economic supremacy.[78] For the next sixty years he was right: the US remained a British economic dependency, exporting cotton and importing manufactured goods.[79] Escape from this pattern came from cotton textiles, an industry that turned the main staple into finished goods. Beginning with a coarse product suited to pioneer conditions, the cotton-textile industry carried the seeds of America's future manufacturing greatness.

Originally, machine shops were adjuncts of the textile mills, their purpose being to make and service mill machinery. Soon the shops were separated from the mills, and a specialized textile-machinery industry was born. Engineers such as those at the Singer Sewing Company (1851), the first American multinational, pioneered improvements in the making of clothing and textiles.[80] In time these engineering companies broadened their output, producing machine tools, locomotives, engines, and other metal products.[81] The US was launched on its mission to revolutionize the world's production techniques.

It is significant that Sweden, the other society that fully escaped the staple trap, also did so via engineering machinery. As noted, that industry began as an adjunct to Sweden's great staple export, forest products, but quickly expanded into other areas. Between 1875 and 1914, Swedish inventors and engineers revived the eighteenth-century tradition and developed or adapted many products at the cutting edge of technology. It was remarkable that such a small country was able to bring together inventors and engineers with financiers and entrepreneurs to found so many companies that are leading international concerns today.

When Gustaf de Laval invented the cream separator in 1878 and organized a company (Separator, later Alfa Laval) to make them, he found a ready market among Sweden's dairy farmers. Within twelve years the company was exporting five-sixths of its production.[82] De Laval also invented a steam turbine and created a company for its manufacture. Several decades later Sven Winquist perfected the modern ball bearing, and in 1907 he founded SKF. The product was of such quality that within five years SKF was the world's leading ball-bearing exporter and had established its first branch plant abroad. Many more subsidiaries were to come.[83] In these two cases Sweden found niches for itself, competing well abroad and dominating the home market.

Other Swedish inventions led to engineering companies with a presence in world markets, but they faced stiffer competition, with exports restricted mainly to more backward societies. They managed to hold the home market, however. Two years before de Laval devised the cream separator, Lars Magnus Ericsson invented the first table telephone (1876) and founded the company LM Ericsson to manufacture phone equipment.[84] The basic technology had been invented earlier that year through the efforts of Alexander Graham Bell, but LM Ericsson made adaptations and became a leading telephone manufacturer.[85] By the late 1890s the company was dominating the domestic market, had set up its first foreign plant, and was exporting over 80 per cent of its equipment.

There were similar experiences with oil and diesel engines for boats and machinery. The first practical internal-combustion gas engines were made in Germany in 1878. Bolinder, a Swedish firm that started in forestry machinery, acquired Swedish patents in 1894 for oil engines, a variant of those using gas. It then began selling marine engines to Sweden's large fleet of smaller vessels and soon began to export. Bolinder was later merged into the Volvo complex. With technology licensed from Rudolf Diesel, a German engineer, the AB Diesels Motorer company, met success about the same time in stationary engines and marine motors; foreign sales became significant by 1914. AB Diesels was a forerunner of the contemporary Atlas Copco company.

An 1880 invention enabled Sweden to utilize another of its great resources: water power. Jonas Wenstrom patented a three-phase electrical system for electrical transmission and generation, allowing electricity to be used for power for the first time.[86] It was a great boon to Swedish industry. Lacking coal, Sweden's iron industry had continued to use charcoal long after other countries had abandoned it, but had begun to import large amounts of coal when the electric forge was introduced around 1900. Coal was still an important source of energy, but electric forges, powered by hydroelectricity, supplemented the imported fuel and were used even more widely in steel production. In other sectors hydroelectricity soon overtook steam in powering industry. 'It is hardly an exaggeration to say that Swedish industry stepped directly from water power to electricity,' stated Jan Kuuse.[87]

ASEA (Swedish General Electric Company) an independent firm, was the main purveyor of these innovations in Sweden. ASEA pioneered electric lighting in the 1880s, power transmission in the 1890s, and hydroelectric generation in the next decade. At first the company struggled in the home market against foreign competition, but by 1914 it had led Sweden to an export surplus in electric generation and transmission equipment.[88]

All of these engineering companies—Alfa-Laval, SKF, LM Ericsson, Atlas Copco, and ASEA—developed from Swedish inventions or adaptations of foreign technology. All became major corporations duly recorded in *Fortune* magazine's 1987 world list of the top 500 non-American companies.[89]

Several other industries benefitted from Swedish inventiveness around the turn of the twentieth century. Gustaf Dalen made a series of inventions involving the use of gas; he was a director of AGA, later a large Swedish multinational specializing in chemicals and transport and engineering products. Carl Johansson developed a method of precision measurement for Sweden's armaments and general mechanical industries, an important building block in the country's reputation for precision manufacturing.[90] In the 1905-20 period a wide variety of agricultural implements were designed and made in Sweden as adaptations of US technology. All this creativity soon led to exports.[91]

Reciting the glittering evidence of Swedish inventiveness and entrepreneurial ability may leave the false impression that engineering had become the leading sector by the turn of the century. But in 1900 agriculture still contributed more to the economy than all of manufacturing, including the engineering sector. Timber and lumber remained the major export items in 1916, while pulp and paper was rising quickly.[92] Nevertheless, the development of engineering goods foretold Sweden's later industrial prowess and its escape from a staple economy.

Engineering goods started to take off in the 1890s, expanding sales mainly in the domestic market. After 1905, the home front having largely been secured, exports fuelled growth. Engineering products made up 10 per cent of imports in 1890, but only 3 per cent of exports. By 1910 the figures were in equilibrium, while six years later exports almost doubled imports.[93] The engineering industry had grown from infancy to lusty adolescence, accounting for 10 per cent of all manufacturing production in 1912 and employing 69,000 (20 per cent) of Sweden's industrial workers.[94] From this foundation engineering emerged as Sweden's foremost export industry in the 1920s. In 1985 it accounted for 45 per cent of all the country's exports.[95]

Export markets

How can we account for Sweden's remarkable success at making and exporting sophisticated products? Three major elements were needed in conjunction: an interest in applying scientific discoveries to everyday uses, financiers willing to bankroll risky and innovative firms and take part in their management, and an orientation to exports.

It had long been a tradition for Sweden to look beyond its borders for markets for its manufactured goods. Eighteenth-century merchant houses engaged in a vigorous import-export trade and extended credit to Swedish industrialists through many of the same revolutionary methods used by Crédit Mobilier in France a century later. Instead of profiting from the interest spread between borrower and lender, in the manner of later British and Canadian banks, Swedish merchant houses offered credit to the industries they bought goods from, to bargain down the price. The merchants therefore became dependent on selling the industrial products of their clients; they could not afford to become passive observers of the industrial scene, as conservative commercial banks are. Merchants often involved themselves in the management of their industrial customers, sometimes taking ownership positions.

The traditional iron industry was the focus of the relationship between merchant, industrialist, and exports.[96] By the late nineteenth century the lustre of primary iron had faded, but the tradition of the merchant-banker lived on. Like the iron industry, Swedish engineering tended to avoid competition in general goods, preferring to find specialist niches in foreign markets. The strategy of exporting specialist products was sufficient economic activity to sustain a small country.

Another element in Sweden's success at making internationally competitive products was the kind of technological creativity we examined in Sweden's early engineering industries. But it was not enough simply to be inventive. In the twentieth century British scientists have been creative while British industrialists have often failed miserably at making and marketing their inventions. Sweden did not have this difficulty in the early part of the century. While it made little headway in Germany and the United States, the technological leaders of the 1880-1914 era, it was successful elsewhere in finding export markets. Britain, already losing its industrial edge, was a little more receptive. And in the more economically backward countries—Russia, including Finland, and Norway (after free trade with Sweden had ended)—Swedish engineering exports received their boost. Since Sweden was just beginning to adopt modern technology, its products were often better suited than those of the advanced countries to the more primitive conditions of the backward nations.[97]

By 1913 czarist Russia imported over a quarter of Sweden's advanced engineering exports. Finland, then a Russian colony, accounted for a further 7 per cent, and the other Scandinavian countries—Norway and Denmark—for 17 per cent. Together, these Baltic countries took half of Sweden's engineering exports. In contrast, the much larger US, German, and British markets bought only one-sixth. The reason had little to do with proximity: far-off Australia, in roughly the same economic phase as Sweden's Baltic customers, took as much as Britain. Clearly Sweden was first able to make its mark in countries just beginning to industrialize.

Between 1905 and 1917 Sweden's most important market was Russia. The strategic question added to Swedish sales: an adversary of Germany, Russia had been dependent on the latter for most engineering goods. But as soon as Sweden began to make products of comparable quality, Russia deliberately bought Swedish wherever possible. The Russian market provided only a temporary bonanza for Sweden—after a massive upsurge during the war, Russia abruptly cut off sales and repudiated debts when the Bolsheviks took power. Nevertheless, pre-revolution Russian sales had helped to bring the products of Swedish engineering to a level where they readily entered the markets of the advanced countries.[98]

By the early twentieth century, therefore, Sweden had escaped from its staple-exporting past, and specialized, state-of-the-art engineering products had led the way. Capitalizing on its early promise, Sweden had an export surplus in engineering and other manufactured goods in the 1980s.[99]

THE POLITICS OF INDEPENDENT DEVELOPMENT

Sweden's rapid transformation was not simply the working-out of preordained laws: state policies and cultural trends were decisive. Sweden could have taken the same path as Norway or Canada, remaining dependent on resource exports and allowing a high level of foreign economic control. All three countries had similar problems and opportunities: a shortage of domestic capital during early industrialization; a comparative advantage in staple exports; and foreign designs on their resources and infant industries. Sweden avoided the fate of its northern brethren in large part because of the unintended consequences of immediate political events during the period of initial industrialization, from 1866 to 1914, as well as a general awareness of the need to protect the country's independence.

In Chapter 2 we saw that reliance on foreign ownership and technology were enticing possibilities for late-follower countries: they represented an easy route to development. Several political tendencies, however, militated against this choice in most late followers: an independent military policy, state frugality, and investment banking. These factors were instrumental for Sweden's independent development.

To understand how these tendencies evolved in Sweden, we must cast the net widely to include examination of defence, taxation, electoral suffrage, credit institutions, nationalism, protectionism, the role of government in the marketplace, and, throughout, the social inequalities that underlay all these issues. This discussion will enable us to consider how Sweden financed industrialization and avoided foreign economic control.

Capitalists and nobles

Sweden is known for its neutrality and its 'politics of compromise', a reputation suggesting an uneventful history, the reading of which could assist insomniacs. But appearances can be deceptive. Swedish politics from 1866 to 1914 were rife with conflicts and passionate controversy.

As already indicated, the numerically tiny nobility, who had held the power in this, the second oldest continuing parliamentary system, since its beginnings in the 1400s, supported economic liberalism and industrial development. On the other hand, the farmers, the main popular-democratic force from the 1860s to 1880s, were economically conservative. In a reversal of French history, Swedish constitutional reforms abolishing the hereditary-estate basis for parliamentary representation (at the late date of 1866), strengthened the landed nobility,[100] and, if anything, weakened the drive to liberal democracy.

Delayed development postponed the growth of an industrial working class, yet Sweden was the first country to elect a socialist government (1920). One of the few nations to achieve parliamentary democracy without a major revolution, Sweden adopted universal suffrage partly because the working class threatened to form rifle associations (1890s) and to emulate the Russian Revolution (1917) if not given the vote. Neutral, 'peaceful' Sweden developed a conservative nationalism with a militaristic bent at the turn of the twentieth century. Such contradictions are not the stuff of bland history.

Dominating the political scene was a struggle between the lower social classes—the vast majority—and the political and economic élites. The latter included the business class (less than 3 per cent of the population) and the few nobles, who were quickly transforming themselves into modern business-men.[101] In 1866 fewer than one-third of the nobles were landowners (243 families), and many of these had become industrialists by using their forest reserves to produce charcoal for the iron industry. Indeed, the majority of ironworks were owned by nobles: unlike the German landed nobility, who opposed industrialization, Sweden's landed nobles were central to the process.

At the time of Louis XIV in France, Sweden's absolute monarchs had created a nobility of officials to counter the independent power of the landowning nobility. By the mid-nineteenth century over 60 per cent of Swedish nobles were senior bureaucrats in the armed forces, the civil service, and the judiciary (515 families). From their urban base, especially in Stockholm and in alliance with the Crown, they dominated political life. Frequently the state nobility helped to finance new industrial firms.[102] Sweden's aristocrats were transforming themselves into new men of privilege as capitalists, bureaucrats, and politicians.

The middle class—merchants, ironmasters, large farmers, and bureau-crats—were surprisingly ready to allow continued aristocratic rule. Unlike their counterparts in France, where aristocrats lost their land or even their heads, and England, where bourgeois reformers had to fight their way into the establishment (in 1832), Swedish capitalists were content to join rather than replace the noble-led élite. Perhaps it was because so many Swedish nobles were not above dirtying their hands in the pursuit of profit. Certainly the nobility's openness to bourgeois power contributed to class harmony at the top. With about 3 per cent of the population, the burghers had had one parliamentary chamber to themselves since the sixteenth century. In 1866 they won, with little struggle, the bourgeois principle of electoral power according to wealth rather than hereditary status. Few aristocrats objected because most had met success in bureaucratic/political positions and business.

A similar acquiescence to noble leadership occurred in Germany under Bismarck, but bourgeois subordination in Sweden had none of Germany's unity-of-the-nation aspect to it. In effect, Sweden experienced a virtual fusion of capitalists and aristocrats into a new élite, intent on the pursuit of progress and profits. R.T. Naylor's merchants-against-industry theme (see Chapter 1) was nowhere in evidence. Erik Dahmen observed:

> The historical connection between commerce and the new manufacturing firms is a conspicuous feature in almost all industries. The first engineering firms that were independent of the old iron works were usually founded by merchants. The same applies to the big new lumber mills, the pulp mills, and to the construction joineries and furniture factories . . . In the early decades of industrialisation . . . twenty or so names appear in connection with at least a hundred of the new firms.[103]

In other words, merchants and noble officials established Sweden's early industries in a fairly monopolistic environment. Industry founders from a craft background emerged in large numbers only after Sweden's engineering breakthrough—in reverse order to Naylor's thesis. The house of capitalism stood united within itself, and with the nobility.

Farmers, politics, and defence

In contrast to the nobles, the ordinary people displayed no such unity, and so the fight for popular democracy was protracted. In a classic example of 'co-option', the 1866 reforms allowed larger farmers and some middle-class burghers to vote, while excluding the masses of the old order—poor farmers and rural landless—as well as those from the new order—urban workers and the lower middle class. This was the intent of Baron Louis De Geer, the author of the reforms; it was necessary, he argued, to 'secure a voice to education and property'.[104] The king had to be assured that abolition of the Estates would not unleash Armageddon. He need not have worried: the new Upper Chamber was dominated by counts and barons (30 per cent), high officials (75 per cent), ironmasters, or factory owners (20 per cent), with many deputies wearing several of these hats.[105]

For two decades after 1866 the larger, middle-class farmers fought the oligarchy over the burden of taxes for defence, but by the late 1880s the tariff question had cut across class lines and broken up their assault on élite power. The class-based struggle for equality soon reasserted itself, however, as previously voiceless elements clamoured to be heard. From the 1890s until 1918 an ever-more-insistent movement to broaden the franchise was led by workers and the lower middle class. Together, these contests over the franchise, taxation, and tariff protection had major implications for defence, foreign ownership, and banking.

Although radical liberal movements, pushed along by an emerging working class, had led much of Europe into mass revolt in 1848, in Sweden these events had only a faint echo. With high hopes, Adolf Hedin—brilliant orator, prolific writer, and able leader—launched the New Liberal Association soon after

1866. He advocated mass democracy, free trade, public education, old-age insurance, an end to harsh poor laws, a people's army—the stock-in trade of liberal-democratic demands at that time.[106] Within three years the party died. In contrast to the situation in Norway and Denmark, radical liberalism made no headway among Sweden's larger farmers, the only sizeable group that could vote.

Political success fell to the more conservative—'let's not share power with the lower classes'—Ruralist Party. Formed as a parliamentary party with no outside membership, the Ruralists were the first modern party in Sweden.[107] By forging an alliance with a few urban radicals they controlled the Lower Chamber (1868-87) but could not choose the government. Sweden was in a similar position to British North America prior to 'responsible government'. Cabinet was selected by the king, mainly from the plutocrats of the Upper Chamber. Many farmers, haunted by a sense of their own inferiority and believing in a separation of powers between executive and legislature, did not challenge this practice.[108] Thus the Ruralist-dominated Lower Chamber could veto policies of the oligarchy but could take little initiative.

During initial industrialization members of the ruling oligarchy, the traditional guardians of national safety, were obsessed with modernizing the armed forces. After the Franco-Prussian war, when improvements to defence became urgent, the Swedish artillery was reputed to be the most antiquated in Europe and the navy had deteriorated. Sweden's integrity depended upon either a balance of power between the major states of the Baltic or a power vacuum in the region.

Power rapidly shifted around 1900 as Germany rose to great-power status, Russia went through tumultuous changes, and Britain's naval dominance was challenged. Great-power alliances altered as states embarked on an armaments race before the First World War. Russia was widely feared in Sweden, pursuing as it was the Russification of neighbouring Finland. Norway did not share this fear, and its nationalist movement created tensions on Sweden's western front until 1905, when Norway gained independence from the Swedish Crown. As a result of these tensions, Sweden was in a precarious position through much of this period. The political question was not whether defence was necessary, but who should pay for it.

Although leery of the oligarchy's history of foreign adventurism, farmers shared its concern about national defence, but they opposed shouldering defence costs all by themselves. Since the mists of time, all landowners except nobles had had to provide supplies for the armed forces. For the Ruralists, removal of inequitable land taxes for defence was the number-one issue, and until it was settled they blocked the oligarchy's schemes to modernize the army and institute conscription. Later, the working and lower middle classes, in the familiar cry that reform must accompany the citizens' duty to defence, demanded the vote if they were to be conscripted. Time and again, the ruling élite's Upper Chamber voted one way on defence issues while the Ruralist-led

Lower Chamber voted the other. The result was deadlock until 1883-85, when the first tax and conscription reforms took effect.[109] After 1904, with all tax inequities removed, farmers assumed their usual role as defenders of the fatherland, and in the winter of 1914 they staged a huge march protesting against low defence expenditures. By then, patriotism had become relatively cost-free.

It is difficult to assess the economic impact of the politics of taxation and defence expenditures because so little has been written on Sweden's munitions industries between 1866 and 1914.[110] We know that the end of the deadlock over defence taxation in the mid-1880s led to a re-equipment of the navy; thirteen warships were built between 1883 and 1903.[111] (In 1911, the year of Wilfrid Laurier's 'tin pot navy', Sweden was rocked by bitter controversy over whether to build a battleship. The pacific Liberal government was supported by the even more pacific Social Democrats, and the F-boat was stopped. But proponents of military preparedness—farmers and Conservatives—pushed on and raised enough money privately to finance the ship.)[112] While the effects of defence expenditures on Sweden's wider economy were probably not extensive, there was certainly a connection between defence, nationalism, and restrictions on foreign ownership.

Both in wartime and in the prelude to it, Sweden took measures to reverse foreign ownership of key economic sectors. In 1916, during the First World War (in which Sweden avoided involvement), the Conservative government passed a law preventing foreign ownership of Swedish resources and the strategic iron and steel industries.[113] It was significant, and typical, that wartime conditions led to the strongest measures. Similar action was taken after the Nazi rise to power in the 1930s, when the Swedish Social Democratic government forced foreign owners out of the armaments and airplane industries. Krupp, the great German armaments company, had bought Bofors, Sweden's large munitions company. By making guns in Sweden, Krupp evaded the Allies' Versailles restrictions on arms manufacture.[114] In the 1930s Sweden forced Krupp out of Bofors, and another German company was compelled to close an airplane factory in Sweden. Hostility to both nazism and militarism meshed with nationalism. Sweden's objective, the Prime Minister declared, was to 'eliminate foreign interests wholly' from the armaments and airplane industries.[115]

Although defence spending was not great at any point in the period from 1870 to 1914, the ebb and flow of Swedish defence spending was beneficial for capital self-reliance.[116] The effect was unintended. Short of domestic capital during the railway boom of the 1870s, Sweden borrowed an enormous amount of foreign capital.[117] Farmer opposition to inequitable defence taxes lessened defence spending and borrowing and hence the need for even more foreign capital. Later, when military spending was more generous, Sweden had developed to the point where it was better able to provide indigenous capital. The need to borrow foreign capital rapidly diminished, and by 1910 Sweden had become a net capital exporter.

Like agrarians almost everywhere, Sweden's farmers resented taxation, believed in economy in government, and opposed public waste. Further investigation is needed, but it is interesting to note that the Riksdag adopted the principle of limiting the speed at which state railways were being built (1871) only three years after the Ruralist Party gained control of the Lower Chamber of the Riksdag.[118] This reduction in the rate of railway construction reduced Sweden's need to import foreign loan capital and released scarce domestic capital for the development of independent manufacturing capacity.

Liberalism and protectionism

Conventional wisdom has it that American branch plants came to Canada as a result of the National Policy tariffs of 1879. Although, as we shall see in Chapter 5, the reasons were much more complicated, there is some truth in that view. Sweden's history, on the other hand, tells of a different connection between tariffs and foreign ownership. In Sweden in the late nineteenth century the protectionists were nationalists who (unlike Canadian protectionists) resisted control of Swedish resources, while free-trade liberals welcomed foreign direct investment. As in Canada, the debate involved philosophic as well as economic issues. Free-market liberals believed in a very limited state and abhorred 'narrow nationalism'. Protectionists, in contrast, while motivated partly by self-interest, viewed the state's economic role positively and were economic nationalists. The contest between the two groups would determine whether the state actively resisted foreign direct investment.

In Sweden, as elsewhere, this debate had its roots in the eighteenth-century enlightenment. In the 1750s and 1760s the middle-class 'Caps' revolted against the upper-class 'Hats', the party of the nobles and the big bourgeoisie. The Caps pressed for political and economic liberalism in their attack on the mercantilist intervention that favoured privileged groups. When they took power for a short period, they favoured importers over exporters, allowed a free press, increased peasants' rights, cut military expenditures, and reduced state aid to industry.[119] The king ended the debate with the 1772 coup d'état that ushered in a mild form of absolutist rule.

As already noted, Sweden's early interest in liberalism gave way to a prolonged rejection of democracy.[120] Political stagnation accompanied economic and scientific stagnation: Sweden's eighteenth-century precocious-ness in all these spheres was gone. The 1848 revolutions badly frightened the country's few radical liberals.

Yet if political liberalism was dead among the middle and upper classes, economic liberalism was not.[121] While the lower social classes were more economically conservative[122]—many, like the craftsmen in the Burgher Estate, represented the old order and not the new industrialism—in the 1850s the king and Crown prince were enthusiastic proponents of industrial development and free trade, and economic liberals came to dominate the Noble Estate. Nevertheless, the élite's economic liberalism was tempered by its social and political conservatism, its strong nationalism, its defence preoccupations, and its fear of social upheaval.

Eventually, mild economic liberalism triumphed over backward-looking interests and led to the removal of barriers to industrialization. In 1846 the guilds were abolished; the first joint-stock banks were established (1863-65); and tariffs were reduced in anticipation of the customs union with Norway.

The constitutional reforms of 1866 did not advance the cause of laissez-faire liberalism. Ruralist Party strength had an economic-conservative influence, although in the 1870s the Ruralists tended to support free trade in principle because grain prices were reasonably good. But the 1880s saw international grain prices halved under the impact of plentiful and cheap New World grain that was moved by new, cheaper transportation. In the face of this threat to grain production a protectionist movement developed.[123] Although reminiscent of Canada's National Policy of 1879, it had a different base of support: certain farm interests provided the initiative, while industry played an important secondary role. (A similar alliance developed in Bismarck's Germany with the 'union of rye and iron'.) As in Canada in the same period, farmers' attitudes were based almost entirely on economic interest rather than ideology: large grain farmers in central Sweden wanted to shut cheap foreign grain out of the domestic market to counteract a drastic fall in land prices. But they could not convince their northern and southern colleagues— who were mainly in animal production and therefore consumers of grain—of the wisdom of high grain prices.[124] In 1888 the Ruralist Party broke apart under the strain of this debate and went into confusion and eclipse for the next twenty-five years. The agrarian movement's decline was also based on its very success at tax and defence reforms. After protectionism ceased to be the primary issue, the farmers were able to develop a new party, the Agrarians, between 1913 and 1921.[125]

Protectionism was a minority force within the rural community. As net consumers of bread grains, small farmers and rural labourers opposed grain tariffs, but stiff property qualifications barred their voices from the Riksdag. Large protectionist farmers, on the other hand, had ample representation, and when they combined with the noble-industrial élite in the Senate they could command a majority in a joint vote between the two chambers. As a result, an agricultural tariff was established in 1888, and industrial protection followed in 1892.[126] Except for a brief interlude in 1905-06, the Protectionists—the main lineal ancestors of the present Moderate party—maintained a majority from 1888 to 1911, a period that saw crucial decisions on foreign direct investment. Thus limitations to democracy allowed a conservative nationalism to triumph.

Economic historians have not agreed on the effects of protectionism on Sweden's economic development. Eli Heckscher, a neo-classical economist, argued that tariffs had little effect on industry.[127] Kurt Samuelsson disagreed: 'Because of the protection afforded by the tariffs, a consumer goods industry based on the home market was enabled to grow faster and to attain a greater scope than would otherwise be the case.'[128] Whatever the role of tariffs in Sweden's development, the 1890s marked the shift from staple exports to expansion of the domestic market for industrial goods.[129]

The rise of left-wing parties

Protectionism triumphed in the 1890s, but at long-term cost to the upper and middle classes. Its victory sparked the first interest in politics among the disenfranchised lower middle and working classes, who wanted to gain the vote to overturn tariffs. With the decline of the Ruralists, class conflict entered a new phase, and universal suffrage became the dominant issue in Swedish politics until 1918.[130]

Inspired by the formation of the German and Danish socialist parties, the Social Democratic Party of Sweden was founded in 1889, at the start of industrialization. From an early point the Social Democrats broke from the anti-nationalist ideology of international socialism and proclaimed their goal to be the creation of a real nation.[131] Although the Social Democrats had fewer members than liberal organizations, they provided a more determined force. They urged workers to join voluntary rifle associations and threatened a general strike if demands for universal suffrage were ignored.

In 1893 the liberals and Social Democrats established a 'people's parliament', the first Swedish assembly elected by universal manhood suffrage. Co-operation in the alternative parliament led to a quarter-century alliance between the Liberal Party (founded in 1900) and the Social Democrats. The Liberals—not a nineteenth-century party of emerging capitalists, but a modern party of the urban lower middle class and progressive farmers—formed governments in 1905-06 and 1911-14 with the support of the ever-strengthening Social Democrats. The Liberal Party's late emergence and its dependence on the Socialists demonstrated the weakness of liberalism during early industrialization.

Between 1900 and 1914 these growing left-wing parties affected some policies but not others. Their opposition to protection had had little effect in the 1890s because few of their supporters could vote, and later the issue lost much of its importance. Similarly, although their opposition to increased defence spending did have some delaying effect, it did not stop a military build-up shortly before the First World War. The emergence of popular forces in the first decade of the twentieth century had a greater effect in increasing the domestic ownership of northern resources and pushing the state towards a more positive role in the economy. Universal suffrage was granted between 1918 and 1921, and the Social Democratic, Liberal, and Agrarian parties dominated governments in the interwar years.

Protectionism, nationalism, and foreign ownership

Despite the rise of left-wing parties, the protectionist victory of the 1890s signalled the upsurge of a conservative nationalism—influenced by Germany's authoritarian and autarkic model—that was partly a reaction to rural decline and the equality demands from the classes created by industrialism. Romanticism in the arts, militarism, and glorification of things Swedish combined with protectionism to produce a reactionary nationalism in ruling circles. Economic liberalism lost ground, and with it tolerance for foreign ownership.

As we have seen, capital-deficient Sweden benefitted from large capital imports during initial industrialization. State railways, municipalities, mortgage banks, and industries all relied heavily on foreign loan capital, and development was accelerated. But unlike Canada, czarist Russia, and Norway, Sweden avoided high levels of foreign direct investment. In 1900 foreign ownership was highest in Sweden's mining sector (20 per cent) and only a little lower in minerals (including the iron industry) and textiles.[132] British and Norwegian capital was significant in sawmills,[133] while leading US machinery manufacturers and German producers of electrical equipment—areas where Swedish-owned firms also showed strength—established themselves in Sweden in this period.[134] Yet in total, foreign ownership of Swedish industry was on a 'trifling scale'.[135] Swedish inventiveness and entrepreneurial ability in manufacturing did not leave much of a vacuum for foreign companies to fill.

In addition, in the words of Eli Heckscher, 'in turning to foreign countries to finance the most capital-absorbing operations of the time, the government released domestic savings for the use of private business which under other circumstances might have had to borrow abroad.'[136] Thus the state's foreign borrowing led to greater domestic ownership of industry. This period was crucial for the future: in contemporary Sweden foreign subsidiaries account for only 4 per cent of the total economy and 6 per cent of manufacturing. In no sector or subsector does foreign ownership exceed 15 per cent.[137]

Low levels of foreign ownership during initial industrialization were not the result of foreign indifference: witness the numerous attempts to establish foreign direct investment in Sweden during that period. Norway, with similar resource endowments but weaker indigenous financial institutions and less development overall, received a great deal of foreign investment at that time, including some from Sweden. (Abundant water power was the main interest.)

In 1909, several years before foreign investment peaked in Norway, foreign ownership reached 39 per cent in resources and manufacturing, exceeded 80 per cent in the chemical and mining industries, and was 32 per cent to 47 per cent in metals, heating and lighting, textiles, and clothing.

In the aftermath of gaining independence from Sweden, and in a climate of anti-industrialism, Norway took steps to curb foreign ownership in 1909. Foreign companies had to receive permission to exploit Norway's resources; property rights to hydroelectricity were to revert to the state within forty to eighty years after the grant of concession and without compensation; foreigners were completely barred from acquiring forest lands.[138] These laws and the nationalist climate that led to them drastically reduced foreign-ownership levels by 1919.[139] British and German investors had been eager to enter similar fields in Sweden as well, but resistance to foreign ownership developed at an earlier point there than in Norway.

Because foreign ownership has not posed a significant problem in Sweden, scholarly interest in the question has not been great—except in the *cause célèbre* of northern iron-ore from the 1880s to 1907—and more primary research is needed. Some of this deficiency is being corrected by Sven Nordlund's study on foreign ownership in Sweden between 1895 and 1950,[140] however, and enough is known to give a general outline of foreign direct investment in Sweden during initial industrialization.

The Crown had a traditional claim to ownership of Swedish lands and resources, including minerals, similar to the British and French traditions (later transferred to Canada): Crown lands were considered to be in the public domain.[141] An 1829 law forced foreigners to obtain royal permission to purchase land, but for the next forty years permission was granted readily, because such requests came mainly from individual settlers wishing to farm in Sweden. Foreign attempts to purchase Swedish minerals and forests after 1870, however, were more controversial.

Indeed, by the mid-1800s the Crown's own claim to mineral resources was eroding as the ideas of possessive individualism began to take hold. This erosion was of little consequence for foreign ownership until the 1870s, when Britain and Germany became industrial and military rivals. Rapid changes in steelmaking made Swedish iron ore highly desirable to both countries' steel industries—especially since it was fairly close to tidewater, and hence to British and German ports. Bessemer steelmaking required phosphorus-free ore, and central Sweden was one of the few areas in Europe where it was available. The Gilchrist-Thomas technique, on the other hand, developed in 1878, required high phosphoric ore, which northern Sweden possessed in large quantities.[142] With each discovery, foreign capitalists looked to Swedish resources.

In the early 1870s, at the beginning of Sweden's industrial transition, German and English firms began to buy Swedish iron mines, ironworks, and forests. Despite the advances of economic liberalism, there was sufficient opposition to foreign ownership—largely from workers, small farmers, and craftsmen—to launch an investigation by a Riksdag committee in 1873. Its report, never published, was critical of foreign ownership of resources, which would lead, it suggested, to an outflow of profits and little reinvestment in Sweden.[143] Without a stake in Swedish society, foreign corporations were seen as a threat to community, and Treffenberg, the chairman of the committee, suggested that Sweden might lose its freedom. New restrictions on foreign ownership were rejected, however, on the grounds that the problem was still minor, and that Sweden needed the capital.[144] This episode was the first skirmish in a longer war that culminated in the removal of foreign owners from most of the iron-ore business and the introduction of tough concession laws.

From the 1880s on, opposition to the government's liberal approach increased as the economic interests of Swedish ironmasters combined with a growing nationalist movement that had its roots among the people. This protectionist sentiment extended to forestry in the north as well, where ruthless exploitation was under way. In this period the protectionist farmers of central Sweden joined forces with manufacturers (including the iron-masters) from that region and reversed the trend to economic liberalism. Sale of forest lands to private farmers ended, and conservation was encouraged.

Although the twists and turns of a twenty-five-year battle to resist foreign control of Sweden's resources need not be fully recounted here, certain events were critical. In the 1880s the British purchased iron mines in Sweden, Spain, and Norway to supply British industry.[145] In addition, to extend their control over Swedish mining, they owned smelting, railway, and steamship companies. A major political storm ensued, and by 1891, three years after the Protectionists took power, the northern iron-ore railway was nationalized and some English ore holdings were regained by the state. It was a victory for ironmasters in central Sweden and mine owners throughout the country, who accepted nationalization on the understanding that they would retain the right to exploit the natural resources.[146]

The final battles over control of iron ore were fought in the early 1900s, when the German industrialists Possehl, Krupp, and Thyssen competed with the British to control Sweden's resources.[147] Public opinion was against foreign ownership, and most newspapers endorsed nationalization. Support for state ownership came from a strange variety of sources. Swedish mine owners and Wallenberg, the banker, wanted the state to buy British-controlled ore mines so that Swedish firms could operate them without making long-term investments. As the issue developed from 1901 to 1907, support for public ownership came most strongly from the rising Liberals and Social Democrats. As in Norway at the same time, anti-capitalist sentiment combined with nationalism to make a potent mixture. Meanwhile, conservative nationalism was on the wane because the economic élite's grip on political power was weakening. As Bo Jonsson put it, as long as the Conservative élite

> were masters of the State apparatus, they took a positive view of the State. But when faced with the prospect that the reform policy would be taken further by a democratized state authority, the Conservatives felt inclined to return to a more individualistic line and to repudiate an extension of State influence.[148]

The Liberals, in power briefly in 1905-06, wanted full nationalization of the Kiruna ore companies, but the Conservative government settled in the following year for 50 per cent ownership of the two largest ore companies.[149] Foreign interests were largely excluded.

Battles were fought over foreign ownership of northern sawmills and forest land as well. By 1901 foreign investors were involved in 46 out of 192 forest companies, holding majority control in ten of them. Farmers from the northern region of Norrland, many of whom owned large forest reserves, feared losing their lands to the forest companies, especially those that were foreign-owned. A farmer-led committee in 1902 advocated prohibition of foreign ownership. It argued that

> it is necessary to change such rules, as allow Swedish land to be sold in rising proportions to foreigners, whose economic calculations will decide how our people and our land is treated ... What future will Norrland have if they are allowed to buy all the land? Those principles ... must be changed, if not, Norrland and our whole native country shall end up under a foreign yoke [and] the population turned into enslaved and indolent company workers. The free and wealthy farmer disappears ... The sawmill owners act like traitors, planning to sell the country to foreigners and exterminate the free farming population.[150]

Norrland farmers failed to have foreign landownership prohibited, but the battle helped to set the stage for general restrictions fourteen years later. No controversy of comparable proportions occurred over the ownership of manufacturing industries.[151]

The 1910 Stock Corporations Act required that all directors of foreign subsidiaries be Swedish citizens.[152] Legislation passed in 1916 was much tougher: foreign companies could not own property, minerals, or mines without permission.[153] This law, the basic legislation on foreign ownership until 1982, was applied largely to primary manufacturing—iron and steel, wood products, and pulp[154]—but also to some secondary industries. In 1931 Ivar Kreuger, an infamous Swedish promoter, sold the giant Swedish telephone company LM Ericsson to ITT, its American competitor. Kreuger made the transaction secret 'since it was legally impossible for a foreign company to control LM Ericsson'.[155] ITT soon lost majority control.[156] It is not known how extensively these bans on foreign ownership of Swedish industry were applied, but certainly major foreign-controlled companies such as Fagersta and Bofors were repatriated in the 1920s and 1930s.[157]

Why was foreign direct investment so low in Swedish manufacturing industries before 1914? There are three possible answers. First, foreign capitalists may have been uninterested in Swedish industry. Second, the state and public opinion may have discouraged foreign investors from entering this sector. Third, Swedish-owned industries may have provided little room for foreign subsidiaries. There is not enough evidence for a definite answer, but the lack-of-interest argument seems implausible. Swedish industrial bonds sold well abroad, and German and British capitalists made large direct investments in nearby Russia, Norway, and Poland during that period. The best answer is probably a combination of the second and third possibilities: internal resistance and the competitiveness of domestically owned industry. At any rate, the state's attitude as shown in the legislation of 1829, 1891, 1907, 1910, and 1916 created an unfavourable climate for foreign ownership.

Sweden's decision not to alienate its resources to foreign interests and instead to utilize them to build up domestic manufacturing was important for the country's economic success. Nationalism was the polemic language of political discourse used by right and left alike to legitimate their interests and ideologies between 1890 and 1914.[158] Economic nationalism was most strongly championed by farmers and workers—although conservative protectionists also offered significant support—and the eventual triumph of controls on foreign ownership coincided with the rise to power of the popular parties as the electoral franchise was extended.

FINANCING INDUSTRIALIZATION

As the pace of industrialization quickened in the 1870s, Sweden lacked sufficient amounts of domestic capital, a problem it shared with other late followers. The way Sweden handled this capital shortage determined its route to late follower-development.

Internal regeneration of industrial capital and short-term bank credits were the primary means used by the early developing countries to finance industrialization; however, they were never fully adequate in the late followers.[159] I therefore take internal reinvestment as a given in late-follower development and focus instead on additional sources to these funds—for it was in those respects that the late followers differed from each other. Shortages of industrial capital required bank loans and what Gerschenkron called 'substitutions' to reinvestment. Four substitutions were possible for late followers. The first two used domestic capital: either the state (1) or financial institutions (2) could unlock domestic capital previously confined to farming, luxury, or savings and channel these funds into industrialization. The second two substitutions involved foreign capital: taking the form of either portfolio (3) or direct (4) investment, foreign capital could add to domestic funds and was readily available in the late 1800s if the host country could provide security and adequate export earnings. The independent route to late-follower development, it will be recalled from Chapter 2, involved a combination of the first three substitutions, while the dependent route relied heavily on foreign direct investment as well. Foreign technology and management usually accompanied the latter substitution.

Sweden, as a late follower, used three methods—with about equal emphasis—to enlarge its pool of development capital sufficiently and so avoided dependence on foreign direct investment. First, it borrowed foreign portfolio capital on a record scale to finance the agricultural revolution, railway building, and urban growth. Second, the state financed the majority of transportation and communications improvements and on occasion aided industry directly, as in the case of northern ores. Third, fundamental changes to Sweden's banking system played a central role in the process of industrialization. This last factor proved crucial.

Despite the monumental work of Rondo Cameron and his associates, the question of how important banking was to development during early industrialization has not been settled.[160] Rather than attempt to decide this issue here, I will focus on the less ambitious issue of how the particular banking system in place affected the choice of late-follower development routes.

The real breakthrough for modern manufacturing in Sweden came between 1897 and 1912, when secondary industry rather than resources set the pace and the value of manufacturing rose 250 per cent.[161] When industry needed large infusions of long-term capital, domestic banks were able for the first time to contribute sufficient amounts. The story of how Sweden's banks shifted to industrial investments starts in the mid-1800s, when the country's modern financial structure was established.

The politics of banking

Banking systems are affected greatly both by legislation and by general ideas about the functions of banks and the security of bank notes and deposits. Considerable controversy surrounded the issues of banking and the role of the state in the early 1800s. Should the state support and direct the credit system as in the past? In Sweden the banking issue was part of a general debate about economic liberalism.

On banking as on other questions, the rural community often took one side, and town, industry, and commerce the other.[162] Two centres of power reflected this division. The Crown and the state had a monopoly over financial legislation, while the Riksdag had unrestricted budgetary power. Banking policy was central to the struggle between these loci of power.[163]

As in the US and Canada, in the Sweden of the mid-1800s banking was a major source of contention between agrarians, urban capitalists, and officials. And the issues were much the same. Agrarians wanted low taxes, low interest rates, and credit for agriculture. They used their Riksdag majority in the Noble and Peasant chambers to further their interests, which they saw as tied to the National Bank of Sweden. The National Bank, established in the seventeenth-century great-power era, had accustomed the populace to using paper money,[164] and in the early 1800s it remained the centre of Sweden's public credit system.

The Crown and state officials, for their part, wanted to modernize Sweden through economic liberalism, and to this end they diminished the National Bank's right to issue paper notes by consistently supporting note-issuing private banks.[165] (The issuing of bank notes, a way of borrowing from the public free of cost, was the main means of profit before deposits and share-issuing became widespread; the funds thus borrowed were put into interest-bearing loans.) The fight over note-issuing between public and private institutions profoundly affected Sweden's banking system.

In countries where private banks gained control over note-issuing, there tended to develop a commercial, short-term lending system. Where the state retained a note-issuing monopoly, banks had to find alternative ways to earn profits, and the German concept of investment banking often took root.[166]

A fairly even balance of opposing forces in Sweden led to a hybrid banking system. Conservative agrarians won on some issues, liberal modernizers on others. The resulting system likely provided more capital for industrial and agricultural progress than would have been available if either side had won outright.

Most accounts portray the conservative agrarians as having lost the banking debates. In 1863-64, several years before the emergence of the Ruralist Party, a series of reforms capped a decade of efforts to modernize banking along British commercial lines. The usury law limiting interest rates and discouraging bank deposits was removed. Banks won the right to establish limited liability if they gave up private note-issuing, but they still could not hold industrial shares—a key element in German investment banking.[167] The publicly supported credit system of the National Bank was shunted aside; new commercial banks, savings banks, and mortgage institutions replaced pre-industrial merchant houses and private loan brokers as sources of credit.

While it appeared that agrarian-based conservatism towards banking had lost on all counts, this was not the case. From the 1830s to the 1860s the social-political strength of noble landowners and wealthy farmers ensured that Sweden's financial institutions would direct credit to agricultural modernization.[168] Compared to farmers in Canada, then, Sweden's propertied agrarians had an easy job getting the financial system oriented to their needs.

Yet not all Swedish farmers received ready credit during the agricultural revolution. Most privately-owned financial institutions were biased against small farmers, who had to rely exclusively on government-assisted rural savings banks.[169] These farmers directed an unsuccessful campaign against the mortgage and commercial banks, but they did achieve another of their goals: retention of a National Bank role in note-issuing.

Note-issuing had consequences for taxation: if the National Bank gave it up, profits would be lost to state revenue and taxes would rise. Since non-noble farmers carried an inordinate tax burden, especially after the tax reforms of 1862, they fought hard for a public note-issuing monopoly.[170] They got their chance in the 1870s and 1880s with the rise of the Ruralist Party. As part of the campaign against unfair defence taxes, farmers successfully reasserted the National Bank's note-issuing monopoly. Private note-issuing was wound down, and in 1903 it ceased. The agrarians had won.

Withdrawal of private note-issuing led banks to issue short- and long-term bonds, thereby linking the short-term money market with the long-term capital market.[171] As well, they began to make more loans on the security of real property, a technique borrowed from mortgage banks. Deposits became important in financing bank credits, especially after Ruralist interventionism succeeded in establishing a Bank inspectorate whose function was to guarantee depositors' funds. These advances in fund-raising enabled banks to make industrial investments. With the agricultural revolution over, surplus funds from farming flowed into banks, and some of them were transferred to industry.

Investment banking

The Stockholms Enskilda Bank (SEB), forerunner of the present Skandinaviska Enskilda Bank,[172] was the pioneer investment bank in Sweden. Given its role as financier and promoter of new industrial sectors, it is ironic that the SEB began as a conservative alternative to investment banks.[173] I will focus on this bank because of its importance in Sweden's industrial breakthrough.

Founded by A.O. Wallenberg, a merchant whose descendants became famous politicians, diplomats, and businessmen, the SEB shifted its investments in ways that paralleled major developments in Sweden's initial industrialization. From Norrland timber (in the 1850s and 1860s), the SEB moved into railways, ironworks, and government loans (1870s); in the 1890s it shifted to electrical industries and northern iron ore. Finally, the SEB turned to timber and wood pulp before withdrawing from industrial development in 1910, when the Stockholm Stock Exchange was established.[174]

The SEB's impact was out of proportion to its size (in 1897 it was Sweden's third largest bank). Instead of waiting for loan applications, the bank's principal owners, the Wallenbergs, sought out new enterprises, investigated them thoroughly, and provided long-term capital and managerial advice to those approved. The SEB remained loyal even during clients' financial difficulties.

Until 1909-11 Swedish legislation conformed to the British model in forbidding banks from acquiring stocks in companies. But the SEB found ways to get around the law. Instead of directly holding shares, as German investment banks did, the SEB gave credit to industrial clients and accepted their bonds in return. It also purchased and earned interest on industrial bonds. To circumvent the prohibition on direct dealing in shares, the Wallenbergs operated as individuals and handled company shares through a subsidiary holding company.[175]

The SEB obtained a lot of foreign capital, continuing a tradition from the old merchant houses. In this way foreign capital went into Swedish industry through a Swedish-controlled bank, helping to avoid the extensive foreign ownership that prevailed in Norway.

As indicated in Chapter 2, the SEB showed entrepreneurial leadership in the crucial electrical engineering sector in its dealings with the troubled engineering firm ASEA. Electrical equipment could not be sold until electrical demand was augmented. Moreover, as was often the case in new economic sectors, one part of the industry could not develop unless another part was developing simultaneously. Instead of stripping ASEA's assets, as British-style banks would have done, the SEB rejuvenated the whole industry to save the company.

The SEB also assisted the inventor Gustaf de Laval, and helped to finance the introduction of electrical rolling-milling, the Swedish-developed marine engine, and other innovations.[176] In fact, the SEB was heavily involved in financing four of the five major Swedish engineering companies discussed earlier.

Although a commercial bank in form, with unlimited liability, the SEB was really a German-style investment bank. The press and farming community criticized it for breaking the spirit of Swedish laws intended to prevent direct bank involvement in industry, but the state offered little resistance. Indeed, it saved the SEB and other banks from foundering in 1878-79.[177]

The SEB contributed more than any other bank to the financing and management of Sweden's industrial breakthrough. It also had a critical influence on the activities of the two large joint-stock, limited-liability banks. Stockholms Handelsbank (later Svenska Handelsbank) began as a breakaway from the SEB in 1871 and at first acted as a commercial bank. Under the influence of financier Louis Fraenckel, however, between 1893 and 1911, the bank moved into investments. Operating like the SEB, Fraenckel and the Handelsbank were involved with eight of the ten largest industrial firms in 1912.[178] The large Skandinaviska Bank also emulated the SEB in financing and restructuring existing firms.[179] As a result of these changes, domestic and foreign funds were channelled through Swedish banks to aid the development of an independent, technologically precocious economy.

As a late follower Sweden experienced considerable shortages of domestic capital during initial industrialization. The ways in which it overcame these shortages affected the direction of its development. Debates between economic conservatives and liberals—partly a struggle between country and town—provided the environment in which *de facto* investment banks emerged. Despite attempts at economic liberalism in the mid-1800s, the state retained a positive role. Using vast amounts of public and foreign capital, it planned and built the main railway system, allowing scarce domestic capital to flow into industry and thereby enhancing domestic ownership and control.

CONCLUSION

All late-follower countries save Canada became independent manufacturing economies by 1914 or shortly thereafter. Sweden has been studied intensively here because of its similarities to Canada: its small population, its northern resource-exporting economy, and the timing and scale of its industrial progress. If Sweden could become an independent manufacturing economy by 1914, there seems no reason why Canada could not have done so.

If economic factors alone cannot explain Canada's divergence from the other late followers, two possibilities remain. Canada's divergence was caused either largely by external conditions or largely by internal social and political factors. The Swedish example throws light on which of these is the most compelling explanation.

As developed countries deficient in cheap raw materials in the late 1800s, Britain and Germany reached beyond their borders to secure supplies. Sweden and the rest of Scandinavia were near at hand, the sea effectively reducing distance. Lightly populated, they were ideal sources of raw materials. British and German interest in Sweden's iron and forest resources was similar to American interest in Canadian resources.

As Scandinavia began to develop, its markets attracted foreign capitalists to secondary industries; prior to 1909 Norway was the preferred area, but some investments made their way into Sweden too. Scandinavia and Canada both developed in an environment in which more advanced countries sought to own and control important sectors of their economies. If external interest in economic domination was not very different for Sweden and Canada, we are left with internal factors as the main basis for Canada's different development. In this regard Sweden is especially instructive for understanding the Canadian case.

Sweden had a long history as an independent nation, developing an effective state that continued to evolve both during its great-power era and after its loss of empire. Over several centuries Sweden developed a coherent national culture despite social and class inequities. Right and left had different conceptions of the Swedish nation during initial industrialization, but each expressed its vision in nationalist terms. A degree of common nationalism could be seen in the responses of both right and left to the northern-ore issue. Special interests, defence considerations, desire for diversification, and support for socialist ideas came together in a nationalist program to regain control of the Swedish economy.

Another notable feature of Swedish society was its long-standing interest in education, scientific advancement, and utilitarian applications of new discoveries. These traditions formed the fertile ground for Sweden's remarkable innovations from the 1870s to 1914. Sweden's technological leadership aided economic growth in a number of engineering products and lessened technological reliance on foreign companies.

The balance of political forces during initial industrialization worked in Sweden's favour. As a country less backward than Japan or Russia, it found that a fair amount of economic liberalism was compatible with successful late-follower development. But a positive state role was also important. The state was heavily involved in a number of areas: improving communication links quickly and cheaply; borrowing foreign capital but maintaining Swedish control; releasing limited supplies of domestic capital for development by importing capital for other projects; and reversing foreign takeovers of strategic sectors. The nature of state intervention was similarly important. Officials could have prevented the emergence of investment banking, but instead they chose to sidestep liberal orthodoxy.

The power of the countryside—nobles and commoners—to restrain business interests from completely dominating the state was important as well. Its influence could be seen in Sweden's heterogeneous banking system, its emphasis on defence, and its generally frugal fiscal orientation. Agrarian power discouraged business interests from exploiting state revenues for their own special ends and thus hurting overall development. All these factors were important for Sweden's late-follower success.

Although Sweden was an old society, it differed less in social structure and ethos from Canada than any other late-follower country. Its parliamentary traditions, its acceptance of the rule of law, and its lack of a genuine feudal past were similar to Canada's. As well, Sweden's New World characteristics—its building of railways through frontier regions and its agrarian movements—contributed as much to independent development as did such Old World features as an established bureaucracy, a standing army, and an orientation to development that went beyond bourgeois materialism.

The Swedish case has allowed us to step outside conventional perspectives on Canada's development possibilities. In trying to understand why Canadian development was peculiar in an international context, we need to keep internal political factors at the centre of the discussion. Sweden's development helps to pinpoint where Canada became sidetracked from independent development.

NOTES

I am grateful to Professor Ulf Olsson of the University of Umea, Sweden, for his incisive review of this chapter. I am also indebted to Sven Nordlund of the University of Umea for permission to use and quote from a preliminary draft of his doctoral thesis. Any errors remaining in fact or interpretation are my own.

Abbreviations in this chapter:
EH: *Economy and History*
JEEH: *Journal of European Economic History*
JEH: *Journal of Economic History*
SEHR: *Scandinavian Economic History Review*
SJE: *Swedish Journal of Economics*
SJH: *Scandinavian Journal of History*
SPS: *Scandinavian Political Studies*

[1] R. Caves began his study this way: 'Most analyses of Canada's secondary manufacturing industries agree . . . these industries are condemned to relatively small-scale operation by the size of the national market and the structure of the nation's international trade. Canada's comparative advantage in primary industries together with the structure of Canadian and foreign tariffs prevent most manufacturers from exhausting the economies of scale' (Caves, 'Diversification, Foreign Investment, and Scale in North American Manufacturing Industries' [Ottawa: Economic Council of Canada, 1975], p. 3). Regarding a Canadian comparative advantage in manufactured goods vis-a-vis the US, the Macdonald Commission lists such sectors as urban transit, office furniture, petrochemicals, forestry products, agriculture, and food processing, and certain subsectors of textiles, clothing and footwear. See Canada, Royal Commission on the Economic Union and Development Prospects for Canada, *Report of the Royal Commission on the Economic Union and Development Prospects for Canada* (hereafter *Macdonald Commission Report*), vol. 1 (Ottawa: Minister of Supply and Services 1985), p. 336.

[2] Canada, *Macdonald Commission Report*, vol. 1, p. 269.

[3] C. Hopkins, *The Canadian Annual Review of 1911* (Toronto: Annual Review Publishing Co., 1912), p. 23; D. Warner, *The Idea of Continental Union* (University of Kentucky Press, 1960), p. 163; M. Wade, *The French Canadians 1760-1911*, vol. 1, rev. ed. (Toronto: Macmillan, 1968), p. 466; R.T. Naylor, *The History of Canadian Business 1867-1914*, vol. 1 (Toronto: Lorimer, 1975), p. 202.

[4]S. Clarkson, 'The Two Solitudes: Foreign Investment through the Prism of Canadian Economists' (unpublished paper presented to the Canadian Economics Association Meetings, Fredericton, N.B., 1977).

[5]Canada, *Macdonald Commission Report*, vol. 1, p. 63.

[6]R. Harris and D. Cox, *Trade, Industrial Policy and Canadian Manufacturing* (Toronto: Ontario Economic Council, 1982), p. 2.

[7]Before the historic free trade debate of 1987-88, John Turner represented the wing of the Liberal Party that accepted a classical liberal approach. See S. Clarkson, *Canada and the Reagan Challenge*, new ed. (Toronto: Lorimer, 1985), p. 352. In the 1980s New Democrats hotly debated a new social contract. Proponents advocated state intervention in the setting of wages and worker participation in management, but many accepted the comparative-advantage notion that Canada should stay with resource exporting. Opponents of a new social contract argued for free collective bargaining, a market-oriented approach. See J. Richards and D. Kerr, *Canada, What's Left? A New Social Contract pro and con* (Edmonton, Newest Press, 1986).

[8]On the left, J. Richards and L. Pratt argued that 'it would be unwise to dismiss the value to Canada of its staple industries', not only for the prairie region for which they made their case most strongly, but for Canada as a whole (*Prairie Capitalism: Power and Influence in the New West* [Toronto: McClelland and Stewart, 1977], p. 313). A. Powis, then President of Noranda and co-chairman of the Business Council on National Issues, said in 1977: 'While we might wish it were otherwise, the simple fact is that Canada's comparative advantage in world trade rests in large measure on our resources' (cited in J. Laxer, *Canada's Economic Strategy* [Toronto: McClelland and Stewart, 1981], p. 42). On the other hand, there is a growing appreciation that resources represent a declining share of the economy. See Canada, *Macdonald Commission Report*, vol. 2, p. 529.

[9]Economic Council of Canada, *Looking Outward: A New Trade Strategy for Canada* (Ottawa: Information Canada, 1975), p. 32. The Macdonald Commission held a less extreme version, recognizing that comparative-advantage theories must be modified by market failure. See R. Harris, *Trade, Industrial Policy and International Competition*, vol. 13, Macdonald Commission research reports (Toronto: University of Toronto Press, 1985), p. 37.

[10]D. J. Daly, *Rationalization and Specialization in Canadian Manufacturing*, vol. 2, Macdonald Commission research reports (Toronto: University of Toronto Press, 1986), p. 178; H.H. Postner, *Factor Content of Canadian International Trade: An Input-Output Analysis* (Ottawa: Information Canada, 1975), pp. 69, 124.

[11]This song is an unofficial national anthem of Quebec.

[12]A.S. Milward and S.B. Saul, *The Economic Development of Continental Europe 1780-1870* (London: George Allen and Unwin, 1973), pp. 481, 493; E. Heckscher, *An Economic History of Sweden* (Cambridge: Harvard University Press, 1954), p. 225.

[13]L. Jorberg, *Growth and Fluctuations of Swedish Industry 1869-1912* (Stockholm: Almquist and Wiksell, 1961), p. 27.

[14]Heckscher, *An Economic History of Sweden*, p. 209.

[15]Its railways (25 km per 10,000 inhabitants) fell short of Canadian experience (57 km), but was not that far off other New World levels: US 41 km; Australia and Argentina 44 km. See L.-E. Hedin, 'Some Notes on the Financing of the Swedish Railroads 1860-1914', *EH* 10 (1967): 5.

[16]G. Williams, *Not for Export* (Toronto: McClelland and Stewart, 1983).

[17]B.R. Mitchell, 'Statistical Appendix', in C. Cipolla, ed., *The Fontana Economic History of Europe*, vol. 4, part 2 (Glasgow: Fontana, 1973), p. 748; M.C. Urquhart and K.A.H. Buckley, *Historical Statistics of Canada*, 2nd ed. (Ottawa: Statistics Canada, 1983), Series A2-14.

[18]A. Maizels, *Industrial Growth and World Trade* (London: Cambridge University Press, 1963), p. 538.

[19]E.H. Phelps Brown and M.H. Browne, *A Century of Pay* (London: Macmillan, 1968), p. 68.

[20]K.G. Hildebrand, 'Labour and Capital in the Scandinavian Countries in the Nineteenth and

Twentieth Centuries,' in P. Mathias and M.M. Postan, eds, *The Cambridge Economic History of Europe*, vol. 7, part 1 (Cambridge: Cambridge University Press, 1978), p. 590; Jorberg, *Growth and Fluctuations*, p. 18.

[21]L. Jorberg, 'The Nordic Countries 1850-1914', in Cipolla, ed., *The Fontana Economic History of Europe*, vol. 4, part 2, p. 404; 72% were involved in farming in 1872 and 48% in 1910.

[22]In 1881, 48% of Canadians were engaged in farming; in 1911, 34% (Statistics Canada, *Historical Statistics of Canada*, 2nd ed. [Ottawa: Minister of Supply and Services, 1983] Series D1-7.)

[23]There are disagreements about whether Norway was poorer or richer than Sweden then, but it was certainly not as rich as Canada. P. Bairoch ranks Norway's per capita GNP considerably higher than Sweden's during this period ('Europe's Gross National Product 1800-1975' *JEEH* 5, no. 2 [1976]: 286). Milward and Saul argue that Norway was poorer and more backward (*Economic Development of Europe*, p. 532).

[24]Jorberg argued that Sweden's limited domestic market in the 1870s was a major obstacle to industrialization (*Growth and Fluctuations*, p. 362).

[25]Williams, *Not for Export*, p. 227.

[26]Ibid.

[27]These words were changed to 'du gamla du fria' (you ancient, you free) (F. Scott, *Sweden: The Nation's History* [Minneapolis: University of Minnesota Press, 1977], p. 326).

[28]Ibid., p. 212; K. Samuelsson, *From Great Power to Welfare State* (London: George Allen and Unwin, 1968), p. 12.

[29]Heckscher, *An Economic History of Sweden*, p. 141.

[30]T. Hamerow, *Restoration, Revolution, Reaction: Economics and Politics in Germany 1815-71* (Princeton: Princeton University Press, 1958), p. 137.

[31]The 'later-industrializing' or 'later-developing' countries include Germany as well as late followers. Germany developed late in relation to England, France and the US and it displayed many features of late-follower development. See K. Hardach, 'Some Remarks on German Economic Historiography', *JEEH* 1 (1972): 37; A. Gerschenkron, *Economic Backwardness in Historical Perspective* (Cambridge: Harvard University Press, 1962), p. 5.

[32]K. Marx and F. Engels, *The Revolution of 1848-9* (New York: International Publishers, 1972).

[33]D. Rustow, *The Politics of Compromise* (Princeton: Princeton University Press, 1955), p. 19; Rustow, 'Sweden's Transition to Democracy: Some Notes Toward a Genetic Theory', *SPS* 6 (1971): 19.

[34]F. Burns (pseud. for Gunnar Hagloff), cited in A.B. Fox, 'Sweden: Armed Neutral', *The Power of Small States: Diplomacy in World War II* (Chicago: University of Chicago Press, 1959), p. 110.

[35]Rustow, 'Sweden's Transition to Democracy,' p. 15.

[36]Heckscher, *An Economic History of Sweden*, p. 29.

[37]Ibid., p. 168; K. Tonnesson, 'Tenancy, Freehold and Enclosure in Scandinavia from the Seventeenth to the Nineteenth Century', *SJH* 6, no. 3 (1981).

[38]Heckscher, *Economic History of Sweden*, p. 130.

[39]Scott, *Sweden: The Nation's History*, p. 252.

[40]W.O. Henderson, *Britain and Industrial Europe 1750-1870* (London: Liverpool University Press, 1954), p. 1.

[41]Scott, *Sweden: The Nation's History*, p. 252.

[42]Milward and Saul, *Economic Development of Europe*, p. 472.

[43]Scott, *Sweden: The Nation's History*, p. 437.

[44]Gerschenkron, *Economic Backwardness*, p. 6.

[45]Water power rather than steam fuelled New England's early textile industry and was important, though secondary, in Lancashire.

[46]Samuelsson, *From Great Power to Welfare State*, p. 73.

[47]Heckscher, *Economic History of Sweden*, p. 183.

[48]For example, A.J. Youngson argues that in iron production 'the emergence of British industrial supremacy, manifest in the years after the close of the Napoleonic War, entailed the decline of Sweden from a very-long established position of economic power' (*The Possibilities of Economic Progress* [Cambridge: Cambridge University Press, 1959], p. 150).

[49]K. Marx, *Capital*, vol. 1 (Moscow: Progress Publishers, 1954), p. 19.

[50]W.W. Rostow, *The Stages of Economic Growth: A Non-Communist Manifesto* (London: Cambridge University Press, 1965).

[51]L. Sandberg, 'The Case of the Impoverished Sophisticate: Swedish Industrialization Before World War I', *JEH* 39, no. 1 (1979): 234.

[52]Samuelsson, *From Great Power to Welfare State*, p. 146. The growth of a pauperized rural proletariat occurred in many backward regions of Europe in the early 19th century. See D. Landes, *The Unbound Prometheus: Technological Change and Industrial Development in Western Europe from 1750 to the Present* (Cambridge: Cambridge University Press, 1969), p. 138.

[53]Heckscher, *Economic History of Sweden*, p. 172.

[54]Ibid., p. 150.

[55]Tonnesson, 'Tenancy', p. 204.

[56]Samuelsson, *From Great Power to Welfare State*, p. 21.

[57]Tonnesson, 'Tenancy', p. 206.

[58]Heckscher, *Economic History of Sweden*, p. 225.

[59]B. Boethius, 'Swedish Iron and Steel 1600-1955', *SEHR* 6, no. 1 (1958): 160.

[60]Wood products were the leading export sector.

[61]Milward and Saul, *Economic Development of Europe*, p. 482. Oats, for London's horses, was the main export crop. In the 1830s one London transport enterprise alone employed more than 300,000 horses. See Jorberg, 'The Nordic Countries', p. 104.

[62]O. Gasslander, *History of Stockholms Enskilda Bank to 1914* (Stockholm: Stockholms Enskilda Banken, 1962), p. 10.

[63]Jorberg, 'Nordic Countries', p. 105.

[64]Sweden has only a small amount of low-grade coal, not suitable for industrial purposes.

[65]Jorberg, *Growth and Fluctuations*, p. 38.

[66]C.-A. Nilsson, 'Foreign Trade and the Breakthrough of the Engineering Industry in Sweden, A Comment' *SEHR* 26, no. 2 (1978); Boethius, 'Swedish Iron and Steel', p. 154; J. Kuuse, 'The Development of the Swedish Engineering Industry: A Rejoinder', *SEHR* 26, no. 2 (1978): 165.

[67]A.R.M. Lower, *Great Britain's Woodyard. British America and the Timber Trade 1763-1867* (Montreal: McGill-Queen's University Press, 1973), p. 59.

[68]T. Williams, ' Heavy Chemicals' in C. Singer et al., eds, *A History of Technology* (Oxford: Clarendon Press, 1958), p. 252.

[69]Milward and Saul, *Economic Development of Europe*, p. 494; Scott, *Sweden: The Nation's History*, p. 447.

[70]Heckscher, *Economic History of Sweden*, p. 228.

[71]J. Kuuse, 'Foreign Trade and the Breakthrough of the Engineering Industry in Sweden 1890-1920', *SEHR* 25, no. 1 (1977): 29.

[72]Soderlund, *Swedish Timber Exports* p. 47; Milward and Saul, *Economic Development of Europe*, p. 485.

[73]Belgium may have been a partial exception. See Milward and Saul, *Economic Development of Europe*, p. 432. There is little information on Belgium's early development.

[74]H. Modig, 'The Backward Linkage Effects of Railroads on Swedish Industry, 1860-1914,' *SJE* 74, no. 3 (1972): 366.

[75]Seventeen per cent of engineering production was directed to the railroads. See B. Holgerson

and E. Nicander, 'The Railroads and Economic Development in Sweden During the 1870s', *EH* 11 (1968): 21; Milward and Saul, *Economic Development of Europe*, p. 486.

[76]In gross domestic capital terms, the level was 29% (1860s), 27% (1870s), and 46% (1880s).

[77]S. Kuznets, 'International Differences in Capital Formation Financing', in National Bureau of Economic Research, *Capital Formation and Economic Growth* (Princeton: Princeton University Press, 1955), pp. 38, 71.

[78]W.A. Williams, *The Contours of American History* (New York: New Viewpoints, 1973), p. 72.

[79]D.C. North, 'Industrialization in the United States', in *Cambridge Economic History of Europe*, vol. 6, p. 678.

[80]M. Wilkins, *The Emergence of Multinational Enterprise: American Business Abroad from the Colonial Era to 1914* (Cambridge: Harvard University Press, 1970), p. 37.

[81]G. Gibb, *The Saco-Lowell Shops, Textile Machinery Building in New England 1813-1949* (New York: Russell and Russell, 1969), p. 167; North, 'Industrialization in the United States', p. 684.

[82]Kuuse, 'Foreign Trade', p. 12.

[83]Ibid., p. 13; Scott, *Sweden: The Nation's History*, p. 453.

[84]J. Kuuse, *LM Ericsson 100 Years* (Orebro: 1976)

[85]Swedish telephone technology was also influenced by Siemens of Germany. See Kuuse, 'Foreign Trade', p. 15; Scott, *Sweden: The Nation's History*, p. 453.

[86]C.M. Jarvis, 'The Generation of Electricity; in Charles Singer et al., eds, *History of Technology*, vol. 5 (Oxford: Clarendon Press, 1958).

[87]Kuuse, 'Foreign Trade', p. 24.

[88]Ibid., p. 24.

[89]*Fortune*, 1 Aug. 1988, pp. D8-25.

[90]Scott, *Sweden*, p. 453.

[91]O.F. Ander, *The Building of Modern Sweden* (Rock Island: Augustanna, 1958), p. 41; Kuuse, 'Foreign Trade', p. 18.

[92]Kuuse, 'Foreign Trade', p. 29.

[93]Ibid.

[94]Jorberg, *Growth and Fluctuations*, pp. 80, 388, 391.

[95]The Swedish Institute, *Sweden's Foreign Trade* (Stockholm: The Swedish Institute, 1986).

[96]B. Boethius, 'Jernkontoret and the Credit problems of the Swedish Ironworks: A Survey', *SEHR* 10, no. 2 (1962); Gasslander, *Stockholms Enskilda Bank*, p. 8; Samuelsson, *From Great Power to Welfare State*, p. 94.

[97]Kuuse, 'Foreign Trade'; in 'Foreign Trade: A Comment', C.-A. Nilsson says Kuuse exaggerated the importance of the Russian market (p. 161).

[98]Kuuse, 'Foreign Trade,' p. 27.

[99]The Swedish Institute, *Sweden's Foreign Trade*.

[100]They had been reduced to a minority, however, within the nobility. See below.

[101]T. Soderberg, *Tva Sekler Medelklass* (Stockholm: Bonniers, 1972), pp. 368-73. The business class was only one component of Soderberg's 'middle class'.

[102]E. Dahmen, *Entrepreneurial Activity and the Development of Swedish Industry, 1919-1939* (Homewood: Richard D. Irwin, 1970), p. 415; Samuelsson, *From Great Power to Welfare State*, p. 163.

[103]Dahmen, *Entrepreneurial Activity*, p. 62.

[104]Samuelsson, *From Great Power to Welfare State*, pp. 22, 141; Verney, *Parliamentary Reform in Sweden 1866-1921* (Oxford: Clarendon Press, 1957), p. 93.

[105]Scott, *Sweden: The Nation's History*, p. 393.

[106]Verney, *Parliamentary Reform*, p. 92.

[107]O. Osterud, ' The Transformation of Scandinavian Agrarianism: A Comparative Study of Political Change around 1870', *SJH* 1 (1976): 203.

[108]Verney, *Parliamentary Reform*, pp. 103, 204.

[109]Rustow, *The Politics of Compromise*, p. 33.

[110]Ulf Olsson has confirmed this in private correspondence. See his *Teknologi, Statsmakt och svensk vapen produktion under fyra sekler En perspektivskiss* (Sartryck ur Ekonomisk - historika studier tillagnade Artur Attman, 1977).

[111]Ander, *The Building of Modern Sweden*, p. 12.

[112]Scott, *Sweden: The Nation's History* p. 12.

[113]H. Johansson, Foreign Business Operating in Sweden', in M. Norgren, ed., *Industry in Sweden* (Halmstad, Sweden: Swedish Institute for Cultural Relations with Foreign Countries, 1967), p. 82.

[114]W. Manchester, *The Arms of Krupp 1587-1968* (Boston: Little, Brown, 1968), p. 352.

[115]B. Braatoy, *The New Sweden* (London: Thomas Nelson and Sons, 1939), p. 88.

[116]In 1912 about 1% of the GNP or about 10% of government expenditures went to the military.

[117]A smaller railway boom in 1900-05 had much weaker effects because Sweden's economy had grown so much. See Hedin, 'Financing Swedish Railroads', p. 9.

[118]I have not seen an analysis of the politics of this legislation. Hedin suggests that state debt then demanded great restraint in expenditure ('Financing Swedish Railroads', p. 13).

[119]S. Carlsson, 'Sweden in the 1760s', in S. Koblik, ed., *Sweden's Development from Poverty to Affluence* (Minneapolis: University of Minnesota Press, 1975); Samuelsson, *From Great Power to Welfare State*, p. 104; Heckscher, *Economic History of Sweden*, p. 202.

[120]For a discussion of middle-class liberal movements see Soderberg, *Medelklass*.

[121]E. Heckscher, 'A Survey of Economic Thought in Sweden, 1875-1950', *SEHR* 1, no. 1 (1953): 105.

[122]T. Ericsson, 'The Mittelstand in Swedish Class Society, 1870-1914,' *SJH* 9, no. 4 (1984): 319.

[123]Heckscher, *Economic History of Sweden*, p. 237; J. Kuuse, 'Mechanisation, Commercialisation and the Protectionist Movement in Swedish Agriculture, 1860-1910', *SEHR* 19, no. 2 (1971): 40.

[124]Kuuse, 'Mechanisation', p. 41.

[125]Rustow, *The Politics of Compromise*, pp. 36, 75.

[126]Ibid., p. 35.

[127]Heckscher, *Economic History of Sweden*, p. 239.

[128]Samuelsson, *From Great Power to Welfare State*, p. 187.

[129]Jorberg, 'Structural Change', p. 129.

[130]Rustow, *The Politics of Compromise*, p. 40.

[131]C. Strahl, *Nationalism and Socialism. Fosterlan Det I Den Politiska Idebatten I Sverige 1890-1914* (Lund: Bibliotheca Historica Lundensis, 1983).

[132]Youngson, *Possibilities of Economic Progress*, p. 180.

[133]S. Nordlund, preliminary draft of doctoral dissertation in economic history, University of Umea.

[134]Johansson, 'Foreign Business in Sweden', p. 80.

[135]Heckscher, *Economic History of Sweden*, p. 249; K.-G. Hildebrand, 'Labour and Capital in the Scandinavian Countries in the Nineteenth and Twentieth Centuries', in H.J. Habakkuk and M. Postan, eds, *The Cambridge Economic History of Europe*, vol. 7, part 1, p. 606.

[136]Heckscher, *Economic History of Sweden*, p. 211.

[137]Skandinaviska Enskilda Banken, *Some Data About Sweden 1983-1984.* (Stockholm: SEB, 1983), p. 59.

[138]T. Bergh et al., *Growth and Development: The Norwegian Experience 1830-1980* (Oslo: Norwegian Institute of International Affairs, 1980), p. 103.

[139]A. Stonehill, *Foreign Ownership in Norwegian Enterprises* (Oslo: Central Bureau of Statistics of Norway, 1965) p. 32.

[140]Nordlund, doctoral dissertation.

[141]H.V. Nelles, *The Politics of Development: Forests, Mines and Hydro-electric Power in Ontario 1849-1941* (Toronto: Macmillan, 1974) p. 1.

[142]M. Flinn, ' Scandinavian Iron Ore Mining and the British Steel Industry 1870-1914' *SEHR* 2, no. 1 (1954): 32.

[143]E.E. Fleetwood, *Sweden's Capital Imports and Exports*, (Geneva: Journal de Genève, 1947), p. 29.

[144]Nordlund, doctoral dissertation.

[145]Stonehill, *Foreign Ownership In Norwegian Enterprises*, p. 31.

[146]Jonsson, *The State and the Ore-fields*, p. 368.

[147]K.-G. Hildebrand, *Banking in a Growing Economy: Svenska Handelsbanken 1871-1955* (Stockholm: Svenska Handelsbanken, 1972), p. 23; Gasslander, *Stockholms Enskilda Bank*, p. 345. A famous financier, Sir Ernest Cassel, owned the largest mining conglomerate in Sweden.

[148]Jonsson, *The State and the Ore-fields*, p. 373.

[149]These companies had the greatest capitalization of any in Sweden then. The state took over the other half share of these companies in the 1950s.

[150]Nordlund, doctoral dissertation.

[151]Government policy on foreign ownership in manufacturing appears to be largely unexplored, 1870 to 1914.

[152]With permission, up to one-third of the board could be foreigners. All shares could be foreign-owned (Nordlund, doctoral dissertation).

[153]If 20% or more of the shares were foreign-owned the company was considered foreign.

[154]Johansson, 'Foreign Business in Sweden', p. 82.

[155]According to the 1916 law (J. Glete, 'The Kreuger Group and the Crisis on the Swedish Stock Market' *SJH* 3 [1978]: 268).

[156]It maintained a strong position in the company until 1960 (B. Gafvert, *Kreuger, Riksbanken och Regeringen* [Stockholm: LiberForlag, 1979] p. 293).

[157]K. Samuelsson, 'The Banks and the Financing of Industry in Sweden, 1900-1927', *SEHR* 6, no. 1 (1958): 176.

[158]Strahl, *Nationalism and Socialism*.

[159]Internal regeneration was very important in Sweden but its exact contribution is unknown (Samuelsson, *From Great Power to Welfare State*, p. 199). Data on the contribution of industrial self-financing during initial industrialization is 'exceedingly meagre' (Kuznets, 'International Differences in Capital Formation Financing', p. 19).

[160]R. Cameron, ed., *Banking and Economic Development: Some Lessons of History* (New York: Oxford University Press, 1972), p. 5.

[161]Jorberg presents these growth rates in current prices, which has the effect of slightly overestimating them in comparison to earlier rates (*Growth and Fluctuations*, p. 38).

[162]S. Bjorklund, *Oppositionen vid 1823 ars riksdag* (Uppsala: Scandinavian University Books, 1964).

[163]I. Nygren, 'Transformation of Bank Structures', *JEEH* 12, no. 1 (1983): 30.

[164]Sweden is the oldest European country to have had continuous circulation of bank notes (Sandberg, 'The Case of the Impoverished Sophisticate', p. 240).

[165]Nygren, 'Transformation of Bank Structures', p. 310.

[166]Britain was an exception (Gasslander, *Stockholms Enskilda Bank*, p. 8).

[167]Fears about risks for depositors and holders of bank notes lay behind rejection of this style of German banking (Gasslander, *Stockholms Enskilda Bank*, p. 274).

[168]Newly emerging credit institutions and the declining system centred on the National Bank were geared towards financing agricultural reform and the export of farm products (Nygren, 'Transformation of Bank Structures', p. 33).

[169]Ibid., p. 38.

[170]T. Hedlund-Nystrom, 'The Finance Act of 1862 and its Effects on the Economy', *EH* 15 (1972): 81.

[171]Nygren, 'Transformation of Bank Structures', p. 36.

[172]The Stockholms Enskilda Bank merged with the Skandinaviska Bank in the 1970s to form the Skandinaviska Enskilda Bank.

[173]Gasslander, *Stockholms Enskilda Bank*, p. 12.

[174]J. Potter, 'The Role of a Swedish Bank in the Process of Industrialization, A Review Article', *SEHR* 11 (1963): 71.

[175]Gasslander, *Stockholms Enskilda Bank*, pp. 289, 510.

[176]Ibid., p. 212.

[177]Ibid., p. 29.

[178]Hildebrand, *Svenska Handelsbanken*, p. 7.

[179]Sandberg, 'Banking and Economic Growth in Sweden', p. 667.

4

The Politics of Dependent Industrialization

The wellsprings of human freedom lie not only where Marx saw them, in the aspirations of classes about to take power, but perhaps even more in the dying wail of a class over whom the wave of progress is about to roll.

Barrington Moore Jr, 1960.

We are bound hand and foot, and lie helplessly at the feet of the Catholic priests of Lower Canada who can laugh to scorn all our convulsive efforts for freedom ... When the civil, political and religious degradation in which we are placed is fully realized, we shall hear very little in Upper Canada of the cry 'Tory' and 'Reformer'. These distinctions will be swept away and another very different organization of parties will be formed.

The North American *(Clear Grit press), 1850.*

Tell us what you want and we will give you what you need. The politician is the little boy who climbs the tree to shake down acorns to the hogs below.

John A. Macdonald in an address to businessmen.

Our colonies are rather too fond of us, and embrace us, if anything, too closely.

The Times *(London), 1864.*

The notable fact is that in all this era of constitution making, and of constitution testing in the decades just after 1867, the voice of democratic radicalism was so weak.

Frank Underhill, 1946.

There are probably not a thousand men in Canada who would call for protection if the United States would consent to free trade.

The Toronto Mail *(Conservative paper), 1878.*

Most observers thought Canada had two choices in the immediate post-Confederation period: it could achieve a limited degree of economic independence and industrial development via the National Policy and the British connection, or it could opt for a resource-oriented strategy through economic integration with the United States. A third possibility—full economic independence—was dismissed as a farce by John A. Macdonald and successive generations of Canadian historians.[1]

Was the achievement of an independent industrial economy a realizable dream for Canada? Economic factors in themselves would suggest it was. As has been noted, Canada was the eighth largest manufacturing country in the world in 1867. Furthermore, Sweden and Japan, starting from weaker economic positions, overcame their respective staple-exporting and colonial-economic handicaps to develop independent industrial economies.

In a seminal article written in the 1960s, Mel Watkins argued that Canada's National Policy of tariff protection for domestic industry, public subsidies for railways to the west, and immigration was little more than a copy of the 'American system' of the 1820s.[2] Henry Clay had conceived the American system to be an alternative to a colonial or 'British system' of free trade. After assessing the Canadian version of the American system as inadequate, because Canada developed later and in an élitist way, Watkins raised the question of a third possibility for Canada: the 'European system'.

By 'European system' Watkins meant the institutional changes that Alexander Gerschenkron has shown were crucial for the independent industrial development of the 'backward' countries of Europe. (This system was discussed as the 'independent route' to late-follower development in Chapter 2.)

In the late nineteenth and early twentieth centuries backward European countries rejected the economic liberalism that was trumpeted as the new religion in the early industrial starters, especially England; instead, they adopted strong state-interventionist strategies for economic development. Yet while the Canadian case may appear similar, Watkins concluded that here the much celebrated intervention of the state to promote development was little more than a response to the American 'threat'. Moreover, the state refrained from ushering in valuable policies for fear of acting against the interests of the ruling élite: 'It is arguable that the Canadian government, rather than being praised by historians for what it has done, should be chastised for what it has failed to do.'[3]

This chapter begins where Watkins left off. It attempts to explain why the post-Confederation Canadian state failed to champion the independent route, or European system, which was more favourable to independent industrial development.

THE AGRARIAN FACTOR

As we saw in Chapter 2, the independent route entailed major institutional changes. Of crucial significance was the invention of investment banking, first successfully developed in Germany, which transformed banks from conservative, no-risk pillars of the establishment to entrepreneurial and technological innovators. One alternative was the system adopted in Japan, where the state took the place of investment banks during the early years of modern development.

Another alternative to the European investment banks that, while not as efficient in transferring domestic capital to the industrialization process, went far beyond the strictly commercial banks, was the system of 'free' or 'unit' banks. Organized as local institutions without ties to national commercial banks, these were the English-speaking world's variant of investment banks. They were present in England during initial industrialization,[4] in the United States from the 1830s, and in Confederation-era New Brunswick and Nova Scotia. Unit banks lent money more readily to local entrepreneurs than did large centralized banks because, as local men, the unit bankers were personally acquainted with their clients and hence with the human risks involved.

American industrial policy was changed in the 1830s by the farmer-led destruction of commercial banking and its replacement by hundreds, and eventually thousands, of small unit banks: this was a modification of the American financial system in the direction of the European model. Thus Watkins' description of Canada's National Policy (1879-1930) as a carbon copy of the American system was accurate in so far as it referred to the original, unreformed American system. But Canada rejected, as we shall see, the modified and more fruitful version.

Government restraint was another element of the independent route. If the state refrained from extravagant spending and ensured cheaply built transportation, communications, and defence systems, the need to import foreign capital would be reduced. Late-follower countries tended towards frugal public spending, while at the same time borrowing foreign money to accelerate development. Foreign direct (ownership) investment, on the other hand, was usually restricted.

A third institutional modification involved technological sovereignty. It meant generating methods of production that fitted a country's unique circumstances, including wage levels, consumer tastes, resource endowments, special skills, and size of markets. Retention of domestic ownership and management of industry was crucial to this process, enabling late-follower countries either to develop a limited range of techniques on their own, as in Sweden, or else to borrow and adapt techniques from the advanced countries, as in Japan and Italy.

There was another route by which late-follower countries could progress. The dependent or easy road to rapid development was the result of failing to adopt the institutional changes of the European system (or its equivalent, as in Japan) during initial industrialization. It was purchased at the price of diminished political, economic, and technological sovereignty. Canada was the only late-follower country that clearly took this route (czarist Russia partly did) and the only one that did not achieve an independent and fully developed manufacturing economy.

Adopting the independent route or European system during initial industrialization would have led to sharp confrontations between ordinary Canadians and the ruling élite. But this fact itself raises further questions. Why did the power of big business remain unchallenged in a new settler society with a broad electoral franchise? Why did Canadian farmers (owner-operators), who comprised the largest component of the labour force from 1870 to 1914, not have the dominant influence on government policies that their counterparts did elsewhere? Why were popular-democratic movements so feeble during the formative period in which the nation-state was established and the industrial structure set in its branch-plant, resource-exporting mould? Why was the Canadian state not strongly nationalist during this time? In asking these questions we go beyond Grant's problem of why Canadian businessmen put profits above country, to an analysis of the weakness of popular economic nationalism in Canada during the age of autarky.

Nationalist/continentalist categories first arose in the National Policy debates a hundred years ago, and they still affect our thinking in unconscious ways. The traditional reasoning holds that the conservative nationalism of Canada's National Policy was predicated on the power of élite elements, a whiggish political philosophy, and the British tie, while continentalism resulted from American liberal and democratic influences among Canada's farmers.[5] I reject this dichotomy and argue instead that the feeble 'nationalism of the National Policy'[6] resulted from the inability of Canada's ordinary people—principally farmers but also workers—to impress themselves on the political system. Nineteenth-century nationalism was born, after all, with the popular struggle for democracy.[7]

It may strike the reader as odd that farmers should be seen as the potential champions of an independent industrial economy. Why would farmers wish to develop an industrial society at all, let alone one controlled by Canadian rather than foreign capitalists? One might think that industrial workers were the obvious alternative to representatives of big business as leaders in Canadian development.

Canadian farmers did not, for the most part, consciously seek to build an independent industrial Canada during initial industrialization. Far from it.[8] Most were simply trying to develop their farms and prevent the incursions of industrial capitalism into their lives and their communities. But that does not mean that the objective consequences of policies advocated by organized farming groups would not have led to a variant of the European system. The outcomes of popular struggles against injustices do not always coincide with the movements' goals; consequence is not the same as intention. We shall see that, in fact, farmer-led movements in Canada, while generally seeking goals unrelated to independent industrial development, advocated policies that might have led to development along the lines of the European system.

This reason alone, of course, does not justify a focus Canada's on farmers: one must ask whether they could have gained state power or shared it with other social classes during initial industrialization. My answer is yes. We know from Canadian history and from comparative studies of other societies that farmers' movements and parties were the main alternative to rule by big business in that phase of development. The reasons why Canadian farmers did not successfully use their potential political strength to gain or share power, then, are the focus of this chapter.

To make relevant comparisons between societies, one must often look at one time period for the first country and a different period for the second. In regard to industrial development, societies should be compared at those economic and social phases when the forces of town and country, farmers, industrial workers, and the various sections of the bourgeoisie were comparable in numbers and in strength. Thus Canada's politics of initial industrialization (1870-1914) should be compared with those of an earlier United States (1825-1860), an even earlier Britain (1760s-1830s), or a later Australia (1900-1940s). To examine the power of farmers' movements in the United States and Canada at contemporaneous periods in the nineteenth century, for example, would be misleading because the industrial revolution created manufacturers and workers as new forces in the US at an earlier point. American farmers and plantation owners had more difficulty influencing the state in post-Civil War, already-industrialized America than they did in the pre-Civil War, early-industrializing years.[9]

In the decades leading up to the 1837 rebellions, strong popular-democratic movements arose in Lower and Upper Canada to challenge the rule of British governors and local merchant-landlord cliques. In Lower Canada the Parti Canadien and Patriote movements—led by professionals such as doctors and lawyers—had their main base of support among the habitant farmers of Lower Canada.[10] In election after election the popular nationalists won overwhelming victories[11] to the largely impotent legislature. In Upper Canada the course of popular democracy was slightly different. The class conflict—between farmers and the urban petite bourgeoisie on the one side, and commercial capitalists and land speculators on the other—was similar. But the Upper Canadian contest lacked the element of national subordination to an alien élite that so heightened the conflict in French Lower Canada. In an economy still based on agriculture and forestry, the Reformers in Upper Canada were led by urban small businessmen and professionals who derived their main support from farm districts. An industrial working class was not yet in evidence, although urban 'mechanics' (artisans and workers) were a secondary element in Reform strength.[12] Upper Canadian Reformers did not enjoy the overwhelming support accorded to their counterparts in Lower Canada and had to settle for alternating electoral victories with the Tory élite.[13] Even when the reformers won at the polls in Upper and Lower Canada, the colonial state never passed into their hands, because Britain continued to rule.

Popular-democratic movements were largely absent in the Maritimes during this period. Unconcerned with any threat from below, New Brunswick's politics revolved around a struggle between small lumbermen and local merchant princes, who were sometimes allied and sometimes at odds with the coterie of officials surrounding the lieutenant-governor. Farmers, the majority of the population, were peripheral to this contest.[14] Nova Scotia was even more quiescent. Political contests ran along two lines: religious divisions and the influence of Halifax versus the outports. The occasional critic of Halifax's oligarchic rule was quickly absorbed into the establishment.[15] Only in Prince Edward Island, the sole Maritime province where agriculture dominated the economy, were there signs of much popular unrest in the early 1800s: between 1834 and 1842 a movement of tenant farmers, the 'Escheat Party', attempted to wrest control of island land from the few powerful alien landowners to which it had been granted in 1767.[16]

The 1837-38 rebellions in the Canadas convinced Britain that a second American revolution was in the making, and democratic home rule was conceded within a decade. Yet when elective government came and popular control of the state was possible, farmer-led movements of reform fell on hard times, for reasons that are at the heart of this chapter. For now, it is sufficient to point out that, despite their weakness, agrarian-based movements continued to be the only alternative to business rule.

After 1837, over the next eighty years of nation-building and industrial transformation, farmers' movements flickered, on occasion brightly. Once, in 1894, the farmers' Patrons of Industry came close to winning office in Ontario. They had numbers on their side in that era: in 1881 the agricultural work force (mainly owner-operators) made up 48 per cent of the total labour force.[17] But as a stratum for itself the agrarian element had little influence on state policy during this formative period.

It was only in the years 1919 to 1922, after initial industrialization was completed and farmers were reduced to one-third of the labour force, that agrarian political movements again held centre stage. Aided by significant numbers of Labour members, these movements took office in three provinces, including Ontario, and showed strength even in such unlikely places as the Maritimes, British Columbia, and Quebec.[18] In the federal election of 1921 the farmers' Progressive Party won a third of the seats, mostly from the Prairie provinces.[19]

No such flowering of political strength was seen among workers and their allies before, during, or after initial industrialization. Individual labour MPs here, a handful of Independent Labour Party members there—even, briefly, the (Marxist) Socialist Party of Canada as official opposition in British Columbia just before the First World War—did not constitute a serious bid for power by working-class movements.[20] Nor was a syndicalist route to power possible, as the 1919 Winnipeg General Strike showed.

Labour demonstrated somewhat greater electoral strength immediately after the First World War, but it was overshadowed by the farmers' surge. The

Co-operative Commonwealth Federation (CCF) was formed in 1933, well after initial industrialization was over. It was as much an agrarian- as a worker-based party, and never came close to winning a national election.[21] Thus in Canada the idea of a government dominated or even heavily influenced by an organized and determined working class during initial industrialization would have been a fantasy.[22] But the possibility of farmer political power was, as Arthur Meighen stressed in 1921, entirely real.[23]

Evidence in other countries confirms the political weakness of the working class during initial industrialization. Only in France, Russia, and Australia did workers develop a precocious organization and consciousness at the stage when their numbers could still be overwhelmed by the rural classes. And even in those countries the working class was far from all-powerful. In highly centralized France, where the initial industrialization phase stretched almost interminably from roughly 1785 to 1870, the Parisian working class could topple governments, but could not make them in its own image: after the 1789 revolution the power of the conservative peasantry stood in the way.[24] The Russian Revolution of 1917 was led by workers and soldiers drawn largely from the peasantry and occurred towards the end of initial industrialization (1880s to 1930s). It succeeded only in the unusual context of state disintegration after defeat at war. Peasant acquiescence and some peasant support were crucial to consolidation of Bolshevik power after the October Revolution.[25] In 1910, at the beginning of manufacturing development in Australia, the Labour Party came to office with a program offering substantial change. The victory of Labour at so early a point in Australian history was due, in part, to the triumph of capitalist agriculture over the family farm. Agricultural workers made up a large part of the labour force and minimized the divisions between town and country that weakened the working class elsewhere.[26]

Yet if the weakness of Canada's working class was not unusual, the weakness of its agrarians was. During the transition period to industrial capitalism, it was no doubt easier for aristocratic landlords to rule in older societies than it was for independent farmers to hold or share elected power in new settler societies. Aristocrats, the ruling class in the pre-industrial order, generally could retain power by holding the line against the rising tide of democracy and popular nationalism. Farmer power in new settler societies, however, required an early and quick victory for a broad franchise and representation in or control of government. This victory came at an early point in the new settler societies of the United States, Australia, and New Zealand, where popular-democratic movements quickly swept away parties openly advocating rule by large property holders.[27] In some older societies, such as Sweden, the transition to democracy did not spell the diminution of agrarian political power, at least for a while: as the power of the Swedish rural nobility began to decline in the 1870s and 1880s, the influence of independent farmers grew.[28] Canada, however, did not share the tendency to agrarian political influence during initial industrialization, and this needs to be explained.

It may seem that the emphasis here on agrarian movements should lead to a focus on the hinterland movements in the Maritimes and the west. For most of initial industrialization, however, the west had a small population and fewer than 10 per cent of the parliamentary seats. It was only in 1903 and 1907 that western representation rose to 15 per cent, reflecting the rapid settlement of the prairies in those years. Prairie populism was just beginning, and its main impact was not felt until after the First World War, by which time the branch-plant structure was firmly established. Since our purpose is to examine state policies leading to branch-plant development, we must look at the period before the rise of western agrarian movements.

What of the Maritimes provinces, which had more people and greater political weight than the west during most of the period (21 per cent of the seats in the 1870s and 16 per cent in 1907)? For the most part they failed to influence the nature of politics in Canada. The major parties had begun to emerge in central Canada in the 1850s, and Maritime politicians, like their western counterparts, were only gradually incorporated into their structures in the quarter-century after Confederation.[29] As a result, the class character of parties from central Canada had the decisive influence on post-Confederation politics.

AGRARIAN POLITICAL WEAKNESS IN CANADA

The Loyalists, the Conquest, and populist movements

Canada has been described as organically conservative, hierarchical, deferential, and not given to the extremes of the republican and liberal experiment to the south. Instead of the triumph of the popular democracy of an Andrew Jackson, we had the victory of people like Sir Francis Bond Head, the lieutenant-governor who put down Upper Canada's agrarian-based rebellion in 1837-38. 'That I was sentenced to contend on the soil of America with Democracy,' said Bond Head, 'and that if I did not overpower it, it would overpower me, were solemn facts . . . evident to my mind.'[30] British appointees were not the only ones with anti-democratic sentiments. In arguing for an unelected Senate, John A. Macdonald contended that 'a large qualification should be necessary . . . in order to represent the principle of property. The rights of the minority must be protected, and the rich are always fewer in number than the poor.'[31]

The common explanation for Canadian conservatism (as opposed to neo-conservatism) is based on Canada's rejection of the ideas of the Enlightenment.[32] As Frank Underhill put it: 'Our ancestors made the great refusal in the 18th century. In Canada we have no revolutionary tradition; and our historians, political scientists, and philosophers have assiduously tried to educate us to be proud of this fact'.[33] Seymour Martin Lipset, an American political sociologist with a lifelong interest in Canada, attributes 'the variations between Canada and the United States' to

> the founding event which gave birth to both, the American Revolution ... English-speaking Canada exists because she opposed the Declaration of Independence; French-speaking Canada ... also sought to isolate herself from the anti-clerical democratic values of the French Revolution. The leaders of both cultures after 1783 and 1789, consciously attempted to create a conservative, monarchical and ecclesiastical society in North America.[34]

Gad Horowitz took up this theme in his famous thesis regarding the un-American and less 'congealed' character of Canada's liberal, 'fragment' culture.[35] The relative strength of socialism in Canada and its weakness in the United States can be explained, Horowitz argued, as a reaction to Canadian tory notions of class hierarchy and organic conceptions of the community.[36] In contrast, reactionary politics in the United States emphasized the liberty of the individual, especially the freedom of enterprise, giving birth not to communitarian ideas of socialism, but to a progressive liberalism, with an individualist emphasis on equality.

While toryism may have eventually led to a later socialist reaction in the twentieth century, as Horowitz contended, agrarian radicalism fared poorly after 1837. This was partly because the Loyalist tradition of associating liberal and democratic movements with Americanization undercut those advocating an agrarian popular democracy. As late as 1946, it could still be said that 'every Canadian movement of the Left ... has had to meet the accusations of Americanism, and in proving its sound British patriotism it has been apt to lose a good deal of its Leftism'.[37] Loyalism was reinforced in every generation in the nineteenth century—during the War of 1812, the 1837 rebellions, the US Civil War, and at the time of American annexationist sentiment in the 1880s and 1890s.

This conservative, anti-American tradition was strengthened by Canada's pattern of immigration and emigration. Despite the presence of many Americans, the character of English Canada was influenced to a greater extent by British immigrants who occupied leading positions in Canadian society in the latter half of the nineteenth century.[38] Orangemen, retired military officers, and younger sons and daughters of the British gentry entered and stayed in large numbers, while those of more liberal and democratic persuasions tended either to avoid the destination in the first place or else to move on after a short stay.[39]

But the rejection of the American Revolution by tory Loyalists is not the place to begin an inquiry into the weakness of agrarian democracy in Canada. We must look to an earlier time in our history. The British Conquest of Quebec was the founding episode to which the later train of events, including Loyalist immigration, must be traced. To explain the formative effect of the Conquest it is best to turn—at least within English Canada—away from historians and political scientists, to the literary critic Northrop Frye. In 1952, even before Michel Brunet,[40] Frye commented on the order of events that made Canada distinctive:

> Historically a Canadian is an American who rejects the Revolution. *Canada fought its civil war to establish its union first, and its wars of independence, which were fought against the United States and not Europe, came later.* The Canadian point of view is at once more conservative and more radical than [the American].[41] (Emphasis added.)

Why did the forced union of English and French in Canada lead to the decline of agrarian-based populism after the 1837 rebellions? To answer that question we must step back and look at the more usual development of liberal democracy in new settler societies.

Liberalism rests on beliefs about private productive property and the market economy, but it does not necessarily imply political democracy. In fact, democracy was added on to liberalism in every Western society that later adopted a liberal-democratic system.[42] The transition from an aristocracy to a liberal democracy usually occurred when substantial property holdings began to replace inherited social position as the key to political rights. This was the period in which whiggery or plutocracy (rule by the rich) was the dominant ideology. An American Federalist (Whig) and friend of Daniel Webster captured the essence of this view: 'As the wealth of the commercial and manufacturing classes increases, in the same degree ought their political power to increase.'[43]

Whiggery usually found fertile soil in older societies with feudal pasts, where aristocratic and plutocratic bases for political rights could co-exist, if uneasily. In new settler societies in temperate climates, where slavery or new types of serfdom could not be established easily, plutocratic ideologies generally withered quickly in the rising tide of nineteenth-century democracy.[44] This was the case in Australia and New Zealand. Even in the United States, where an 'aristocracy' of slave-owning planters arose in the southern states, the Federalist and Whig parties died by the 1840s. Canada was the exception. Even though feudalism never had deep roots here,[45] plutocratic ideology—often referred to as the British conservatism of restraint—had a surprisingly long life. The question is why this was so.

The unusual character of nineteenth-century Canadian politics was not the result of a peculiar class structure. Canada's social formation was typical of new settler societies (with small aboriginal populations) transplanted from northwestern Europe. Rather, Canada's political divergence was based on non-class factors related to the Conquest of Quebec and, for a time, the economics of British colonial preference.

During the American Revolution the merchants had joined forces with southern planters and free agrarians to demand independence from colonial rule and a broadening of democratic rights. This was the usual stance of emerging capitalists in the age of revolutionary liberalism. From the time of the French Revolution of 1789 until the 1848 uprisings, pre-industrial bourgeoisies in northwestern Europe made alliances with the more numerous classes—farmers, artisans, shopkeepers, and urban plebeians—with the aim of ending autocratic power.[46] To be sure, capitalists were most often on the moderate wing of democratic movements, fearing that mass democracy might lead to a revolution from below. Nevertheless, as a rule they favoured an extension of the franchise and an elected rather than appointed executive.

In Canada the bourgeoisie started off in the usual way. A small number of British-American merchants moved to Montreal between the Conquest (1760) and the Constitution Act (1791), took over most of the fur trade from the French merchants, and began to make the political demands typical of their class: representative government for the middle class and an end to British military rule. But as soon as their campaign for a legislative assembly succeeded in the 1790s, they abruptly reversed their position and henceforth provided the strongest support for continued British colonialism and the arbitrary rule of appointed officials.[47] Why the sudden change of heart?

In what was to become a firm pattern in Canadian history, the ethno-national question overshadowed political divisions along class lines. By carving out a separate colony for Loyalist settlers in Upper Canada in 1791, Britain left the growing number of English-speaking merchants in Montreal surrounded by a sea of French Canadian habitants in Lower Canada. Even though the British were greatly over-represented, French Canadians controlled the legislature of Lower Canada. John Richardson, the leader of the Montreal merchants, expressed his frustrations as an elected representative in the new legislature: 'Nothing can be so irksome as the situation of the English members—without numbers to do any good—doomed to the necessity of combating the absurdities of the majority, without hope of success.'[48]

The attitude of French Canadian politicians disturbed Richardson and his friends. Instead of pushing for freedom of enterprise and capitalist progress, as Montreal's big capitalists expected of a parliament, the francophone majority used representative government to win recognition for their national rights and to champion the class interests of small-holding farmers who opposed many of the aims of commercial business.[49] The merchants' answer was to help curtail the power of the colonial legislature. They turned against liberal democracy and supported a reactionary and colonial brand of whiggery.

British reaction to American secession after 1783 reinforced the stance of Canada's nascent bourgeoisie. British industrialists had as yet little influence on government policy, and colonial strategy was based on defence of the Empire. In this early period (1783-1846) colonial resources, even if more expensive, were favoured over those from non-Empire sources. Montreal merchants prospered; it was quite natural that for economic reasons they would oppose movements for colonial independence and popular democracy that threatened colonial preference.

Yet, despite these factors contributing to the longevity of whig ideas in the Canadas, there were strong popularly based movements for the extension of political democracy and greater home rule in the 1820s and 1830s. These movements expressed the petit-bourgeois class interests of the farmers, professionals, tradesmen, and artisans, interests that clashed with those of the big merchants on several issues. Popular movements wanted public expenditures redirected from canals for commerce to roads for agriculture.[50] The level of expenditures was another point of contention. The corrupt practices of local ruling cliques were bitterly resented by reformers and added to state costs. Would the taxes to pay for government expenditures be imposed on commerce (tariffs) or agriculture (land taxes)? Land, the major resource of unsettled areas, was at the centre of the debate. Farmers wanted cheap land for family farms, while colonial officials and commercial interests favoured speculation and vast land grants for private land companies, the established churches, and the state. Finally, questions about the nature of credit institutions tended to divide along debtor (farmer) versus creditor (commerce) lines.

Class conflicts over these issues formed much of the basis for the great battle between commerce and agriculture that was fought out in the 1837-38 rebellions in Lower and Upper Canada.[51] As well, these conflicts reflected political ideas prevalent abroad. The reform movement in Britain, the democratic ferment in neighbouring American states, and the French Revolution of 1830 inspired reformers in both colonies to campaign for democracy, local government, and greater autonomy.[52] The popular movements were spearheaded by the farming community and their professional and artisanal allies in the towns. On the opposing side, the merchant colonial-official faction generally stood for restrictions against popularly elected assemblies, for government-granted privileges to the wealthy, loyalty to Britain, and the unity of the Canadian provinces. Agricultural crisis added a sense of urgency to the reformers' political grievances.[53]

Division between the representatives of commerce and farming occurred in both Upper and Lower Canada. Common class interests overrode those of ethno-nationality as the rebellions approached, and popular movements in both Upper and Lower Canada favoured an alliance between reformers in the two provinces.[54] Although many of the leaders of the insurrectionary movement in Lower Canada were of Irish or American origin, the class conflict there was deepened by national divisions paralleling the class cleavages, with the Anglo-dominated business élite and its allies on one side and the French Canadian rural and middle classes on the other. Papineau's Parti Canadien stood for the national rights of French Canada as well as for the farming majority.

The events of the rebellions are well known and need not be repeated here.

The consequence of their collapse was that the whig philosophy and the political power of business became entrenched and remained dominant in Canada throughout the second half of the nineteenth century—the very time when the state was established and industrialization began. The main drive for Canadian independence was taken up by the plutocratic commercial capitalists. This was to have major implications for the kind of economic strategy Canada would pursue.

SECTIONALISM AND POPULAR-DEMOCRATIC MOVEMENTS

Canadian farmers and workers did not step aside after 1837-38 and allow the plutocrats to prevail unopposed. In almost every decade from the 1850s until the First World War, significant popular-democratic movements challenged the power of commercial and industrial capitalists. Unfortunately, most of these movements fell into the trap of French/English division. In this context big business ruled with ease and even allowed itself the luxury of public expressions of internal divisions—manufacturers versus bankers and railway magnates, for example.[55]

Things started off on a familiar footing in the 1850s. Agrarian radicalism had been temporarily eclipsed in the previous decade when moderate whigs led the campaign for responsible government and democratic home rule. But once responsible government was achieved in 1848 and the former leaders of the rebellions returned from exile, it seemed that class divisions would again dominate politics. Small independent farmers began to rally against the whiggery of big commerce.

This was a time when a railway clique ran the government and granted itself public largesse on an enormous scale. Allan MacNab, tory land speculator, hunter of rebels, and future premier of the united Province of Canada, captured the essence of the era when he boasted, 'All my politics are railroad'.[56] Nine of the nineteen directors of the Grand Trunk, the major railway of the province, were government members. The chief solicitor for the railway, George-Étienne Cartier, changed hats when he entered Parliament to become chairman of its Railway Committee.

It was against this union of state and capital that popular movements began to rally. In Upper Canada the Clear Grits carried the flame for popular democracy; in Lower Canada, the Rouges. Several issues inspired these agrarian-based groups. To the farmer, the state represented the rich, with its government-sponsored projects, its defence of the last vestiges of serfdom in Lower Canada, and its granting of public lands to the established churches. As debtors, agrarians wanted freer credit. They also saw the extension of elective government as a way of breaking down class rule.

Before the Clear Grits and the Rouges could make common cause, however, a sectional battle between English and French eclipsed those class-based issues. In the aftermath of the rebellions Upper and Lower

Canada had been merged into the single Province of Canada to further Lord Durham's aim of 'altering the character' of French Canada in order to assimilate it.[57] The union forced the question of how English and French would co-exist within a unitary state now consisting of Canada West and Canada East.

The anti-democratic élite of Montreal—composed of Scots, Americans, Englishmen, and a sprinkling of French Canadians—together with business interests in Canada West, found they could still rule under responsible government if they made concessions to the French Canadians.[58] Moderate reformers in Canada West led by Baldwin and Hincks joined the new élite alliance. Under this conservative *modus vivendi* English Canadian big business would recognize French Canadian rights as long as conservative, Church, and entrepreneurial elements in French Canada supported its schemes.[59]

In contrast to the élites in French and English Canada, which did manage to forge alliances, the early popular-democratic movements found it difficult to establish working relations across ethno-national lines. Élite unity and popular disunity have been constant elements in Canadian history ever since. It was the Clear Grits of Canada West who first raised the cry of 'French domination' in 1850 and so contributed to the development of political cleavage along sectional rather than class lines. Their press forecast such a development: 'We are bound hand and foot, and lie helplessly at the feet of the Catholic priests of Lower Canada ... When the civil, political and religious degradation in which we are placed is fully realized, we shall hear very little in Upper Canada of the cry "Tory" and "Reformer".'[60] The Clear Grits championed the sectional issues of the day, opposing a publicly supported Catholic school system in Canada West and calling for 'representation by population' as soon as it was discovered that such a principle would make French Canada a minority within a unitary state.[61]

The Rouges were not disposed towards an alliance with a xenophobic and anti-Catholic movement in English Canada. Despite their anti-clericalism, and in some cases their agnosticism, the Rouges 'believed in Catholicism as ... a national institution. They rejected its doctrines and beliefs, but they preserved an almost unshakeable confidence in the institutional role of religion.'[62] Although their support was based mainly in the farming districts of the Montreal region and the Eastern Townships, the Rouges were more than simply another North American agrarian movement.[63] In conquered Lower Canada they were the nationalists, hostile to British rule and to assimilation. They criticized

> that perfect labyrinth of laws, of manners and of language, which imposes on us a double nationality, so as to render the one necessary, the other useless ... to make us lose ours and adopt the other ... We only wish for one thing, the preservation of our language, our laws and our customs.[64]

Thus, despite the remarkable similarity in their political philosophies and programs, the possibility of a broad class-based alliance between the Rouges and the Clear Grits was remote.[65]

In this situation the popular movements of the two Canadas weakened each other. Under severe pressure from a reactionary and theocratic church, the Rouges were seen to be splitting the unity of French Canada in the face of anti-French campaigns in Canada West. For their part, the Clear Grits buried their class differences with big commerce in order to strengthen the campaign against 'French domination'; to this end they joined with their former enemy, George Brown of the *Globe* (after his 'no Popery' campaign). Brown represented the emerging merchants of southern Ontario, who were beginning to rival Montreal's élite for economic and political dominance. The Brownites and Clear Grits created the Reform Party (later the Liberal Party), in which big-business interests and whiggery prevailed over small-business populism.[66] Sectionalism had triumphed over class as the basis for political struggle.

In the 1870s and again in the 1890s, two farmer movements emerged to challenge the policies of the capitalist-oriented state and the power of Canada's big-business class. The Dominion Grange (Patrons of Husbandry), with 31,000 members in the late 1870s, was succeeded by the Patrons of Industry, which claimed double those numbers in 1894. Both movements were based mainly in Ontario, but they also showed strength in Manitoba and the Maritimes, and among Anglophone farmers in Quebec.[67]

These organizations were typical of movements of small versus big business at the time. The Grange wanted an end to the monopoly aspects of capitalism but not to capitalism itself. It opposed the exactions of the middlemen, who stood between agrarian producers and urban consumers. Lack of access to farm credit was another major concern, leading the Grange to advocate government ownership of all banks as a way of breaking the monopoly of the commercial banks.[68] It urged public ownership of railways, telephones, and telegraphs for similar reasons.

The concerns of the Patrons of Industry were much the same. At base there was resentment over the maldistribution of wealth. It seemed to the Patrons that those who engaged in physical toil, the 'producers', earned the least, while those employed in non-physical occupations did not create wealth but earned the most.[69] The Patrons favoured low-cost government, tariffs for revenue but not for industrial protection, and an extension of democratic rights. They opposed railway control of prairie land.[70] (The Patrons entered the Ontario election in 1894 and to their own surprise almost captured the government. Seventeen members were elected; a 3 per cent swing in their favour would have led to a plurality of Patron members.)[71]

Agrarian movements in Canada from the 1850s to the 1930s were overwhelmingly petit-bourgeois in character, representing the interests of owner-operators in the struggle to preserve the family farm. Other participants in agriculture—farm labourers, tenant farmers, seigneurs, forced labourers—played an insignificant role. Early forms of forced labour had fallen into disuse in the early 1800s,[72] and the seigneurs lost their privileges in the mid-1850s, while tenant farmers were few in number and usually on the way to becoming proprietors.[73] Farm labourers, comprising about one-fifth of the male agricultural work force in 1891 and less than that earlier, were the only group of significant size apart from the agricultural small-business class. They failed, however, to form cohesive communities and bring their weight to bear on the political system. The majority were irregular or seasonal labourers who moved in and out of an agricultural working class, while another large portion were the sons (rarely the daughters) of farm proprietors. Only a small number were permanent hired hands. Thus agrarian movements in Canada were of and by the small business class, the latter comprising all family members.[74]

Labour shared many of the objectives of farmers, and attempts were made to forge a farmer/labour alliance to strengthen the 'producing classes' against the 'monopolists'. In 1886 and again in 1893-94 serious efforts were made to unite the two groups. But although some co-operation did occur around Patrons of Industry candidates in the 1894 Ontario election, an alliance was not to be.[75] The failure of those efforts may have been due partly to their timing: in 1886 labour was at its zenith and the farmers' movement at a low ebb, while in 1893-94 the reverse was true. More important, however, were the differences in the two groups' class interests. As self-employed businessmen, farmers found labour's demand for an eight-hour day hilarious, and, as occasional employers of casual labour, costly. Similarly, labour opposed government-assisted immigration, a cheap source of agricultural labour but a threat to workers.[76] Thus class differences in Canada prevented the formation of farmer-labour alliances—which had achieved limited success in the United States at the same time, but which also revealed similar class tensions.[77]

Although the Grange and the Patrons attracted wide support, they could not topple national governments. Several decades later, after the First World War, agrarian parties scored considerable electoral success by championing these same issues, even though farmers had by then become a minority of the population. Ironically, at the time when farmers comprised a plurality of Canadians, their movements were politically ineffective.

Ethno-national division was in large part responsible for their failure. Sectional tensions were running high in the early 1890s, when the Patrons emerged. The second Riel rebellion, in 1885, and the subsequent hanging of Riel had set the English and French communities at each other's throats. Fifty thousand people, about one-third of the French population of Montreal, attended rallies where all shades of opinion condemned the execution as an injustice and an attack on their race. Honoré Mercier, soon to become premier of Quebec, called for a national party to unite everyone opposed to Riel's execution. The crowd endorsed the idea, and thus was born the remarkable alliance between the former anti-clerical and populist Rouges with the ultra-Catholic and conservative 'Castors'. In response the Toronto *Mail*, until then the unofficial Conservative Party paper, thundered that 'as Britons we believe the Conquest will have to be fought over again. Lower Canada may depend upon it there will be no treaty of 1763. The victors will not capitulate next time.'[78]

Tempers had flared again in 1888, when Mercier offered monetary compensation to the Jesuits to settle the order's longstanding claim to estates seized after the Conquest. Most English Canadians were incensed when the Quebec premier requested that the Pope determine how the compensation should be divided between Jesuits and other Church bodies.[79] Despite the offer of some compensation to Protestant education, Orange reaction to papal 'interference' in Canadian affairs was swift. D'Alton McCarthy, the head of the Imperial Federation League and a promising young Conservative, joined with the Grand Master of the Orange Lodge to form the Equal Rights Association—an organization determined to combat the influence of the Catholic Church, to end French domination of Canadian political life, and to abolish separate schools in Ontario and Manitoba. McCarthy and twelve other members urged the House of Commons to disallow Quebec's Jesuits' estates legislation, but failed. Undeterred, McCarthy carried his anti-Catholic, anti-French campaign into Manitoba and scored a major victory. In direct violation of the Manitoba Act of 1870—the act under which Manitoba entered Confederation—the province abolished Catholic schools and the use of French in the legislature. The teaching of French was sharply curtailed in Manitoba schools.[80]

Despite concerted attempts by its leaders, the Patrons of Industry could not stay out of these conflicts.[81] Shortly after the formation of McCarthy's Equal Rights Association, the Protestant Protective Association (PPA), an even more militantly anti-Catholic organization, was born. With connections to the Conservative Party's Orange wing, the PPA sought to drive Catholics out of political office and boycott Catholic-owned businesses. Fourteen PPA members were elected in the 1894 Ontario election, in most cases standing as members of other parties as well, and they elected—on a straight PPA ticket—mayors in Hamilton, London, and other cities.[82] The PPA caused problems for the Patrons because many farmers supported both. In Ontario's 1894 election seven candidates nominated by the PPA announced that they were Patron candidates as well.[83] The result was that the Patrons became associated in the public's mind with the PPA. In Manitoba the Patrons campaigned federally against the restoration of separate schools and thus alienated their Catholic supporters.[84] They also endorsed prohibition, another issue dividing Protestant and Catholic, English and French.

As a result of the ethno-national and religious discord of this era, the populist dream of forming a national party to fight for the rights of farmers was not realized. The Patrons of Industry, like the Dominion Grange before them, did not develop into a pan-Canadian movement. They made little headway among French Canadian habitants, who instead joined Church- or government-led agricultural associations.[85] Sectionalism was not conducive to farmers' politics. When ethno-national issues predominate, as they did in the late nineteenth century, it is difficult to appeal to class unity; in fact, class politics suffered an eclipse in the US at a similar point in its class formation, when Civil War issues held the stage.

Canadian politics, then, had two peculiar features during national unification and early industrialization. First, anti-democratic ideas lived on for an unusually long time in the new settler society. Second, the largest class, the independent farmers, made little political impact when their numbers and economic strength were at a peak. Related to these odd features, however, was a third: the lack—in contrast to the Australian experience—of a strong, popularly based Canadian nationalism. Why did Confederation arouse so little enthusiasm among ordinary Canadians?

Robert Haliburton, the poet of the Canada First movement who created the myth of 'Canada as a northern country inhabited by descendants of northern races', lamented the prosaic manner in which British North America was unified: 'Confederation . . . created as little excitement among the masses as they would feel in the organization of a joint stock company.'[86] Young intellectuals in both English and French Canada wanted to provide Canada with the patriotic fire it so desperately lacked.

Canada First was an Ontario-centred nationalist movement founded in 1868 by young followers of the assassinated D'Arcy McGee. Four years later the Parti National emerged out of the anti-Confederation Rouges party in Quebec and embraced the new, enlarged Canada. Both movements wanted to throw off the colonial past and develop an independent spirit in Canada:

> We are a national party because, before all, we are attached to our nation, and because we have pledged our unswerving loyalty to Canada above the whole world: Canada against the world . . .[87]

> The Citizen of the United States has a flag of his own, a nationality of his own—the Canadian has ever had to look abroad for his. For years British policy isolated the Provinces, to prevent their absorption in the neighbouring Republic, and in so doing stunted the growth of national sentiment.[88]

Both movements espoused popular-democratic reforms such as the secret ballot, a broadening of the franchise, an end to patronage and corruption, tariffs to foster industry, and greater independence in setting foreign policy.[89] Another loose group of nationalists in English Canada—people like Phillips Thompson, A.W. Wright, and E.E. Sheppard—were more progressive than Canada First, had connections with the emerging labour movement, and, except for Sheppard, joined in the Patrons crusade.[90] Why did these nationalist movements not form a pan-Canadian alliance and develop a popular-democratic version of the National Policy, perhaps along the lines of the European system?

Once again, the problem was the chasm in ethno-national relations in Canada. Before the Canada Firsters could get very far in creating myths that would provide 'some cement more binding than . . . a mere community of profit', they became embroiled in the Métis question in Manitoba.[91] The issue was whether the west would become a settlement of 'French half-breeds' or an extension of Ontario. Colonel Denison, a leading member of Canada First, advocated an 'armed emigration' of Ontarians to the west, to stamp a British character on the new region, and the group rushed to the defence of the 'Canadian Party' in the Red River, taking up the cause of Thomas Scott, an Orangeman executed by Riel's provisional government. On the other side was the Parti National, which in the 1872 federal election campaigned with some success on the maltreatment of Riel.[92]

The nationalist movements had well-defined, if differing, views on Canada's identity and could appeal emotionally to popular sentiments in their respective sections of the country. But these ethno-national—at times, racist—appeals led only to national conflict, not to national unity. The only cause that could excite the imagination was the opening of the Canadian west. And the only Canada-wide nationalism that did emerge in those years, centred on John A. Macdonald's National Policy, confined its pitch to such prosaic symbols as the tariff and the promotion of home industry. Pan-Canadian nationalism has had, until recently, the same uninspiring quality: an obsessive emphasis on geography—or 'mappism', to use Abraham Rotstein's phrase—and economic prosperity.

In the absence of any popular pan-Canadian independence movement, the minimalist stance of the National Policy was the only nationalist possibility remaining. It was designed, as Mel Watkins has argued, to ward off full absorption into the United States, but, unlike the European system, it was not a strategy designed to lead to an independent industrial economy. The National Policy was promoted by the factions of Canadian big business that stood to benefit from commercial and manufacturing protection and government subsidies and bonusses. Nova Scotia coal interests, most manufacturers, and—reluctantly at first—the majority of central Canadian merchants and bankers backed the National Policy. The Canadian Pacific Railway and the primary steel industry, offspring of the strategy, were vociferous supporters. National Policy advocates attracted popular support by appealing to loyalty to Britain, economic benefits, and preservation of the Canadian west. But even this minimalist program was challenged by sections of big and small business who favoured closer integration with the United States.

CLASS POWER AND STATE POLICIES

Canadian politics, then, diverged from that of other advanced capitalist countries during initial industrialization. The forces of big business were politically ascendant and faced little challenge because the class that could have ousted them in this era—the farmers—was seriously divided by ethno-national issues. How did the peculiarity of weak agrarian power affect state policies and foreign ownership? Let us look at agrarian influence in other countries.

Studies of class have usually focussed on the conflicts between lord and peasant in older societies, or between slave owners and free farmers in the US. Though mundane compared to the French Revolution or the American Civil War, the conflicts between agricultural classes and the classes based on manufacturing (industrialists and workers) were nevertheless important as well. Town and country stood against each other on many important issues such as industrial protection and taxation levels, and the conflicts between them had profound effects in shaping distinct national patterns during the industrial revolution.[93] For example, the victory for free trade in agricultural goods in England (abolition of the Corn Laws), won by urban manufacturers with the help of urban workers, stands in sharp contrast to the agricultural protectionism in France, backed by a strong peasantry, that continues to this day. The European Common Market is still bedevilled by these historically based differences.

During initial industrialization agrarians of all classes in capitalist countries displayed several common political tendencies bearing on economic development: they supported defence, low taxes, low state expenditures, and liberal access to credit. Each of these subjects will now be reviewed in turn.

Defence

Aristocrats, slave-owners, independent farmers, and landholding peasants provided the strongest support for defence and territorial expansion into nearby areas. They were not so strongly in favour of overseas empires. Their stance is not surprising. Capital has no upper limits, is relatively mobile, and can be utilized intensively; land, in contrast, is finite in quantity, fixed in place, and must be used on an extensive basis. Hence the landholders' emphasis on defence of the homeland and expansion into neighbouring territories.[94]

The military character of aristocratic landlords is legendary—they were a warrior class. Less well-known is the similar tendency among peasants and free farmers during initial industrialization. Marx argued that French peasants, victorious in 1789, were the backbone of 'French gloire' under Napoleons I and III.[95] In the US free farmers and southern planters provided the main force behind the relentless drive westward at the expense of Amerindians, France, Spain, Mexico, and British North America.[96] On the other hand, northeastern capitalists tried to block rapid agricultural expansion to the west, fearing that a class of labourers could not be retained when the alternative of free land was available. A similar military orientation was evident among agrarians in Sweden, Japan, and Russia during initial industrialization.[97]

The political implications are clear. In countries retaining a large dose of 'feudalism', the military factor led to spectacular reversals. In several societies aristocrats surrendered their own privileges in order to meet military threats. Aristocratic states abolished serfdom as follows: Prussia in 1807, after defeat by Napoleon; Russia in 1861, after the Crimean War; and Japan from 1868 to 1873, after the Unequal Treaties with Western powers.[98] These were 'revolutions from above', to use Barrington Moore's phrase. The primacy of a military orientation was not confined to aristocratic countries, however. In the US, for example, President Andrew Jackson (1829-37), the hero of the Battle of New Orleans, was an agrarian-based advocate of low tariffs who made an exception to this principle for armaments in order to build up an American defence industry.[99]

The economic implications of an military preoccupation on the part of agrarians were less obvious. For strategic reasons the state fostered a domestically controlled process of industrialization. Because today's ally could be tomorrow's enemy in the late nineteenth and early twentieth centuries, strategic industries had to be free from foreign ownership, technology, and suppliers. In that era the strategic sectors included basic steel and coal, engineering goods and machinery, chemicals, railways, and sometimes shipbuilding. Thus state interest in an independent army, supported by agrarians, led unintentionally to the creation of a domestically controlled engineering sector.

War or the threat of war sparked innovation: interchangeable parts and line assembly, for instance, were introduced in the manufacture of small military arms. It was in the US, with its 'turbulent frontier' of agriculture, as William A. Williams put it, that these innovations were first applied.[100] Earlier, the British Navy had provided a great demand for iron when the first breakthroughs in iron-making occurred. Government contracts came in blocks and had to be filled on time, providing an incentive for innovation.[101] Military preparedness led to the development of heavy industry in late-follower countries too, and although Japan did not innovate, its first factories produced war goods.[102] For defence reasons, governments shifted development towards strategic industries by providing them with capital and stable markets.

The agrarian emphasis on defence was closely related to a nationalism that often had an exclusivist character. Though by no means the only patriotic elements in society, agrarian nationalists did have their peculiar tendencies: opposition to foreign ownership, support for independent strategic technologies, and often advocacy of their own brand of protectionism. The build-up of the German army starting in the early 1890s was the result of militarism and protectionism marching together, partly under the banner of the Union of Agriculturalists, a vocal centre for Junker propaganda.[103] At the same time the noble-led Protectionist Party in Sweden allied with protectionist independent farmers to campaign for a stronger army and against foreign ownership of Sweden's resources.[104]

In Japan and Russia aristocratic governments also blocked foreign investment on nationalist and strategic grounds. Fearing a compromise of its independence, Japan refused foreign loans between 1874 and 1896, a period of severe capital shortage.[105] The czar reversed German branch-plant incursions into Russian Poland in the late 1880s.[106] Even agrarians in the US modified their laissez-faire views for similar reasons: during the first agrarian attack on commercial banking in the early 1800s, they criticized English ownership of the Bank of the United States, despite laws forbidding foreigners from voting by proxy and restricting bank directorships to American citizens.[107] These agrarian tendencies shifted economic development towards autarky.

Agrarian tax revolt

Except in regard to defence outlays, politically powerful agrarians tended to support government restraint, and they did so for a simple reason: high taxes placed a greater burden on agrarians, who were usually cash-poor, than on commercial or industrial capitalists. Their stance promoted the independent route to industrialization, because whereas a frugal state would reduce the need for foreign investment, a spendthrift one would increase it. Agrarian attitudes towards taxes were also influenced by the level of benefits provided by the state to industry and agriculture. To establish a benchmark for comparison with Canada, we will review the level of state expenditures by agrarian-influenced governments during initial industrialization.

Aristocratic Prussia supervised railway building closely, avoided waste, and constructed lines for one-third the cost of British lines.[108] The US built railways even more cheaply, and government railway expenditures were held down by opposition from agrarians. While most agrarians supported railway construction to improve access to markets, many, especially in the South, blocked a federal role in railway building, fearing the imposition of higher taxes by means of tariffs; they also suspected that the metropolis would gain the greatest benefit.[109] Sweden's non-noble large farmers were economy-minded as well: three years after the Ruralist Party gained ascendancy in the Lower Chamber, a law was passed limiting the speed of state railway building to a level that would not increase the debt. Perhaps because noble lands were tax-exempt until the 1880s, aristocratic governments in Sweden did not display such a passion for state economy. Nevertheless, in contrast to Canada, Sweden was not extravagant during initial industrialization, and government trunk lines were cheap: one-seventh the price per mile of British railways.[110]

Agrarian political frugality contrasted sharply with commercial business extravagance. With its quick succession of regimes, the 1848 revolution in France threw into relief the political tendencies of the various classes. According to Marx, the finance aristocracy—'bankers, stock-exchange kings, railway kings, owners of coal and iron mines and forests, a part of the landed proprietors'—had ruled France under the July monarchy (1830-48) and 'had a *direct interest in the indebtedness of the state.* The *state deficit* was really the main object of its speculation and the chief source of its enrichment. At the end of each year, a new deficit' (author's emphasis).[111]

The finance aristocracy was overthrown in the February revolution of 1848 by an alliance of the industrial bourgeoisie, the petite bourgeoisie, and the working class. The revolution looked secure until the provisional government committed the unpardonable sin of saving the Bank of France from ruin by raising taxes. 'Who was to be taxed. . . . Who was sacrificed to bourgeois credit? *Jacques le bonhomme, "the peasant".*'[112] From this point on, the peasants viewed the republic as the tax collector, and it was quickly ousted by the coup d'état of the peasants, bringing Louis Napoléon to power. Although the peasants did not control his government, Louis Napoléon's policies displayed the usual agrarian tendencies: railways were rationalized to avoid duplication, but there was no restraint on military adventures (the hallmark of his reign).

Similar tendencies were evident in other countries during early industrialization. Except for military spending, agrarian classes usually preferred that the government keep its expenditures low. If their policies held sway, the need for foreign investment was lessened.

Industrial credit and agrarian political power

Perennially short of cash, agrarians usually sought freer credit and favoured state control of note-issuing (paper money). The break-up of commercial banking systems was related to the political power of agrarians. Although farming classes tended to pursue their own economic interests, their desire for credit was congruent with the greater supply of domestic capital for industry. The relations between agrarian political power and modifications to the American and European banking systems will now be examined, since they were the alternatives to the commercial banking that prevailed in Canada and England.

In the US, northeast commerce and industry were the political backbone of whiggish Hamiltonian banking policies. The whigs set up the Bank of the United States (1791-1811 and 1816-36), a central bank designed to conduct commercial business, expand the money supply, and sustain government credit. Like the Bank of England, it was supposed to ensure stable commercial banking. But the emphasis on stability masked another feature: the favouring of creditors over debtors. In the early nineteenth century private commercial banks did not lend readily to farmers, who needed capital to mechanize agriculture. The result was that the agrarian-based movement that swept Andrew Jackson to office also destroyed the Bank of the United States and the whole commercial banking system.[113] Upon the ashes of the old system new unit banks proliferated, and later several large industrial investment banks rose as well. Besides lending more readily to farmers, the new system increased credit to industry.[114]

European investment banks had their most important start in Germany, where they developed in a dialectical relationship with Junker-controlled Prussia. These banks originated in the Rhineland, an economically advanced region of Prussia where they had to deal with an aristocratic state that was at best indifferent to capitalist development. The framework for monetary and banking activities in Prussia was different from that in England and the US, where banking profit was derived mainly from the issuing of private bank notes. Because the note-issuing monopoly was a major source of state revenue, aristocratic-statist Prussia refused to give it up, and private Rhenish bankers had to find alternatives to note-issuing. Investment banking was their answer. Taking an interest in the management of their industrial clients, the new banks profited from purchasing industrial shares, acting as stockbrokers, and speculating on stock markets with the aid of insider knowledge. After 1870 they dominated the German banking system. It is unlikely that investment banking would have developed in the Rhineland, however, if bankers rather than aristocrats had controlled the state and ended the note-issuing monopoly.[115]

England adopted a purely commercial banking system once industry had overtaken agriculture's economic predominance. Because England was the only advanced manufacturing country for over half a century after the 1770s, profits were high, and a surplus of domestic industrial capital had developed by the time commercial banking became entrenched. The situation had been different during initial industrialization, when agrarian political power was greater. Then Britain had a heterogeneous banking system in which numerous country (unit) banks were important. According to Phyllis Deane:

> When the pioneers of the industrial revolution went in search of capital, they could hope to find local bankers who had access to enough personal knowledge about the borrower on the one hand, and enough practical knowledge of the trade or industry concerned on the other, to be able to take risks which a less personally involved banker would find incalculable and therefore out of range. Probably the English banks have never been so ready to assist innovation or to finance long-term investment in industry as they were in the period 1770-1830 when the Industrial Revolution took shape.[116]

Soon after Britain had passed through initial industrialization, most local banks disappeared and, with them, capital for small, innovative industry. The move to commercial banking occurred during the tumultuous changes that took Britain from aristocratic to plutocratic rule between the 1820s and the 1840s. Merchants and large manufacturers were the strongest critics of the old, 'unstable' English banking system.[117] In these and other cases, availability of domestic capital for new industry had been dependent on the power of agrarians, whether independent farmers or land-holding aristocrats.[118]

CANADIAN FARMERS AND STATE POLICIES

It is commonly thought that Canadian farmers were laissez-faire liberals. Were this so, greater influence on the part of farmers would have led to a diminished state role during initial industrialization. Since laissez-faire policies were inimical to the European system, agrarian political dominance in Canada would have hurt, not helped, the development of independent secondary manufacturing in Canada.

The idea of farmer hostility to government intervention is based on several misconceptions. Regarding the tariff, the most controversial issue, farmers often lined up on one side and the Canadian Manufacturers Association on the other. Together, farmer support for Alexander Mackenzie's 'laissez-faire' government (1873-78) and opposition to government expenditures for canal and railway projects give the impression that farmers opposed state intervention. Reginald Whitaker, for instance, argued that 'toryism', the creed of the dominant capitalists, favoured intervention, whereas the popular liberal-democracy of the petite bourgeoisie held to the unregulated freedom of enterprise.[119] The historical evidence, however, shows that Canadian farmers favoured intervention, though of a different kind than that supported by commercial and industrial capitalists. Since farmers' organizations were out of power throughout initial industrialization (1870-1910), their role in opposition can be misconstrued to suggest that they opposed government intervention in principle.

Farmers in Canada were ambivalent about tariffs in the 1840-1914 period. They tended, as in other countries, to support duties on agricultural imports and oppose tariffs on manufactured goods. After a ten-year battle for protection waged by the farmers, Canada's first tariffs (1843) were raised against US farm produce, not against manufactured imports.

Farmers' attitudes towards industrial protection were influenced by the type of farming they did. Of those who produced for the home market, many could support industrial protection, but most of those who sold their produce for export were opposed. When Ontario farmers moved into animal husbandry to supply the growing Canadian cities, the Tory call to build up the home market through the National Policy had—for a time—wide support in the farming community, and it is likely that a majority of Dominion Grangers voted Conservative in the National Policy election of 1878. Economic depression and massive emigration in the late 1880s weakened the credibility of the home-market idea, and many farmers changed their minds, but the Dominion Grange did not support reciprocity with the United States in 1891. On the other hand, western farmers, who depended on wheat exports, naturally supported free trade.[120]

On other forms of intervention the farmers' position depended on class interest, not ideology. In the 1830s the agrarian-based Reformers of Upper Canada fought for more-competitive banking, while fifty years later the

Grangers pushed for state-owned banks. These policies seem contradictory, but both were attempts to break the commercial banking monopoly, which provided inadequate farm credit. Farmers displayed the same ideological flexibility towards intervention in transportation projects, supporting cheap government and opposing many of business's railway projects, yet demanding government-owned railways and more road building.[121] Farmers, in sum, did not adhere to laissez-faire in principle. If they viewed state intervention as beneficial to their interests, they often supported it; if not, they often stood in opposition. The same was true of farmers in the US and Australia in the 1800s.[122]

The peculiar political weakness of Canadian farmers did not alter the degree of state intervention pursued by Canadian business élites. Instead, it altered the character of that intervention. It is not clear what policies farmers would have implemented had they held power—the policies that parties or groups advocate when out of office are not always good indicators of what they will do when in. Nevertheless, we can project the main direction of such policies both from the platforms of contemporary Canadian farmer movements and from agrarians' experiences in other countries where they did hold power.

Upper and Lower Canada had modelled their credit systems after the commercial Hamiltonian banks of the United States. When American agrarians, allied with a strong working-class movement and some New York banks, assaulted and ended this system in the 1830s, Upper Canadian farmers were impressed.[123] By this time they had begun to adopt new farming techniques, increasing their need for capital.[124] Reformers advocated a similar system of unit banks and easy credit for Upper Canada. For reasons to be explained in Chapter 5, they did not succeed.

The new Dominion entrenched Canada's commercial banking system in 1870-71. The unit banks of New Brunswick and Nova Scotia and the 'French banks' of small-town Quebec failed in the next few decades. From this point on, the banking system was set in its centralized, investment-shy mould. Large commercial banks were too powerful to be changed radically by the assault of western farmers in the early twentieth century.

Unlike the European investment banks, Canadian banks did not make substantial long-term investments in domestic industry, nor did they participate in manufacturers' managerial decisions. It was not that Canadian banks were bereft of domestic capital; in fact, they were so powerful that they expanded abroad on a major scale in the 1900-13 period, at precisely the time when American branch plants first established their hold on Canada.[125] Canadian industry did receive the necessary capital, but much of it was not from domestic sources. And because farmers were defeated in their attempts to bring about credit reform, the lending orientation of the banks did not move towards a policy of financing domestic industry. Canada's failure to adopt either the American or the German banking system was not related to peculiar tendencies of Canadian farmers, but simply to their political weakness.

A similar situation existed regarding state expenditures. Farmers repeatedly tried to scale down Canada's grandiose railway schemes between the 1850s and the First World War, but without success. With capitalists firmly in control, the state encouraged the squandering of enormous amounts of capital. In consequence, Canada borrowed record amounts of British portfolio capital, especially on the eve of the First World War.

The result was a complicated triangular adjustment in which, as Jacob Viner put it, 'the capital borrowed by Canada in Great Britain entered Canada largely in the form of American commodities'.[126] Tariffs and patent restrictions, however, hindered many large US firms in exporting to Canada: their solution was to jump over the border and set up branch plants. In effect, therefore, as will be discussed in the next chapter, by rapidly boosting the size of the Canadian market, those capital imports from Britain fostered the establishment of American branch plants in Canada. And to the extent that the need for such borrowing can be attributed to extravagant railway spending, the failure of Canadian farmers to impose frugality on the government did in fact contribute to Canada's heavy reliance on foreign investment, both portfolio and direct.

Finally, there was the strategic factor. In contrast to their counterparts in other countries, Canadian farmers were not especially military-minded. To understand why, one must examine the way the state was created. Agrarian-based reform groups did not spearhead the movement for Canadian independence. Instead, it was the commercial capitalists of central Canada who led reluctant peoples from Canada East and the Maritimes into Confederation in 1867. They saw the new Dominion not as an independent country, but rather, in the words of Alexander Galt, scion of the Lower Canadian business community and the first politician to propose Confederation, as a 'Dependency of the Empire'. Furthermore, the new nation was to be anti-democratic and whiggish: 'Confederation . . . does not profess to be derived from the people but would be the constitution provided by the imperial parliament.'[127] These views were echoed by George Brown, the 'Reform' father of Confederation. Referring to universal manhood suffrage in the United States, he opined that 'the balance of power was held by the ignorant, unreasoning mass'.[128] Such was the ideology of the statesmen who pushed the Confederation scheme through the colonial legislatures, deliberately avoiding holding a vote on the matter whenever they could.[129] These were hardly the means to arouse popular nationalism among ordinary people.

Unpalatable as the idea may seem, the advent of mass democracy was related to the development of modern armies. Revolutionary France had the first armed people, when the 'levée en masse' was raised to defeat the professional armies of émigré nobles who sought to restore the ancien régime. But the relation between democracy, popular nationalism, and mass armies was not confined to Old World societies. The historian William A. Williams has argued persuasively that the farming majority provided the driving force behind American expansionism during most of the nineteenth century, believing as it did that freedom was connected to an expanding frontier.[130] In Australia it was the Labour Party, imbued with a sense of Australianism, that in its first term in office (1910-13) established a navy and created a citizen force for home defence through a system of universal and compulsory military training.[131]

We have seen that it was precisely in the new industries of twentieth-century technology that American manufacturers came to dominate Canadian industry. The creation of an independent armaments and engineering sector was not a strategic requirement, because Canada did not develop its own armed forces to an appreciable level before the First World War. This was one of the main reasons why Canada encouraged the branch-plant route to import advanced technology, while the other late-follower countries tended to reject it.

Confederation in 1867 came at roughly the same time as the unification of Italy (1870), the modernizing Meiji restoration in Japan (1868), the emancipation of the serfs in Russia (1861), and the abolition of the estates in the Swedish Parliament (1865-66). On the surface it seems that all late-follower countries were establishing modern, unified states in the same era. But the Canadian state was different. Although Confederation came about partly as a response to a military threat from the United States in the aftermath of its civil war, Canadian foreign and military policy remained under British authority. This position was not foisted on Canada by the British Empire; in fact, the predominant opinion in official London was that Canada was a burden and a nuisance—the quicker it stood on its own, the better. Although aware of this opinion, Canada opted for 'dominion' status in 1867, a mid-point between colony and full nationhood.

After Confederation British regular forces[132] left Canada (in 1871), and a voluntary militia of moderate size was raised. Instead of establishing a substantial standing army, however, Canada relied on protection behind the British shield. In 1865, when Edward Cardwell, the colonial Secretary, had had assurances from Canada that 'that Province is willing to devote all her resources both in men and money to the maintenance of her connexion with the Mother Country . . . the Imperial Government fully acknowledged the reciprocal obligation of defending every portion of the Empire with all the resources at its command.'[133] The commitment Cardwell made to Canada was reconfirmed by British officials later in the century. But the American military threat to Canada was largely removed in 1871 with the Treaty of Washington.[134] By 1900 Canada's former enemy, the United States, had come to be seen as an additional guardian. Prime Minister Laurier summed up the view that Canada had no need to protect itself: 'You must not take the Militia seriously, for though it is useful for suppressing internal disturbances, it will not be required for the defence of the country, as the Monroe Doctrine [proclaiming American military hegemony in the Americas] protects us against enemy aggression.'[135]

Canadians opposed both standing armies and all but token military expenditures. When it looked as if Russia might go to war with the British Empire in 1877, and ports in the Canadian Maritimes could be threatened, some government ministers thought it would be less expensive to let the Russians destroy everything than to mount a sufficient defence.[136] By the First World War even Australia had a credible navy, while Canada had only legislation and two out-of-commission ships.[137] Yet when Britain declared war on Germany on 4 August 1914 Canada was automatically at war too. Canada's voluntary position as a dependency of the Empire until near the end of the First World War—when Canadian generals were finally put in command of Canadian soldiers—and the absence of a real military threat from the Americans coincided with the period when the industrial structure was established in its branch-plant mould. The result was clear: Canada had no strategic logic, and no compelling motive to block foreign ownership of munitions and related industries, before 1914.

Until that time Canada had only a very modest armaments industry, producing uniforms, cartridges, artillery shells, and rifles.[138] Instead of developing a domestically owned and innovative engineering industry under the protective care of an independent military policy, it relied almost exclusively on foreign technology, which was a major factor in the emergence of the branch-plant structure.[139] If Canadian Confederation had been an agrarian-democratic project, it is likely that Canada would have been more independent from Britain and would have developed larger and more independent armed forces before the First World War.

CONCLUSION

Despite a good industrial beginning, Canada failed to adopt the European system that in other late-follower countries led to independent development. Rather than point a finger at Canadian capitalists for not protecting their own bailiwick, this chapter has indicted the whole of the social formation. For capitalists everywhere, profits come first: what marked Canada off from other advanced countries was that other classes did not gain state power and guard the domestic ground for native capitalists. Foreign ownership and a truncated manufacturing sector were the results.

The Canadian state missed the opportunity of moving to independent industrialization largely because of the ways class and ethno-nationality intersected. Inequalities between the two nations, starting with the Conquest, led to a sectional politics that strengthened big capital and weakened popular-democratic forces. Canada's situation was a peculiar one for a new settler society in the democratic age. Popular forces, primarily agrarians, failed to take a leading role in creating the state and transforming the economy during the initial phase of industrialization. The usual strategies of late-follower countries were not pursued. Credit remained stultifyingly commercial, and state indebtedness grew enormously at the hands of those who benefitted from it. These factors slowed the development of the domestically owned industry that could have more easily kept out foreign subsidiaries. As well, the state discarded the first line of defence against foreign ownership and technological dependence by choosing to be a British dependency.

In the present age, when serious challenge to the power of capitalists is weak in most Western countries, the idea that business must dominate the political system has become almost axiomatic. This unfortunate assumption results from a lack of historical perspective, and it is especially dangerous when we examine the period in which industrial capitalism was first taking shape. The reason the Canadian state did not defend domestic ownership of Canadian industry is ironic: the capitalists were too powerful.

NOTES

This chapter is a revised version of 'Class, Nationality and the Roots of the Branch Plant Economy', *Studies in Political Economy* 21 (Autumn 1986).

[1] See W.T. Easterbrook and Hugh Aitken, *Canadian Economic History* (Toronto: Macmillan, 1956), pp. 381-408, for a standard discussion of Canada's economic alternatives.

[2] Mel Watkins, 'The American System and Canada's National Policy', *Bulletin of the Canadian Association for American Studies* (1966).

[3] Ibid., p. 41.

[4] Phyllis Deane, *The First Industrial Revolution* (Cambridge: Cambridge University Press, 1965), pp. 191-8.

[5] J.M.S. Careless, 'Frontierism, Metropolitanism and Canadian History', *Canadian Historical Review* 35, no. 1 (1954): 8-14; Fred Landon, *Western Ontario and the American Frontier* (Toronto: Ryerson Press, 1967); Goldwin Smith, *Canada and the Canadian Question* (Toronto: University of Toronto Press, 1971).

[6] This term was first used by Craig Brown, 'The Nationalism of the National Policy', in P. Russell, ed., *Nationalism in Canada* (Toronto: McGraw-Hill Ryerson, 1966).

[7] Eric Hobsbawm, *The Age of Revolution: Europe 1789-1848* (London: Weidenfeld and Nicolson, 1962).

[8] Thomas Crerar, House leader of the Progressives, urged Canada to develop 'the natural resources of the country' (W.L. Morton, *The Progressive Party in Canada* [Toronto: University of Toronto Press, 1978], p. 116).

[9] Richard Hofstadter, *The American Political Tradition And The Men Who Made It* (New York: Alfred A. Knopf, 1951).

[10] Fernand Ouellet, *Economic and Social History of Quebec 1760-1850* (Carleton Library, no. 120, [Toronto: Macmillan 1980]), pp. 318-31; Stanley Ryerson, *Unequal Union: Confederation and the Roots of Conflict in the Canadas 1815-1873* (Toronto: Progress Books, 1968), pp. 69-84.

[11]Until 1836, when a moderate wing of the Patriotes split from the majority.

[12]Ryerson, *Unequal Union*, p. 109; Donald Creighton, *The Commercial Empire of the St. Lawrence 1760-1850* (Toronto: Ryerson Press, 1937), pp. 255-88; Charles Lipton, *The Trade Union Movement of Canada 1827-1959*, 2nd ed. (Montreal: Canadian Social Publications, 1968), pp. 11-16.

[13]Edgar McInnis, *Canada: A Political and Social History* (Toronto: Holt, Rinehart and Winston, 1969), pp. 252-6.

[14]Graeme Wynn, *Timber Colony: A Historical Geography of Early Nineteenth Century New Brunswick* (Toronto: University of Toronto Press, 1981), pp. 49, 113-49; W.S. MacNutt, *The Atlantic Provinces, 1712-1857* (Toronto: McClelland and Stewart, 1965), pp. 185-6.

[15]J.M. Beck, *Joseph Howe: Conservative Reformer 1804-1848*, vol. 1 (Kingston: McGill-Queen's University Press, 1982). By 1867 political cleavage revolved around a nation-building group led by professional versus liberal anti-Confederate mercantile interests. See D.A. Muise, 'Parties and Constituencies: Federal Elections in Nova Scotia, 1867-1896', *Historical Papers 1971* (Canadian Historical Association).

[16]F.W.P. Bolger, ed., *Canada's Smallest Province: A History of PEI* (Ottawa: PEI 1973 Centennial Commission, 1973), pp. 95-114.

[17]George Haythorne, *Land and Labour* (Toronto: Oxford University Press, 1941) p. 29.

[18]In Nova Scotia, farmer-labour parties won a quarter of the seats in the provincial legislature in 1920 and formed the Opposition. See Ernest Forbes, *The Maritimes Rights Movement, 1919-1927. A Study in Canadian Regionalism* (Montreal: McGill-Queen's University Press, 1979), p. 47. The Progressives ran twenty candidates in Quebec in the 1921 election and received 18.5% of the vote in those constituencies (Chief Electoral Officer, *General Election 1921* [Public Archives of Canada, 1977], M-4212).

[19]Morton, *Progressive Party*; Louis Wood, *A History of Farmers' Movements in Canada* (Toronto: Ryerson Press, 1975), pp. 301-9; Ernest Forbes, *Aspects of Maritime Regionalism 1867-1927* (Ottawa: Canadian Historical Association, Historical Booklet no. 36, 1983), p. 15. In Ontario the United Farmers (UFO) won 43 seats to Labour's 12, while in Manitoba the United Farmers (UFM) won 28 seats to Labour's 6 (Morton, *Progressive Party*, pp. 85, 228). See R. James Sacouman, 'The Differing Origins, Organization, an Impact of Maritime and Prairie Co-operative Movements to 1940', in Robert Brym and R.J. Sacouman, *Underdevelopment and Social Movements in Atlantic Canada* (Toronto: New Hogtown Press, 1979), regarding the weakness of popular-democratic movements in the Maritimes at that time.

[20]Literature on early labour and socialist parties is scattered. For a start, consult A. Ross McCormack, *Reformers, Rebels and Revolutionaries: The Western Canadian Radical Movement 1899-1919* (Toronto: University of Toronto Press, 1977), pp. 53-97; Gregory S. Kealey and Bryan D. Palmer, *Dreaming of What Might Be: The Knights of Labour in Ontario, 1880-1900* (London: Cambridge University Press, 1982) pp. 204-47, and Martin Robin, *Radical Politics and Canadian Labour* (Kingston: Industrial Relations Centre, 1968).

[21]There was the famous poll in September 1943 showing the CCF at 29%, slightly ahead of the Liberals and Tories, but by the time of the 1945 election the surge had abated. See David Lewis, *The Good Fight: Political Memoirs 1909-1958* (Toronto: Macmillan, 1981); Derek Black, *Winners and Losers: The Book of Canadian Political Lists* (Toronto: Methuen, 1984).

[22]Greater agrarian compared to working-class political power in Canada during initial industrialization (1870-1914) was reinforced by greater numbers, a property qualification for male suffrage through the early part of the period, and electoral districts weighted toward rural constituencies. See Gregory Kealey, *Toronto Workers Respond to Industrial Capitalism 1867-1914* (Toronto: University of Toronto Press, 1980), pp. 367-8; Norman Ward, *The Canadian House of Commons: Representation* (Toronto: University of Toronto, 1950), pp. 32-5, 211-32.

[23]Morton, *Progressive Party*, p. 114.

[24]Marx, 'Excerpts from the Class Struggles in France, 1848 to 1850' in L. Feuer, ed., *Marx and Engels* (Garden City, N.Y.: Anchor Books, 1959), p. 287.

[25]Note the Bolsheviks' early reliance on the Left Social Revolutionaries. See E.H. Carr, *The Bolshevik Revolution 1917-1923*, vol. 2 (Harmondsworth: Penguin Books, 1966), pp. 35-61.

[26]Gordon Greenwood, *Australia: A Social and Political History* (Sydney: Angus and Robertson, 1955), pp. 157-8.

[27]G. Laxer, 'The Political Economy of Aborted Development: The Canadian Case', in Robert Brym, ed., *The Structure of the Canadian Capitalist Class* (Toronto: Garamond Press, 1985), p. 87.

[28]Dankwart Rustow, *The Politics of Compromise* (Princeton: Princeton University Press, 1955), pp. 9-47.

[29]Escott Reid, 'The Rise of National Parties' in H. Thorburn, ed., *Party Politics in Canada* (Toronto: Prentice-Hall, 1963); George Hougham, 'The Background and Development of National Parties' in Muise, 'Parties and Constituencies', pp. 20-1.

[30]Quoted in F. Underhill, 'Some Reflections on the Liberal Tradition in Canada', in Underhill, *In Search of Canadian Liberalism* (Toronto: Macmillan, 1960 [1946]), p. 3.

[31]Joseph Pope, ed., *Confederation: British North America Act* (Toronto: Carswell Law Publishers, 1895).

[32]The term 'conservative' is confusing. It used to convey the aristocracy's pre-liberal-democratic values of inequality, obligation, and leadership but has recently come to mean support for classical (19th-century) liberalism, emphasizing economic liberty. Milton Friedman, father of neo-conservatism (*Capitalism and Freedom* [Chicago: University of Chicago Press, 1982]), still calls himself a 'liberal' (p. 6). I use the terms 'conservative' and 'liberal' in their traditional senses.

[33]Underhill, *Canadian Liberalism*, p. 12.

[34]S.M. Lipset, 'Canada and the United States: The Cultural Dimension,' in C.F. Doran and J. Sigler, eds., *Canada and the United States* (Toronto: Prentice-Hall, 1985), p. 3.

[35]Gad Horowitz, 'Conservatism, Liberalism and Socialism in Canada: An Interpretation', *Canadian Journal of Economics and Political Science* 32 (1966) and 'Notes on Conservatism, Liberalism and Socialism in Canada', *Canadian Journal of Political Science* 11, no. 2 (1978).

[36]The tory version of collectivism is, according to Horowitz, 'a community of hierarchically ordered communities or classes ('estates') and not fundamentally an association of primordially free and equal individuals' ('Notes on Conservatism', p. 393).

[37]Underhill, *Canadian Liberalism*, p. 15.

[38]T.W. Acheson, 'Changing Social Origins of the Canadian Industrial Elite, 1880-1910,' *Business History Review* 47, no. 2 (Summer 1973).

[39]Landon, *Western Ontario*, pp. 185-92; Smith, *The Canadian Question*, p. 183.

[40]Michel Brunet, 'The British Conquest: Canadian Social Scientists and the Fate of the Canadiens' in Carl Berger, ed., *Approaches to Canadian History* (Toronto: University of Toronto Press, 1967).

[41]Northrop Frye, *The Bush Garden* (Toronto: Anansi, 1971), p. 14.

[42]C.B. Macpherson, *The Life and Times of Liberal Democracy* (Oxford: Oxford University Press, 1977), p. 23.

[43]A. Schlesinger, *The Age of Jackson* (Boston: Little, Brown, 1945), p. 13.

[44]Louis Hartz, *The Liberal Tradition in America* (New York: Harcourt, Brace and World, 1955), p. 89.

[45]R.C. Harris, *The Seigneurial System in Early Canada* (Madison: University of Wisconsin Press, 1967) p. 7.

[46]Hobsbawm, *Age of Revolution*, pp. 82, 141.

[47]Ouellet, *History of Quebec*, pp. 15, 52; Creighton, *The Empire of the St. Lawrence*, pp. 22-55; Mason Wade, *The French Canadians 1760-1967*, vol. 1 (Toronto: Macmillan, 1968), pp. 93-7.

[48]Wade, *The French Canadians*, vol. 1, p. 97.

[49]P.E. Trudeau, *Federalism and the French Canadians* (Toronto: Macmillan, 1968), p. 104.

[50]Farmers west of the Welland Canal were an exception: they benefitted from the opening of the canal in 1829.

[51]Gerald M. Craig, *Upper Canada The Formative Years 1784-1841* (Toronto: McClelland and Stewart, 1963), pp. 220-1; Creighton, *Empire of the St. Lawrence*, pp. 255-87.

[52]J.E. Rea, 'William Lyon Mackenzie – Jacksonian?' in J.M. Bumsted, ed., *Canadian History Before Confederation* (Georgetown Ont.: Irwin-Dorsey, 1972); Craig, *Upper Canada*, pp. 197-200; Fernand Ouellet, *Louis Joseph Papineau: Divided Soul* (Ottawa: Canadian Historical Association Booklet no. 11, 1972), pp. 10-11.

[53]John McCallum, *Unequal Beginnings: Agriculture and Economic Development in Quebec and Ontario until 1870* (Toronto: University of Toronto Press, 1980), pp. 4-15.

[54]S.D. Clark, *Movements of Political Protest in Canada* (Toronto: University of Toronto Press, 1959), p. 362.

[55]S.D. Clark, *The Canadian Manufacturers' Association* (Toronto: University of Toronto Press, 1939), p. 10.

[56]P. Baskerville, 'Sir Allan Napier MacNab', *Dictionary of Canadian Biography*, vol. 9 (Toronto: University of Toronto Press, 1976), p. 524.

[57]Lord Durham, *Lord Durham's Report: An Abridgement*, ed. G.M. Craig (Ottawa: Carleton University Press, 1982 [1839]), p. 151.

[58]Gerald J.J. Tulchinsky, *The River Barons* (Toronto: University of Toronto Press, 1976), pp. 9-32.

[59]J.M.S. Careless, *Canada: A Story of Challenge* (Toronto: Macmillan, 1970), p. 225; Brian Young, *Promoters and Politicians: The North-Shore Railways in the History of Quebec 1854-1885* (Toronto: University of Toronto Press, 1978), p. 4.

[60]*North American*, 2 July 1850.

[61]J.M.S. Careless, *Brown of the Globe*, vol. 1, *The Voice of Upper Canada 1818-1859* (Toronto: Macmillan, 1959), p. 124.

[62]Ouellet, *History of Quebec*, p. 485.

[63]Jean-Paul Bernard, *Les Rouges* (Montreal: Les Presses de l'Université du Québec, 1971), p. 97.

[64]Wade, *The French Canadians*, vol. 2, p. 262.

[65]Bernard, *Les Rouges*, pp. 91-2, 197.

[66]Careless, *Brown of the Globe,* vol. 1, pp. 311-22.

[67]Wood, *Farmers' Movements*, pp. 60-4, 109-32.

[68]Ibid., pp. 87-8.

[69]Russell Hann, *Farmers Confront Industrialism: Some Historical Perspectives on Ontario Agrarian Movements*, 3rd rev. ed. (Toronto: New Hogtown Press, 1975), pp. 12-20.

[70]Wood, *Farmers' Movements*, p. 114.

[71]S.E.D. Shortt, 'Social Change and Political Crisis in Rural Ontario: The Patrons of Industry, 1889-1896', in Donald Swainson, ed., *Oliver Mowat's Ontario* (Toronto: Macmillan, 1972), p. 222.

[72]H.C. Pentland, *Labour and Capital in Canada 1650-1860* (Toronto: Lorimer, 1981), pp. 8-23.

[73]Haythorne, *Land and Labour*, p. 199.

[74]Ibid, p. 213.

[75]John Smart, 'The Patrons of Industry in Ontario' (M.A. thesis, dept. of history, Carleton University, 1969), p. 47; Hann, *Farmers Confront Industrialism*, p. 21; Kealey and Palmer, *Dreaming*, pp. 387-91.

[76]Wood, *Farmers' Movements*, p. 103; Shortt, 'Political Crisis in Rural Ontario,' pp. 225-9; Paul Craven and Tom Traves, 'The Class Politics of the National Policy', *Journal of Canadian Studies* 14, no. 3 (Fall 1979): 19-20.

[77]S.M. Lipset, *Agrarian Socialism*, rev. ed. (Berkeley: University of California Press, 1971), pp. 20-8.

[78]Wade, *The French Canadians*, vol. 1, p. 419. See O.D. Skelton, *The Life and Letters of Sir Wilfrid Laurier*, vol. 1 (Toronto: Carleton Library, 1965), p. 89; A.R.M. Lower, *Colony to Nation* (Toronto: McClelland and Stewart, 1977), p. 383.

[79]Paul-André Linteau et al., *Quebec: A History 1867-1929* (Toronto: Lorimer, 1983), p. 251.

[80]McInnis, *Canada*, p. 430; W.L. Morton, *Manitoba: A History* (Toronto: University of Toronto Press, 1957), p. 241-50.

[81]James Watt, 'Anti-Catholicism in Ontario Politics: the Role of the Protestant Protective Association in the 1894 election', *Ontario History* 59, no. 1 (March 1967).

[82]James Watt, 'Protestant Protective Association of Canada: An Example of Religious Extremism in Ontario in the 1890s', in B. Hodgins and R. Page, eds., *Canadian History Since Confederation*, 2nd ed. (Georgetown, Ont.: Irwin-Dorsey, 1979), p. 280.

[83]Smart, *The Patrons of Industry*, p. 63.

[84]Brian R. McCutcheon, 'The Patrons of Industry in Manitoba, 1890-1898,' in Donald Swainson, ed., *Historical Essays on the Prairie Provinces* (Toronto: McClelland and Stewart, 1970), p. 163.

[85]Firmin Létourneau, *Histoire de l'agriculture (Canada Français)*, 2nd ed. (Montreal: L'Imprimerie populaire, 1952), pp. 146-62; Linteau et al., *Quebec*, pp. 421-6.

[86]R.G. Haliburton, *The Men of the North and Their Place in History* (Montreal: John Lovell, 1869), p. 1.

[87]Cited by Skelton, *Sir Wilfrid Laurier*, p. 172.

[88]William Foster, 'Canada First or Our New Nationality' (Canada: Public Archives, 1968 [1871]), p. 27.

[89]Carl Berger, *The Sense of Power: Studies in the Ideas of Canadian Imperalism 1867-1914* (Toronto: University of Toronto Press, 1970), pp. 68-77; Robert Rumilly, *Honoré Mercier et son temps*, vol. 1 (Montreal: Fides, 1975), pp. 70-6.

[90]Russell Hann, 'Brain workers and the Knights of Labor: E.E. Sheppard, Phillips Thompson and the Toronto News, 1883-1887', in Gregory Kealey and Peter Warrian, eds., *Essays in Canadian Working Class History* (Toronto: McClelland and Stewart, 1976).

[91]Foster, 'Canada First', p. 29.

[92]The Parti National's leader, Louis Jette, personally defeated G.E. Cartier on the Riel issue.

[93]Barrington Moore, Jr., *The Social Origins of Dictatorship and Democracy: Lord and Peasant in the Making of the Modern World* (Boston: Beacon Press, 1966).

[94]Max Weber, 'The Economic Foundations of "Imperialism" ', in H.H. Gerth and C.W. Mills, eds. *From Max Weber* (New York: Oxford University Press, 1958), p. 165.

[95]Karl Marx, 'Excerpts from the Eighteenth Brumaire of Louis Bonaparte' in L. Feuer, ed., *Marx and Engels*, p. 338.

[96]W.A. Williams, *The Roots of the Modern American Empire* (New York: Random House, 1969) p. 69.

[97]See Rustow, *The Politics of Compromise*, regarding independent farmers and the landed nobility in Sweden; E.H. Norman, *Japan's Emergence as a Modern State* (New York: US Institute of Pacific Relations, 1940) regarding Japan, and Gerschenkron, *Economic Backwardness*, pp. 130-42, for czarist Russia.

[98]Stein's decree abolishing serfdom was made in 1807 but most manorial peasants were not properly freed until 1850 (Knut Borchardt, 'The Industrial Revolution in Germany 1700-1914,' in C.M. Cipolla, ed., *The Emergence of Industrial Societies*, vol. 4, part 1 (London: Fontana, 1973), p. 97; R.P Dore, *Land Reform in Japan* (London: Oxford University Press, 1959), p. 14.

[99]Beards, *New Basic History of the United States*, p. 243.

[100]David Landes, *The Unbound Prometheus: Technological Change and Industrial Development in*

Western Europe from 1750 to the Present (Cambridge: Cambridge University Press, 1969), pp. 307-8.

[101]Hobsbawm, *Industry and Empire*, p. 50.

[102]Norman, *Japan's Emergence*, p. 117, 112.

[103]Alexander Gerschenkron, *Bread and Democracy in Germany* (New York: Howard Fertig, 1966).

[104]Bo Jonsson, *The State and the Orefields: A Study in Swedish Orefields Politics at the Turn of the Century* (Stockholm: Almquist and Wiksell, 1969), p. 367.

[105]Norman, *Japan's Emergence*, p. 114.

[106]Olga Crisp, 'French Investment in Russian Joint Stock Companies 1894-1914', *Business History* 2 (June 1960), p. 78.

[107]Ross Robertson, *History of the American Economy* (New York: Harcourt, Brace and World, 1964), p. 160.

[108]Hobsbawm, *Industry and Empire*, p. 113.

[109]Williams, *Modern American Empire*, p. 58.

[110]J.H. Clapham, *Economic Development of France and Germany 1815-1914* (Cambridge: Cambridge University Press, 1961), p. 156.

[111]Marx, 'Class Struggles', p. 283.

[112]Ibid., p. 296.

[113]The movement was agrarian in its appeal, but urban workers and intellectuals provided much of its leadership and thought. See Schlesinger, *The Age of Jackson*.

[114]Bray Hammond, *Banks and Politics in America: From the Revolution to the Civil War* (Princeton, Princeton University Press, 1957).

[115]Richard Tilly, *Financial Institutions and Industrialization in the Rhineland 1815-1870* (Madison: University of Wisconsin Press, 1966).

[116]Deane, *First Industrial Revolution*, p. 179.

[117]William Bowman, *The Story of the Bank of England* (London: Herbert Jenkins, 1937), p. 238.

[118]This relationship appears to have held in Japan and Sweden during industrialization. See G. Laxer, 'The Social Origins of Canada's Branch Plant Economy' (Ph.D. dissertation, University of Toronto, 1981) p. 590.

[119]Reginald Whitaker, 'Images of the State in Canada,' in L. Panitch, ed., *The Canadian State: Political Economy and Political Power* (Toronto: University of Toronto Press, 1977), p. 32.

[120]J.M.S. Careless, 'The Toronto Globe and Agarian Radicalism 1850-1867', in C. Berger, ed., *Upper Canadian Politics in the 1850s, Canadian Historical Readings*, no. 2 (Toronto: University of Toronto Press, 1967), p. 50; Wood, *Farmers' Movements*, pp. 92, 128.

[121]Fernand Ouellet, *Lower Canada 1791-1840. Social Change and Nationalism* (Toronto: McClelland and Stewart, 1980), p. 153; Wood, *Farmers' Movements*, p. 104.

[122]Henry Broude, 'The Role of the State in American Economic Development', and N. Butlin, 'Colonial Socialism in Australia, 1860-1900,' both in H. Aitken, ed., *The State and Economic Growth* (New York: Social Science Research Council, 1959), p. 38.

[123]Hammond, *Banks and Politics*.

[124]Robert L. Jones, *History of Agriculture in Ontario, 1613-1880* (Toronto: University of Toronto Press, 1946), p. 93.

[125]Naylor, *History of Canadian Business*, vol. 2, p. 218.

[126]Jacob Viner, *Canada's Balance of International Indebtness 1900-1913* (Toronto: McClelland and Stewart, 1975 [1924]), p. 288.

[127]O.D. Skelton, *The Life and Times of Sir Alexander Tilloch Galt* (Toronto: Oxford University Press, 1920), p. 243.

[128]Careless, 'The Toronto Globe and Agrarian Radicalism', p. 59.

[129]The advocates of Confederation were able to prevent an election on the issue in the two sections of Canada and in Nova Scotia, but did not succeed in New Brunswick, where they were soundly trounced in 1865. Nova Scotia elected an overwhelming contingent of anti-Confederation

members at the first opportunity (1867). PEI and Newfoundland turned down the Confederation scheme outright. See McInnis, *Canada*, p. 349.

[130]Williams, *Modern American Empire*.

[131]Greenwood, *Australia: Social and Political History*, pp. 157-8.

[132]The British maintained naval garrisons at Halifax and Esquimault until 1906.

[133]Desmond Morton, *Ministers and Generals: Politics and the Canadian Militia 1868-1904* (Toronto: University of Toronto Press, 1970), pp. 4-5.

[134]Morton, *Ministers and Generals*, p. 13.

[135]Earl of Dundonald, *My Army Life*, new ed. (London: Edward Arnold, 1934), p. 191.

[136]Morton, *Ministers and Generals*, p. 44.

[137]C.P. Stacey, *The Military Problems of Canada: A Survey of Defence Policies and Strategic Conditions Past and Present*. (Toronto: Ryerson Press, 1940), pp. 70-4.

[138]Morton, *Ministers and Generals*, pp. 44-6, 172.

[139]For the connections between defence, foreign ownership, and technological dependence see Laxer, 'Aborted Development'.

5

The Making of a Branch-plant Economy

For the most part, Canadian banks did not force capital accumulation in the way common in the United States, squeezing it out by tax in the form of depreciated currency . . . [This] means that Canadian banks contributed even less to fixed capital investment than American ones. On the whole, it seems regrettable that Canadian development in the nineteenth century had to be undertaken with the aid, alone, of so unsuitable a financial instrument as the commercial banking system. Its control of resources, and preference for short advances, tended to perpetuate an extractive economy at the expense of agricultural and industrial development.

H.C. Pentland, economic historian, 1950.

All my politics are railroad.
Allan MacNab, Prime Minister of the Province of Canada, 1853.

Americans built railroads to develop their country, Germans for purposes of war, but Canadians apparently just for the fun of building them.
A.R.M. Lower, historian, 1946.

You must not take the Militia seriously, for though it is useful for suppressing internal disturbances, it will not be required for the defence of the country, as the Monroe doctrine [proclaiming American military hegemony in the Americas] protects us against enemy aggression.
Wilfrid Laurier, Prime Minister, 1902.

At its peak, in 1913, foreign investment took over half the total of British savings, at its peak too, in the years between 1908 and 1913, foreign borrowing financed over half the total addition to the stock of capital in the largest borrower—Canada.
A.K. Cairncross, economic historian, 1953.

I am very glad to see . . . that you are going to publish something about the tariff . . . This is a love affair for me . . . I love my two boys, my only sons, and they are living in a big city of the United States. My heart is aching to have them home again in some Canadian city. I am afraid they will marry American girls and settle down there, almost forgetting their mother . . . You will say, 'What has all this to do with the question of high tariff?' I will tell you just what. I got a letter two weeks ago from one of my boys. They both work in the same factory. The letter said, 'What do you think, mother? We may be back in Canada before long. I heard our manager say yesterday . . . that if the Dominion Government should raise the Canadian tariff as high as the American tariff it would be necessary for our company to start a big branch factory in Canada. Over one-third of the work done in our great factory now is for export to Canada . . . I guess there would be quite a lot of branch factories started in Canada if the tariff should be raised and there would be lots of work for Canadians at home.' Now, Mr. Editor, do you see why I am interested in the tariff question? I want my boys to come home, because I think Canada is a purer and better country.

Elizabeth J.C. in a letter to the Montreal Family Herald and Weekly Star, *1902.*

The branch factory, by and large, is merely a more intensive method of selling an American product in foreign markets; the branch factory, theoretically at least, takes up the work where the ordinary sales methods stop.

US Senate Report, 1931.

In the last chapter we examined the social and political context of dependent industrialization. The next step is to outline the part played by state policies in the making of a branch-plant economy. Several conventional theories appear to provide simpler explanations for the preponderance of foreign direct investment in Canadian development, and it might be argued that there is little need to examine the phenomenon from a perspective emphasizing Canadian state policies. This chapter will argue otherwise.

We will start with a review of the conventional arguments, which lean, typically, on external influences, geographical factors, and market determinism. For the most part these arguments are not wrong, merely inadequate. As Richard Pomfret, writing more broadly of Canadian economic history perspectives, put it, they are unable 'to present a satisfactory general explanation of Canada's economic development.'[1] Following that review I will set out a novel political perspective that accounts for the defeat of free banking from the 1830s to 1870s, delayed prairie settlement in the 1890s, and the building of two superfluous transcontinental railways in the early 1900s. All three of these seemingly unconnected episodes had important repercussions for Canadian industrial development, ranging from a shortage of domestic long-term capital to slow growth of the internal Canadian market to the inflationary effects of borrowing massive amounts of British capital to finance the unneeded transcontinentals. And the outcomes of all three episodes had a common political cause: the defeat of the agrarian political agenda.

CONVENTIONAL WISDOM

Conventional explanations of Canada's branch-plant economy point to factors like the National Policy tariffs and the Patent Act, Canada's proximity to the United States and the 'spillover' phenomenon, the unique development of the American corporation, the triumph of market forces in Canada's high-wage economy, and Canadian conservatism in the sense of risk aversion and the influence of the British connection. (Another major factor, the encouragement of foreign direct investment as deliberate policy, will be discussed in the next chapter.)

Tariffs and foreign investment

National Policy tariffs are commonly cited as a prime cause of American direct investment in Canadian manufacturing.[2] This view is not new; in 1904 Finance Minister W.S. Fielding proclaimed that 'the Tariff, without being excessive is high enough to bring some American industries across the line'. The tariff argument appears unassailable. To avoid tariffs, US industrialists set up branch plants in Canada and affixed 'Made in Canada' labels to their products to overcome consumer resistance. US exports from Canadian subsidiaries to British Empire markets were enhanced as well.[3] Thus tariffs were undoubtedly related to foreign direct investment.

Such relationships were not confined to Canada.[4] In Chapter 2 we saw that tariffs attracted German branch plants into Russian Poland. As well, in the mid-1900s many Latin American countries used tariffs to induce direct foreign investment in a strategy known as 'import substitution'.[5] Thus the tariff inducement may appear to be a case of self-determination. After all, Canadians have been free to set tariff levels since the 1850s, and debate about tariffs was intense throughout the National Policy era. But what seems obvious need not be the truth. Tariffs can be considered a cause of foreign ownership only if external dominance and geographic determination are assumed.

Tariffs were neither necessary nor sufficient to induce foreign ownership. Many Norwegian industries, for instance, came under foreign control early in this century despite negligible tariffs.[6] In other situations tariffs attracted foreign ownership only in the context of other favourable policies. Most countries erected tariffs during initial industrialization, yet, unlike Canada, avoided high levels of foreign ownership.

Canadian tariffs were neither high nor exceptional. US tariff levels were higher in almost every year between 1867 and 1913 than Canadian ones.[7] When Canada raised its tariffs in 1879 protective duties were rising in many other nations in response to similar conditions of overproduction, falling prices, and rising nationalism:

> Austria raised its duties in 1878, 1882 and 1887 . . . Germany raised its rates in 1879, 1885 and 1888; France, in 1881, 1885, 1887 and 1892; Belgium, in 1887, Italy, in 1878, 1887 and 1891; and Russia, in 1877 and 1892. . . . Only the Netherlands, Denmark, Finland, Turkey and Great Britain retained their free trade systems.[8]

Since tariffs are more restrictive in small countries than in large ones, comparisons can be misleading. Sweden and other small countries, however, had policies that combined tariffs, successful exportation of manufactured goods, and retention of domestic ownership. If protective tariffs were commonplace, this factor alone cannot explain Canada's unique level of foreign ownership.

The patent 'working clause'

The patent 'working clause' was an adjunct to Canada's protective tariffs. It was a clause in the 1872 Patent Act stipulating that the protection afforded to inventors would be withdrawn unless they or their assignees began preparations for manufacture in Canada within two years.[9] In the absence of the working clause, a foreign firm had been able to obtain a Canadian patent and export from its home base. The philosophy behind the working clause was the neo-mercantilist doctrine of enlarging domestic output. And this was the doctrine that underlay the National Policy.

Canada's Patent Act has been widely cited as a major cause of early foreign ownership in Canada. The first to make this argument was Edward Porritt, in 1908. Canada's Patent Act, he said, 'has been as instrumental as the high duties on manufactured articles imported from the United States in compelling American manufacturers to establish branch factories in Canada—even more directly in many instances than the tariff.'[10] Cleona Lewis and R.T. Naylor have repeated Porritt's argument.[11]

There is considerable truth in these observations. The working clause provided an incentive either to establish foreign branch plants in Canada or to license new technologies to Canadian entrepreneurs (licensing arrangements were often a prelude to foreign ownership). Patent laws had these effects outside Canada too. Gillette, an American razor company, established a branch plant in Germany in the early 1900s because of Germany's working clause.[12] Similarly, Siemens of Germany founded a French subsidiary in 1878 to comply with France's working law.[13] Thus the working clause, like protective tariffs, invited foreign direct investment.

Again, however, this is not the whole story. R.T. Naylor has given the impression that Canada was unique in the way its patent working clause affected foreign investment. But in fact the US was the only country without such a clause.[14] Working clauses date from fourteenth-century Europe. Britain's patent law of 1624, which included a working clause, was a model for other countries. Although in the eighteenth century Britain gradually abandoned the obligation to work a patent, most other countries did adopt the rule.[15] The compulsory working provision was a major clause in the first International Convention for the Protection of Industrial Property in 1884.

Although Canada did not join the international body until 1924, the wording of its 1872 statutes is almost identical to that of the 1884 International Convention.[16]

Naylor has pointed out that the Canadian law prohibited imports of articles patented in Canada, whereas some countries restricted imports and others had no import curbs at all.[17] The Canadian law, however, was just a stronger expression of the widely accepted principle of requiring a patentee to make the article in the country granting patent privileges. The question posed in regard to tariffs must be raised here too. If Canadian law was not unique, why did Canada receive unique levels of foreign direct investment?

Geography and external influences

At this point geographic determinism,[18] external influences, and market forces are usually brought in to bolster the tariff and patent arguments. In *The Emergence of Multinational Enterprise: American Business Abroad* Mira Wilkins devoted chapters to the spillover effects to both Canada and Mexico.[19] American trade and investment spread to neighbouring Mexico and Canada, she observed, after the US frontier closed in the late 1800s. Incentives for Americans to invest in nearby resources included cost savings, convenience, and, it was assumed, security of supply. America's northern and southern neighbours were the two largest recipients of US direct investment shortly before 1914.

This pattern would seem to clinch the proximity argument—at least until Mexico's nationalist revolution of 1911 is considered. Before that date Mexico was the leading recipient of American direct investments abroad; after it, Mexico receded from this position and Canada became the leading recipient. Internal changes in Mexico overcame the 'push' factors of proximity and external influence. Similarly, as already noted, Sweden and Norway resisted nearby German and British direct investment forays during the same era. In all these cases, internal policies counteracted the expansionism of nearby economic giants. Thus proximity and external desire to invest were not sufficient explanations of foreign ownership either.

Supporters of the proximity thesis have one remaining card to play: it seems to have been more difficult for less-developed countries to resist foreign ownership in the manufacturing sector than in the resource field. Perhaps, then, geographic and external factors were sufficient conditions to account for high levels of foreign ownership in manufacturing.

In the early 1900s manufacturers established branch plants abroad to stimulate sales or to hold on to existing markets threatened by tariffs or other restrictions. Thus foreign ownership followed trade, and high-income markets were of more interest than poor ones: the lucrative Canadian market, for instance, was more attractive to US manufacturers than the Mexican one, where poverty restricted market size. Often a firm would start with a sales branch and later set up a branch factory. Companies establishing foreign subsidiaries usually had advantages in technology, or in novel products or marketing techniques.[20]

Foreign branch plants represented more than movements of capital. They were primarily transfers of technology, know-how, and entrepreneurship. Such transfers had occurred earlier as individuals migrated abroad, taking their knowledge with them.[21] But foreign branch plants were different because they remained satellites of headquarters' operations and were integral to their marketing strategies. Companies did not establish foreign subsidiaries in significant numbers until the 1870s to 1890s, when national markets emerged and industries became consolidated in the advanced countries.

From a late twentieth-century perspective it would appear obvious that the transnational subsidiary was an American creation, while Europe was still engaged in the older patterns of portfolio investments and exports, often to captive markets in old-style empires. After all, the US was the home of the majority of transnationals after 1945. That being so, it was natural that Canada, its only affluent neighbour, should receive branch plants at an early point. No other industrial country was situated beside the United States. In contrast, Europe was shielded by the Atlantic Ocean from the brunt of the American economic invasion until after 1945, and by then it had generated mature industrial structures, mainly under the stewardship of domestic capitalists.

This logic rests on flawed assumptions. The US was not the only innovative power, nor was it the only country to establish branch plants abroad prior to 1914. Germany was also conquering foreign markets in the new technologies (as discussed briefly in Chapter 2). On the eve of the Great War German electrical exports were greater than those of the US and Britain combined,[22] while in chemicals Germany was the world's leader, a position achieved through technical excellence.[23] German branch plants appeared in nearby countries in electrical and chemical goods, metal-working, and engineering. So great was German dominance in chemicals that the US industry was largely German-owned until the US government took it over for strategic reasons during the war with Germany.[24]

In the late nineteenth century corporations in Germany and the US underwent remarkably similar changes through diversification and functional integration.[25] As Jurgen Kocka observed, 'In both cases, the large firms clustered in capital-intensive, technologically-advanced industries, especially those producing iron, steel and other metals, on the one hand, and machinery, instruments and transportation equipment, on the other.'[26] The original structure of the firm and the types of goods produced were similar in both countries—and in marked contrast to Britain, which had already lost its technological lead. Germany relied more heavily on science and technology than did the US, but its industry was less geared to mass-marketing.

Still, despite the similarity of German and American firms, Germany failed to develop transnationals on a scale to rival the US. Conclusions about the causes of that failure must remain tentative, since extensive research on early German foreign direct investment has only recently begun,[27] but two reasons seem paramount: the devastation of two world wars and greater resistance to German subsidiaries in neighbouring countries. As the loser in both world wars, Germany experienced great discontinuities in its development. Wilkins noted that

> World War I marked a dividing point . . . German, direct foreign investors lost control over their investment strategies: German subsidiaries in the United States and Britain were taken over . . . As a consequence of war, Krupp lost its ore fields in Lorraine, Spain, and Latvia, but . . . part of its loss may have been recouped . . . Numerous German concerns had substantial pre-war investments in Russia that they never regained; important German properties in Poland passed to other nationalities as a result of German defeat. *Of all direct investments abroad, those of German companies appear to have been most seriously, hurt by the war.*[28] (Emphasis added.)

Because Germany lost substantial territory and population in both wars, its per capita production was almost stagnant, growing at only 0.4 per cent per annum from 1913 to 1950.[29]

Yet the wars only partly explain the relative dearth of German transnationals. Neighbouring countries resisted German investments before 1914: czarist Russia's opposition to German branch plants was examined in Chapter 2, and Sweden's and Norway's restrictions on German and British foreign ownership in Chapter 3. In these instances the internal politics of host countries affected the establishment of foreign branch plants.

In sum, like the other arguments already discussed, proximity and external influences alone cannot account for Canada's unique level of foreign ownership. Since Russia, Sweden, and Norway were able to resist the incursion of German branch plants, we are still left with the question of why Canada did not do the same.

Market forces and Canada's high-wage proletariat

A variation of the market determinism/external influences theme has been advanced from a Marxist perspective by Leo Panitch.[30] Parting company with Marxists preoccupied solely by Canadian capitalists—commercial or industrial—Panitch focusses on the role of working-class struggles in the making of a branch-plant economy. For Panitch the strength of a high-wage proletariat was crucial to Canada's dependent development (an argument reminiscent of the 'white dominion model' discussed in Chapter 1).

According to Panitch, high Canadian wages had contradictory effects. An expanding domestic market for mass-produced goods was favourable for industrialization, but it created opportunities for American rather than Canadian capitalists. High wages, won through the 'very struggles of the Canadian working class',[31] came in several forms: a shorter work week, restricted immigration, and resistance to factory discipline and wage cuts. These working-class victories limited the extraction of surplus value (akin to profits), argues Panitch, and forced employers to adopt labour-saving technologies, with severe consequences for Canadian-owned manufacturing. The reduction of industrial profits affected Canadian manufacturers more than their American competitors, who were 'experiencing the same or worse at home', because the latter aimed not to expand their profit level but to enlarge their market. Only Canadian capitalists 'had to worry about rates of return to invested capital in manufacturing in Canada', presumably because they confined their activities to Canada.[32]

Panitch's focus on groups outside the economic élite is a welcome change, but the particulars of his argument are confused. He assumes that because Canada developed later, its manufacturing productivity was much lower than that of the US. From this it follows that to compensate for low Canadian productivity, Canadian workers would have had to accept lower wages than they did. (Although lower than American wages, Canadian wages were still high by international comparison.) Panitch cites H.A. Logan's US-Canadian comparisons of manufacturing wages. According to Logan, US wages were about 60 per cent higher in 1890; the gap narrowed to about 25 per cent in 1910 and widened slightly in the 1920s.[33] Logan's figures have long since been replaced: recent estimates show the wage gap to have been greater especially in the immediate pre-First World War period of branch-plant invasion.

But the main issue was whether Canada's productivity or efficiency was comparable to that of other countries, and labour is only one factor in overall productivity; Logan himself noted that wage levels and labour efficiency cannot tell us about comparative efficiency.[34] Panitch fails to examine this question. Subsequent to Panitch's article, J.R. Baldwin and A.G. Green calculated that by 1929 productivity in manufacturing was almost equal in the two countries—Canadian total factor productivity was only 3 to 5 per cent lower.[35]

Contrary to Panitch's assumption, manufacturers adjusted rationally to Canadian conditions of lower wages by combining more labour with other inputs. Canadian industry used less capital, less fuel, and fewer materials per worker, thus making Canadian productivity roughly equal to American.[36] If Baldwin and Green are right, capitalists in Canada did precisely what Panitch argued they were not able to do: impose a higher rate of 'absolute exploitation of the Canadian working class'[37] by paying lower wages.

The argument about relatively high Canadian wages seems to owe more to Marx's discussion of relative and absolute surplus value (involving class struggles over the length of the working day) in Volume 1 of *Capital*[38] than to economic history. History cannot be explained by deduction from theory. Adam Smith and the American free-traders of the 1820s made a similar deduction from theory when they argued that the fact that higher wages were paid in the more backward US than in Britain posed an insuperable obstacle to US manufacturing exports, and even to the establishment of manufacturing altogether.[39] In the next several decades they were proven wrong: far from leading to reduced profits and foreign industrial domination, higher US wages led to an explosive search for new technologies and new ways to organize work to reduce its labour content.[40]

High Canadian wages did not preclude manufacturing exports to Europe. The 1890s and 1900s were Canada's golden period of exporting farm implements: before 1902 only one US firm exported more than Canada's Massey-Harris,[41] which exported more than half its production by 1911 and sold more binders in Germany in 1905 than all local manufacturers combined.[42] The main markets for Canadian light binders, thresher-reapers, ploughs, and seed drills were in the advanced countries; Britain and Australasia, areas of relatively high wages, each took about a quarter of these Canadian exports in 1899.[43] The cases of lower-wage Germany and France are more interesting. Although industrially more developed than Canada at that time, Germany and France together took about one-third of Canadian exports of farm implements, despite their lower wages.[44] Sweden developed under similar conditions: although its industrial wages were 10 to 20 per cent above those in Germany from the 1880s to 1914, it competed increasingly well with Germany in Baltic markets.[45]

Finally, there is the curious argument about lower industrial profits in Canada. (Panitch weakens his case by referring to comparable US working-class resistance to capitalist exploitation, a state of affairs that, according to his reasoning, should have led to low profits there as well.) If Canada achieved comparable levels of overall productivity with more labour power in as broad a sector as manufacturing, the extraction of surplus value would, according to Marxist theory, be higher in Canadian than in US industry.[46]

Is there evidence that industrial profits were lower in Canada? The important test is from history. No one has made a systematic survey, but fragmentary information shows good profit levels for American and Canadian industry in Canada from 1900 to 1914.[47] Jacob Viner referred to US direct investments in Canada as 'offering a chance at unusually high profits as well as losses'.[48] Rapid growth in Canada's total productivity and domestic market size provided favourable conditions for both domestic and foreign direct investment.

Canadian workers were not as influential in raising wages as Panitch suggests. Except for gaining restrictions on Oriental labour after the Canadian Pacific Railway was completed, union opposition to massive immigration was totally ineffectual. In-migration peaked in the years 1900-14, the first period of high US branch-plant entry into Canada. Immigration likely served precisely the purpose that organized labour feared: suppression of wage increases. Manufacturing expanded more rapidly than at any time in Canadian history, yet real wages appear to have remained stationary.[49] Unions were powerless to restrict immigration.

In attributing so much power to organized workers, Panitch erred on the voluntarist side. But the rest of his argument is the familiar blend of market determinism, external influence, and geographic proximity. Consider this statement:

> American capital came to dominate Canadian industry because [of] the balance of class forces in a continental capital and labour market which the National Policy could not alter ... Canada's early history of simple commodity production, its proximity to the United States geographically and culturally, and above all perhaps the timing of its industrial 'takeoff' determined aspects of Canada's trajectory to a 'rich dependency'.[50]

In summary, we have seen that tariffs were neither a sufficient nor a necessary condition for the establishment of foreign direct investment. The tariff and Patent Act arguments, if they have any validity, can be made only in conjunction with assumptions of geographic determinism or external domination. But geographic determinism and external control are questionable assumptions. Canada was not coerced into accepting US direct investments during the National Policy era. Nor did investment inevitably 'spill' across borders. Finally, high wages did not price Canadian-owned industries out of the market either at home or abroad.

State policies—as well as the inclinations of Canadian businessmen—were crucial in turning an American predisposition towards Canada into actual investments. It is to these policies and inclinations that we now turn to account for the predominance of US direct investment in Canada's productive sectors.

THE ROLE OF BANKS

Banks and state revenue

Late-follower Canada could not rely on accumulating industrial capital through reinvestment of profits. Instead, it could develop a financial system to gather dispersed capital and direct it into long-term investment in industry—the investment-banking route of other late-follower countries—or it could invite foreign capital to do the job.

There were two routes to the adoption of investment banking. One was the German system, in which state control over the issuing of bank notes forced privately owned banks to look for new ways to turn a profit. The other was the (early) British and (later) American system in which privately owned banks held the note-issuing right. This is the route to be discussed here.

Where privately owned banks won the right to issue notes there were two contrasting patterns: the right could be monopolized by large banks, or it could be spread among numerous small banks. Where, as in nineteenth-century Canada, large banks captured a monopoly, conservative, commercially oriented banking systems tended to emerge; in that case, if the state needed funds to pay for infrastructure, it often borrowed foreign capital on a massive scale. In the second form, by contrast, many small banks could issue bank notes. This pattern prevailed during Britain's initial industrialization (but not after the 1820s), in the US from the late 1830s, and in pre-Confederation New Brunswick and southern Nova Scotia in the latter half of the nineteenth century.

When numerous small banks could issue notes, the result was a form of investment banking. Money was lent to industry as revolving (usually three-month) loans and covered working capital, but usually not fixed capital. Small banks did not allocate capital to industry as effectively as German investment banks, but they were much better in this regard than commercial banks. Canada, therefore, developed the worst system for a late-follower country. Large commercial banks controlled note-issuing, and the state lacked the resources to finance infrastructure. While German investment banking would have suited Canadian conditions, it was never seriously considered. The Canadian state's failure to gain control over the issuing of bank notes at an early point may have precluded the emergence of German-style investment banking in Canada. Many Canadians equated investment banks with corruption: 'This is an age of grab. . . . An age . . . of the [US] Crédit Mobilier, the Tammany Ring.'[51]

The fight for free banking

Debate was intense during the formation of the Canadian banking system, from the 1830s to the 1870s, over whether Canada should retain the early American commercial banking system, which avoided risky long-term investments, or adopt the later American system of 'free' (unit) banking, with its greater emphasis on long-term investments. Ironically, British authorities sided with the early American system and opposed the later changes in that country.

The first banks chartered in Canada (1817-22) were modelled after American commercial banks, whose philosophy was stability and conservatism. Merchants set up most early Canadian banks for their own use, not for lending to farmers or mechanics. As the US moved to a freer credit system in the 1830s, however, the influence of its banking system waned and a strong British presence prevailed. The implications were enormous. From the 1830s to the 1860s, when farm mechanization and emerging industry required long-term investments, the banks increasingly emphasized liquidity, and loan terms were shortened. Canadian banks shunned railway financing and public debt until the 1880s.

A far-ranging debate on banking policy took place in Britain and the US from the 1820s to the 1840s, after which the two banking systems were set firmly on different paths. The main issues in the debate were banking security, currency uniformity and stability, banking monopoly, social privilege, regulation, and public versus private revenue from note-issuing.

The panic of 1825, in which sixty country banks in England failed, led to changes culminating in the Bank Act of 1844, the foundation of modern British banking. The Bank of England, founded 150 years earlier, became a truly central bank with a near-monopoly over note-issuing.[52] A restricted number of large regional banks with numerous branches became entrenched, virtually killing small country banks. Risk capital for industry, so plentiful in the first fifty years of industrialization, began to dry up after the crash of 1837.[53] Three episodes of bank failures—in 1847, 1857, and 1866—taught the surviving banks the importance of liquidity, and by the 1870s Britain had a commercial banking system that avoided long-term investments in industry. Having passed through initial industrialization, British manufacturing was not impeded in the short run, but in pre-industrial Canada the entrenchment of commercial banking had different effects.

The US moved in the opposite direction. Starting with a more conservative system than England's, it destroyed its central bank and the near-monopoly of large commercial banks in the 1830s. Unrestricted banking allowed the number of state banks to mushroom to 1,562 by 1860.[54] For a time the new American system favoured debtors over creditors, and capital flowed more freely into farming and industry. In these years the United States became an industrial country.

The British and American debates spilled over to British North America. The American advocates of 'free' banking and 'no' banking (many farmers opposed banks altogether) had their counterparts in Upper and Lower Canada in the 1830s. Most were reformers who tended to represent farmers, the main class supporting banking changes in the US.

'Of all the devices now at work to harm the country's interests, the most powerful is the bad administration of the Banks,' declared Louis-Joseph Papineau in 1834, in terms indistinguishable from the agrarian attacks that would continue throughout North America for the next century:[55] banks favoured the 'monopoly of a political coterie' and were run simply for their own gain. Papineau and the Parti Patriote directed their hostility against the Bank of Montreal, which represented Montreal's British merchants and enjoyed a near-monopoly in the province. Along with the British Governor, the Bank's directors virtually ran the government from the unelected Legislative Council.[56] Yet, fearing the economic consequences, the Patriotes did not attempt to destroy the Bank as the Jacksonians were then doing to the Bank of the United States.

There was much less agitation for new banks among French Canadians than among Upper Canadians and Americans during the tumultuous and speculative 1830s. Lacking capital because of their land tenure system and a severe farm crisis, most French Canadians were loath to take on debt.[57] But even in Lower Canada new banks were proposed to break the British Tory monopoly. The Banque du Peuple was the most ambitious alternative, founded by promoters associated with the Parti Patriote to assist farmers.[58]

Supported on nationalist grounds by French Canadians, the new bank prospered, and two other independent rural banks were operating along similar lines on the eve of the 1837 Rebellion.[59]

Upper Canadian farmers cast envious glances at American prosperity and freer credit. Desperately short of capital, farmers supported easy credit and attacked the monopoly of the Bank of Upper Canada, the preserve of the unelected executive. (According to Adam Shortt, it was 'virtually a private corporation of the Family Compact backed by the funds of the Provincial Treasury'.)[60] As in the neighbouring American states, banking was a major political question in Upper Canada. Reformers caused a run on the Bank of Upper Canada in an attempt to ruin it. They created their own bank, the Bank of the People, named after its counterpart in Lower Canada,[61] and local banks were also established to provide credit to farmers.[62] From 1831 to 1835 three measures were introduced in the Assembly to deregulate banks, and a few new banks were chartered. But the Family Compact had friends in high places. Alarmed by the danger of corruption from American influences, the Colonial Office in 1836 refused any act on banking and currency without prior royal assent. The legislature retaliated, increasing banking capital by 900 per cent and approving nine new banks,[63] but royal assent was withheld. Before the legislature could react, the 1837-38 rebellions broke out, and the large number of American bank failures in the same years made Canadian élites less receptive to bank expansion.

After the rebellions were defeated, agrarian radicalism was muted for a decade. In Upper Canada reform leadership passed to pro-commerce moderates, merchants, financiers, and landowners, while in Lower Canada Lord Durham's challenge to French Canadian nationality became the central issue. In the 1840s the quest for responsible government (democratic home rule) united Upper Canadian reformers with Lower Canadian nationalists. Agrarian demands were largely absent until responsible government was won in 1848, when free-banking proposals were again put forward.

The defeat of free banking

Soon after the union of Lower and Upper Canada in 1841, a debate arose over state revenue and banking changes. A united province, long demanded by Montreal merchants, now made it possible to improve St Lawrence shipping: defeat of the rebellion and Durham's challenge to French Canadian nationality had neutralized French Canadian opposition to canal-building at public expense. But an obstacle remained. High Upper Canadian debts hamstrung government involvement. The state needed more revenue.

Lord Sydenham, first governor of the united province, was central to the banking changes then taking place in England. As former President of the Board of Trade, and a close associate of Lord Overstone—the leading exponent of the currency principle embodied in the conservative 1844 Bank Act in England—Sydenham proposed a public bank of note-issue for the Province of Canada. Through such a bank the chartered banks' lucrative note-issuing business could be transferred into state coffers to finance transportation improvements. Merchants and contractors would have benefitted to the detriment of banks. But politics did not break along these lines because many big merchants were also involved in banking. As well, many legislators were sceptical of any proposal coming from the Governor because of his opposition to responsible government.

Although Sydenham was supported by Francis Hincks, former cashier of the People's Bank and a moderate Reformer, and George Moffatt, a founder of the Bank of Montreal, his bill was defeated. No debate on banking could be disentangled from the main issue of responsible government. Some opposed any scheme strengthening the revenues of the unelected executive; others were leery of a public note-issuing monopoly, remembering the Family Compact's connection with the Bank of Upper Canada. Chartered banks and ultra-conservatives also fought the scheme.[64]

The defeat of public note-issuing had serious consequences for state debt. Since most Canadian banks held back from lending to governments, railways, farmers, and industry in the 1840s and 1850s, continuing instead to fund the staples trade, the state was forced into massive capital imports. The enormous debt thus incurred led to the contentious issue of higher tariffs for revenue, as well as a loss of investor confidence. Proposals for public note-issuing were made without success until the bank acts of 1870-71.[65]

In the 1840s, during the low ebb of agrarian radicalism, several changes consolidated commercial banking. Having adopted a conservative banking philosophy in England, the Colonial Office and British Treasury interfered increasingly in Canadian affairs to ensure that British practices prevailed.[66] A uniform commercial banking system was taking shape in the united province, note-issuing was increasingly confined to the large chartered banks, and the People's Bank merged with the Bank of Montreal. Thus the reformers' failure to achieve self-determination in the 1830s had important consequences for banking.

With responsible government achieved in 1848, exiled reformers returned—as did agrarian radicalism. Amidst widespread agitation for more banking capital, Hincks and William Merritt supported a 'freedom of banking' bill in the Canadas, modelled after New York State laws, that was intended to set up unit banks. The bill passed in 1850, but did not meet expectations because it was fashioned by a section of commercial capitalists more concerned with provincial debt than with farmers' need for credit. Finance Minister Hincks forced the free banks to tie up their capital in low-yield government securities, a requirement not made of chartered commercial banks. As a result free banks could not compete with the chartered banks. (In the US, by contrast, the Jacksonian movement of agrarians, workers, and New York bankers had been able to sweep away the chartered banking system.)[67]

Hincks's interest in state revenue was not purely altruistic: public largesse to the Grand Trunk Railway netted him personally over $1 million.[68]

It is not clear why legislators got away with penalizing the 'free' banks. The positions of the Clear Grits and Rouges towards free banking have not been adequately researched, but we know that the British Treasury issued a strong rebuke of the 'unsound' banking law, and chartered banks protested loudly. On the other hand, the Toronto and Hamilton Boards of Trade opposed repeal of the Free Banking Act in 1857, arguing that more banking capital was needed.

The British-owned Bank of British North America, established in 1837, also helped the triumph of commercial banking in Canada. Operating under a royal, not a colonial, charter, its directors had powerful connections in the City of London and the Colonial Office. With its enormous prestige, the Bank introduced some Scottish banking practices that were soon copied by Canadian banks. It also brought to Canada several generations of Scottish bankers who knew much more about Scottish and English than American banking.[69] This was a new element. Until the late 1830s Canadian bankers and businessmen had been more familiar with US banking practices.[70]

The final attempt to introduce unit banking occurred after Confederation on the initiative of the Bank of Montreal. With almost one-quarter of central Canadian (paid-up) capital, it had been the exclusive Canadian banker to the government and the Grand Trunk, Canada's main railway.[71] The Bank proposed a public note-issuing monopoly and a system of local banks, the latter a long-standing demand of farmers. The few large commercial banks would handle Canada's mercantile and foreign trade, while smaller commercial banks would lean on the stronger Bank of Montreal for assistance.[72] The ensuing system would have resembled the early English pattern, with many small country banks, a few large commercial banks, and the Bank of Montreal functioning like the private, central Bank of England. Although not fully adequate for late-follower development, this system had favoured industry and innovation during England's early development.

Macdonald's government supported the Bank of Montreal's scheme—which would have meant using Canadian capital to finance infrastructure and, to a lesser extent, industry—because it promised greater state revenue and access to capital. But except for the Maritime unit banks, all banks, cities, and boards of trade resisted the proposal.[73] (Farmers, urban workers, and manufacturers took little part in this historic battle.) Instead, the scheme's opponents wanted to use Canadian capital only to move staples, and to rely on British capital to build railways and canals.[74] Jealousy of Montreal's dominance, especially from Toronto, threatened to split the Conservative Party, and the government retreated. The victory of the opponents' proposal led to an overemphasis on staple extraction and capital imports during initial industrialization.

Both the politics and the timing of crucial turning points in Canadian banking history have been unfortunate. Just as American banking took a more favourable direction, it lost its influence in central Canada, and the colony adopted British banking practices only after they had become less useful for late-follower development. Internal politics contributed to the ebb and flow of external influence. Agrarian radicals campaigned for free banking but defeat of the rebellions cut their movement short, and British influence increased as the commercial element made political gains. The 1850s revival of agrarian radicalism was stillborn, mired in sectional conflict. Free banking was allowed to die.

By the 1870s the commercial banking system was well entrenched and immune to later attacks by western farmers. In the years to come, Canadian banks failed to effectively fund industrial development, leaving a void for foreign capital and foreign management to fill. The federal government, deprived of note-issuing revenue, relied more heavily on prairie land sales, huge imports of British portfolio capital, and tariffs to finance development.

THE IMPACT OF DELAYED PRAIRIE SETTLEMENT

The west and the National Policy

'We are the nation of human progress,' cried John L. O'Sullivan, creator of the idea of American Manifest Destiny. It was 'the right of our manifest destiny to overspread and to possess the whole of the continent which Providence has given us for the ... great experiment of liberty'.[75] When the separatist traditions of the US South were destroyed in civil war, his dream, the dream of the American North, seemed about to triumph. Only a few small British colonies stood in the way of its realization. When they banded together defensively in Confederation, the prospects of their remaining outside the great union seemed poor. They were largely concentrated in small numbers along the St Lawrence and the Atlantic fringe, confined to the eastern part of the continent by the Canadian Shield. Hopes of building an empire from sea to sea to rival the US depended on the British northwest. If the new Dominion could lay effective claim to it, success was assured; without it, Canada could not resist absorption for long.

Confederation was a response to political, economic, and strategic crises. When, by the mid-1850s, most of the arable land in the older provinces had been settled, British North Americans began to emigrate in increasing numbers to the American west in search of new land. To stem this loss of people Canada needed to develop a new frontier. Settlement of the Canadian west would, it was hoped, not only satisfy Canadians' appetite for virgin farm land, but also stimulate manufacturing in eastern Canada by rapidly expanding the domestic market. As soon as the Canadian Pacific Railway reached the prairies in 1883, however, settlement slowed to a trickle; homestead entries were down until 1899, and did not become really large again until 1903.[76] The effect, I will argue, was to slow the development of Canadian manufacturing in eastern Canada in the 1880s and 1890s, leaving Canadian industry vulnerable to the invasion of American branch plants from 1900 to 1914.

The staples approach viewed the pre-1914 wheat boom as the main cause of Canadian growth and manufacturing development at that time. In 1956 W.T. Easterbrook and Hugh Aitken reflected the common wisdom: 'wheat production sparked this industrial development and ... prairie settlement created a strong demand for Canadian manufacturers.'[77] Although in 1966 Chambers and Gordon questioned the connection between western settlement and eastern industry, calculating that the wheat boom contributed at most 8.4 per cent to growth in per capita income between 1901 and 1911,[78] subsequent studies have disputed this argument.[79] According to the critics of Chambers and Gordon, an investment boom preceded the wheat boom in anticipation of the latter and stimulated Canadian manufacturing development.[80] Thus the staples explanation linking prairie settlement to Canada's industrial growth stands up well. Given this, we can move on to the main question: why settlement, and therefore the wheat boom, was delayed.

Since the Dominion of Canada had been created largely from above, for reasons of convenience, rather than from below, by popular will, prosperity was crucial to success. There was no common bond of nationality to hold the allegiance of all Canadians. The British connection was a binding force for most people of British origin, but was divisive vis-à-vis French Canada. At the same time, the value of the British tie had to compete against the attractions of continental union. The very existence of Canada would be imperilled if economic opportunities fell too far behind those in the buoyant US.[81]

Shortly after Confederation, John A. Macdonald pulled together elements of past policy into a coherent vision known as the National Policy that was to last into the 1930s. Tariffs were central to it, but to reconcile two contradictory purposes it was important that they be moderate: they had to be high enough to encourage the location of manufacturing in Canada, but not so high that imports ceased—otherwise tariff revenues would also cease.[82] Our ancestors may have been reconciled to death, but to income taxes they were not. There was no need: duties on imports, the federal government's main revenue source, made direct taxation (including income taxes) unnecessary.

Macdonald foresaw the National Policy stemming a disastrous exodus in the 1870s. Exaggerating a little for effect, he said:

> We have no manufactures here. We have no work-people; our work-people have gone to the United States. They are to be found employed in the Western States, in Pittsburg ... Canadian artizans are adding to the strength, to the power, and to the wealth of a foreign nation instead of adding to ours ... If Canada had had a judicious system of taxation [a protective tariff] they would be toiling and doing well in their own country.[83]

A protective tariff and a transcontinental railway would ensure that a rapidly growing west would be a captive market for eastern manufactured goods.

The concept was bold, and for a time it seemed to work. Manitoba boomed in anticipation of a Canadian transportation link with the east. But, as noted above, when the CPR connected Winnipeg with the Great Lakes, in 1883, the settlement boom ended. This is one of the great puzzles of Canadian history. Why did prairie settlement slow down just when the CPR was completed, and why did it take almost twenty years to pick up again?[84]

Conventional explanations

Historians have perhaps spent as much energy debating why settlement was delayed as the politicians of the time spent wringing their hands over it. An older literature from the 1930s used the traditional explanations: the low international price of wheat, the competition of the American frontier, and an inhospitable climate that hindered settlement of the west in the nineteenth century. This debate has been taken up anew by economic historians applying econometric methods. Both groups of scholars have much to say, but typically they have formulated the question too narrowly, neglecting the political aspects. I will argue that the availability of railways and the terms of land sales—fundamental influences on the rate of settlement—were, as in the US west, greatly affected by political decisions. My purpose is to introduce a new political perspective to see how far it can illuminate the question.

Many people sought land in unsettled regions of the New World in the 1880s and 1890s. Many Europeans emigrated to wheat lands in the US, Argentina, and Australia; over 750,000 came to the US in 1882 alone.[85] Internal migration from settled to frontier regions was brisk too; over 250,000 eastern Canadians moved west between 1870 and 1900. But barely more than half ended up in the Canadian west: the rest went to the American plains.[86] If so many immigrants were available, why did so few come to and stay in the Canadian frontier during this crucial era of industrial development?

Let us look first at the traditional arguments. In 1935 W.A. Mackintosh argued that

> the tide of world markets was running strongly against settlement on the Canadian plains in those years. The settlement boom of the early eighties made headway against it only for a time before being converted into a recession. The decline of wheat prices was particularly sharp after 1882, and it accounts in large measure for the decline in settlement after that date. Contemporary with the great period of prairie settlement, the trend of wheat prices was steeply upward from 1895 to 1920.[87]

This argument is not correct regarding the movement of prices;[88] nor does it take into consideration the fact that as transport costs fell drastically from the 1870s to the early 1900s, farmers received a higher proportion of the international price for wheat. At Regina, for example, the farm price of wheat declined only 7 per cent from 1880-84 to 1895-99, while the international price fell 35 per cent.[89]

A full understanding of the incentives to settle the Canadian prairies would include an examination of farm-gate prices and comparative costs in unsettled lands in North America. Unfortunately, information is spotty on these questions for the 1880s to 1890s period.[90] We do know, however, that wheat farming expanded rapidly in the US, Russia, Argentina, and Australia in the nineteenth century, and that farmers in those countries were subject to similar prices and, likely, similar costs. Consequently, an explanation of delayed prairie settlement in Canada based on world wheat prices and other economic disincentives is inadequate.

Then there is the second explanation: American competition. 'The most decisive factor in relegating Canada to a very minor role in the world migration and capital movements', wrote Easterbrook and Aitken, 'must be sought in the weight and momentum of United States expansion westward.'[91] This idea that the American frontier had to be filled before Canada could have its turn seems to imply a mystical pull to the American dream—a questionable assumption. At any rate, the argument flies in the face of an incontrovertible fact: the US frontier did not close when the boom in Canada began. Homestead entries from 1901 to 1910 were nearly twice as great in the US as in the previous ten years.[92]

Kenneth Norrie restored the American-frontier argument to economic orthodoxy by removing its non-rational assumptions. He argued that settlers on both sides of the border avoided semi-arid lands (where annual rainfall averaged a precarious 10 to 20 inches) as long as sub-humid lands (20 to 30 inches of precipitation) were still available. Sub-humid lands could be farmed by traditional methods,[93] but semi-arid ones could not. It was not until the late 1890s that techniques to cope with semi-arid conditions were developed and widely diffused, at which time many settlers took up the dry lands on either side of the border. Norrie concludes that 'since there was a much greater supply of sub-humid land in the US it was inevitable that the American boom after 1879 would dwarf the Canadian one, and that many Canadians would be attracted to the US'.[94] With this argument Norrie linked the second traditional explanation (the end of available land in the American west) with the third (climate as a barrier to settlement).

There is no disputing the precarious nature of farming in the Canadian prairies at the turn of the century. Drought and variable rainfall in the south, frost in the north, little wood on the open plains, hail storms, high winds, and grasshopper infestations were hazards requiring new techniques.[95] Since the Canadian plains developed late, settlers there were able to borrow the innovations of American plains farmers by the 1880s: the chilled-steel plough, roller-milling, Appleton's twine binder, mechanical grain elevators, summer fallowing, the sod house, and other dry-farming techniques.[96] Still, Norrie is undoubtedly correct in claiming that few settlers ventured into semi-arid lands while moister, sub-humid lands were available on the continent.[97] As he points out, settlers were averse to risk, preferring consistent yields to gambling, even if long-term averages were high.[98]

Canadian settlement patterns confirm the Norrie hypothesis. The CPR main line cut through Palliser's triangle, the semi-arid region that includes southwestern Saskatchewan and southern Alberta.[99] Run by a shrewd management interested in the railway business, the CPR promoted settlement. (Its attitude contrasted with that of the Union Pacific, a US railway that concentrated on the sale of railway lands rather than on rail traffic.) The CPR encouraged settlement by building a massive irrigation project and selling lands at lower rates than other large western landholders.[100] Increased settlement near the railway meant more rail traffic; thus in some respects the interests of the CPR and settlers were complementary.

The Dominion government also promoted settlement, advertising extensively and establishing agents in the US, Britain, and Europe. It increased its efforts after 1896, but there were still few takers by 1901.[101] Ten years later, after the rush of settlers pushed the prairie population to over 1.3 million, Palliser's triangle was still only 'thinly settled'.[102] Rail transportation, fairly benevolent land policies, and vigorous promotion had not been enough to overcome the climatic problems. Thus technical barriers defeated the best efforts of the state and business to hasten settlement of Palliser's triangle.

Settlement of the Park Belt—the area north of the triangle, including Saskatoon and Edmonton—was different. Early surveys indicated that the area was preferable to the dryer southern region; in the 1850s Captain John Palliser called it the 'fertile belt' and the semi-arid region (named for him) an extension of the 'American desert'. In the case of the Park Belt it was railways and governments rather than technical factors that affected the rate and timing of settlement; however, as it will be argued here, those efforts did not quicken settlement but impede it.

Recent literature on the rate of settlement concentrates primarily on Palliser's triangle. This is surprising, because it had the least-promising farm land and attracted the fewest settlers. The Canadian prairies contain a lot of land with moisture levels similar to those of the sub-humid areas in the US where settlement proceeded quickly before 1900.[103] After people had finally come to western Canada in large numbers, Palliser's triangle was the most thinly settled area; in 1911 half the area had fewer than two people per square mile and very little of it had more than five. In contrast, the Park Belt showed much higher densities. Very little of this region had fewer than two people per square mile, the most common density being two to five persons; large areas had five to ten. It would appear that the northern Park Belt had about twice the population of the more arid southern region in 1911. Nor did the southern region achieve a better balance later.[104]

Revisionist studies of the National Policy's failure to settle the prairies have focussed on the area with the fewest people. This is hardly a test of the rate of settlement of the whole prairies. What needs to be explained is why the

northern Park Belt was not heavily settled between 1885 and 1900, after the
CPR had been completed. This is where the real settlement delay
occurred.

Many recent historians accept a climatic argument for the Park Belt too:
the danger of frost. Norrie, for example, dismisses the region's pre-1900
possibilities:

> The northern Park Belt region does not have the same aridity problems as
> further south, in part because of lower evaporation loss, but its growing season
> is significantly shorter. Thus until the development of earlier ripening varieties
> of wheat after 1900 this northern area was beyond the feasible margin of
> settlement.[105]

Is Norrie right that the danger of frost was great enough to deter settlement at
that time? It is true that frost was a hazard in the Park Belt before hardy new
wheat strains were developed and widely available: Marquis (1911), Garnet
(1926), and Reward (1929).[106] Manitoba settlers had experienced severe fall
frosts from 1883 to 1885, at the start of the downturn in migration. (There was
also a severe drought in 1886.)[107] Nevertheless, the evidence indicates that the
risk of frost did not deter Park Belt settlement altogether.

In fact, the Park Belt was essentially settled before 1911, when Marquis
wheat, which shortened maturation by about a week, was first commercially
available. A more important advance had occurred earlier: Red Fife, the
dominant wheat strain of the prairies 1885 to 1910, had shortened the growing
season by about twenty days, 'greatly expanding the frost free growing
area'.[108] As Vernon Fowke noted, Marquis wheat

> contributed little to the conquest of the West, for it was not available until the
> end of the period of phenomenal western settlement ... Had Marquis wheat
> been developed in 1870 instead of forty years later it would have hastened
> western settlement only slightly.[109]

It was not frost but lack of railways that hindered Park Belt settlement. If few
settlers had come to the Park Belt before 1902, the year the Grand Trunk and
Canadian Northern railways announced plans to construct transcontinental
lines through the area, it was because only the Regina to Prince Albert (1890)
and Calgary to Edmonton (1891) lines poked their way into the region. Those
who made the trip streamed into the northern reaches of the lines, undaunted
by frost.[110] So great was the interest in farming the area that the prospect of
two transcontinental lines across the Park Belt was enough in itself to spark a
settlement boom.[111] When the Canadian Northern completed its main line
from Manitoba to Edmonton by 1906 and vigorously built branch lines,
settlers flocked to the area. And their main crop was still Red Fife wheat.

Norrie is correct that settlement of sub-humid lands preceded that of
semi-arid lands. The Park Belt was settled without a completed railway, while
Palliser's triangle received little settlement despite good rail connection and
encouragement for twenty years.[112] Thus the climate-as-barrier argument has

limited validity: climatic obstacles undoubtedly delayed southern settlement, but they created no insuperable problems in the northern Park Belt, where population density was greater in any case.

Railway land grants

From an early date railway land grants were seen as impediments to settlement. 'What we have in the shape of a land monopoly is this,' cried Clifford Sifton, Laurier's energetic minister of the interior (immigration) from 1896 to 1905:

> We have millions of acres in that country owned by railway companies and these companies are not required to do any work or spend any money. They sit down; they toil not, neither do they spin. But the farmers toil and the farmers spin. The farmers do their work: they cultivate their lands and make their roads and bridges and pay their taxes and improve their land. And the land goes up in value for the benefit of the railway companies.[113]

No populist, Sifton nevertheless expressed the grievances of prairie farmers. He charged that railways were sitting on 67 million acres of land—an area twice the size of England—in 1898, because they had not yet selected government land grants. Settlement could not occur until the railways picked their land, which in the end amounted to 32 million acres.[114]

Railway land grants did block settlement: rail lands were sold rather than given to settlers, discouraging those without substantial capital. CPR president William Van Horne recognized this fact in 1894: 'We sell practically no lands at all to people newly arrived in the country, our sales being almost entirely to people who have already made a start on Government lands and who wish to add to their holdings.'[115] Similarly, despite flawed estimates of farming profitability in Manitoba and North Dakota in the 1880s and 1890s,[116] Charles Studness was justified in concluding that in Manitoba 'Canadian settlers occupied the good homestead land that was within a reasonable distance of railroads, and then turned to homestead land in northern North Dakota rather than purchase more productive Canadian land from the CPR or the Hudson's Bay Company'.[117] An astonishing number of Canadians made the long trek out to the Canadian west only to end up a few miles south of the border. In North Dakota's five organized counties along the border Canadian-born populations ranged from 17 per cent to 35 per cent in 1890.[118]

A more serious obstacle to prairie growth before 1900 was the blocking of railways and settlement in the Park Belt. A peculiar Canadian policy allowed railways to choose land far removed from their main lines, where it was not in their interests to build new lines or encourage early settlement. Most such lands were in the northern Park Belt.[119] J.B. Hedges analyzed the CPR's policy in this area:

The Canadian Pacific's first thought was to settle and develop the lands which were reasonably close to its main line . . . It gave little thought to the Northern Reserve [in the Park Belt] during the nineties . . . There was little incentive to make the outlays necessary for construction in the North, and, in the main, the lands were ultimately served by other lines of railway . . . The Canadian Pacific Company was placed in the position, then, of having land not only far removed from its own lines, but actually tributary to rival railways . . . Every settler placed on the lands meant business for the other companies, not for the Canadian Pacific . . . The zeal which the Company displayed in the work of settling the South was largely absent in the North, where ordinary business sense dictated a policy of waiting for the enjoyment of the unearned increment.[120]

Why did the Conservatives, architects of the National Policy, countenance this bottleneck in prairie settlement? After all, slow progress in the west reflected badly on their design for Canadian prosperity and independence. Inadequate land and railway policies were the result of two factors: enormous government debts incurred when the CPR was built, and ineffective agrarian opposition to railway land monopoly. The fiscal crisis of the late 1860s and 1870s deterred the state from paying for a transcontinental railway through open-ended loan guarantees, the method used earlier. Instead, the state gave the railways fertile prairie land, causing the twin deterrents to settlement: lack of free homestead land and the blocking of railway building in the Park Belt.

Railway building responded more to political decisions than to market forces. Expected profits from rail haulage were not enough to induce construction of transcontinental railways in Canada; market forces would have led to Canadian prairie connections with St Paul and Chicago. Hence government incentives were necessary for the building of all-Canadian routes and for the attraction of foreign capital to finance them.[121]

Even the CPR route was a political decision. Originally the main line was to go through the Park Belt. But a southerly route across Palliser's triangle was chosen in 1881 because of a more optimistic assessment of its farming potential and a perceived US threat to the Canadian claim to the west.[122] (A northern CPR route would be of little use in defending Canadian territory in the southern prairies.)[123] This political decision had consequences for the rate of settlement.

Railway overbuilding and government debt

State policies in the 1880s and 1890s were made in the context of a large debt that had a major political dimension. This section will examine the politics of the fiscal crisis and the initial failure of the National Policy.

The 1850s brought the railway era and its companion industrialism to Canada. This was typical for later-developing countries. What was not typical was the extent of waste in Canadian railway building. Canada frequently copied British promoters who discovered that profits were made in building, not operating, rail lines.[124] For Britain, with capital to burn and dense settlement, such extravagance had few adverse effects. The situation was different in Canada, which was short of domestic capital and sparsely settled. In Britain capitalists financed railways; in Canada, by contrast, governments guaranteed private railway loans.

After the 1850s railway extravaganza the Canadian government debt was $54 million; in the US, a country fifteen times as populous, government debt was only 50 per cent higher.[125] Yet even that debt was so high that President Lincoln had difficulty raising funds to finance the North's effort in the Civil War. The Canadian debt was so large by the late 1850s that the government could barely meet the interest payments and took decades to liquidate it.[126]

Canada had entered the railway era in the 1840s, when American railway building had begun to pose a serious economic threat. Montreal and Toronto merchants hoped to get part of the US midwest trade by building rail lines to the Atlantic. A commercial slump in 1846-49, however, made it impossible for three major Canadian railways to obtain private capital to complete their lines. The colonial government stepped in with the 1849 Railway Guarantee Act, setting the framework for railway finance in the 1850s: the state guaranteed financing, but did not regulate the rates charged.[127] Passed unanimously before the brief revival of agrarian radicalism in 1850, it was a contractor's dream, and succeeded in creating over 2000 miles of railways in the 1850s.

With a state guarantee for just about any line, the railway mania was on. By 1860 southwestern Ontario had three main trunk lines; competing lines ran northwards from Cobourg and Port Hope, which were eight miles apart; two parallel lines ran from the Ottawa Valley to the St Lawrence; Montreal had two railways, twelve miles apart, connecting Canada East and the US.[128] Duplication on such a scale was a disaster. When the Great Western was completed through southwestern Ontario, in 1855, it showed a handsome dividend; by 1860, when the Grand Trunk ran over the same territory, both lines operated at a loss. The railway boom brought unparalleled temporary prosperity. As much foreign capital per capita was invested in the 1850s as in the record 1904-14 period, unleashing inflationary pressures that pushed railway costs higher still.

The lack of planning was complemented by expensive building methods. Under the influence of the Grand Trunk, operating out of England,[129] British methods of railway construction were used. Developed in the context of a glut of capital, the British philosophy was to construct, at high original cost, railways that would last and be cheaper to operate because they would require less maintenance. The American railway philosophy, in contrast, was to build cheaply and make improvements as revenues allowed.[130]

The consequences of all this confusion and extravagance were predictable.

By 1860 the Grand Trunk was virtually bankrupt and other railways were in trouble. Many municipalities defaulted on their payments, and British investors lost confidence in Canada.[131] In a vain attempt to regain British confidence, the government honoured the defaulted railway and municipal loans. The resulting debt led to tariff increases in 1858-59, to repeated efforts to gain public control over the issuing of bank notes, and to a weakened ability to finance railways.

Two points should be made about the railway boom of the pre-Confederation era. First, railway extravagance had a political basis. In the 1850s Canada came close to becoming Marx's ideal/typical capitalist state: 'the executive committee of the ruling class'. Those running the state and the largest firms, the railways and the banks, were virtually one and the same. For example, four directors of the Grand Trunk Railway were cabinet ministers when the line was guaranteed large sums by the legislature.[132] Moreover, because the first railway boom occurred at the onset of industrialization, most Canadian capitalists were financiers, promoters, land speculators, and merchants rather than industrialists. With little effective opposition from farmers, the Canadian state was virtually the captive of one class—commercial capitalists—and that class had an interest in encouraging public debt to subsidize their projects (see Chapter 4).

Second, state debt and reduced access to foreign loans meant that when the CPR was built, the government could not give much cash help. Instead, it provided enormous land grants, a railway monopoly, and virtually unregulated railway rates. These and other palliatives succeeded in financing the CPR, but at the cost of delaying western settlement and slowing the development of eastern manufacturing.

Strategic versus economic railways

Hugh Aitken has characterized Canadian development as 'defensive expansionism'.[133] Always several decades ahead, the US forced the Canadian pace before the country was ready, and so Canada's development was distorted. This kind of forced, premature development—characteristic of all late-follower countries in varying degrees—was the result of strategic considerations.

After Confederation Canada had to establish a transportation system to unify its regions and thwart the American challenge. But strategic considerations often conflicted with economic ones: inexpensive transportation improved competitiveness, while strategic routes, which were usually more costly, protected territory. The ways in which the Canadian government responded to the strategic challenge, I will argue, placed an unnecessary burden on prairie farmers and contributed to the delay in settlement.

Two periods of railway overbuilding in Canada, in the 1850s and between 1904 and 1915, were encouraged by generous state support. Between these periods two major railways were built to serve political, strategic, and economic purposes: the Intercolonial and the Canadian Pacific. The conflict between economic and strategic routes bedevilled both lines. In the end, strategic routes were chosen—for valid reasons—but ways to reduce costs were not devised.

The Intercolonial connected the Maritimes with central Canada. Backed by a British guarantee, the line was built after 1867 for political and military purposes by the federal government. It was never conceived as a paying proposition, and should not be evaluated in those terms.[134] American expansionism after the US Civil War dictated that a northern military route be chosen, a justifiable decision; as well, the promise to build the line did help to encourage the Maritimes to federate with Canada. But the railway was built according to extravagant British standards. Iron bridges instead of wooden ones, and steel rails instead of iron, were unnecessary. By 1876 costs had reached $34 million, almost $50,000 per mile. Canada could not afford such waste.

The Canadian Pacific Railway was the most important project ever undertaken in Canada. Like the Intercolonial, it served political, strategic, and economic needs, and, here again, evaluation of the line must consider these multiple purposes. When defeat of the US south ended that region's veto on acquiring vast stretches of northern lands, the Civil War government approved the Homestead Act, with its free-land provision, and the construction of two transcontinental railways, one of which was the Northern Pacific. Building west from Lake Superior in 1869, the railway was designed to, among other things, acquire Canadian traffic and territory. In response to this threat, Canadian 'defensive expansion' meant the financing of a long transcontinental railway through difficult and almost unoccupied terrain by a country short of domestic capital; however it was done, costs would be great. Nevertheless, there was considerable latitude regarding cost, land grants, tax exemptions, and the duration of the project.

During negotiations for British Columbia's entrance into Confederation in 1870, Macdonald promised a completed railway to the Pacific within ten years. But opinions differed as to the route the new railway should take. At one extreme, the Grand Trunk offered to extend its line to Chicago, to veer north to Manitoba, and then to run west to the Pacific. This route reflected Montreal's historic interest in the traffic of the US midwest. On the other hand, after the Pacific Scandal revealed the political dangers of a close association with American railroad promoters, the Conservative Party broke radically from the Grand Trunk conception to favour a line solely on Canadian soil.[135] Finally, the Liberals—the advocates of cheap government—skirted a path between these two options, arguing that although a north-of-Superior line would have to be built eventually, in the meantime Canada should use Great Lakes shipping in summer and US railways in winter.

The first Pacific Railway contract in 1872 specified an all-Canadian route. This scheme fell apart along with the Conservative government in the Pacific

Scandal of 1873. The Liberals took over and began building rail lines as public projects—a Lakehead to Manitoba connection, a western extension from Winnipeg, a rail connection from Manitoba to US railways, and a few miles in British Columbia to keep that province happy—but things proceeded slowly. When Macdonald was returned in 1878, he resurrected the enormously expensive and unproductive north-of-Superior line, and a contract was signed with a private CPR syndicate in 1881.

Railways cost more to build north of Lake Superior than in BC, and the distance was greater. Was it necessary to build the Canadian Shield section simultaneously with the prairie and BC sections? The question must be considered from strategic, commercial, and political angles.

Strategically, it was important to establish Canadian sovereignty over the west quickly by means of a railway—the American threat was real. But there was no immediate challenge to the uninhabited area north of Lake Superior. Would running a line south of Lake Superior have lost western Canadian commerce to the Americans? In theory, no. Canada had made an agreement with the US in 1873, whereby Canadian goods could travel in bond across US territory from one part of Canada to another. Of course, this arrangement gave the US leverage to threaten withdrawal of these privileges.[136]

The CPR used the bonding arrangement in 1890—for a short route across Maine to New Brunswick—without loss of trade.[137] The 1880 Liberal proposal of a line from 'the Soo' to Manitoba, passing through the US, would probably have been similar to the short line in Maine. The Grand Trunk's proposed line through Chicago, in contrast, might well have made that city the centre of western Canadian trade. Thus the commercial question was strongly linked to the strategic one. If Canada could not dominate western Canadian trade, the area would be ripe for annexation.

There was no pressing commercial imperative for a north-of-Superior line. Large grain elevators were completed at the Lakehead in 1884-85, and by 1894, a decade after the CPR main line was finished, 80 per cent of goods were moving by combined rail/Great Lakes shipping, rather than by the all-rail route north of Lake Superior.[138]

The north-of-Superior line added great costs, and the price was paid by future prairie farmers. Building this section required rapid completion of the whole railway: 'Built through a long stretch of unproductive territory, the road required a large outlay of fixed capital, which in turn necessitated the most rapid possible prosecution of construction of the main line and of branch lines.'[139] Rapid construction raised labour and material costs and forced the CPR to sell 2.2 million acres to land speculators in 1883, inflating land prices for settlers.[140] At the same time, it was necessary to admit imported material for the original construction duty-free, and this reduced the industrial benefits of railway construction.

Nor was this all. The 1881 clause giving the CPR a twenty-year monopoly on all traffic south of its main line produced a series of reactions that led to the building of the two unnecessary transcontinental rail lines between 1904 and 1915. The CPR monopoly clause was justified by the railway's need 'to support the long, unprofitable line along the north shore of Lake Superior'.[141] The CPR monopoly was seen as responsible for high freight rates, and Manitoba chartered competing lines—the forerunners of the Canadian Northern, one of the transcontinentals built on the eve of the First World War. Meanwhile the CPR monopoly slowed the building of branch lines for settlement.[142] After first disallowing Manitoba's competing lines, Ottawa gave in to the enormous pressure exerted by the province and in 1888 cancelled the monopoly clause. But the CPR retained a *de facto* monopoly on trunk traffic in the west until the early 1900s.[143]

The CPR's western freight rates were raised to cover the running expenses of the long unproductive line north of Superior and were virtually immune from government regulation.[144] As soon as the CPR took over the Manitoba-to-Superior line in 1883, freight rates increased by 59 per cent.[145] The CPR charged 30 per cent to 75 per cent more to ship wheat than its US competitor, the St Paul, Minneapolis, and Manitoba Railway,[146] and its rates were still higher eleven years later. The CPR, though, claimed that its combined rail and Great Lakes shipping rates were cheaper than US rail rates.[147]

Forty per cent of the cash subsidy and 25 per cent of the CPR's land grant—all of it located on prime prairie land—were intended as compensation for building the North-of-Superior section.[148] We cannot know the terms needed for a railway without a north-of-Superior line, but it is certain that much more prairie land would have been available for free homesteading if the line had not been built between 1881 and 1885.

The CPR, land policies, and delayed settlement

There was another controversial element to the Macdonald government's transcontinental railway scheme: the manner in which it was financed. And this, in turn, was directly related to the financial mess in which the government found itself in the years just after Confederation. In 1867 the Dominion government took over most of the debts of the four original provinces, debts resulting mainly from the canal- and railway-building of the 1840s and 1850s.[149] Interest payments on the debt took a third of federal revenue.[150] Financing the Intercolonial Railway raised the debt substantially, but the prosperity of the early 1870s meant that tariff receipts more than offset the increased debt. By 1875, when major public expenditures on the CPR began, interest on the debt had dipped to a little over a quarter of revenue, but a depression at that time significantly reduced tariff receipts, and land grants replaced cash subsidies as public aids to railways.[151] 'The most resolute opponent of "monopoly" and "landlock" in later years', wrote Chester

Martin, was prepared to concede that to 'get the railway and keep our public land' was 'impracticable'.[152]

The public was adamant that taxes not be raised to pay for the Pacific railway. A House of Commons' resolution in 1871 stated that public aid 'should consist of such liberal grants of land, and such subsidy in money, or other aid, not increasing the present rate of taxation'.[153] The Liberal government reiterated the promise in 1873,[154] and as late as 1882 Macdonald boasted that the CPR would not cost Canadians a 'farthing'.[155] Cash subsidies to the CPR would have to depend on sales of Crown land in the prairies and on the level of current state revenue. In the end these measures were not enough: tax and tariff exemptions and the monopoly clause had to be added to pay for the railway. Most of the burden for financing the CPR would rest on prairie settlers in the form of land costs and freight rates.

In the late 1870s prospective promoters of the CPR were discouraged by the international depression, by pessimistic forecasts for the west, and by the fact that many expensive sections of the line were little used. Although prosperity returned in 1879,[156] and higher tariffs brought in much higher revenue, the government had to wait two years to find a private syndicate willing to take over the CPR.

The terms were very generous. The railway was granted 25 million acres of prairie land—an area more than three-quarters the size of England—$25 million in cash, and completed sections of the government-built railway (which had cost $37.8 million). As well, the government became the holder of $25 million in CPR bonds, issued on security of the land grant. Equipment and capital stock were excluded from taxation forever, while the land itself was tax-exempt for twenty years. Material for original construction was admitted free of duty, and the CPR was granted a twenty-year monopoly (rescinded in 1888) on railways from the main line to the border. The line was to be completed by 1891.[157]

These terms created resentment, and hatred of the CPR became part of western folklore. Consistently high profits led to speculation that the public aid to the CPR had been excessive.[158] While after-the-fact profits cannot prove that inducements were unnecessary to attract private investment in the first place, some provisions turned out to be more important to long-term profit rates than to the short-term needs of financing the original line. Allowing a 10 per cent profit rate before freight rates could be regulated and giving the railway the right to select land anywhere in the west may have been needlessly generous—but this is difficult to prove. For seven years after the Pacific Scandal, no syndicate was ready to take on the project despite equally favourable provisions. Even with the 1881 terms, the CPR came close to bankruptcy several times during the construction phase, and the state had to stave off disaster.[159] In any case, whether the 1881 terms were necessary or not, they certainly contributed—especially when combined with other land policies pursued by the government—to the delay of prairie settlement.

A public line might have been less costly, if not in construction costs at least in the cost of land for settlers. The farmers' Dominion Grange and the Trades and Labour Congress both favoured public railways, an established Canadian tradition: the Intercolonial and the first sections of the CPR had been public projects, as were the St Lawrence canals. Moreover, public ownership of railways was common in Sweden and Germany. But in Canada the social economy was against it. Farmers and workers were politically ineffective in the late nineteenth century, and business ideology opposed public ownership, while the political corruption resulting from the state's relation to business led to public rejection of state enterprise.[160] Certain managerial and technical difficulties also stood in the way.[161]

The effect of land policies on settlement

Not only did Canada have to build a railway at a pace set by US competition, but it had to match the American opportunities for settlers. In effect, US policy was setting Canadian policy. Speculation, land monopoly, and free homestead had been subjects of intense and bitter struggle for over fifty years before the US Homestead Act of 1862. In contrast, the Canadian Homestead Act of 1872, modelled on the US legislation, passed with little debate. It was not that Canadians cared less about these issues—land was at the centre of conflicts in British North America before 1867. But the national emergency of gaining and holding the west brought a consensus around US-styled land policies.[162]

Because farmers' movements were weak, opportunities for settlers in the Canadian west did not equal those in the US from the 1870s to the 1890s. The free-land policy of the Canadian Homestead Act was virtually cancelled at its inception by the land-grant terms offered to the first Pacific Railway Company. In contrast to western American farmers, Canadian farmers did not articulate intense opposition to railway incursions against the homestead system. A clause in the CPR contract offered land to the railway that was 'fairly fit for settlement', meaning that the CPR itself would be able to choose the best land anywhere in the prairies rather than be restricted to selecting land near its main line.[163]

In 1880 John Macoun, a CPR botanist, made an optimistic report on wheat farming in Palliser's triangle. But the CPR could not have believed him, for it chose as little land as possible along its main line in this area, preferring instead the northern Park Belt. It also chose Manitoba, a more humid area than the southern regions farther west. The CPR was right: as explained above, heavy settlement of Palliser's triangle did not begin until after the Park Belt was occupied.

The government was just as generous with the colonization railways, which were branch lines built to foster settlement. Before 1900 a further 13.5 million acres of prairie land 'fairly fit for settlement' was ceded to them, an area more than half the size of the CPR grant.[164] In this way 'nearly half of the agricultural land then available in western Canada . . . had passed, or were destined when finally located, to pass into the administration of the railways'.[165]

The 'fairly fit for settlement' clause—a departure from American practice—proved disastrous. It took years for the CPR and colonization railways to locate all their land: final selections were not made until 1908, and homestead entries were long delayed in certain areas.[166] Even worse, as noted above, CPR ownership of lands far removed from its own main line and in the midst of projected rival lines led it to hinder settlement in those areas. These lands were in the productive Park Belt.

In the US more than 150 million acres of public land was given to the railways,[167] while in Canada the figure was just under 32 million acres. Since Canada had much less fertile land than the US, its land policy was disastrous. Railway land grants totalled 14 per cent of the US public domain, whereas in Canada they exceeded 24 per cent.[168] As if this were not bad enough, a further 5 per cent of prairie land, plus an area around its forts, was given to the Hudson's Bay Company in exchange for its relinquishing its claim to Rupert's Land in 1870. As well, schools received one-eighteenth of all prairie land in compensation for federal control of land (usually a provincial responsibility). Although neither the Bay Company nor the schools had the right to select the lands, together these areas equalled about half the railway grants, and they were held off the market for many years, postponing settlement. In the end, they brought very high prices.

Canada could not be so cavalier with public lands and remain competitive with the American west. In addition to giving twice the proportion of available land to private railways that the US did, Canada let the rail companies have the choicest land. In the US, by contrast, all the grants were along the railway lines, which meant that the land was of varying quality. Farmer pressure had led to the US Homestead Act of 1862, offering free western land, and nine years later the US Granger movement was powerful enough to end railway land grants altogether.[169] At this point Canada adopted the abandoned American system and added the peculiar twist of giving the railway its choice of land. American farmers were not able to end land speculation, and less than half the land acquired by settlers was free. But as long as free land was available in the US, it was not possible to sell much private or public land in Canada.

No similar farmer pressure existed in Canada. In Ontario the Clear Grits who had fought for cheap land and western expansion in the early 1850s had been incorporated into the business-dominated Liberal Party by the end of the decade. By the 1880s the initiative to provide more free-homestead land in the prairies came not from farmers but from the Conservative government, which in 1882 adopted the policy of free homestead—on half the prairie land. The government did not believe in free homestead as a matter of principle—it simply wanted to match the American competition for settlers. In the 1870s governments had thought the sale of Crown land would cover public costs. By the 1880s, however, the state realized that it would receive more revenue from rapid immigration stimulated by the offer of free land than from public land sales that discouraged settlement. Tariff collections of $16 per capita in Manitoba in 1885 meant that over $2000 per year per mile of railway was available to amortize the government subsidy.[170] In the 1880s and 1890s, however, the government's free-homestead legislation was too little, too late. It could not counteract the absence of railways in the good land of the Park Belt.

As for the CPR, once its land grants were secured it also came to favour free homestead, since settlement of adjacent Crown lands raised the value of CPR lands. Settlers, though, would not buy CPR land, because—inexpensive as it was in southern Manitoba and southeastern Saskatchewan in the 1880s and 1890s—it was still too costly for most pioneers. Moreover, the CPR took a different attitude towards its Park Belt land, located far from the main line: there its policy was simply to profit from land speculation and to hinder the building of rival railroads. The 'fairly fit for settlement' clause, allowing the railways to choose the best agricultural land, was the basis for the CPR's schizophrenic land policies.

Other terms of the CPR contract also deterred settlers. Tax exemption of CPR property, capital stock, and unsold land placed the whole burden of financing local infrastructure on new settlers at a time when they needed money to establish their farms; taxation, even at low rates, discouraged settlement.[171] As well, the *de facto* CPR monopoly of western Canadian traffic was not significantly changed by the cancellation of the monopoly clause in 1888, the Crow's Nest Pass Agreement in 1897, or the creation of a Board of Railway Commissioners in 1903.[172] Thus CPR land grants, tax exemptions, and freight rates continued to discourage western settlement. These were the costs of building the CPR on terms laid down by governments in which agrarian influence was weak.

Land and railway policies were dictated largely by the state's fiscal position. When revenues were good and enthusiasm contagious, the state abandoned limited cash subsidies and land grants and instead guaranteed railway bonds on insanely optimistic projects, such as the Grand Trunk in the 1850s and the two extra transcontinental lines shortly before 1916—all of which later went bust. On the other hand, when the state faced a fiscal crisis, as in the 1870s and 1880s, it promised land instead of open-ended loan guarantees.

The burden of misplaced investment during the booms, encouraged by the state in every case, weighed heavily on the next generation in the form of debt and limited options during economic depressions. It was after one such investment binge that the CPR itself was conceived of and built.

Delayed development

Canadians emigrated in large numbers from the 1860s to the 1890s—a discouraging turn for a new settler society just beginning on nationhood. Not until 1901 did Canada again have a positive immigration balance. But natural increases more than counterbalanced the outflow, and the population grew by 12 and 11 per cent respectively in the 1880s and 1890s, compared with 25 and 20 per cent increases in the US in the same decades. During the wheat boom in the first decade of the twentieth century Canada grew by almost two million, or 34 per cent, with the prairies accounting for nearly half the increase.[173] Economic growth corresponded to population growth: the GNP rose 29 per cent in the 1880s, 31 per cent in the 1890s, and 67 per cent from 1900 to 1910.[174] Manufacturing growth, too, tracked population increase, though not so closely.[175]

Economists claim that Canadian manufacturing came of age in the early 1900s, when productivity increased rapidly and industries diversified.[176] Manufacturing growth was based mainly on the Canadian market, the tariff reserving much of the west for domestic goods. The National Policy was finally beginning to work. Disappointment and massive emigration turned into unparalleled optimism and expansion. In 1902 Laurier declared that the twentieth century belonged to Canada.

Unfortunately for Canada, however, the great expansion took place just when US economic influence began to burst beyond its domestic confines. American companies started to move abroad around the turn of the century, accompanying a surge of US manufacturing exports. The trickle of US branch plants into Canada in the 1880s and 1890s turned into a flood in the 1900-14 period. Through a combination of branch plants and licensing arrangements, US manufacturers developed a decisive grip on Canada's industries of the 'second industrial revolution'.

What would have happened if massive settlement of the Canadian prairies and an accompanying resource export boom had occurred in the 1880s and 1890s? It is probable that Canadian industries—then growing slowly compared to those in the US and Europe—would have been that much larger and better able to withstand the assault of US branch plants when it came. Perhaps the new mass-production industries would have developed earlier in Canada than they did. Had the settlement boom in Manitoba (1876 to 1882) spread further west, the manufacturing growth rates of the 1880s and 1890s would very likely have turned from relatively slow to spectacular;[177] US manufacturing in these decades increased by 112 per cent and 51 per cent, roughly double the Canadian rates.[178]

As it was, the 1900-13 boom raised demand to such an extent that Canadian industry could not satisfy it. Increases in both imports and foreign branch plants were the result. Demand for capital similarly outstripped Canadian supply by 1904, leading to unprecedented borrowing of foreign capital, much of which entered Canada in the form of imported machinery. A less hectic western boom, long enough to allow domestic industry to catch up, would have aided the development of Canadian-controlled manufacturing.

TRANSCONTINENTAL MANIA AND FOREIGN CAPITAL

When settlers finally streamed into Canada, 'the last best West', in the early twentieth century, Canadian spirits soared so high that governments lost their heads and approved grandiose railway projects that made little sense. Later generations of Canadians paid for these miscalculations, which resulted not only in the debt on bankrupt railways, but also in the indirect effect of encouraging US branch plants to enter Canada.

Between 1904 and 1915 Canada built two transcontinental railways for which—since the CPR was already in place to connect the prairies with eastern Canada and the Pacific—there was no need. Kenneth Buckley wrote: 'One traffic bridge over the Canadian Shield [the CPR] may have been justified on non-economic grounds, but hardly two, and certainly not three.'[179] A.R.M. Lower was more colourful: 'Americans built railroads to develop their country, Germans, for purposes of war, but Canadians apparently just for the fun of building them.'[180]

The railways were constructed at the insistence of the state; as was the case with the CPR, market forces would not have led to their creation. Unlike the CPR, however, these lines served no strategic or national-unity purpose. Their creation can be explained only by short-sighted politics.

Railway extravagance

With the wheat boom well under way by 1902, more rail capacity was needed to carry the grain to European markets. The short season for moving wheat added to the strain on the single CPR line from Winnipeg to the Lakehead, where water transport began. In addition, rail lines were needed quickly in Saskatchewan and Alberta to provide for incoming settlers. No such increase in rail capacity was needed north of Superior, though: it had been repeatedly demonstrated that grain would go more cheaply by lake transport than by an all-rail route.[181] Nevertheless, the Laurier government approved and helped to finance two totally new transcontinental lines: the Grand Trunk Pacific-National Transcontinental and the Canadian Northern. The decision was a triumph of immediate politics and speculative enterprise in a context of boundless optimism. And it once again reflected the farmers' failure to make the state heed 'economy in government'.

The origins of the new transcontinentals can be easily summarized. The Canadian Northern started out as a small independent line in Manitoba, completed a link to the Lakehead in 1902, and soon had ambitions in eastern Canada.[182] At the same time the Grand Trunk, central Canada's main railway, wanted an extension to the west to compete with the rival CPR, which had invaded Grand Trunk turf in the east. The greatest recipient of public largesse in the 1850s, the Grand Trunk had twice before proposed a transcontinental line, only to be turned down because it refused an all-Canadian route. With the CPR's success, however, the Grand Trunk overcame its reluctance to build a north-of-Superior line.

The government could have scuttled both lines. Both depended on government charters and massive public funding, and nothing could have been more logical than to allow all railways to use the CPR's north-of-Superior line. But instead, the Laurier government tried half-heartedly to merge the Grand Trunk with the Canadian Northern, a proposal that made less economic sense. The attempt failed, and both railways were allowed to proceed.

To add to the folly, the government insisted on routes that added to the costs of the Grand Trunk line. The original plan had been to run the new line from the Pacific to North Bay to link with the Grant Trunk's extensive central Canadian lines. But the government rejected this plan because it would mean carrying the traffic to Portland, Maine, rather than to a Canadian port. The government made an astounding counter-offer: it would build another eastern section—the National Transcontinental—from Moncton to Winnipeg and lease it to the Grand Trunk Pacific, which would then run from Winnipeg to the west coast. The government route for the National Transcontinental could not have been more extravagant: the line was to head west from Quebec City, and so far north that it was closer to James Bay than to the Great Lakes, with no major centre lying along the route. The length of the difficult and expensive northern Ontario section would be doubled.

The route to New Brunswick was equally foolish. Rather than follow the Grand Trunk suggestion to link up with the underused Intercolonial Railway, Ottawa decided to build a second trunk line from Quebec City through New Brunswick, shortening the distance to the Atlantic by only sixty miles.[183] To add further extravagance to this wilderness line, the National Transcontinental reverted to the British philosophy of expensive initial construction, and was equipped with modern and complete rolling stock. Except for the Panama Canal, it was the largest public project of the time.[184]

Total cost of the National Transcontinental was about $160 million, 250 per cent more than the original estimate.[185] The awarding of expensive contracts to the party faithful, scamping, and doctored accounts added to the costs.[186] In the end, the completion of the Grand Trunk Pacific-National Transcontinental brought the whole Grand Trunk Company to bankruptcy.[187]

Manitoba's intense battle to break the CPR's monopoly in the west created an opportunity for two railroad contractors, Mackenzie and Mann. They gathered unused railway charters and land grants, assembled local lines, and received generous loans, guarantees, and subsidies from all levels of government to build yet another transcontinental line across northern Ontario.[188] They built their lines cheaply,[189] but were rebuffed in their attempts to avoid duplication with the Grand Trunk Pacific. From Edmonton to the Yellowhead pass, for instance, the two railways ran side by side.[190]

By 1914 the Grand Trunk and the Canadian Northern were heavily in debt. They generated little income, not only because of the duplication of lines, but also because few branch lines had been built. By the time the two lines were completed in 1914-15 Canada had one mile of railway for every 250 people. Both lines were financed on the London capital market backed by Canadian government guarantees.[191] The war cut off British funds, and the Canadian government, burdened by enormous war-related outlays, refused to continue subsidizing the lines. After initially acquiring shares in the Canadian Northern, the federal government decided to nationalize both lines, giving birth to the Canadian National Railway.

Having failed to merge the two railways at the beginning of the project, the government was forced to merge them in bankruptcy after a great deal of capital had been thrown away. The enormous expenditures on railways from 1904 to 1915 contributed heavily to Canada's unprecedented level of capital imports.

There were good electoral reasons for the Liberal government to support and take credit for the Grand Trunk's transcontinental line. It had become a Canadian tradition for the Liberals and the Conservatives each to 'have' their own railways. The CPR was grateful to the Conservatives for generous government support and regularly got their employees out for them at election time. And when Macdonald rejected the Grand Trunk's first Pacific railway concept (to go through Chicago) the company naturally sided with the Liberals. In the reciprocity election of 1891 the Grand Trunk brought back, free of charge, thousands of Canadian emigrants from Michigan to vote Liberal.[192] But that was not enough to counterbalance the help given the Tories by the CPR. A continental line would help the Liberals more than would the original Grand Trunk, confined as it was to central Canada. Important interest groups also benefitted from large-scale railway construction: banks, contractors, construction suppliers, railway-equipment industries, and local communities en route. As well, railway construction on a grand scale provided employment for workers and newly arrived immigrants anxious for cash to finance the first years of pioneer farming.

Other factors were at work too. The Liberals, as the party of provincial rights, were sensitive to regional demands, which on the issue of railways were many and diverse. In Quebec the Roman Catholic Church, reacting against the effects of urban industrial life on the piety of French Canadians, favoured a northern colonization railway to open up new rural areas.[193] At the same time Quebec City, represented by Laurier, had declined in economic influence in relation to Montreal, and many people hoped that a transcontinental railway terminating in Quebec would revive its port; with Quebec City as a terminus, a northern route through central Canada was inevitable. But strong pressure also came from the Maritimes to extend the line beyond Quebec City, with the terminus in Moncton so as to favour neither Halifax nor Saint John.[194] And if a northern route was planned, it might as well go through the newly discovered clay belt of northern Ontario. Thus an unnecessary transcontinental railway, which a late-follower country could ill afford, grew by accretion. It was ward-heeling politics carried to the national level.

The Liberal government favoured the Grand Trunk over the Canadian Northern, but ultimately found it politically expedient to support the Canadian Northern's transcontinental plans. After all, the Canadian Northern had the support of five provinces, and there were the precedents of generous federal assistance to the CPR and the Grand Trunk.

Opposition to monopolies, distrust of public ownership because of the inevitable party appointments, and emulation of the US, with its several transcontinental lines, prevented a more sensible solution. Opposition leader Robert Borden offered a plan better suited to Canada's needs as a late-follower country: he wanted the government to buy the existing CPR line between North Bay and the Lakehead, operate it under an independent commission, and lease running rights to the CPR, the Grand Trunk, the Canadian Northern, and the Intercolonial. That way there would be only one line north of Superior, not three. As well, the Canadian Northern and Grand Trunk Pacific would operate over common track from Edmonton to the Pacific.[195] Borden's plan would have satisfied the transportation needs of prairie settlers, offered competition where needed, and saved enormous expense. Why, then, did the Conservatives not triumph in the 1904 election?

The largest class numerically, the farmers, favoured farm expansion, increased transportation facilities, and competitive railways, but they also wanted cheap government. The latter concern might have led them to support the Conservative plan had it not been for one thing: the Tories were the high-tariff party. Ironically, the extravagant Liberal railway policy raised government debt substantially, contributing to the maintenance of the high tariffs that were still a major source of government revenue. A well-developed farmers' movement might have been able to discern the implications of such mammoth waste on redundant railways, but in the early 1900s farmers were divided on national and regional lines and lacked any effective federal political organization.

Big business, on the other hand, subscribed to a strategy of expanding a protected Canadian market tied to British trade and capital. More railways, capital imports, and government debt would benefit strong interests within big business and could do no harm to the rest—or so it was thought.

As a government operating in a vacuum of ideas about industrialization, the Laurier administration was unable to override the interests of particular capitalists and regional interests promoting the railways. Essentially, it lacked the intellectual awareness that would have enabled it to act in the long-term interests of an independent Canadian state and business class. Instead, ideology was uncritically imported from the US and Britain, much of it inappropriate to late-follower development. In this context the government pursued growth rather than development, catering to regional demands and the politics of bribing the people with their own money. Unrealistic optimism—many predicted that Canada's population would one day nearly equal that of the US—contributed to the policy of mammoth railway overbuilding.

Railways, capital inflows, and branch plants

The age of imperialism, stretching from 1870 to 1914, witnessed the greatest international capital flow in economic history. Britain, the greatest lender, invested abroad about as much as the entire value of its fixed industrial and commercial capital. (By 1913 British foreign investment was thirty times as great in relative terms as was US capital outflow during the Marshall plan.)[196] By 1908-13—the period of the two unnecessary transcontinentals—Canada was the largest recipient of British capital. A.K. Cairncross has written that 'at its peak, in 1913, foreign investment took over half the total of British savings, at its peak too, in the years between 1908 and 1913, foreign borrowing financed over half the total addition to the stock of capital in the largest borrower—Canada'.[197] Most of this capital took the form of portfolio, not direct, investment.[198]

It is impossible to calculate the exact amount that railway expenditures contributed to capital imports because much of the capital borrowed by federal and provincial governments was poured into the railways indirectly. It is likely, however, that the two new transcontinentals attracted about half of the capital imported in the peak years of Canadian borrowing, from 1908 to 1913.[199] Some domestic savings also found their way into financing the government's railroad debt.[200] Had the unproductive transcontinentals not been built, part of the domestic capital diverted to them could have flowed into the sectors that, without those funds, ended up receiving large amounts of foreign direct investment.

In 1924 Jacob Viner analyzed how Canada's huge capital imports led to the importation of US manufactured goods and the establishment of US branch plants.[201] Although Viner made pre-Keynesian assumptions and largely ignored the income effects of capital borrowing, the associations he demonstrated between capital imports and commodity imports retain considerable validity.

Viner showed that enormous capital imports from Britain had the effect of raising the price of Canadian-made goods and reducing that of imported goods. Prices in Canada rose much more quickly than in Britain, and somewhat more quickly than in the US. Price increases were most pronounced for the manufactured goods that were produced largely for the domestic market. Naturally, the inflationary rise had the effect of decreasing Canadian exports and increasing foreign imports. This in turn led to a rough balance of international payments: the outflow of Canadian money to pay for the trade deficit balanced the inflow of borrowed foreign currency.[202] The net result was a dramatic increase in industrial imports (particularly from the US), which more than trebled from 1899 to 1913 while exports rose by only 50 per cent (see Chapter 1). This was the period in which Canada's export/import ratio of finished goods diverged sharply from that of other late-follower countries, and Canada began heading down the road towards a dependent and truncated manufacturing economy.

As noted earlier, the fact that most of these new imports came from the US rather than Britain meant a triangular adjustment in international payments: 'The capital borrowed by Canada in Great Britain entered Canada largely in the form of American commodities.'[203] Thus American industry became the great beneficiary of British capital exports to Canada—a development that contributed to the United States' overtaking of Britain's world lead in exporting manufactured goods in the early 1900s.

In the absence of many barriers to foreign direct investment, proximity brought the impact of US industrial development to Canada sooner than to other countries. Canada's early reliance on American techniques, specifications, and parts, together with its closer resemblance to American than to British styles of goods and standard of living, led it to import more from the US.

The movement of US branch plants into Canada between 1900 and 1913 was part of an American business strategy to capture foreign markets. Hindered by Canadian tariffs and patent restrictions, many US firms set up branch plants in Canada to reduce their surplus production. A Senate report in 1931 viewed the 'branch factory' abroad as 'merely a more intensive method of selling an American product in foreign markets; the branch factory, theoretically at least, takes up the work where the ordinary sales methods stop'.[204] US branch plants in turn stimulated the importation of US equipment, machinery, and materials.[205] It was during this period (1900-13) that American subsidiaries became dominant in most of Canada's growth industries.

Thus the importation of enormous quantities of British portfolio capital, in large part to finance the two unnecessary transcontinental railways, encouraged the establishment of US branch plants in Canada. Once they were set up, the value of the branch plants and resource subsidiaries grew enormously through reinvestment of profits generated in Canada rather than through new infusions of foreign capital.[206] Capital imports accounted for 57 per cent of net capital formation in Canada from 1901 to 1915, but only 9 per cent from 1916 to 1930.[207] Nevertheless, from 1916 to 1930, when domestic savings were able to supply over 90 per cent of Canada's net capital demand, the value of US ownership capital trebled.[208] The 1901-15 period—the very years when the new transcontinentals were built—was the crucial time when foreign direct investment gained a foothold in Canada.

Besides encouraging branch plants, railway overbuilding stimulated resource exports. According to Harold Innis, the two new transcontinentals helped to perpetuate a staples orientation in the Canadian economy:

> They involved heavy unit costs of operation and maintenance, which were accentuated by heavy sunk costs of construction. Expansion of mining and of the pulp and paper industry, and settlement in Northern Ontario and Northern Quebec, were of first rate importance in reducing costs and meeting the deficit of the Canadian National Railways.[209]

It should be pointed out that railway overbuilding did have some short-term benefits. In contrast to the tariff-protected CPR, for which English rails were imported, these new lines used Canadian rails.[210] Real output in iron and steel products rose 12.4 per cent per year from 1900 to 1910; a healthy Canadian-owned steel industry was established; and the rail-equipment industry also expanded rapidly.[211] The income-generating effects of Canada's huge capital imports stimulated demand for domestic as well as foreign manufactured goods—as long as the boom lasted. Unfortunately, the violent increase in demand, coming over a short period, greatly outstripped Canadian capacity, and much of the potential benefit was lost to domestic producers.

In the long run, enormous misplaced investments in unproductive railways—a direct result of public policy—contributed to Canada's failure to develop along independent lines during the formative period of initial industrialization.

CONCLUSION

Conventional explanations of the extraordinary levels of foreign ownership and control of the Canadian economy lead one to believe that the outcome was inevitable. Canada was situated next to the United States, the most dynamic economy in the first half of the twentieth century and the cradle of that new business organization, the transnational corporation. In these circumstances, how could Canada have resisted American penetration? The issue seems so cut and dried that it is no wonder there has been little inquiry into the origins of Canada's branch-plant economy.

This chapter has examined three major episodes that contributed to Canada's transformation into a branch-plant economy. First, the defeat of agrarian attempts to replace commercial banking with free banks affected development profoundly. It meant that when Canada began to industrialize it had to look to foreign corporations for investment, technology, and innovative management. Canadian banks had a lot of capital, but they invested little of it in risky new Canadian businesses—the stereotype of the conservative Canadian, loath to take economic risks, owes much to the economic role played by Canadian banks. The failure of nineteenth-century farmers to free up credit has had lasting effects.

Second, the twenty-year delay in settling the prairies was also conducive to the entry of US branch plants. Delayed settlement slowed the pace of manufacturing development in eastern Canada so that when US companies began to search for markets and investment opportunities after 1900, Canada presented a favourable environment. Had agrarians won their demands for free land grants for settlers only, population and industry would likely have grown rapidly before US corporations were ready to go abroad on a massive scale. Canada would not have been such an easy target.

Finally, the addition of two transcontinental railways accentuated domestic capital shortages for industrial development and added little to Canada's industrial capacity. Inflation and increased manufacturing imports were the result, producing ideal conditions for the entry of branch plants. The folly of embarking on such mammoth and misplaced investments at the very time when Canada began importing capital in the form of US subsidiaries cannot be exaggerated. It was the last thing a late-follower country needed. Farmers' calls for economy in government fell on deaf ears. In none of these episodes was it inevitable that Canada embrace the least-promising choice for independent development. The results could have been different if agrarian influence had been greater.

NOTES

[1]R. Pomfret, *The Economic Development of Canada* (Toronto: Methuen, 1981), p. 200.

[2]Canada, Royal Commission on Canada's Economic Prospects, *Canada-United States Economic Relations*, prepared by I. Brecher and S.S. Reisman (Ottawa: Queen's Printer, 1957), p. 117; J. Dales, *The Protective Tariff in Canada's Development* (Toronto: University of Toronto Press, 1966), p. 109; H.F. Marshall et. al., eds., *Canadian-American Industry* (Toronto: McClelland and Stewart, 1976), p. 199.

[3]G. Williams, *Not For Export* (Toronto: McClelland and Stewart, 1983), p. 88. Marshall, *Canadian-American Industry*, p. 202. Bilingual labels were another minor incentive to locate in Canada.

[4]M. Wilkins, *The Emergence of Multinational Enterprise* (Cambridge: Harvard University Press, 1969), pp. 45, 55, 59.

[5]A.O. Hirschman, 'The Political Economy of Import Substituting Industrialization in Latin America', *Quarterly Journal of Economics* no. 82 (February 1968).

[6]A.S. Milward and S.B. Saul, *The Economic Development of Continental Europe 1780-1870* (London: George Allen and Unwin, 1973), p. 529.

[7]Measured by the ratio of duties to total imports for consumption (O. McDiarmid, *Commercial Policy in the Canadian Economy* [Cambridge: Harvard University Press, 1946], p. 181); F.W. Taussig, *The Tariff History of the United States* (New York: G.P. Putnam's Sons, 1910), p. 409.

[8]S.B. Clough, *Economic History of Europe* (Boston: D.C. Heath, 1952), p. 611.

[9]R.T. Naylor, *History of Canadian Business*, vol. 2 (Toronto: Lorimer, 1975), p. 45.

[10]Edward Porritt, *Sixty Years of Protection in Canada, 1846-1907* (Toronto: Macmillan, 1908), p. 410.

[11]Cleona Lewis, *America's Stake in International Investments* (Washington: Brookings

Institution, 1938), p. 311; and R.T. Naylor, *History of Canadian Business*, vol. 2, p. 45.

[12]Wilkins, *Emergence of Multinational Enterprise*, p. 101.

[13]P. Hertner, 'Financial Strategies and adaptation to foreign markets: The German electro-technical industry and its multinational activities: 1890s to 1939' in A. Teichova et al., eds, *Multinational Enterprise in Historical Perspective* (London: Cambridge University Press, 1986), p. 147.

[14]It has been argued that very high US tariffs had a similar effect to the working clause, by discouraging the importation of patented articles (E.T. Penrose, *The Economics of the International Patent System* [Baltimore: Johns Hopkins, 1951], p. 140).

[15]In 1907 Britain restricted imports of patented goods. Patents were not required to be worked but could be revoked if the patented product was 'exclusively or mainly' manufactured outside Britain (A. Thornton, *Thornton on Patents: British and Foreign* [London: Charles Jones, 1910], p. 46).

[16]Statutes of Canada, 'An Act respecting Patents of Invention', CAP. XXVI, June 14, 1872; Penrose, *International Patent System*, p. 56; Thornton, *Thornton on Patents*, pp. 378, 392. In 1872 Canada required that patents be worked within two years, whereas the International Convention for the Protection of Industrial Property eleven years later allowed a three-year period. Subsequently Canada allowed an additional six or twelve-month extension to the two-year period.

[17]Thornton, *Thornton on Patents*, p. 46; Naylor, *History of Canadian Business*, vol. 2, p. 62.

[18]For a geographic interpretation of foreign direct investment, see D.M. Ray, 'The location of United States Subsidiaries in Southern Ontario,' in R.L. Gentilcore, ed., *Geographical Approaches to Canadian Problems* (Scarborough Ont.: Prentice-Hall, 1971).

[19]Wilkins, *Emergence of Multinational Enterprise*.

[20]M. Wilkins, 'Multinational Enterprises', in H. Daems and H. Van Der Wee, eds., *The Rise of Managerial Capitalism* (The Hague: Martinus Nijhoff, 1974), p. 214.

[21]W.O. Henderson, *Britain and Industrial Europe 1750-1870*, (London: Liverpool University Press, 1954).

[22]In 1913 Germany produced 34% of the world's electrical products, compared to 29% for the US (K. Pinson, *Modern Germany*, 2nd ed. [New York: Macmillan, 1966], p. 227).

[23]David Landes, *The Unbound Prometheus* (Cambridge: Cambridge University Press, 1969), p. 75.

[24]United States, *American Direct Investments in Foreign Countries*, Trade Information Bulletin No. 731 (Washington: 1930), p. 39.

[25]US corporations began to adopt multidivisional, 'decentralized' structures in the 1920s, after establishing a strong presence in Canadian manufacturing. See A. Chandler, *Strategy and Structure: Chapters in the History of the American Industrial Enterprise* (Cambridge: MIT Press, 1962).

[26]J. Kocka, 'The Rise of Modern Industrial Enterprise in Germany', in A. Chandler and H. Daems, eds., *Managerial Hierarchies* (Cambridge: Harvard University Press, 1980), p. 99.

[27]For a start into this literature see Wilkins, 'Multinational Enterprises'; Teichova et al., eds, *Multinational Enterprise in Historical Perspective*; H. Schroter, V. Schroter, and P. Hertner, 'How they changed their Strategy: German electro-technical industry in the Italian market before 1914 and between the two wars' (Florence: European University Institute, Papers 159/84 [1987]).

[28]Wilkins, 'Multinational Enterprises', p. 223.

[29]R. Tilly, 'The Growth of Large-Scale Enterprise in Germany since the Middle of the Nineteenth Century', in Daems and Van Der Wee, eds, *Managerial Capitalism*, p. 148.

[30]Leo Panitch, 'Dependency and Class in Canadian Political Economy,' *Studies in Political Economy* no. 6 (Autumn 1981).

[31]Ibid., p. 19.

[32]Ibid., pp. 19-20.

[33]H.A. Logan, 'Labor Costs and Labor Standards', in H.A. Innis, ed., *Labor in Canadian-American Relations* (Toronto: Ryerson Press, 1937), p. 86.

34Ibid., pp. 88-1.

35J. R. Baldwin and A.G. Green, 'Productivity Differentials Between the Canadian and American Manufacturing Sectors as of 1929: A Reexamination' (paper presented at the Bellagio conference entitled 'Productivity: International comparisons and Problems of Measurement in the 19th and 20th centuries', March 1986, revised Feb 1986), p. 19. With permission of the authors.

36Ibid., p. 13. Such calculations have not been made for the period before 1929. Marxists measure productivity in a similar way. Higher productivity comes about through an increase in the amount of constant capital (the value of plant and resources consumed) per worker employed.

37Panitch, 'Dependency and Class', p. 19.

38K. Marx, *Capital*, vol. 1 (Moscow: Progress Publishers, 1954).

39H.J. Habakkuk, *American and British Technology in the Nineteenth Century. The Search for Labour-Saving Inventions* (Cambridge: Cambridge University Press, 1962), p. 8.

40Ibid., p. 45; D. North, 'Industrialization in the United States,' in H.J. Habakkuk and M. Postan, eds, *The Cambridge Economic History of Europe*, vol. 6, part 2 (Cambridge: Cambridge University Press, 1965).

41International Harvester was created by mergers at that time.

42M. Denison, *Harvest Triumphant. The Story of Massey-Harris*, (Toronto: McClelland and Stewart, 1948), p. 166.

43In 1900-03 Australia's real income per head was a little lower than in Canada, while Britain's was a little higher (C. Clark, *The Conditions of Economic Progress*, 3rd ed. (London: Macmillan, 1960), pp. 90, 109, 139.

44For European/American industrial-wage comparisons see E.H. Phelps-Brown and M.H. Browne, *A Century of Pay* (London: Macmillan, 1968) p. 30.

45Ibid., p. 30.

46Surplus value is derived entirely from labour power (Marx, *Capital*, vol. 1, parts 3-5). Strictly speaking, the rate of surplus value is determined in the economy as a whole.

47See discussion of Ford's profits in the Introduction. Marshall, in *Canadian-American Industry*, shows interest and dividend payments on US capital invested in Canada from 1914 to 1932. Most were direct investments. In 1914 dividend and interest payments totalled $39 million on a total investment valued at $881 million, a rate of return of 4.46% per annum. The rate of return was the same on US investment in Canada from 1915 to 1929. Dividends represent only a portion of total profits. For profits in Canadian-owned industries in the late 1920s, see Canada, Royal Commission on Price Spreads, *Report* (Ottawa: King's Printer, 1937).

48J. Viner, *Canada's Balance of International Indebtedness 1900-1913* (Toronto: McClelland and Stewart, 1975 [1924]), p. 286.

49This was true at least in the Toronto region, the centre of US branch-plant activity. See M. Piva, *The Condition of the Working Class in Toronto 1900-1921* (Ottawa: University of Ottawa Press, 1979), p. 44. Real wages did not rise in the highly unionized building trades in Toronto. The effects of immigration on wage rates for unionized workers in the industrial sectors where US branch plants were concentrated needs to be studied. Cairncross calculated wage increases at 49% and cost of living increases at 43%, 1900-13 (*Home and Foreign Investment 1870-1913* (Cambridge: Cambridge University Press 1953), p. 59).

50Panitch, 'Dependency and Class', p. 21.

51The Canada First movement said this in 1875 (Carl Berger, *The Sense of Power: Studies in the Ideas of Canadian Imperialism 1867-1914* [Toronto: University of Toronto Press, 1970] p. 72).

52W. McCaffrey, *English and American Banking Systems Compared* (Syracuse: Kingsport Press, 1938), p. 25. The Bank of England obtained the exclusive right to issue notes in the 1890s.

53The period 1827-37 saw an increase in the availability of capital as regional banks jockeyed for position. I am indebted to David Moss, History Department, University of Alberta, for insights into the English banking system from the 1820s to 1840s.

[54]H. Vatter, *The Drive to Industrial Maturity: The U.S. Economy 1860-1914* (Westport, Conn.: Greenwood Press, 1975), p. 22.

[55]F. Ouellet, *Economic and Social History of Quebec 1760-1850*, English ed. (Toronto: Carleton Library, 1980), p. 388.

[56]A. Shortt, 'A History of Canadian Currency', *JCBA* 8, no. 2: 161.

[57]Ouellet, *Economic and Social History of Quebec*, p. 368.

[58]L.-M. Viger, founder of the Banque du Peuple, was a cousin of J. Viger and D.-B. Viger, leaders of the Parti Patriote.

[59]Shortt, 'History of Canadian Currency', *JCBA* 9, no. 1: 7.

[60]Ibid., p. 39.

[61]C.L. Vaughan, 'The Bank of Upper Canada in Politics, 1817-1840', *Ontario History* 60 (1968).

[62]Shortt, 'History of Canadian Currency', *JCBA* 9, no. 1: 6.

[63]R.M. Breckenridge, *The Canadian Banking System 1817-1890* (Toronto: Macmillan, 1895), p. 77.

[64]Shortt, 'History of Canadian Currency', *JCBA* 10, no. 1.

[65]Proposals for a public bank of issue were made in 1850 and 1860, and for exclusive state note-issue in 1866 and 1869. The bank acts of 1870-1 gave the state the exclusive right to issue notes of less than $4 (Merrill Denison, *Canada's First Bank: A History of the Bank of Montreal*, vol. 2 (Toronto: McClelland and Stewart, 1966) p. 142).

[66]Shortt, 'History of Canadian Currency,' *JCBA* 10, no. 1.

[67]Bray Hammond, *Banks and Politics in America from the Revolution to the Civil War* (Princeton: Princeton University Press, 1957), pp. 597, 667.

[68]G. Myers, *History of Canadian Wealth* (Toronto, Lorimer, 1975), p. 171.

[69]Denison, *Canada's First Bank*, vol. 1, p. 320.

[70]Shortt, 'A History of Canadian Banking and Exchange', *JCBA* 8, no. 2.

[71]Breckenridge, *The Canadian Banking System*, p. 175; Denison, *Canada's First Bank*, vol. 2, p. 130.

[72]J. Schull, *100 Years of Banking in Canada: A History of the Toronto Dominion Bank* (Toronto: Copp Clark, 1958), p. 34.

[73]B.H. Beckhart, 'The Banking System of Canada', in H.P. Willis and B.H. Beckhart, eds, *Foreign Banking Systems* (New York: Henry Holt, 1929), p. 300.

[74]Naylor, *History of Canadian Business*, vol. 1, p. 68.

[75]A. Schlesinger, Jr., *The Age of Jackson* (Boston: Little, Brown, 1945), p. 427.

[76]W.A. Mackintosh, *The Economic Problems of the Prairie Provinces* (Toronto: Macmillan, 1935), p. 282.

[77]W.T. Easterbrook and H.G.J. Aitken, *Canadian Economic History* (Toronto: Macmillan, 1956), p.483.

[78]E.J. Chambers and D.S. Gordon, 'Primary Products and Economic Growth: An Empirical Measurement', *Journal of Political Economy* 64, no. 4 (Aug. 1966).

[79]M.C. Urquhart, 'New Estimates of Gross Domestic Product, Canada, 1870 to 1926', Institute for Economic Research, Queen's University, Discussion Paper no. 586, 1986, p. 27; R. Pomfret, *The Economic Development of Canada*, p. 157; R. Caves, 'Export-Led Growth and the New Economic History', in J.N. Bhagwati et al., eds, *Trade, Balance of Payments and Growth* (Amsterdam, 1971); G. Bertram, 'The Relevance of the Wheat Boom in Canadian Economic Growth', *Canadian Journal of Economics* 6, no. 4 (Nov. 1973).

[80]R.E. Ankli and R.M. Litt, 'The Growth of Prairie Agriculture: Economic Consideration', in D.H. Akenson, ed., *Canadian Papers in Rural History* (Gananoque: Langdale Press, 1978), p. 78.

[81]H. Aitken, 'Defensive Expansion: The State and Economic Growth in Canada', in W.T. Easterbrook and M.H. Watkins, eds, *Approaches to Canadian Economic History* (Toronto: McClelland and Stewart, 1967).

[82]Ibid.

[83]Quoted in M. Bliss, 'Canadianizing American Business: the Roots of the Branch Plant', in I. Lumsden, ed., *Close the 49th Parallel Etc.* (Toronto: University of Toronto Press, 1970).

[84]J. Dales argues the National Policy failed to function for twenty or thirty years ('Some Historical and Theoretical Comment on Canada's National Policies', *Queen's Quarterly* vol. 71 [1964]: 302).

[85]Easterbrook and Aitken, *Canadian Economic History*, p. 396.

[86]C.M. Studness, 'Economic Opportunity and the Westward Migration of Canadians in the Late Nineteenth Century', *Canadian Journal of Economics and Political Science* 30 (Nov. 1964): 571.

[87]Mackintosh, *Problems of the Prairie Provinces*, p. 8.

[88]G. Laxer, 'The Social Origins of Canada's Branch Plant Economy, 1867 to 1914 (Ph.D. dissertation, University of Toronto, 1981), p. 509.

[89]C.K. Harley, 'Transportation, the World Wheat Trade, and the Kuznets Cycle, 1850-1913', *Explorations in Economic History* 17 (1980): 220. Calculations made from Part A series.

[90]W. Marr and M. Percy, 'The Government and the Rate of Prairie Settlement', *Canadian Journal of Economics* 11 (Nov. 1978): 759; M. Percy and T. Woroby, 'American Homesteaders and the Canadian Prairies, 1899 and 1909', *Explorations in Economic History*, 1986, p. 402; J.C. Stabler, 'Factors Affecting the Development of A New Region: the Great Plains, 1870-1897', *Annals of Regional Science*, June 1973. C.K. Harley argues that wheat prices were high enough in the 1880s to encourage settlement, but that at times in the 1890s it was too low ('Western Settlement and the Price of Wheat 1872-1913', *Journal of Economic History* 38, no. 4 [1978]: 874).

[91]Easterbrook and Aitken, *Canadian Economic History*, p. 396.

[92]Stabler, 'Development of a New Region', p. 85.

[93]K.H. Norrie, 'The National Policy and the Rate of Prairie Settlement', *Journal of Canadian Studies* 14, no. 3 (1979): 67.

[94]Ibid., p. 67.

[95]H.E. Briggs, *Frontiers of the Northwest: A History of the Upper Missouri Valley*, (New York: D. Appleton-Century, 1940), p. 535.

[96]W.A. Mackintosh, *Prairie Settlement: The Geographical Setting*, vol. 1 (Toronto: Macmillan, 1934), p. xii.

[97]K. Norrie, 'The Rate of Settlement of the Canadian Prairies, 1870-1911', *Journal of Economic History* 35, no. 2 (1975): 419.

[98]Norrie, 'National Policy', p. 68.

[99]Mackintosh, *Prairie Settlement*, p. 33. In Alberta the semi-arid region is south of a line midway between Red Deer and Calgary.

[100]John Eagle, 'The Canadian Pacific Railway and the Development of Western Canada 1896-1914' (manuscript in press, McGill-Queen's, 1988), chapter 8.

[101]Marr and Percy, 'The Government and the Rate of Prairie Settlement', p. 760.

[102]Mackintosh, *Prairie Settlement*, p. 69.

[103]Norrie, 'Rate of Settlement', p. 423 note.

[104]See Mackintosh, *Prairie Settlement*, for his time-series maps on population densities (p. 62).

[105]Norrie, 'National Policy', p. 66.

[106]A.S. Morton, *History of Prairie Settlement* (Toronto: Macmillan, 1938), p. 148.

[107]W.L. Morton, *Manitoba: A History* (Toronto: University of Toronto Press, 1955), p. 210.

[108]Ankli and Litt, 'The Growth of Prairie Agriculture', p. 39.

[109]V.C. Fowke, *Canadian Agricultural Policy: The Historical Policy* (Toronto: University of Toronto Press, 1947), p. 237.

[110]Morton, *History of Prairie Settlement*, p. 96.

[111]Mackintosh, *Prairie Settlement*, p. 69.

[112]Ibid., p. 53.

[113]D.J. Hall, 'Clifford Sifton: Immigration and Settlement Policy 1896-1905', in H. Palmer, ed., *The Settlement of the West* (Calgary: University of Calgary Press, 1977) p. 63.

[114]C. Martin, *'Dominion Lands' Policy*, (Toronto: McClelland and Stewart, 1973), p. 50.

[115]Eagle, CPR.

[116]See Norrie, 'Rate of Settlement', p. 425 and Ankli and Litt, 'The Growth of Prairie Agriculture', p. 38.

[117]Studness, 'Economic Opportunity', p. 582.

[118]Ibid., p. 574.

[119]Less than half the CPR land grants were in the railway belt, about 8,500,000 acres when Alberta irrigation lands are included. Northern Reserve lands were about 7 million acres and Southern Reserve lands along the Manitoba-US border about 2,500,000 acres. See J.B. Hedges, *The Federal Railway Land Subsidy Policy of Canada* (Cambridge: Harvard University Press, 1934).

[120]Hedges, *Railway Land Subsidy Policy*, p. 47.

[121]Aitken, 'Defensive Expansion'; K. Buckley, *Capital Formation in Canada, 1896-1930*, (Toronto: McClelland and Stewart, 1974), p. 51.

[122]D. Owram, *Promise of Eden: The Canadian Expansionist Movement and the Idea of the West, 1856-1900* (Toronto: University of Toronto Press, 1980), p. 162.

[123]V.C. Fowke, *The National Policy and the Wheat Economy*, (Toronto: University of Toronto Press, 1957).

[124]Easterbrook and Aitken, *Canadian Economic History*, p. 317.

[125]H. Innis and A.R.M. Lower, *Select Documents in Canadian Economic History 1783-1885* (Toronto: University of Toronto Press, 1933), p. 629.

[126]Denison, *Canada's First Bank*, vol. 2, p. 129.

[127]The government guaranteed the interest, at a rate of not over 6%, on half the bonds of any railway over 75 miles long if half the line had already been built. An 1851 amendment limited government support to main lines, but the Municipal Loan Fund, a consolidated fund guaranteed by the central government, allowed cities and towns to subsidize feeder lines. See Easterbrook and Aitken, *Canadian Economic History*, p. 298; Denison, *Canada's First Bank*, vol. 2, p. 63.

[128]George Glazebrook, *A History of Transportation in Canada*, vol. 1, (Toronto: McClelland and Stewart, 1964), pp. 157-164

[129]The Grand Trunk employed English contractors—Peto, Brassey, Betts and Jackson—to build the majority of the line.

[130]See Glazebrook, *A History of Transportation in Canada*, vol. 1, p. 66. The following railways were built according to the expensive British methods: the Grand Trunk and the Great Western in the 1850s (see ibid., p. 166); the Intercolonial in the 1870s (see Easterbrook and Aitken, *Canadian Economic History*, p. 412); and the National Transcontinental (see Glazebrook, *History of Transportation*, vol. 2, p. 137). On the other hand, the CPR and Mackenzie and Mann's Canadian Northern were built according to the American standard. See Glazebrook, *History of Transportation*, vol. 2, p. 145; Harold Innis, *A History of the Canadian Pacific Railway* (Toronto: McClelland and Stewart, 1923), p. 102.

[131]Innis and Lower, *Select Documents*, p. 649; D. Paterson, *British Direct Investment in Canada 1890-1914* (Toronto: University of Toronto Press, 1976), p. 23.

[132]Myers, *History of Canadian Wealth*, p. 176.

[133]Aitken, 'Defensive Expansion'.

[134]H. Innis, *The Problems of Staple Production in Canada* (Toronto: Ryerson Press, 1933), p. 31.

[135]A.A. Den Otter, 'Nationalism and the Pacific Scandal', *Canadian Historical Review* 69, no. 3 (Sept. 1988).

[136]O. McDiarmid, *Commercial Policy in the Canadian Economy* (Cambridge: Harvard University Press, 1946), p. 134. The US threatened to withdraw bonding privileges in the late 1880s, a period of high support for annexation. See M. Wade, *The French Canadians 1760-1967*, vol. 1, *1760-1911*, rev. ed. (Toronto: Macmillan, 1968), p. 467.

[137]Innis, *Canadian Pacific Railway*, p. 136.

[138]Ibid., pp. 134, 183.

[139]Ibid., p. 129.

[140]Ibid., p. 107.

[141]Ibid., p. 175.

[142]Morton, *History of Prairie Settlement*, p. 67.

[143]Innis, *Canadian Pacific Railway*, p. 82; Pomfret, *Economic Development of Canada*, p. 108.

[144]'The freight rates charged ... were to be free from Parliamentary regulation until 10% profit had been earned on the capital expended on construction' (Easterbrook and Aitken, *Canadian Economic History*, p. 429); see also Morton, *History of Prairie Settlement*, p. 66.

[145]Innis, *Canadian Pacific Railway*, pp. 111, 176.

[146]Glazebrook, *History of Transportation*, vol. 2, p. 113.

[147]Innis, *Canadian Pacific Railway*, p. 183.

[148]Ibid., p. 302. The cash was to be raised largely by government sale of western land.

[149]J.R. Perry, *Public Debts in Canada* (Toronto: University of Toronto Librarian, 1898), p. 11.

[150]Ibid., p. xxx.

[151]K.W. Taylor and H. Michell, *Statistical Contributions to Canadian Economic History*, I (Toronto: Macmillan, 1931), p. 11.

[152]Martin, *'Dominion Lands' Policy*, p. 233.

[153]Easterbrook and Aitken, *Canadian Economic History*, p. 420.

[154]D. Thomson, *Alexander Mackenzie: Clear Grit* (Toronto: Macmillan, 1960), p. 196.

[155]Martin, *'Dominion Lands' Policy*, p. 44.

[156]Urquhart, 'New Estimates', p. 93.

[157]Innis, *Canadian Pacific Railway*, p. 98.

[158]P.J. George, 'Foreword' to H. Innis, *A History of the Canadian Pacific Railroad* (Toronto: University of Toronto Press, 1971), p. viii.

[159]Innis, *Canadian Pacific Railway*, p. 105.

[160]Government positions were usually party appointments.

[161]Technical skills in Canada were inadequate for railway building on this scale and public enterprises had difficulty attracting skilled personnel. See Innis, *Canadian Pacific Railway*, p. 90.

[162]Martin, *'Dominion Lands' Policy*, p. 116.

[163]Hedges, *Railway Land Subsidy Policy*, p. 31.

[164]Martin, *'Dominion Lands' Policy*, p. 49.

[165]Ibid., p. 50.

[166]Fowke, *The National Policy and the Wheat Economy*, p. 59.

[167]Martin, *'Dominion Lands' Policy*, p. 38.

[168]Ibid., p. 158.

[169]Hedges, *Railway Land Subsidy Policy*, p. 5.

[170]Studness, 'Economic Opportunity', p. 584.

[171]Morton, *History of Prairie Settlement*, p. 66.

[172]Innis, *Canadian Pacific Railway*, p. 293.

[173]Mackintosh, *Problems of the Prairie Provinces*, p. 281.

[174]O.J. Firestone, *Industry and Education: A Century of Canadian Development* (Ottawa: University of Ottawa Press, 1969), p. 261.

[175]Manufacturing output rose 60% (1880s), 27% (1890s), and 78% (1900-1910). See G.W. Bertram, 'Historical Growth and Structure in Manufacturing in Canada 1870-1957', in J. Henripin and A. Asimkopoulos, eds., *Canadian Political Science Association Conference on Statistics* (Toronto, 1962).

[176]Urquhart, 'New Estimates', pp. 15, 27.

[177]For a revised view of slow manufacturing growth in the 1870s and 1880s see M. Altman, 'A revision of Canadian economic growth: 1870-1910 (a challenge to the gradualist interpretation)', *Canadian Journal of Economics* 20, no. 1 (Feb. 1987).

[178]Vatter, *Drive to Industrial Maturity*, p. 134.

[179]Buckley, *Capital Formation in Canada*, p. 52.

[180]Lower, *Colony to Nation*, p. 427.

[181]Glazebrook, *History of Canadian Transportation*, vol. 2, p. 138.

[182]G.R. Stevens, *Canadian National Railways*, vol. 2 (Toronto: Clarke Irwin, 1962), p. 43.

[183]Glazebrook, *History of Transportation*, Vol. 2, p. 132.

[184]Stevens, *CNR*, p. 227.

[185]Easterbrook and Aitken, *Canadian Economic History*, p. 440.

[186]Naylor, *History of Canadian Business*, vol. 1, p. 287.

[187]Stevens, *CNR*, p. 149.

[188]Naylor, *History of Canadian Business*, vol. 1, p. 292; Martin, *'Dominion Lands' Policy*, p. 59.

[189]Glazebrook, *History of Transportation*, vol. 2, p. 145.

[190]Ibid., p. 44.

[191]Glazebrook, *History of Transportation*, vol. 2, p. 136.

[192]Naylor, *History of Canadian Business*, vol. 1, p. 279.

[193]R.C. Brown and R. Cook, *Canada, 1896-1921: A Nation Transformed* (Toronto: McClelland and Stewart, 1974), p. 149.

[194]Glazebrook, *History of Transportation*, vol. 2, p. 129.

[195]Stevens, *CNR*, p. 145.

[196]Cairncross, *Home and Foreign Investment* p. 3.

[197]Ibid., p. 2.

[198]S. Kuznets, 'International Differences in Capital formation Financing', in National Bureau of Economic Research, *Capital Formation and Economic Growth* (Princeton: Princeton University Press, 1955), pp. 38-9, 71.

[199]The portion going directly to the railways would appear to have been well over 35%. As well, much of the capital borrowed by federal and provincial governments was used to subsidize railroad construction. See Laxer, 'Social Origins,' p. 555.

[200]Buckley, *Capital Formation in Canada*, p. 103.

[201]Viner, *Canada's Balance*. For criticisms of Viner see J.A. Stovel, *Canada in the World Economy* (Cambridge: Harvard University Press, 1959), and H.C. Eastman's introduction to the 1975 edition of Viner's book.

[202]Viner, *Canada's Balance*, pp. 213-55.

[203]Ibid, p. 288.

[204]United States, *American Branch Factories Abroad*. Senate Document #260, 71st Congress, 3rd Session (Washington, 1931).

[205]Viner, *Canada's Balance*, p. 288.

[206]Buckley, *Capital Formation in Canada*, p. 103.

[207]Ibid., p. 99.

[208]The exact contributions of reinvestment, the borrowing of Canadian capital, and capital imports have not been calculated for this period.

[209]H. Innis, *Essays in Canadian Economic History* (Toronto: University of Toronto Press, 1973) p. 152.

[210]W.J. Donald, *Canadian Iron and Steel Industry* (Boston: Houghton Mifflin and Co., 1915).

[211]G.W. Bertram, 'Economic Growth in Canadian Industry, 1870-1915: The Staple Model and the Take Off Hypothesis', *Canadian Journal of Economics and Political Science* 29 (1963).

6

Open Door to Foreign Ownership

By 1914 Canada clearly had more US-controlled manufacturing plants than any other foreign nation.

Mira Wilkins, business historian, 1970.

It is of small moment where the capital comes from that may be employed in developing our industries. When it is thus invested it at once becomes Canadian capital. Don't worry . . . about the annexation business. There cannot possibly be enough American capital invested in Canadian mining industries to enable the transfer of one acre of Canadian soil to Yankee jurisdiction. Meantime we gladly welcome all American capitalists who desire to join our procession in our march to industrial development and national greatness.

The Canadian Manufacturer, 2 March 1894.

I agree with every member of this House and every citizen of Canada that we like to see American capital brought in to establish industries in this country. But, if I am to make a choice as between a large factory built in Canada with United States capital, and a large factory built in Canada with Canadian capital, I will every time choose the latter. And why? Because every manufacturing establishment is built to secure to the owners a net profit. In the case of a factory backed by American capital it is true, money from outside will be spent in erecting the building and paying wages, but *the net profit from that American institution will be taken to the United States to further develop that country*, while in the case of the factory built with Canadian capital, the net profit will remain in Canada for the development of our own country. (Emphasis added.)

H.H. Miller, Liberal MP, 1911.

John McKay, Russian historian, noted that the rulers of most countries before the First World War were apprehensive about foreign investment. 'If the choice must be between either foreign domination with rapid growth or national integrity with slower economic progress,' he wrote, 'few nations will hesitate to pick the latter.'[1] Czarist Russia increasingly discriminated against foreign direct investment from the 1890s on, while Japan went so far as to forbid the borrowing of foreign capital for over two decades. Sweden was more hospitable, but skirmishes over foreign ownership of resources continued from the 1870s until 1916, when tough concession laws restricted foreign ownership (see the discussions in Chapters 2 and 3). Canada, it seems, was the exception.[2] During the National Policy era Canadians chose, or thought they were choosing, rapid progress when they encouraged foreign direct investment.

Foreign ownership was opposed and restricted in certain instances in the first years after Confederation, but it was not until the 1920s that significant general criticisms of foreign investment were made—mainly, then as now, by the left.[3] By then foreign ownership was already well entrenched, accounting for almost 40 per cent in the manufacturing and mining and smelting sectors.[4] There were no restrictions on the general flow for another half-century. The questions for us are why this was so, and how Canadian actions led to a branch-plant economy.

During initial industrialization, restrictions on foreign direct investment in Canada were either limited in scope, temporary, or loosely enforced. That bastion of economic nationalism and opponent of reciprocity with the US, *The Canadian Manufacturer*, the official organ of the Canadian Manufacturers Association, only stated the consensus on American direct investment when it claimed in 1894: 'It is of small moment where the capital comes from that may be employed in developing our industries . . . we gladly welcome all American capitalists. . . .'[5] All three levels of government lured investment into the country, paying scant attention to whether such investment was ownership or loan capital. They cared little, except in rare circumstances, whether capital was foreign or domestic.

The revenue-poor municipalities were the most aggressive promoters, offering all kinds of enticements to any manufacturers—foreign or domestic—who would establish plants in their communities. Would-be investors were showered with gifts, including free sites, money bonusses, loans, tax exemptions, and free water and electricity.[6] A few examples from R.T. Naylor's extensive list indicate the tenor of the times. In 1878 Ottawa gave a New Yorker $10,000, a free ninety-nine-year lease on a site, and a ten-year exemption from taxes to move his textile mill there. Two decades later, in 1897, Vancouver rewarded an American copper and gold company with a bonus of 50 cents for each ton of ore it smelted (up to 100,000 tons). In Nova Scotia the provincial government joined the bonussing craze in 1879 by decreeing that any cotton mill built in the province within three years would get a twenty-year tax exemption at the provincial, municipal, and local levels.[7] As early as 1900, ninety-five Ontario municipalities had granted such aid to Canadian, American, and British factories.

Municipalities in the central provinces were the most generous towards factories that, for the right terms, were willing to locate anywhere. Ontario concentrated on American investors, while Quebec directed its largesse mainly at domestic companies—perhaps because its plentiful supply of cheap and unskilled labour suited the demands of older Canadian-owned industries, such as textiles and boots and shoes.[8] Ontario, on the other hand, attracted secondary metal factories, a pioneering sector of early American transnationals. (American foundrymen had been emigrating to southwestern Ontario to establish their ventures since the 1830s).[9] Although Maritime municipalities got involved as well, they offered fewer concessions, and Manitoba actually frowned on the idea of companies—American or Canadian—requesting bonusses.[10] The geographic distribution of generosity was consistent with the later pattern in which American branch plants were concentrated in southern Ontario, with a smaller number in Quebec and very few in the eastern and western provinces. But it cannot be concluded that municipal bonusses were the cause of these regional differences in branch-plant concentration.

More important were the actions of first the federal and later the provincial governments. The Dominion government encouraged foreign investment in a number of ways: it created a favourable climate for foreign investment, it promoted industrial protection, and it opened up the newly acquired western territories.

The first order of business for the Fathers of Confederation was to restore the confidence of British investors who had lost money in the railway-building spree of the 1850s. Part of their plan involved having the low-debt Maritime provinces share the enormous railway debts that Canada East and West had incurred. The main intent was to attract portfolio capital to finance transportation projects, rather than to bring direct investments, and it was only partly successful: it was not until the late 1890s that Britain's international investments focussed once again on Canada.[11]

In the 1870s a coherent development strategy evolved that went beyond the mere provision of railways and the occupation of the west. It was hoped that the National Policy would help Canada match American growth and prosperity, and that that in turn would generate loyalty to the Dominion in the regions. Industrialization was a means to those ends, not the final goal; the most important thing was to effect a transformation quickly, so that the newly united country could resist the absorptive pull of the United States.

It mattered little to the architects of the National Policy whether Canadian or foreign entrepreneurs did the job. To speed up industrialization, many of the factors of production were to be imported: capital, technology, management, and skilled labour. We have seen this passive philosophy at work in the tariffs that encouraged the importation of foreign management and capital and in the Patent Act, which encouraged the importation of foreign technology to the detriment of domestic technology.

The same passivity soon extended to the provinces. They were happy to let the federal government bring in skilled immigrants, since provincial obligations to educate and train native-born citizens would thus be reduced. As the level of government responsible for resource industries (except in the prairies)[12] the provinces extended the National Policy's philosophy to the new resource industries in forestry, hydroelectricity, and mining.

Ontario took the lead when it adopted its own mini-version of the National Policy, the 'manufacturing condition'—an appropriate name for a policy of passive development. The idea was to ensure the processing of Ontario's new raw materials prior to export to the United States. If that meant that American capitalists had to shift some of their production to Canada, so much the better. The location of activity was the question, not the nationality of capital (except in the celebrated case of Niagara Falls hydro-power).

Ontario's policy was brilliantly documented in H.V. Nelles's *The Politics of Development: Forests, Mines and Hydro-electricity in Ontario 1849-1941*.[13] To achieve a northerly migration of resource industries, Ontario needed a scheme that would be the obverse of the National Policy. Instead of reducing the inflow of manufactured imports through tariffs, the province restricted the export of resources in their raw state so as to encourage resource-processing in Canada.

The new strategy was first applied to Canada's main non-farm crop, forest products. In 1897, during one of the recurring trade disputes between Canada and the US over forest products, the US passed the Dingley tariff—a measure that placed a duty on Canadian lumber but allowed the free entry of Canadian logs. The Americans wanted to import the raw material cheaply and keep out the semi-finished Canadian product.[14] Lumbermen in western and northern Ontario demanded retaliation. Unable to move the reciprocity-oriented Laurier government in Ottawa, they turned to Ontario, the Crown owner of most of the vast timber lands. Although reluctant at first, Ontario imposed a ban on the export of saw logs from all Crown land in 1898. Two years later a similar ban was extended to the export of pulpwood, the raw material for the rapidly expanding pulp and paper industry.[15]

Other governments followed Ontario's example in banning the export of raw forest products. In its capacity as custodian of prairie resources, the federal government was the first, in 1907; Quebec followed in 1910, New Brunswick in 1911, and British Columbia in 1913.[16] As a result of these actions, much of the American lumber industry in the Great Lakes region transferred production north across the border.

Pulp and paper was a tougher case. The American industry established itself in Canada only after the American newspaper lobby had succeeded in getting newsprint on the US list of duty-free imports in 1911-13.[17] Before this time US imports of newsprint were only 1.5 per cent of domestic production (1909). By 1921 total US imports had reached 65 per cent, with Canada alone supplying 35 per cent of the American market, and about three-quarters of the capital invested in the Canadian pulp and paper industry was of American origin.[18]

Rather than being alarmed at the extent of foreign control over domestic resources, provincial governments were overjoyed at the new levels of economic activity, employment, and provincial revenue. They established resource departments and bureaus that, among other things, promoted American and British interest in Canadian resource investments.[19] Their only misgivings were about American companies that avoided locating their processing facilities in Canada by extracting the raw pulpwood on privately owned lands where provincial restrictions did not apply. The Canadian Pulp and Paper Association accused these holdouts of neglecting conservation practices.[20]

THE STATE AND CANADIAN OWNERSHIP

Canada's four largest banks are among the top sixty banks in the world,[21] and Canadian railways, airlines, and hydroelectric and telephone companies play major and independent roles both at home and abroad. Predominantly Canadian owned and controlled, these sectors—finance, utilities, and public-carrier transportation—lend Canada the appearance of an advanced and autonomous capitalist power. On the other hand, branch plants and subsidiaries of foreign multinationals account for almost half the value of manufacturing and resource industries in Canada; foreign subsidiaries in these industries are on average much larger than domestically owned companies, whose role often is to swim around the bigger fish. Those who point to these sectors characterize Canada as an economic dependency or semi-peripheral country.

Observers have long pondered the pattern of Canadian dominance in the commercial sectors and foreign dominance in the industrial and resource industries. To explain this phenomenon, Naylor developed a theory that revolved around the conflict between commerce and industry (see Chapter 1). Many have discounted his argument but failed to produce an alternative explanation.

In Chapter 4 it was argued that the conservatism of Canadian banks and Canada's failure to develop independent defence and military procurement policies were major determinants of this pattern of Canadian and foreign dominance.[22] But there was another, thus far neglected, factor as well: the Canadian state protected certain sectors from foreign control while it allowed—indeed, promoted—foreign investment in others during the formative period of the National Policy. Given the interest that, since the mid-1950s, the issue of foreign ownership has aroused, it is surprising that the state's early role has received so little attention. Because most of the detailed primary work remains to be done, conclusions can only be tentative. Still, it is clear that in most of the sectors where early regulations restricting foreign control remained in force, or where the economic sector was considered so vital that public ownership was common, Canadian control has generally prevailed. These sectors include banking, mass-transportation railways and airlines, utilities, telegraphs and cables, and newspapers and radio. Where there were no early restrictions, or where restrictions were temporary or sporadic, foreign control has tended to dominate. Manufacturing and most resource industries fall into this category.[23]

Alien landownership

At various times from the War of 1812 to the First World War, restrictions were placed on foreign ownership of resources. Among the areas restricted were the ownership of land, the staking of placer gold claims, and petroleum exploration on Crown lands. These provisions were aimed mostly at Americans.[24]

In Canada the first instance of controls on foreign ownership had to do with land, the main source of wealth in a newly settled territory. The implications were enormous. Land- and resource-ownership regulations in Sweden and Norway restricted the activities of foreign capitalists in the whole range of resource industries, from minerals to hydroelectricity to the forest sector. Controls on alien landownership in the US applied not only to farms but also to mines. If similar regulations had survived in Canada, the whole pattern of development and ownership of Canadian resources would have been different.

The landownership issue was raised in the aftermath of the War of 1812, a war that had provoked concern among the Loyalist elements regarding the allegiance of recent American settlers. In 1815 Lord Bathurst, the secretary for the colonies, directed the lieutenant-governor of Upper Canada to refuse land grants to incoming Americans and to prevent their settling in Canada (Lower Canada already had a similar regulation.)[25] This ordinance caused a great deal of agitation among settlers because it implied that non-Loyalist Americans were somehow inferior. Restrictions on American immigrants were repealed in 1828; from that point on, Americans could own land once they became British subjects. Nevertheless, the law had succeeded in diverting all but a trickle of American westward migration away from the province. British emigrants soon made up the vast majority of new entrants, changing the character of Upper Canadian society.

The alien landownership issue did not die in 1828, when American settlers were once more welcome in the province. Absentee landownership by foreigners (that is, the non-British) was still prohibited, and this prohibition had implications for the forest and other resource industries. In 1836 the Montreal *Gazette*, the voice of the English Tory clique in that city, strenuously objected to a Kingston-based scheme to encourage American lumbermen to buy up real estate without becoming British subjects. They were acting 'the cat's paw' for American capitalists, the *Gazette* contended, by attempting to end Upper Canada's restrictions on foreign landholdings. Such a change would allow Americans or other foreigners 'to come here . . . buying up our lands, engrossing our trade, sending their profits to their own countries, and having nothing in common with us'.[26] It is unclear when Upper Canada removed its controls on the leasing or acquisition of forest land, but the anti-American policy had clearly started to break down by the time of the Kingston scheme. The land restrictions do not seem to have survived into the period of the union of Lower and Upper Canada in 1841.[27]

In New Brunswick there were no restrictions on foreign landownership, and the colony boomed when American capital flooded in during the 1830s.[28] Protests were heard, but they failed to stem the tide. The economic benefits of large infusions of American capital and Yankee technical know-how in the forest industry were just too enticing to business interests, property holders, and governments for British allegiance to stand in the way.

Thus the restriction of landownership to nationals, a common practice in other countries, did not extend into the National Policy era of Canadian industrial development (though, in an apparent throwback to the early land restrictions, federal grazing leases on the prairies were made only to British subjects at the time of the First World War).[29] It has been estimated that more than half the capital in mining in Ontario and Quebec in the 1880s was American; US interests also controlled substantial assets in the lumber industry across the country.[30] Americans and other foreigners were barred from locating placer gold claims in Canada until 1900, but this handicap had little effect on their extensive participation in the numerous gold rushes of the late nineteenth century.[31] The early removal of prohibitions on land sales to foreigners left Canadian resources wide open to foreign capitalists, who quickly took advantage of the opportunities. By 1921, 46 per cent of Canadian mining securities were held abroad, and in the nickel-copper and silver-cobalt sectors foreign control was dominant.[32]

Foreign ownership and oil

The early twentieth century witnessed rapid transformation from the age of coal and steam to the age of electricity and the internal-combustion engine. These new techniques demanded new fuels—oil and hydroelectricity—which Canada eventually provided in abundance. Canada's oil resources were destined to fall largely into foreign hands, while electricity was retrieved from American interests through the establishment of public power utilities. State regulations were critical to the outcome in each case.

From the time North America's first producing oil well was drilled in Lambton County (near Sarnia, Ontario), in 1858, until the First World War, there were no restrictions on foreign ownership in petroleum. But for many years the huge oil finds of the future were only a dream. Since Canada had to import most of its oil (98 per cent in 1917), the Canadian industry was largely confined to the downstream activities of refining and marketing. The industry was dominated by Imperial Oil, bought in 1880 by Standard Oil, the Rockefeller company that monopolized the American market.[33] The industry seemed destined to follow the path of other Canadian resource industries: to be developed largely under the auspices of American management and technology. But strategic concerns arising from the international tensions that led to the First World War threatened to alter the scenario.

The Dominion government was awakened from its somnolent, hands-off policy towards ownership and control of the petroleum industry by the British Admiralty, which as early as 1905 was alive to the possibility of oil's being found in Alberta. Faced with the growing threat to its naval dominance by a resurgent Germany, and dependent upon the US for about 80 per cent of Britain's oil supply, the Admiralty was casting anxious glances at all possible sources of oil within the Empire. Admiral Lord Fisher was a believer in Alberta's potential twenty years before that province began to produce significant supplies;[34] with Winston Churchill, then first lord of the Admiralty, he pressured Canada to adopt a pro-Empire oil policy and exclude the Americans from controlling oil in the Canadian northwest. The British state had come to see oil as a strategic resource for which security of supply took precedence over the free market. Since prairie resources were still under federal jurisdiction, it was Ottawa that would have to act.

Six months before the outbreak of the First World War, Canada adopted a new petroleum policy to stimulate exploration and to ensure that western Canadian oil (on Crown land) remained largely in Canadian and British hands. The 1914 ordinance required that

> any company acquiring by assignment or otherwise a lease under the provisions of these regulations, shall at all times be and remain a British company, registered in Great Britain or Canada and having its principal place of business within His Majesty's Dominions, and the chairman of the said company and a *majority of the directors shall at all times be British subjects*, and the company shall not at any time be or become, directly or indirectly, controlled by foreigners or by a foreign corporation.[35] (Emphasis added.)

This law came into effect just before the first significant oil find in Alberta. The Dominion government went beyond Britain's request for wartime or emergency powers and applied the provisions to peacetime as well.

There was strong support for a state role in the oil industry, and not just for reasons of war. The public power movement that led to the creation of Ontario Hydro was at its height, and many influential voices, including that of Senator James Lougheed, minister of the interior, advocated a publicly owned oil industry.[36] But economic nationalism and public ownership did not triumph. A combination of forces pushed the federal government to retreat to its former passive, open-door policy.

Despite the 1914 regulation prohibiting foreign corporations from exploration on western lands, Standard Oil of New Jersey had obtained a dominant position in Alberta by the end of the First World War through its subsidiary Imperial Oil. The multinational got around the federal ordinance, which applied only to Crown land, by purchasing the CPR's subsurface rights to its extensive land-holdings. It also gained access to Crown land reserves by purchasing a controlling minority interest in the Northwest Company, a Canadian-owned front company for Imperial.[37]

The US pressured Canada to revoke the ordinance, since the stakes involved control of the petroleum industry world-wide. With less than 5 per cent of the world's production in 1919, British companies had acquired more than half the world's estimated future reserves, threatening American dominance in the industry.[38] Australia, India, and other countries and territories of the British Empire also restricted oil activity to British subjects. The Americans retaliated against the British Empire with its mineral-leasing law of 1920, which denied ownership rights in the US to citizens or corporations of countries with restrictive ownership laws against Americans.[39] The final pressure on federal oil policy came from the populist movements that swept across the Canadian prairies at the end of the First World War: they demanded provincial control over resources.[40]

As the weak link in the British Empire's armour, Canada was the first state to cave in under American pressure. In 1920 the ordinance restricting non-British ownership and control was scrapped; it was replaced by a face-saving gesture that gave the government notice of any alteration in 'the British character' of the company and allowed cancellation of a foreign takeover at the discretion of the government.[41] Apparently, though, the government never acted on its discretionary power. Thus the prohibition on foreign ownership in Crown lands in the west joined the other 'might-have-beens' of Canadian history.

Public power

While there was a wholesale retreat from prohibitions on foreign ownership of land and resources, hydroelectric power was regained from early American domination through a public power movement. Ontario showed the way in the first two decades of the twentieth century, and its example was later copied by most provinces.[42] Led by small manufacturers, Ontario's public power movement was inspired by a combination of economic self-interest (cheap power), municipal boosterism, anti-corporate sentiment directed against the practices of American monopolies, and—in the conservative, statist tradition of politics in the National Policy era—belief in public ownership as the means to right a number of wrongs. (The influence of the public power movement spread to the three prairie provinces in the same era, when the telephone companies also came under provincial or municipal control.)[43] Whatever the motivation, the results were clear: public ownership meant, among other things, Canadian ownership of an important sector of the Canadian economy.

The main industrial region of Canada, stretching from Montreal to Windsor, was at a disadvantage compared to most of the advanced industrial areas of the world. Not having a domestic supply of coal near at hand, it had to import most of its fuel from the US. But electricity promised to wipe out this handicap. The invention of electrical generators and arc lights in the 1870s ushered in a new age of decentralization, instant communications, and new and finer production techniques.[44] Southern Ontario was fortunate in possessing the larger part of Niagara, the greatest water falls in the world, while the Montreal region had its own bountiful supplies of water power.

But a cloud hung over the rosy future of industrial Ontario. What nature had provided, man threatened to take away. Three power companies had obtained a monopoly over the Canadian side of Niagara Falls and were in a position to make a king's ransom on what was widely seen as the public's natural heritage. Prominent American industrialists and financiers owned two of these companies, which had obtained rights to the Canadian side of the falls and exported most of their output to the US.[45] The third firm, the Electrical Development Company, was owned by members of Canada's 'haute bourgeoisie': William Mackenzie, of Canadian Northern Railway fame; Henry Pellatt, a financier of utilities in South America and Toronto; and Frederick Nicholls, an electrical-equipment manufacturer.[46] This company, known as 'the syndicate', owned the Toronto Street Railway and the Toronto Electric Light Company. It seemed to small manufacturers and politicians in cities and towns throughout southern Ontario that the only Canadians to benefit from Niagara's great power would be those in the grasping metropolis of Toronto. This ill use of nature's bounty could not be countenanced, and a powerful coalition of small business interests and municipal boosters was formed to change the situation.

The story of how the public power movement gathered popular support through a series of municipal referenda and pressured reluctant Ontario governments, both Liberal and Conservative, to create Ontario Hydro has been told elsewhere and need not be repeated here. In this important episode in Ontario's history a movement of middle-class elements successfully took on a five-headed élite composed of Toronto/Montreal financiers, American power trusts, British financiers, and the Ontario and federal governments—a most significant and surprising turn of events. Their success in this campaign was all the more remarkable because it set alarm bells ringing in London financial markets about the political and investment climate in Ontario and Canada. The words 'socialism' and even 'confiscation' were bandied about. In spite of opposition from both Canadian and foreign élites, the public power movement forced Ontario to complete the move to public ownership.[47]

The creation of Ontario Hydro tipped the balance of ownership in power companies in Canada's favour. In the early 1930s American-owned power companies supplied 34 per cent of the electricity in Canada, and almost all of their control came from outside Ontario.[48] Gradually most of the other provinces followed the example of Ontario Hydro, which supplied power to industry at prices competitive with private companies in Quebec and in the 1930s had the lowest residential and small-user rates anywhere in North America.[49] By the late 1980s all provinces but Alberta and PEI had taken the public power route, and American control had diminished to negligible proportions.[50] The creation of these public power companies was not, for the most part, motivated by Canadian economic nationalism. Nevertheless, provincial power companies are among the largest corporations in Canada, and their control by the state has precluded foreign ownership of a major sector of Canadian resources.[51]

Banks and the British-subject clause

While domestic ownership of hydroelectric companies was largely a by-product of the public power movement, Canadian control of banks was a result of legislation. The 1821 act incorporating the Bank of Montreal, Canada's first bank, allowed foreigners to hold shares but prohibited them from being directors of the bank; directors had to be British subjects resident in Montreal.[52] The British-subject clause appeared in the legislation incorporating subsequent banks in Lower and Upper Canada and became part of the first comprehensive banking legislation of the new Dominion in 1871. Major bank revisions in 1890 relaxed the British-subject requirement from 100 per cent to a majority of bank directors, and this clause survived through later banking changes in 1906, 1934, 1954, and 1980.[53]

The exact effect of the restriction on foreign control in banking is unknown, but circumstances suggest that it was important in preventing American incursions into the Canadian business. Several Canadian banks in the early nineteenth century had strong American connections, among them the Bank of Montreal, of which over 40 per cent of the original subscribers were American, as was one of the four chief officers (all the directors were British subjects). One of the prime movers behind the bank was Horatio Gates, an American who refused to take the full oath of allegiance to the king because doing so would require him to bear arms against his American kin.[54] Other American-dominated banks were the Bank of Canada (not the later central bank of the same name) and the Bank of Upper Canada at Kingston.[55] The Family Compact, Upper Canada's cozy élite of government place-holders and keepers of the Loyalist tradition, reacted to the American incursion into British North America: one of their prime motives in establishing the Bank of Upper Canada at York (later Toronto) was to lessen American economic influence. To do this, they restricted directorships to British subjects resident in the province.[56]

Probably as a result of the British-subject requirement, early American influence in banking soon vanished; banking became and remained the strongest bastion of Canadian capitalism. In the 1930s the authors of *Canadian-American Industry* attributed the lack of US control in Canadian banking to fundamental differences between the systems in the two countries and to the statutory requirement of majority control by British subjects domiciled in Canada.[57]

As noted earlier, although the Canadian and American banking systems diverged sharply in the 1830s, British North America copied early American banking legislation. The Bank of Montreal Act of 1821 was derived directly from the Act of Congress that chartered the First Bank of the United States—the federal government bank—in 1791.[58] Concerned that Britain would continue its economic dominance even after the Revolution, and under pressure from agrarians who in 1785, for example, opposed 'admission of foreigners to investment in America', the Bank of the United States charter barred foreign nationals from holding directorships.[59]

Canada's first bank bill, introduced in Lower Canada in 1808, was, with minor revisions, a clause-by-clause copy of the wording of Alexander Hamilton's Bank of the United States charter.[60] In place of clause 3 of the US charter, restricting directorships to US citizens, the Lower Canada bill substituted the British-subjects-resident-in-Montreal requirement. (See Appendix, p. 234.) Although the bill failed to pass in 1808, it was the basis of the Bank of Montreal Act of 1821.[61]

Such was Canada's first restriction on foreign economic control: a straight copy of US foreign control legislation born of anti-British, anti-aristocratic, American nationalism. It is doubtful that the British Colonial Office originated the British-subject clause, because it was not included in the acts setting up New Brunswick and Nova Scotia banks in the 1820s and 1830s.[62] Moreover, while the Bank of England, the state bank founded in 1694, did restrict directorships to British subjects, there were no such provisions for other banks in England.[63]

The Bank of Montreal Act was copied by other banks in Upper and Lower Canada and formed the basis of Dominion bank legislation after Confederation. And though the 'British-subject' clause was later changed to 'Canadian-citizen', it survived otherwise intact into the early 1980s. Thus Alexander Hamilton, author of the American Constitution, was the inadvertent father not only of the Canadian banking system, but of the first restrictions on foreign economic control in Canada.[64]

The British-subject clause seems to have been extended from banking to include all federally incorporated companies. In the 1890s, we find, the Dominion Companies Act required that 'the majority of board of directors must . . . be British subjects resident in Canada'.[65] The restriction may not have had much effect, however, since it could be easily bypassed: in British Columbia, Ontario, and perhaps other provinces, companies could register under provincial, British, or foreign incorporation.[66] The effects of the restriction in areas of federal jurisdiction need further research, but it would appear that few if any such rules were enforced. For example, Canada's main telegraph companies were US-controlled until 1923, when they came under the newly created Canadian National Railway's system,[67] and about one-third of the insurance business, another area of federal jurisdiction, was US-controlled in the early 1930s.[68]

In banking American capitalists did not circumvent foreign-control legislation, but British capitalists did. The Bank of British North America (founded in 1836) was chartered in England—in order to overcome the difficulty of obtaining charters in each of the colonies—and run from there, as was the Bank of British Columbia (founded in 1862). (Both were later absorbed by larger Canadian banks.)[69] American and other foreign bankers, however, did not have the option of incorporating at home and operating in Canada, at least for a while after 1851, when foreign banks were prohibited from maintaining offices in the province of Canada.[70] By the mid-1850s, in contrast, British capital was encouraged to invest in Canadian banks, which in turn were permitted to transfer their stocks and pay their dividends in Britain.[71]

It is interesting to note how little debate the British-subject clause aroused in nineteenth-century Canada. In 1818, for instance, when the Bank of Montreal was largely owned by Americans, the bank's board objected to the clause limiting the voting rights of alien stockholders, and their objections were overruled by the drafters of the 1821 Act.[72] But the matter could not have been considered important, for there was very little discussion about it. The same was true of the latter part of the nineteenth century. In contrast to banking legislation in the US, which was always hotly contested, in Canada between Confederation and the First World War it was largely a matter of bankers making suggestions and the minister of finance complying with their wishes.[73] The 1890 revision modifying the restriction to a majority of British subjects seems not to have been debated either: in 1895 Breckenridge stated merely that the revision was made 'in deference to the convenience of banks near the northeastern frontier of the United States'.[74] Perhaps even more interesting than this near-silence is the fact that twentieth-century historians have shown scarcely more interest in Canada's first foreign-control legislation.

After two centuries, despite their obscurity, restrictions against foreign control of banks seem to have had an effect. Eighty-eight per cent of the assets of banks in Canada were domestically controlled in 1986.[75] The 1989 bilateral trade agreement with the United States, however, threatens to erode Canadian control in the long run by removing virtually all investment and control restrictions on American but not other foreign banks. Under the agreement foreign-ownership restrictions are also removed for American residents in the financial fields of insurance, investment, and loan and trust companies.[76]

Transportation

In the nineteenth century American control of canals and railways was an issue of concern to Canadians largely for strategic reasons. In 1824 the Welland Canal, joining Lake Erie to Lake Ontario on the Canadian side, was owned largely by Americans. To end this threat the Family Compact, 'anxious to preserve the management of the [Welland Canal] Company under British influence', assumed control of the firm. They required that the directors be residents of Upper Canada and that only one-quarter of the company's shares be sold in the US. (Half of them were to be sold in Britain.)[77]

The same issue reappeared fifty years later regarding the Canadian Pacific Railway. As we have seen, John A. Macdonald's answer to the threat of US annexation of the western territory was to build a transcontinental railway. But it would not be easy. The country lacked capital for such an enormous project, and commercial pressures were strong to route the line through the US to the Canadian prairies rather than along the barren northern shores of Lake Superior. Canadian and American railwaymen and promoters schemed to secure links with American railroads and to drop the idea of an all-Canadian route.

One of these schemes led to the downfall of the first Canadian Pacific Railroad in the political furore known as the Pacific Scandal, which brought down John A. Macdonald's government in 1873 and nearly ended his career. It involved large campaign contributions by Hugh Allan and his American associates to the Conservative election campaign the previous year. Allan, a prominent Montreal shipowner, financier, and industrialist, was attempting to buy influence with the government for his CPR scheme. In his plan the Canadian line would essentially be a subsidiary of the Northern Pacific—the very line, then under construction, that the US Senate hoped would lure the Canadian west into the American union. Particularly damaging to Sir John was a letter from him that found its way into the press, requesting campaign funds from Hugh Allan.[78]

Although Macdonald was compromised by Allan's campaign contributions, it was not his intention to allow American control of the line, and he resolutely turned his back on a US route south of Lake Superior after the Pacific Scandal. Macdonald had no qualms about the involvement of American capital in the line; indeed, he encouraged Allan to seek it out. This was not unusual: Canadian railways habitually went to London to obtain capital, and the US would do just as well. But neither Macdonald, nor most of his Cabinet, nor public opinion, especially in Ontario, would countenance American control of the CPR.[79] When the Conservatives returned to power in 1878 they made their position clear: any new CPR syndicate must be Canadian-controlled.

Yet if the CPR was to be a Canadian-controlled line, other railways were a different matter. In 1926 foreign residents held 55 per cent of the capital invested in railways in Canada.[80] And many American railways, such as the New York Central, the Delaware and Hudson, the Wabash, the Pere

Marquette, the Burlington Northern, and the Northern Pacific, had fully US-controlled extension lines in Canada. By the 1920s a majority of the CPR itself was foreign-owned, with shares held in large amounts by Britons, Americans, and continental Europeans.[81] Control of the CPR, however, remained in Canadian hands.

CONCLUSION

Most early controls on foreign ownership were gone by the 1840s, including those on the sale or leasing of land to Americans for farming or forestry. (The restrictions that were later imposed on placer gold and grazing leases in the west appear to have been a throwback to the earlier policy, but more research is needed to confirm this.) In any case, they were as ineffective as the land and resource restrictions in barring American ownership and control. The only regulation of Loyalist vintage to survive as an effective restriction on foreign economic control concerned banking. It is likely that Canadian control of this important sector was enhanced by the British-subject clause. But this control came at a high price for the rest of the economy, because Canadian banking was dominated by an economic élite that was able to withstand populist pressure to extend credit. Because of their conservatism, Canadian banks showed little interest in extending domestic capital and domestic control into manufacturing and modern resource industries.

The other effective policies affecting foreign control were in the areas of hydroelectricity and transportation. The Ontario public power movement, although led by well-to-do elements, was of populist, small-business origin; it was opposed by the élites and must be seen as an eruption 'from below'. That it made an impact on both the Liberal and Conservative parties was despite the best efforts of the leadership of those parties.

Domestic control of the CPR was inspired by the strategic question vis-à-vis the United States. Since, in the late nineteenth century, Canada was a British dominion with little control over its defence and foreign policy, the strategic question was confined to the race to lay effective claim over the great, largely unoccupied, northwest. Much as in the Arctic sovereignty issue of the 1980s, Canadian nationalism showed itself as defence of the land, the homestead.[82]

Broader strategic issues did not lead to restrictions on foreign control in Canada, except for the temporary prohibition against foreign oil companies on federal Crown lands from 1914 to 1920. There were no restrictions on foreign control in industrial fields, which other late-follower countries saw as strategic.

Despite the range of restrictions against foreign control in the nineteenth and early twentieth centuries, Canada was remarkably open to foreign direct investment. It was partly a matter of timing, partly a matter of the way the nation developed. By the time the country began to industrialize, Loyalist-based anti-Americanism was largely gone. Thus a true Canadian nationalism, as opposed to a continuing allegiance to Britain, was weak during the first half-century of Canadian nation-building.

NOTES

[1]John McKay, *Pioneers for Profit: Foreign Entrepreneurship and Russian Industrialization 1885-1913* (Chicago: Chicago University Press, 1970), p. 21.

[2]I have no information regarding Italy's policies towards foreign ownership before 1914.

[3]A.A. Heaps, Labour member from Winnipeg North, did not want to 'see the Canadian people become, in the language of the Bible, hewers of wood and drawers of water to American capitalists' (*House of Commons Debates*, 20 Feb. 1928, p. 637); see also J. M. Van Der Hoek, 'The Penetration of American Capital in Canada', *Canadian Forum* 71 (Aug. 1926); J. F. White, 'Oil and Opportunism', *Canadian Forum* 64 (Jan. 1926); and Research Committee of the League for Social Reconstruction, *Social Planning for Canada* (Toronto: University of Toronto Press, 1975 [1935]), p. 52. The Canadian Pulp and Paper Association claimed that those American pulp companies operating in Canada to extract raw pulpwood were refusing to participate in conservation (Canada, Royal Commission on Pulpwood, *Report of the Royal Commission on Pulpwood* [Ottawa: King's Printer, 1924] p. 256).

[4]A.E. Safarian, *Foreign Ownership of Canadian Industry* (Toronto: University of Toronto Press, 1973), p. 14.

[5]*The Canadian Manufacturer*, 2 March 1894, p. 188.

[6]Cleona Lewis, *America's Stake in International Investments* (Washington: Brookings Institution, 1938), p. 312.

[7]R.T. Naylor, *The History of Canadian Business, 1867-1914*, vol. 2 (Toronto: Lorimer, 1975), pp. 134-46.

[8]John McCallum, *Unequal Beginnings: Agriculture and Economic Development in Quebec and Ontario until 1870* (Toronto: University of Toronto Press, 1980), pp. 91-2.

[9]These ventures were not branch plants but firms set up by American entrepreneurs who immigrated to Canada. See John C. Weaver, 'The Location of Manufacturing Enterprises: the Case of Hamilton's Attraction of Foundries, 1830-1890', in Richard Jarrell and Arnold Ross, eds, *Critical Issues in the History of Canadian Science, Technology and Medicine* (Thornhill: HSTC Publications, 1983).

[10]Ibid., p. 145.

[11]A.K. Cairncross, *Home and Foreign Investment 1870-1913* (Cambridge: Cambridge University Press, 1953), chap. 3, and Donald Paterson, *British Direct Investment in Canada 1890-1914* (Toronto: University of Toronto Press, 1976).

[12]The federal government controlled resources in the prairies until 1930. There was little forestry and mining in this area during the National Policy era in any case.

[13]H.V. Nelles, *The Politics of Development: Forests, Mines and Hydro-electricity in Ontario 1849-1941* (Toronto: Macmillan, 1974).

[14]Ibid., pp. 66-7.

[15]Ibid., pp. 70-87.

[16]H. Marshall et al., *Canadian-American Industry* (Toronto: McClelland and Stewart, 1976), pp. 36-7.

[17]Constant Southworth, 'The American-Canadian Newsprint Industry and the Tariff', *Journal of Political Economy*, Oct. 1922: 681.

[18]Ibid., pp. 682, 694. By the 1930s two of the three largest newsprint companies, Abitibi and Consolidated, had changed from American to Canadian control (Marshall et al., *Canadian-American Industry*, p. 40).

[19]Ontario's Bureau of Mines was established in 1891 with promotion of foreign investment as one of its main objectives; see Nelles, *The Politics of Development*, pp. 26, 122.

[20]See note 3 re *Royal Commission on Pulpwood*.

[21]*Fortune*, 4 Aug. 1986, p. 207; *Standard and Poor's: Industry Surveys*, April 1987, p. B16.

[22]H.C. Pentland, R.T. Naylor, and others have previously made the point about Canadian banks.

[23]Some unregulated sectors, such as retailing, have had moderate levels of foreign ownership.

[24]In the case of placer gold, the restrictions may have been directed at Orientals.

[25]Adam Shortt, 'Founder of Canadian Banking: Horatio Gates, Wholesale Merchant, Banker and Legislator', *Journal of the Canadian Bankers Association* (henceforth *JCBA*) 30 (1922): 34.

[26]*Montreal Gazette*, 27 Aug. 1836, cited in H. Innis and A.R.M. Lower, eds, *Select Documents in Canadian Economic History 1783-1885* (Toronto: University of Toronto Press, 1933), pp. 253-4.

[27]Ontario, Dept. of Lands and Forests, *A History of Crown Timber Regulations* (Ontario, 1957) pp. 201, 209. Very little primary research has been done on this question.

[28]Graeme Wynn, *Timber Colony: A Historical Geography of Early Nineteenth Century New Brunswick* (Toronto: University of Toronto Press, 1981), pp. 144-5.

[29]David Breen, *The Canadian Prairie West and the Ranching Frontier 1874-1924* (Toronto: University of Toronto Press, 1983), p. 200.

[30]Marshall et al., *Canadian-American Industry*, pp. 5-10.

[31]Lewis, *America's Stake in International Investments*, p. 207.

[32]E.S. Moore, *American Influence in Canadian Mining* (Toronto: University of Toronto Press, 1941), p. 85.

[33]W.A. McRae, 'Open Your Mouth and Shut Your Eyes And We'll Take Your Oil Land Wherever It Lies', part 2, *Saturday Night*, 22 March 1919; W.T. Easterbrook and Hugh Aitken, *Canadian Economic History* (Toronto: Macmillan, 1956), p. 548; Marshall, *Canadian-American Industry*, p. 107.

[34]E.H. Davenport and Sidney Russell Cooke, *The Oil Trusts and Anglo-American Relations* (New York: Macmillan, 1921), p. 9.

[35]*Canada Gazette*, Jan.-June 1920, 6887-038 (P.C. 105).

[36]David Crane, *Controlling Interest: The Canadian Gas and Oil Stakes* (Toronto: McClelland and Stewart, 1982), p. 43.

[37]Imperial held minority ownership in the company until 1919, when it boosted its share to over 99% (D.H. Breen, 'Anglo-American Rivalry and the Evolution of Canadian Petroleum Policy to 1930', *Canadian Historical Review* 62, no. 3 [Sept. 1981]: 293, 299).

[38]Ibid., p. 294.

[39]St Joe Minerals Corporation threatened to use this law in 1981 to block a takeover attempt by Seagram's during the National Energy Program (Stephen Clarkson, *Canada and the Reagan Challenge*, updated version [Toronto: Lorimer, 1985], pp. 26-7).

[40]David Breen argues that the federal government shifted its emphasis towards hoped-for discoveries in the Northwest Territories in order to avoid the provincial-control issue. Its optimism about large finds in the north was premature ('Anglo-American Rivalry', pp. 299-301).

[41]*Canada Gazette*, Jan.-June 1920, 6887-038 (P.C. 105).

[42]American interests controlled the first two hydro companies on the Canadian side of Niagara. They were active in setting up Shawinigan Water and Power and other power companies in Quebec. US power companies held strong positions in the Maritimes and the West as well. See Marshall, *Canadian-American Industry*, pp. 139-52.

Manitoba embarked on public power at the same time as Ontario, but public ownership did not succeed in replacing private power interests as fully as in Ontario before the Second World War. See H.V. Nelles, 'Public Ownership of Electrical Utilities in Manitoba and Ontario, 1906-1930', in Bruce Hodgins and Robert Page, eds, *Canadian History Since Confederation* (Georgetown, Ont.: Irwin-Dorsey, 1979), pp. 512-34.

[43]There are a number of excellent studies on the creation of Ontario Hydro. See Nelles, *The Politics of Development*, chapters 6, 7; Merrill Denison, *The People's Power: The History of Ontario Hydro* (Toronto: McClelland and Stewart, 1960); W.R. Plewman, *Adam Beck and the Ontario Hydro* (Toronto: Ryerson, 1947). Regarding public telephone companies and the reaction against private utility monopolies, see Christopher Armstrong and H.V. Nelles, *Monopoly's Moment: The Organization and Regulation of Canadian Utilities 1830-1930* (Toronto: University of Toronto Press, 1988).

[44]John Dales, *Hydroelectricity and Industrial Development: Quebec 1898-1940* (Cambridge, Mass.: Harvard University Press, 1957), pp. 156-7.

[45]Denison, *The People's Power*, p. 61.

[46]Nelles, *The Politics of Development*, p. 230.

[47]Public ownership included municipal ownership of local utilities.

[48]Marshall, *Canadian-American Industry*, p. 141.

[49]Dales, *Hydroelectricity and Industrial Development*, p. 47. See Clinton White, *Power for a Province: A History of Saskatchewan Power* (Regina: Canadian Plains Research Center, 1976), p. 17, for the influence of Ontario's example on Saskatchewan.

[50]Newfoundland still retained a major private company in Newfoundland Light and Power. In 1987, during the free-trade negotiations, Utilicorp United of Kansas City bought West Kootenay Light and Power (of British Columbia).

[51]In 1985 provincial utilities ranked high in the *Financial Post*'s top 500 companies: Ontario #16, Quebec #17, B.C. #51, Sask. #108, N.B. #110, Manitoba #166, Nfld. #235.

[52]Merrill Denison, *Canada's First Bank: A History of the Bank of Montreal*, vol. 1 (Toronto: McClelland and Stewart, 1966), p. 142.

[53]*Statutes of Canada*, 34 Vict Chap V; R.M. Breckenridge, *The History of Banking in Canada* (Washington: Government Printing Office, 1910), p. 217; E.L. Stewart Patterson, *Canadian Banking*, rev. ed. (Toronto: Ryerson, 1941), p. 31.

[54]Shortt, 'Founder of Canadian Banking'.

[55]The Bank of Canada began in 1818 and folded in the early 1820s. Its articles of association copied those of the Bank of Montreal but dropped the British-subject clause for obvious reasons. The Kingston Bank operated without a charter between 1819 and 1822.

[56]Adam Shortt, 'The Early History of Canadian Banking', *JCBA* 4, no. 4: 351-5, and 5, no. 1: 9.

[57]Marshall, *Canadian-American Industry*, p. 266.

[58]See Appendix, p. 234.

[59]Bray Hammond, *Banks and Politics in America from the Revolution to the Civil War* (Princeton: Princeton University Press, 1957), pp. 53, 114.

[60]Hamilton was influenced most by the Bank of England, founded in 1694, but also by the experience of other English, Scottish, and early state banks in America. He had earlier drawn up the Constitution of the Bank of New York (Hammond, *Banks and Politics*, p. 128).

[61]The Act also prohibited lending money to any foreign prince or state. This clause was omitted in 1871 (Denison, *Canada's First Bank*, vol. 2, p. 185).

[62]Bank of Nova Scotia, *History of the Bank of Nova Scotia 1832-1900* (Toronto: n.p., 1900).

[63]W.M. Acres, *The Bank of England From Within*, vol. 1 (London: Oxford University Press, 1931) p. 37. Hamilton may have got the idea for his restriction from his study of the Bank of England, but the Bank of the US charter did not follow the Bank of England charter clause by clause as the Bank of Montreal Act copied Hamilton's charter.

[64]Shortt, 'Early History of Canadian Banking', *JCBA* 4, no. 1 (1896). Hamilton's influence was also felt in the BNA Act.

[65]George Shepley, 'The Power of Directors', *JCBA* 3, no. 4 (July 1896): 349. There was no restriction on directors in Canada's first Railway Act in 1868 (Canada, *Statutes*, cap. 68, 14.7 1868).

[66]I am indebted to Donald Paterson of the University of British Columbia for this point.

[67]*Monetary Times*, 4 July, 1879, p. 41; 2 Dec. 1881, p. 868; Marshall, *Canadian-American Industry*, p. 123.

[68]Marshall, *Canadian-American Industry*, p. 163.

[69]The Bank of BNA was absorbed by the Bank of Montreal in 1918 and the Bank of BC was absorbed by the Bank of Commerce in 1901. The Royal Bank of Canada, founded in 1859—not the bank now bearing that name—was chartered and directed from England. See Denison, *Canada's First Bank*, vol. 1, p. 313; Victor Ross, *History of the Canadian Bank of Commerce*, vol. 1 (Toronto: Oxford University Press, 1920-34), p. 251.

[70]Foreign banks were prohibited from maintaining offices for discount or deposit, or for circulation of bank notes. See Ross, *Canadian Bank of Commerce*, vol. 2, p. 413.

[71]Adam Shortt, 'History of Canadian Currency', *JCBA* 9, no. 2: 114.

[72]Denison, *Canada's First Bank*, vol. 1, pp. 137-40.

[73]Francis Hincks, 11 March 1870, *House of Commons Debates*, p. 373; Denison, *Canada's First Bank*, vol. 2, p. 243.

[74]R.M. Breckenridge, *The Canadian Banking System 1817-1890* (Toronto: Macmillan, 1895), p. 349.

[75]Kirk Falconer, 'The Trade Pact, Deregulation and Canada's Financial System', in D. Cameron, ed., *The Free Trade Deal* (Toronto: Lorimer, 1988), p. 158.

[76]Canada, *The Canada-US Free Trade Agreement* (Ottawa: External Affairs Canada, 1988), article 1703.

[77]Hugh Aitken, *The Welland Canal Company* (Cambridge, Mass.: Harvard University Press, 1954), p. 79.

[78]W.K. Lamb, *History of the Canadian Pacific Railway* (New York: Macmillan, 1977), pp. 18-35.

[79]A.A. Den Otter, 'Nationalism and the Pacific Scandal', *Canadian Historical Review* 69, no. 3 (Sept. 1988); Harold Innis, *A History of the Canadian Pacific Railway* (Toronto: McClelland and Stewart, 1971), pp. 79-83. Ontario's concern with American domination was more than altruistic nationalism. Toronto was a bitter rival of Montreal for control of the Pacific railway and for the future commerce of the west. The problem with Allan, for Toronto capitalists, was that he represented Montreal as well as American capital.

[80]Safarian, *Foreign Ownership*, p. 14. Foreign-ownership levels in railways fell continually from this point.

[81]Marshall, *Canadian-American Industry*, pp. 113-23.

[82]This concept was first articulated by Abraham Rotstein.

7

Conclusion

In 1983 a United Nations survey found that the value of foreign direct investment was higher in Canada than in any other country in the world. There was more such investment in Canada in absolute, quantitative terms than there was in the United States, making Canada's level of foreign ownership more than ten times as great on a per capita basis.[1] With 0.5 per cent of the world's people, Canada was the recipient of 17 per cent of all global foreign direct investment.[2] In this regard Canada was clearly different from the other advanced countries.

How can we account for this difference? This question has been the subject of academic inquiry since the 1930s. Standard theories have been developed, all resting on one essential fact: Canada's location in North America.

With the rise of anti-colonial struggles in the early 1960s, a favourite explanation for Canada's curious economic position was derived from Third World dependency theories. Based on the theme of external domination, this theory has several variations. One has to do with the modern corporation—an American invention. The new corporate structure allowed for better administration of geographically dispersed units of production and sales; its flexibility and decentralization enabled businesses to expand abroad as well as into different economic sectors. Thus, according to the theory, it was only natural that Canada, sitting next to the United States, would be subject to early and massive intrusion of American subsidiaries. Other variations on the theme of external domination focus on pressure exerted by the US state and the alliances between local élites and imperial powers that are a standard element in dependency theories: in this case, corporate alliances formed with Canadian élites. In the dependency view, however, the latter—the only domestic contribution to the scenario—have involved so few Canadians that they cannot be considered evidence of self-determination on Canada's part.

Geographic proximity to a greater power provided an older explanation. In the 1920s Canadian academics discovered the importance of geography, climate, and economics in the determination of history. These factors were added to the narrow and stuffy early interpretations of Canadian history, which had been confined to laws, constitutions, political institutions, and great leaders. Linked to the American-frontier thesis, these new factors crowded out competing explanations.

Cultural similarity, an argument put forward by Goldwin Smith in the 1890s, is the oldest theory of Canadian dependence. According to this line of reasoning, it was because Canadians did not view Americans as foreign that they did not resist US economic control. With the relatively free movement of peoples across the border and the spillover of American culture into Canada through periodicals and, later, radio, movies, and television, Canadians failed to develop a very distinct consciousness.

All these theories accept what has become the dominant theme in Canadian culture: that Canada has been a passive entity moulded by overwhelming natural forces and by equally overwhelming external human forces. They are inadequate because the Canadian people themselves barely enter their purview. During the years when Canada went through its own industrial revolution, between Confederation and the First World War, the government had the capacity to take action on many issues, including the extent and type of foreign investment. The effectiveness of restrictions on foreign control of banks was testimony to the country's ability to choose its own economic destiny. Canada's recent difficulties in extricating itself from foreign ownership, notably in the oil and gas sector, do not prove that, from the beginning, Canada never had a choice. It is much easier for a country to avoid massive levels of foreign ownership and control at an early point in its development, as did Japan, or to reverse the process at an early stage, as did Norway, than to remove vested foreign interests once they have become well entrenched.

Another flaw in the external-domination theme is that American business did not even begin to undergo the changes that gave birth to the modern corporation until the 1920s—that is, not until American subsidiaries had already gained a decisive grip on Canadian manufacturing and resource sectors. Thus the development of the modern corporation was not a necessary condition for the establishment of transnational corporations.

Proximity to the United States does not in itself explain investment penetration either. Mexico received a large amount of early American attention, but it was able to reverse the situation in the 1911 revolution and later in the 1930s, with the creation of Pemex, the state-owned oil company. If Mexico had sufficient autonomy to decide whether or not it wanted American investment, can it be argued seriously that Canada did not? Nor was the United States the only technologically dynamic society to control production in adjacent countries (the heart of the argument about Canada's unique geographic position); Germany, too, set up branch plants in neighbouring countries in the several decades before the First World War, but it did not go on to dominate them economically.

This leads us to the oldest argument: cultural and linguistic similarities. Perhaps Canadians so identified with their neighbours to the south that they did not care to be economically independent. Canadians have often seemed to favour close economic ties with the American giant, and English, if not French, Canadians have been uncertain about their cultural distinctiveness. There is little doubt that Canada would have enacted tougher investment restrictions if the Japanese had bought as much of Canadian industry as the Americans did. But this argument gets us only so far. Canadian political leaders generally resisted the overwhelming pull of the United States during the National Policy period, from 1879 to the 1930s, and Canadians—though at times only a bare majority—supported them. If national autonomy had been of little importance, would Canada have gone to the trouble of building the Canadian Pacific Railway entirely through Canadian territory? Would voters have rejected reciprocity with the United States in 1891 and again in 1911? Would farmers have broken from the American Grangers in the 1870s or from the American Patrons of Industry in the 1890s? These episodes and others demonstrate that English-speaking Canadians valued their distinctive nationality even though they spoke the same language as Americans.

The whole question of nationality and cultural similarity poses other questions, questions that lead away from the standard explanations to the effect that Canada was not the master of its own destiny. If it is accepted that ideas and culture can have a determining influence on history, resistance to US economic penetration must have been possible; Canadians must have been able to determine their own fate. Why, then, did Canada not restrict American direct investment in Canadian resources and manufacturing industries during the National Policy era? This question moves us to the heart of the matter—to the internal politics that underlay state policy formation.

To gain perspective, I have used a comparative framework in this book. The standard explanations for Canada's unusual degree of foreign ownership rely too heavily on the Canadian data and Canadian perspectives to shed light on why domestic policies diverged from those of other countries in similar economic circumstances. The archives, the statistics, the events, and the personalities of Canadian history are the invaluable tools of Canadian historians. They explain the choices, the influences, and the context within which state policies were made. But, as crucial and insightful as these forms of inquiry are, they cannot explain why Canadians apparently never considered, let alone implemented, policies adopted by other countries in similar dilemmas.

Students of Canadian history have generally held the same narrow assumptions about the Anglo-American world as did the leaders, the classes, and the communities they studied. The examples of development in other advanced capitalist societies have usually been assumed to be inapplicable to Canada. Even the American experience has not been fully assimilated by Canadian historians. The myriad ways in which American society has influenced Canada have been explored in depth, but the ways in which the US broke out of a staple-exporting relationship with industrial Britain have barely been acknowledged. Largely absent, too, has been any examination of the political controversies surrounding American banking, land, and railway policies. Whereas in the US such policies have given rise to high political drama, in Canada they have usually been treated as nothing more than tiresome technical matters in which ordinary Canadians could have no influence. Finally, Canadian scholars have largely neglected the American populist movements of the 1800s: it was populist nationalism that put the issues of foreign ownership of banks, western lands, and mines on the US political agenda in the nineteenth century.

Moreover, if important elements of American history have been neglected in explaining Canadian economic dependence, the experiences of European countries and of Japan have been ignored almost entirely. This book breaks with the tradition by analyzing Canadian industrial development from the perspective of European experience.

We know that Canada adopted the National Policy as the means to achieve economic and political independence within North America. And we know that in part it failed. The failure was greatest in the area of foreign investment, which acted as a bridgehead for later threats to Canadian economic, political, and cultural sovereignty. The National Policy was a carbon copy of the original 'American system' of Henry Clay, created sixty years earlier. I have argued that, in the altered conditions of development in the late nineteenth century, the 'European system' was more appropriate for Canada.

The European system of late-follower development evolved in particular international circumstances and in response to internal pressures. By the late nineteenth century there were already several advanced industrial countries competing for the markets and even the real estate of the world. Industrial progress had improved transportation and communications so dramatically that the world was becoming a single economic and political system. Less-developed countries either created independent industrial economies of their own or fell into economic dependence on the already-developed powers. Leaders of the late-follower countries saw the risk clearly enough and determined to maintain their sovereignty. Canadians' desire not to continue as 'hewers of wood and drawers of water' for the industrial nations was felt as strongly as similar sentiments elsewhere.

Several institutional modifications of England's laissez-faire model were at the heart of the European system (and its Japanese variant). Banks now engaged in long-term lending, and domestic capital was gathered in new ways to finance risky new industries. There was no basic conflict of the type R.T. Naylor has outlined between commercial and industrial capitalists. The state generally refrained from encouraging the wasteful use of scarce domestic capital on unneeded infrastructure, and some degree of technological independence was achieved through native invention or the imitation of foreign technologies in domestically controlled businesses. The desire to keep armed forces independent of foreign, possibly enemy, supplies underlay much of the late-follower state's drive to industrial independence.

Canada followed none of these patterns, and it was the only late follower to rely so heavily on foreign-controlled inputs in its development. Foreign ʟ investment, management, and technology, and reliance on big power milit. protection, became substitutes for the European system.

Could Canada have succeeded in fully breaking free from its hewer-of-wood role had it adopted the European system? Here we run up against two enduring myths that have been used to explain Canada's continued economic dependence. The first contends that Canadians were too conservative or unenterprising to develop industry by themselves. The second holds that the population was too small and scattered for the creation of a market suitable for efficient development.

The image of nineteenth-century Canada as a land of rustic backwardness is as false as the myth it supports. Before the American branch plants arrived in significant numbers (between 1900 and 1914), Canada was already the eighth largest manufacturing country in the world, no mean feat for a nation with a small population. American capital and know-how did not make Canada an advanced country—it was the other way round. The developed nature of Canada's industry, labour force, and standard of living attracted American subsidiaries northward. At the turn of the century—*before* Canada became a branch-plant economy—Canadians were enterprising enough to export sophisticated industrial goods, developed and made in domestically owned businesses, to such markets as Germany, Britain, and France.

The second myth, that the small size of the domestic market was an obstacle to independent development, is an excuse for failure. The examples of the small industrial countries of Western Europe are relevant. Sweden was chosen here for intensive study because it provides the ideal model for comparison with Canada. Other small European countries, such as Switzerland, Belgium, and the Netherlands, were more developed at an earlier point than Canada and so had advantages for independent development that Canada did not share; Austria was the centre of an important empire in the late nineteenth century, hardly a comparable situation to Canada's. Sweden, however, began industrial development as late as Canada and with a domestic market as small or smaller (even if Norway is included); in fact, it was the only other late-follower country with a small population. Finally, Sweden's northern character, its resource-exporting relationship with Britain in the 1800s, and its social and cultural similarities to Canada add to the power of the comparison.

Sweden broke out of its dependence on exporting staple products to metropolitan countries and became an important centre of manufactured exports itself. It made this transition in the same period in which the National Policy was in effect in Canada and without recourse to much foreign direct investment. During these years Sweden adopted a variant of the European system. Investment banks contributed to Swedish development by making long-term investments in domestic industry and technology. In addition, both the education system and the risk-taking banks encouraged invention. Frugality in state expenditures, especially in railway building, helped Sweden

s voracious appetite for foreign capital, which came almost
form of loans. Foreign ownership was discouraged by strong
sition as well as by the vigour of internal development.

state was central to Sweden's success in the European system, but the
country's development was not an automatic or even a very deliberate
process. The interplay of class forces in the context of a well-developed and
relatively homogeneous national consciousness led to the adoption of various
components of Sweden's economic policies. Rural classes had an important
political influence on the shape of industrial policies. The nobility had been in
transition for some time from a rural base to leadership in commerce,
industry, and, of course, the state. Early industrialization also saw the rise in
importance of independent farmers—both large and small—in the political
system. All these rural classes helped to push state policies in the direction of
the European system. Such influence was most notable in the areas of
government expenditures and economic nationalism, but it was also evident
in the evolution of investment banking and in Sweden's emphasis on military
preparedness.

The Swedish case tells us several important things about Canada's
possibilities at the time of the National Policy. First, a late-follower country
with a small market and population could make a successful transition to
independent industrial development. Second, dependence on staple exports
need not have inhibited such a course. Internal politics and national
consciousness, however, did affect the outcome, and classes outside
commerce and industry played decisive roles in determining state economic
policies.

If the European system, adopted in some form by all other late-follower
countries, could have helped it achieve the goals of independent development,
why did Canada not adopt it? This question leads to consideration of the
politics of Canadian development at the time of the National Policy, a line of
inquiry treated as unimportant in the standard explanations of Canadian
economic dependence.

Canada's failure to adopt a variant of the European system was in large part
the result of the weakness of agrarian influence in early development.
Although the industrial revolution eventually relegated agriculture to a minor
place in the economic scheme of things, agrarian classes usually had a major
impact on the direction of early industrialization before their influence ebbed
away. The implications of the peculiar weakness of agrarians in Canada
during this early period lies at the heart of the new perspective presented in
this book.

Farmers did have considerable impact on politics in Canada, as in all new
settler societies, but their influence was at its strongest before and after initial
industrialization. During the period when industry began to transform
Canadian society—roughly from just before Confederation to the First World
War—independent and organized agrarian voices were strangely quiet. It was
in the latter part of this period that American direct investment established a

solid hold on the Canadian economy. This was also the time in which the Canadian state was formed. The lack of independent agrarian input affected the nature of both processes. Agrarian weakness was the political peculiarity that, I have argued, accompanied the economic peculiarity of Canada's heavy reliance on foreign ownership for development.

It is impossible to know the exact impact of the political weakness of organized farmers on the course of Canadian industrialization. The best we can do is attempt to recognize the directions in which effective pressure by independent farmers' movements might have led. The politics of farmers before the 1837 rebellions, when their voice was strong in central Canada, and the re-emergence of agrarian populism immediately after the First World War, in Western Canada and Ontario, give us a lot to go on. So too do the sporadic agrarian movements in the 1850s, 1870s, and 1890s, during initial industrialization. The political impact of agrarians in the same economic phase in the United States and other countries also indicate the general nature of farmer politics in that economic phase.

All of these sources indicate that the effect of organized agrarian movements was to push politics in the direction of the European system. Two elements in particular stand out in the program of agrarian movements in nineteenth- and early twentieth-century Canada: the repeated attempts to free up banking and credit and to promote economy in government. These demands ran consistently through farmers' movements as the locus of organization shifted from east to west and the economy was transformed from pre-industrial to industrial. They were also characteristic of agrarians in other countries during initial industrialization.

Further elements of agrarian impact were evident in other societies where agrarians held or shared power, but were either absent or barely noticeable in Canada. These were opposition to foreign economic penetration and an emphasis on military defence of the homeland. Both emanated from agrarians' attachment to the land, which went beyond mere economic rationality. Agrarian reaction was generally strong both to threats to the land from invasion and to the exploitation and control of natural resources by foreign capitalists. Perhaps holding power or being able to influence the political agenda led agrarians outside Canada to these statist tendencies. The only counterparts to the latter in Canada have been a general concern with threats to the territorial sovereignty of Canada and a greater opposition to foreign ownership of resources than to other types of foreign ownership, and these reactions have not been confined to farmers. The fact that Canadian farmers—indeed, all ordinary citizens—had little to do with the formation of the state probably accounted for the weakness of populist nationalism. The contrast with the United States in this respect is striking.

If farmers' influence would have pushed the National Policy in the direction of the European system, why then were Canadian farmers so weak? This was the period in which their influence should have been at its peak. By the late nineteenth century farmers in central and eastern Canada had gone beyond the pioneering phase and made up almost half the population. A wide franchise and the achievement of self-government in the late 1840s also created favourable conditions for strong populist influence. One of the curious aspects of Canadian history was the blossoming of agrarian strength after the First World War, when the number of farmers had already declined in relative terms as a result of industrialization and urbanization.

Farmer influence was weak during the formative period of early industrial development, I have argued, for two reasons. The British connection and fear of US manifest destiny cast populist influences in Canada as disloyal. More important, the intensity of sectional tensions between English and French, Protestant and Catholic, relegated class conflicts and class movements to a secondary level of importance. Ethno-national tensions occurred not only in central Canada but also in the west with the Riel rebellions and the Manitoba schools question; they were in evidence in New Brunswick as well. These tensions hurt several farmers' movements in English Canada, most notably in the 1850s and 1890s. Victory seemed at hand in the 1921 federal election—the farmers' Progressive Party won the largest number of seats of any party in English Canada—but in failing, as always, to make a significant bridge across ethno-national lines to Quebec, the agrarians lost the election. Sectional conflict between English and French diverted Canadian politics away from class-based issues and divisions.

The weakness of farmers' movements affected a number of policies, all contributing to the victory of a branch-plant economy. The banks successfully resisted a century of agrarian assaults and failed to change their conservative approach to financing industry, while the state either encouraged the most foolish schemes or supported sensible projects but at the highest costs. In both cases the need for foreign capital was accentuated. Second, because farmer opposition to unfavourable land and railway policies had little effect, settlement of the prairies was delayed for about twenty years—which in turn slowed the pace and scale of Canadian industrial progress in the decades immediately preceding the first major invasion of American branch plants. Finally, the weakness of populist nationalism set the stage for open-door policies in regard to foreign investment.

One might ask whether the history of the social origins of foreign ownership has any relevance for Canada as it nears the twenty-first century. It does. If Canada is to plan successfully for the new economy in the years ahead, an understanding of how it got to its present situation is essential. In this book I have challenged several enduring myths that have confused Canadians. The idea that Canada would have remained an economic backwater if not for the massive intrusion of American capital and know-how is false. So too is the deeply held notion that Canada's fate lies in the hands of external human powers and overwhelming natural forces. Lastly, the belief that Canada has too small a population to make an important and independent contribution to the new international economy is also false.

Above all, we can learn from Canadian history that economics cannot be understood without reference to the social life of the people. Internal problems arising from tensions among Canadians along anglophone/francophone and regional or other lines must be settled on an equitable basis of mutual respect, so that Canadians do not stand divided on questions of economic development and the penetration of foreign corporations. If internal inequities continue to plague Canada, domestic élites will be free to look after their own interests—even though these usually conflict with the best interests of Canada and its people.

NOTES

[1]The Americans considered a corporation foreign-controlled when foreign assets reached 10 per cent, whereas Canada waited until foreign ownership reached 50 per cent before designating the company foreign-controlled.

[2]United Nations Centre on Transnational Corporations, *Salient Features and Trends in Foreign Direct Investment* (New York: United Nations, 1983), p. 34.

Appendix

A comparison of Alexander Hamilton's Charter of the Bank of the United States (1791) with the proposed Charter of the Bank of Lower Canada (1808) reproduced from Adam Shortt's 'The Early History of Canadian Banking', *Journal of the Canadian Bankers' Association* 4, no. 1 [Oct. 1896].

Charter of the Bank of the United States

1. The number of votes to which each stockholder shall be entitled, shall be according to the number of shares he shall hold, in the proportions following, that is to say: For one share and not more than two shares, one vote; for every two shares above two, and not exceeding ten, one vote; for every four shares above ten, and not exceeding thirty, one vote; for every six shares above thirty, and not exceeding sixty, one vote; for every eight shares above sixty, and not exceeding one hundred, one vote: and for every ten shares above one hundred, one vote. But no person, co-partnership, or body politic, shall be entitled to a greater number than thirty votes. And after the first election, no share or shares shall confer a right of suffrage, which shall not have been holden three calendar months previous to the day of election. Stockholders actually resident within the United States, and none other, may vote in elections by proxy.

Proposed Charter of the Bank of Lower Canada

1. The number of votes to which each stockholder or stockholders, body politic or corporate, holding stock in the said corporation, shall be entitled on every occasion when in conformity to the provisions and requirements of this Act, the votes thereof are to be given shall be in proportion following, that is to say: For one share and not more than two, one vote; for every two shares above two, and not exceeding ten, one vote, making five votes for ten shares; for every four shares above ten and not exceeding thirty, one vote, making ten votes for thirty shares; for every six shares above thirty and not exceeding sixty, one vote, making fifteen votes for sixty shares; for every eight shares above sixty and not exceeding one hundred, one vote, making twenty votes for one hundred shares; and for every ten shares above one hundred, one vote, making thirty votes for two hundred shares; but no person or persons, body politic or corporate, shall be entitled to a greater number than thirty votes. And all stockholders resident within this province or elsewhere, may vote by proxy, if he, she or they shall see fit, provided always, that such proxy shall be one of His Majesty's subjects, as hereafter designated, and do produce a sufficient authority from his constituent or constituents for so representing and voting for him, her or them. Provided also that after the first election of directors, no share or shares of the capital stock of the corporation shall confer a right of voting, either in person or by proxy, which shall not have been holden during three calendar months, at the least, prior to the day of election or of the general meeting where the votes of the stockholders are to be given.

2. Not more than three-fourths of the directors in office, exclusive of the President, shall be eligible for the next succeeding year. But the director who shall be president at the time of an election may always be re-elected.

3. None but a stockholder, being a citizen of the United States, shall be eligible as a director.

4. No director shall be entitled to any emolument, unless the same shall have been allowed by the stockholders, at a general meeting. The stockholders shall make such compensation to the President, for his extraordinary attendance at the bank, as shall appear to them reasonable.

5. Not less than seven directors shall constitute a board for the transaction of business, of whom the president shall always be one, except in case of sickness, or necessary absence: in which case his place may be supplied by any other director whom he, by writing under his hand, shall nominate for the purpose.

6. Any number of stockholders, not less than sixty, who together, shall be proprietors of two hundred shares or upwards, shall have power, at any time, to call a general meeting of the stockholders, for purposes relative to the institution, giving at least ten weeks notice, in two public gazettes of the place where the bank is kept, and specifying, in such notice, the object, or objects, of such meeting.

2. Not more than nine (exclusive of the president or vice-president) of the directors in office, at each of the cities of Quebec and Montreal, shall be eligible for the next succeeding twelve months: but the directors who are president and vice-president at the time of an election, may always be re-elected.

3. None but a stockholder actually resident in this province and holding at least twenty shares in the capital stock, and being a natural born subject of His Majesty, or a subject of His Majesty naturalized by Act of the British Parliament, or a subject of His Majesty's having become such by the conquest and cession of this province, shall be capable of being elected or chosen a director of the said corporation, or shall serve as such.

4. No director shall be entitled to any salary or emolument unless the same shall have been allowed to him by a general meeting of the stockholders; but the stockholders shall make such compensation to the president and vice-president for their extraordinary attendance at the bank as shall appear to them reasonable and proper.

5. Not less than five directors shall constitute a Board for the transaction of business at each of the branches of the Bank at Quebec and Montreal, whereof the President or Vice-President shall always be one, except in case of sickness and necessary absence, in which case their places may be supplied by any other directors whom the President or Vice-President so absent, shall respectively by writing under their hands, appoint for that purpose. The President and Vice-President shall vote at their respective Boards as directors, and in case of there being an equal number of votes for and against any question before them, they respectively shall have a casting vote.

6. Any number of stockholders not less than _____, who together shall be proprietors of _____ shares, or upwards, shall have power at any time, by themselves or their proxies, to call a general meeting of the stockholders for purposes relative to the corporation, giving at least six weeks notice thereof in at least one of the newspapers published at Quebec and at Montreal respectively, and specifying in such notice the time and place of such meeting, with the object or objects thereof: and the said directors or any seven of them shall have the like power at any time (upon observing the like formalities) to call a general meeting as above said, and if the object for which any general meeting called either by stockholders or directors as above said, shall be to consider of a proposal for the removal of the President, Vice-President or other director or directors for maladministration, then and in such case the person or persons so proposed to be removed shall from the day on which such notice shall first be

7. Every cashier or treasurer, before he enters upon the duties of his office, shall be required to give bond, with two or more sureties, to the satisfaction of the directors, in a sum not less than fifty thousand dollars, with condition for his good behavior.

8. The lands, tenements and hereditaments, which it shall be lawful for the said corporation to hold, shall be only such as shall be requisite for its immediate accommodation, in relation to the convenient transacting of its business, and such as shall have been bona fide mortgaged to it by way of security, or conveyed to it in satisfaction of debts, previously contracted in the course of its dealings, or purchased at sales upon judgments which shall have been obtained for such debts.

9. The total amount of the debts which the said Corporation shall, at any time, owe, whether by bond, bill, note, or other contract, shall not exceed the sum of ten millions of dollars, over and above the moneys then actually deposited in the bank for safe keeping, unless the contracting of any greater debt shall have been previously authorized by a law of the United States. In case of excess, the directors, under whose administration it shall happen, shall be liable for the same in their natural and private capacities; and an action of debt may, in such cases, be brought against them, or any of them, their, or any of their heirs, executors or administrators, in any court of record of the United States, or either of them, by any creditor or creditors, of the said Corporation, and may be prosecuted to judgment and execution; any condition, covenant or agreement to the contrary notwithstanding. But this shall not be construed to exempt the said Corporation, or the lands, tenements, goods or chattels of the same, from being also liable for and, chargeable with, the said excess. Such of the said directors who may have been absent when the said excess was contracted, or created, or who may have

published, be suspended from the execution of the duties of his or their office: and if he be the President or Vice-President, his place shall be filled up by the remaining directors, to serve during the time of such suspension.

7. Every cashier and every agent and clerk of the bank, before he enters upon the duties of his office, shall give bond, with two or more sureties, to the satisfaction of the directors, that is to say, every cashier in a sum not less than _____ thousand pounds, with conditions for his good and faithful behavior, and every agent and clerk with the like condition and sureties in such sum as the directors shall consider adequate to the trust to be reposed in him.

8. The lands and tenements which it shall be lawful for the corporation to hold shall be such only as are hereinbefore prescribed and limited. Provided always that the corporation may hold mortgages or hypothecations on all kinds of property which can by law be mortgaged or hypothecated, by way of security for debts contracted with the corporation in the course of its dealings, and also may hold such lands and tenements as shall be purchased at sales made upon judgments and executions, which shall have been obtained at the suit of the corporation for debts so contracted; or where the corporation, for debts so contracted, shall be an intervening party in any suit brought by any other person or persons; or where for such debts the corporation shall lodge an opposition with the sheriff *afin de conserver*; but in all such cases of purchase, the corporation shall be bound to sell the lands and tenements within _____ years after the date of the purchase respectively so made by the corporation.

9. The total amount of the debts which the said Corporation shall at any time owe, whether by obligation, bond, bill or note, or other contract whatsoever, shall not exceed treble the amount of gold and silver actually in the bank arising from their capital stock (but exclusive of a sum equal in amount to that of the gold and silver actually in the bank arising from other sources than the said stock, as also exclusive of a sum equal in amount to the notes of the Government of this province, held by the Corporation as part of the general stock), unless thereunto authorized by an Act of the Legislature of this province; and in case of excess the directors under whose administration it shall happen, shall be liable for the same in their private capacities (unless such excess shall have arisen in consequence of any of the agents hereafter mentioned having acted contrary to the regulations and instructions of the directors), and an action of debt in every such case may be brought against them, or any of them, their heirs, executors, administrators, and curators, and be prosecuted to judgment and execution, according to the laws of this province. But this shall not exempt the said corporation, or the lands, tenements, goods or

dissented from the resolution or act, whereby the same was so contracted, or created may, respectively, exonerate themselves from being so liable, by forthwith giving notice of the fact, and of their absence or dissent, to the President of the United States, and to the stockholders at a general meeting which they shall have power to call for that purpose.

10. The said Corporation may sell any part of the public debt whereof its stock shall be composed, but shall not be at liberty to purchase any public debt whatsoever; nor shall, directly or indirectly, deal or trade in anything, except bills of exchange, gold or silver bullion, or in the sale of goods, really and truly pledged for money lent, and not redeemed in due time: or of goods which shall be the produce of its lands. Neither shall the said Corporation take more than at the rate of six per centum per annum, for or upon its loans or discounts.

11. No loan shall be made by the said Corporation for the use, or on account, of the government of the United States, to an amount exceeding one hundred thousand dollars, or of any particular State, to an amount exceeding fifty thousand dollars, or of any foreign prince or state, unless previously authorized by a law of the United States.

12. The stock of the said Corporation shall be assignable and transferable, according to such rules as shall be instituted in that behalf, by the laws and ordinances of the same.

13. The bills obligatory, and of credit, under the seal of the said Corporation, which shall be made to any person, or persons, shall be assignable, by endorsement thereupon, under the hand or hands of such person or persons, and of his, her, or their assignee, or assignees, and so as absolutely to transfer and vest the property thereof in each and every assignee, or assignees, successively, and to enable such assignee, or assignees, to bring and maintain an action thereupon, in his, her, or their own name, or names. And bills or notes which may be issued by order of the said

chattels thereof, from being also liable for such excess. Such directors, however, as shall have been absent when the said excess was contracted, or shall have entered their protest against it upon the records of the Corporation, may respectively exonerate and discharge themselves therefrom, by pleading and proving such absence or showing such record.

10. The said Corporation shall not directly or indirectly deal in anything excepting bills of exchange, gold or silver bullion, or in the sale of goods really and truly pledged for money lent, and not redeemed in due time or in the sale of stock pledged for money lent, and not so redeemed : which said goods and stock so pledged and not so redeemed may be sold by the said Corporation at any time not less than ten days after the period for redemption without judgment first obtained, any law or usage to the contrary notwithstanding ; and if upon such sale of goods or stock there shall be a surplus (after deducting the expenses of sale) over the payment of the money, such surplus shall be paid to the proprietors thereof respectively. Neither shall the said Corporation take at the rate of more than six per centum per annum for or upon its loans or discounts.

11. The corporation is hereby empowered to make any loan or loans for the use or on account of this province that shall be previously authorized by a law or laws of the Provincial Parliament.

12. The stock of the said Corporation shall be assignable and transferable according to such rules and forms as shall be established in that behalf by the by-laws, ordinances and regulations of the same, but no assignment or transfer shall be valid or effectual unless such assignment or transfer shall be entered or registered in a book or books to be kept by the directors for that purpose, nor until the person or persons making the same shall previously discharge all debts due by him, her or them to the said Corporation, which may exceed in amount the remaining stock belonging to such person or persons, and in no case shall any fractional part of a share or other than a complete share or shares be assignable or transferable.

13. Bank obligations, bank bonds, bank bills, obligatory and of credit under the common seal of the said Corporation, signed by the President or Vice-President, and countersigned by a cashier which shall be made to any person or persons, shall be assignable by indorsements thereupon without signification thereof, any law or usage to the contrary notwithstanding. And bank bills or bank notes which shall be issued by order of the said Corporation, signed and countersigned as above said, promising the payment of money to any person or persons, his, her or

Corporation, signed by the President, and countersigned by the principal cashier, or treasurer, thereof, promising the payment of money to any person, or persons, his, her or their order, or to bearer, though not under the seal of the said Corporation, shall be binding and obligatory upon the same, in the like manner and with the like force and effect, as upon any private person or persons, if issued by him or them in his, her or their private or natural capacity, or capacities; and shall be assignable or negotiable, in like manner, as if they were so issued by such private persons; that is to say, those which shall be payable to any person or persons, his, her, or their order, shall be assignable by endorsement in like manner, and with the like effect, as foreign bills of exchange now are; and those which are payable to bearer shall be negotiable and assignable by delivery only.

14. Half-yearly dividends shall be made of so much of the profits of the bank as shall appear to the directors advisable; and once in every three years the directors shall lay before the stockholders, at a general meeting, for their information, an exact and particular statement of the debts which shall have remained unpaid after the expiration of the original credit, for a period of treble the term of that credit; and of the surplus of profit, if any, after deducting losses and dividends. If there shall be a failure in the payment of any part of any sum subscribed by any person, co-partnership, or body politic, the party failing shall lose the benefit of any dividend which may have accrued prior to the time for making such payment, and during the delay of the same.

15. It shall be lawful for the directors aforesaid to establish offices whersoever they shall think fit, within the United States, for the purposes of discount and deposit only, and upon the same terms, and in the same manner, as shall be practised at the bank; and to commit the management of the said offices, and the making of the said discounts, to such persons, under such agreements, and subject to such regulations, as they shall deem proper;

their order, or to bearer, although not under the seal of the Corporation, shall be binding and obligatory upon the same, and shall be assignable and negotiable in like manner as if they were issued by private persons ; that is to say those which shall be payable to any person or persons, his, her or their order shall be assignable by indorsement in like manner and with the like effect as foreign bills of exchange now are : and those which shall be payable to bearer shall be negotiable by delivery only.

14. Half yearly dividends shall be made of so much of the profits of the bank as shall appear to the directors advisable, and shall be payable at such place or places as the directors shall appoint, of which they shall give public notice in a Quebec and Montreal newspaper at least four weeks before; and the directors shall every year at the general meeting for election thereof lay before the stockholders for their information, an exact and particular statement of the debts due to and by the bank, specifying the amount of bank notes then in circulation, and such debts as in their opinion are bad or doubtful, as also stating the surplus of profit if any remaining after deduction of losses and provision for dividends:

If there shall be a failure in payment of any part of the sum or shares subscribed by any person or persons, body politic or corporate, the party or parties failing in paying the first instalment of ten per centum succeeding the deposit of ten per centum hereinbefore required to be made at the time of subscribing, shall respectively forfeit the said deposit, to and for the use of the said corporation, and on failure of paying the other instalments or any of them, the party or parties failing therein shall lose the benefit of dividends (as well on the deposit as on the instalments paid by him, her or them) which shall have accrued prior to the time for making such payment and during the delay of the same, but shall not forfeit the principal sum of the said deposit excepting in the instance above said.

15. It shall be lawful for the directors of the bank to establish offices, for the purpose of deposit and discount only, in such places in the provinces of Lower and Upper Canada as they shall think advisable, upon the same terms and in the same manner as shall be practised at the bank, and to commit the management thereof to such agents under such agreements and subject to such regulations as the directors shall deem proper, the same not being contrary

not being contrary to law, or to the constitution of the bank.

16. The officer at the head of the treasury department of the United States shall be furnished, from time to time, as often as he may require, not exceeding once a week, with statements of the amount of the capital stock of the said Corporation, and of the debts due to the same; and shall have a right to inspect such general accounts in the books of the bank as shall relate to the said statements: *Provided*, that this shall not be construed to imply a right of inspecting the account of any private individuals, with the bank.

to the constitution or laws of this province, or to this Act.

16. And be it further enacted by the authority aforesaid that the Governor, Lieutenant-Government or person administering the Government of this province for the time being, shall be furnished (at such times as he shall require the same) with statements of the amount of the capital stock of the Corporation, of the amount of debts due to and by the same of the amount of monies deposited therein, of the amount of notes in circulation, and of monies on hand belonging to the said Corporation : and shall have authority himself, or by a person or persons for that purpose by him authorized and appointed, under his hand and Seal at Arms, to inspect the general accounts of the bank : provided that such inspection shall not extend to any right or authority to inspect the account of any individual or individuals with the bank.

TABLE A

FINISHED MANUFACTURES AS PERCENTAGE OF TOTAL TRADE IN
MANUFACTURES IN THE MAIN NON-COMMUNIST INDUSTRIAL
COUNTRIES, PLUS AUSTRALIA, 1899, 1913, 1955

	EXPORTS			IMPORTS[1]		
	1899 %	*1913* %	*1955* %	*1899* %	*1913* %	*1955* %
Britain	75	76	79	69	64	43
Early followers						
Belgium (Luxembourg)	47	46	44	67	62	75
France	78	76	60	60	59	62
Switzerland	81	79	83	54	59	63
US	63	62	77	80	69	50
Middle follower						
Germany	73	63	76[2]	43	43	41[2]
Late followers						
Canada	83	52	22	76	75	80
Italy	41	70	76	58	63	67
Japan	39	63	73	68	62	68
Sweden	50	57	63	55	55	69
Others						
Netherlands[3]	4	4	63	4	53	63
Australia[5]	4	4	50[6]	81	77	75

SOURCE: Maizels, *Industrial Growth*. Figures for 1913 and 1955 taken from Table 3.7; 1899 figures and those for Australia derived from Tables A15-19, A20-27, A47-65, A69.

[1] From other industrial countries and India (details: Maizels' Appendix A).
[2] West Germany.
[3] It could not be determined if the Netherlands was a late-follower country.
[4] Figures are not available
[5] Australia was not a late-follower country. See Chapter 1.
[6] An exact figure was not available. The approximate figure was derived from Maizels' Table 3.2.

TABLE B

TRADE IN FINISHED MANUFACTURED[1] GOODS (FMG) BY INDUSTRIAL COUNTRIES
(1899 AND 1913 FIGURES IN US 1913 $MILLIONS 1955 FIGURES IN US 1955 $MILLIONS)

	1899				1913				1955			
	$(000,000) Exports FMG	% Total exports	$(000,000) Imports FMG	Ratio exports/imports	$(000,000) Exports FMG	% Total exports	$(000,000) Imports FMG	Ratio exports/imports	$(000,000) Exports FMG	% Total exports	$(000,000) Imports FMG	Ratio exports/imports
UK	995	(39.6%)	372	2.7	1492	(34.4%)	490	3.0	5270	(23.2%)	665	7.9
Early followers												
Belgium (Luxembourg)	80	(3.2%)	106	0.75	149	(3.4%)	157	0.95	965	(4.3%)	835	1.2
France	395	(15.7%)	100	4.0	595	(13.7%)	191	3.1	1845	(8.1%)	689	2.7
Switzerland	104	(4.1%)	53	2.0	162	(3.7%)	94	1.7	994	(4.4%)	474	2.1
US	265	(10.5%)	201	1.3	528	(12.1%)	287	1.8	6418	(28.3%)	1621	4.0
Middle follower									(W. Germany)			
Germany	569	(22.6%)	123	4.6	1094	(25.2%)	173	6.3	3999	(17.6%)	547	7.3
Late followers												
Canada	15	(0.6%)	66	0.23	22	(0.5%)	222	0.10	464	(2.0%)	2286	0.20
Italy	53	(2.1%)	36	1.5	148	(3.4%)	103	1.4	873	(3.8%)	509	1.7
Japan	24	(1.0%)	45	0.53	96	(2.2%)	73	1.3	1281	(5.6%)	175	7.3
Sweden	13	(0.5%)	12	1.1	51	(1.2%)	34	1.5	577	(2.5%)	670	0.86
Totals for the above	2513	(99.9%)	1114	2.3	4337	(99.8%)	1948	2.3	22686	(99.8%)	8471	2.7
Others (information incomplete)												
Australia	–	–	133	–	–	–	179	–	100	–	979	0.11
Netherlands	–	–	80	–	–	–	124	–	822	–	1000	0.82
Russia	–	–	89	–	–	–	185	–	[2]	–	[2]	–

SOURCE: Derived from A. Maizels, *Industrial Growth and World Trade* (London: Cambridge University Press, 1963), Tables A15-19, A20-27, A39, A47-65, A69.
[1] For classification of 'finished manufactured' goods, see Maizels' definition in Appendix A.
[2] Figures for imports and exports for the USSR were given by Maizels, Table 3.4; however, comparable estimates of production and trade could not be made accurately in US dollars. The same was true of Czechoslovakia, East Germany, Hungary, and Poland. In rough terms, these countries had manufacturing exports worth $4 billion US in 1955.

TABLE C

TRADE IN FINISHED MANUFACTURED¹ GOODS (FMG) EXCLUDING TEXTILES AND CLOTHING², BY INDUSTRIAL COUNTRIES (1899 AND 1913 FIGURES IN US 1913 $MILLIONS; 1955 FIGURES IN US 1955 $MILLIONS)

	1899				1913				1955			
	$(000,000) Exports FMG	% Total exports	$(000,000) Imports FMG	Ratio exports/imports	$(000,000) Exports FMG	% Total exports	$(000,000) Imports FMG	Ratio exports/imports	$(000,000) Exports FMG	% Total exports	$(000,000) Imports FMG	Ratio exports/imports
UK	365	(29.1%)	170	2.1	685	(25.9%)	260	2.6	4480	(23.0%)	523	8.6
Early followers												
Belgium (Luxembourg)	60	(4.8%)	57	1.1	117	(4.4%)	111	1.1	744	(3.8%)	741	1.0
France	169	(13.5%)	61	2.8	309	(11.7%)	147	2.1	1474	(7.6%)	651	2.3
Switzerland	44	(3.5%)	30	1.5	79	(3.0%)	54	1.5	860	(4.4%)	400	2.2
US	224	(17.8%)	60	3.7	463	(17.5%)	104	4.5	5942	(30.4%)	1207	4.9
Middle follower									(W. Germany)			
Germany	336	(26.8%)	81	4.1	814	(30.8%)	121	6.7	3704	(19.0%)	407	9.1
Late followers												
Canada	12	(1.0%)	46	0.26	21	(0.8%)	154	0.14	449	(2.3%)	2078	0.22
Italy	23	(1.8%)	25	0.92	65	(2.5%)	82	0.79	638	(3.3%)	476	1.3
Japan	10	(0.8%)	30	0.33	38	(1.4%)	58	0.66	662	(3.4%)	167	4.0
Sweden	13	(1.0%)	8	1.6	50	(1.9%)	22	2.3	563	(2.9%)	554	1.0
Totals for the above	1246	(99.1%)	568	2.2	2641	(99.9%)	1113	2.4	19516	(100.1%)	7204	2.7
Others (information incomplete)												
Australia	–	–	61	–	–	–	110	–	³		727	–
Netherlands	–	–	42	–	–	–	88	–	649		867	0.75
Russia	–	–	82	–	–	–	167	–	⁴		⁴	–

SOURCE: see Table B.

¹ See Maizels' Appendix A.
² Textiles and clothing made up 50.0% of total finished manufactured exports of the eleven industrial countries in 1899. This proportion fell to 39.1% in 1913 and 14.2% in 1955.
³ Maizels did not break down Australia's manufacturing exports by commodity for any year.
⁴ See footnote 2, Table B. Maizels did not break down USSR manufacturing by commodities for 1955.

Index